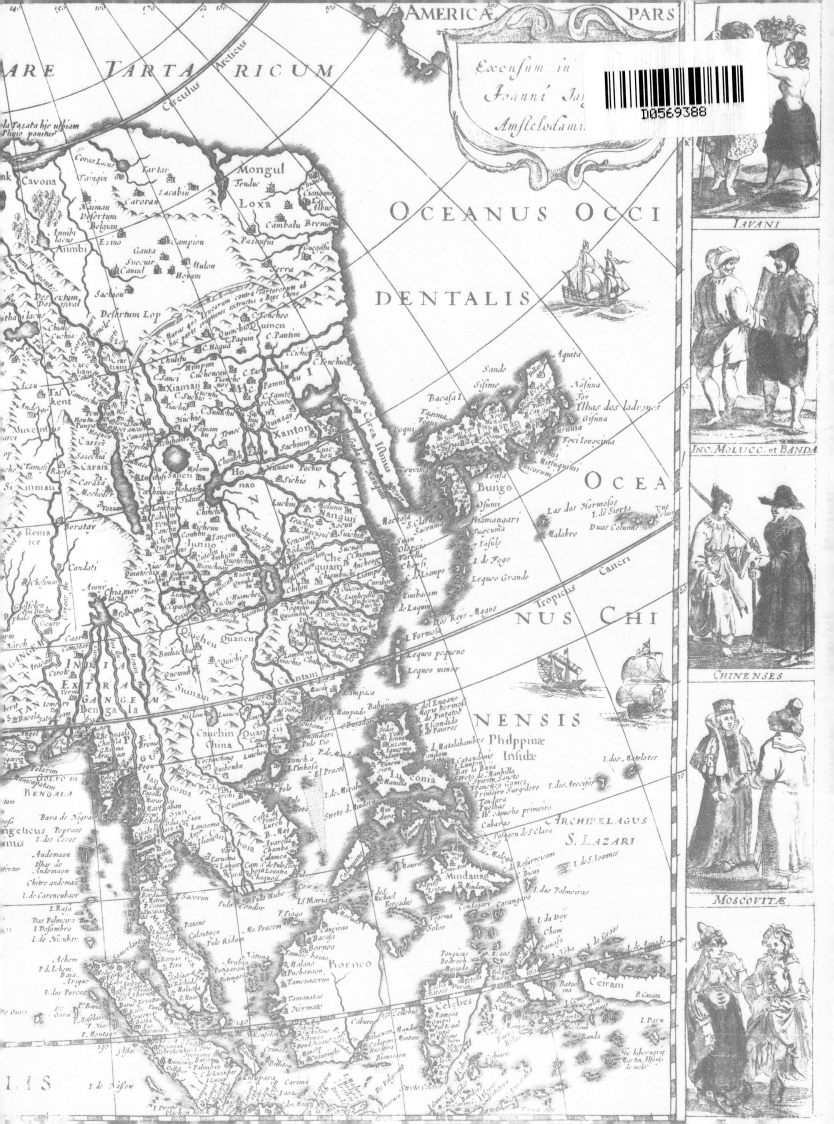

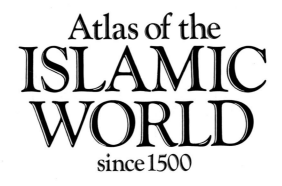

Atlas of the
ISLAMIC
WORLD
since 1500

For Pat, Andrew and
Eleanor

Editor Graham Speake
Art editor Andrew Lawson
Map editors Liz Orrock, Zoë
Goodwin
Picture research Christine
Forth
Text editor and index Jennifer
Drake-Brockman
Design Adrian Hodgkins
Production Clive Sparling

AN EQUINOX BOOK

Library of Congress Cataloging in
Publication Data

Robinson, Francis
  Atlas of the Islamic World.

  Includes index.
  1. Islamic countries –
  Historical geography – Maps.
  I. Title.
  G1786.S1R5   1982   911'.17671
                         82–675002
  ISBN 0–87196–629–8   AACR2

Published by Facts On File, Inc.
460 Park Avenue South
New York, N.Y. 10016

Origination by MBA Ltd,
Chalfont St Peter, Bucks., Siviter
Smith Graphics, Birmingham,
and York House Graphics,
Hanwell, London

Maps drawn and originated by
Lovell Johns Ltd, Oxford,
England

Filmset by Keyspools Ltd,
Golborne, Lancs., England

Printed in Spain by Heraclio
Fournier S.A. Vitoria

Frontispiece A *rakat* of prayer,
illustrating the sequence of
movements a Muslim is required
to make at his devotions.
Normally the worshiper would
stay facing in the same direction,
towards Mecca; we have
portrayed some movements from
the side for the sake of clear
illustration. Repeated movements
have been omitted.

Atlas of the
ISLAMIC
WORLD
since 1500

by Francis Robinson

Facts On File®

CONTENTS

8 Chronological Table
10 Rulers of the Islamic World
12 Preface
16 Introduction: Western Attitudes to Islam

Part One: Revelation and Muslim History

22 The First Nine Centuries from 622 to 1500
44 The Empires of the Heartlands in the 16th and 17th Centuries
88 The Further Islamic Lands from 1500 to the 18th Century
110 Decline, Reform and Revival in the 18th and 19th Centuries
130 The Rise of Europe and the Response of Islam until the mid-20th Century
158 The Reassertion of Islam in the Later 20th Century

Special Features

40 Belief and Practice
50 The Safavid World
64 The Mughal World
80 The Ottoman World
92 Javanese Culture and Islam
106 Madrasas of Central Asia
108 Mosques of the Further Islamic Lands
146 Political Cartoons
163 Modern Arab Art
176 Islam in the West

Part Two: To be a Muslim

RELIGIOUS LIFE
180 The Quran
182 At the Mosque
186 At the Shrine
188 The Stages of Life
190 The Believer's Year
192 Pilgrimage to Mecca

ARTS OF ISLAM
200 Calligraphy
204 Ceramics
206 Carpets

SOCIETY AND THE MODERN WORLD
212 Nomadic Life
214 The Village
216 The Town
218 The House
220 The Position of Women

224 Glossary
226 List of Illustrations
229 Bibliography
232 Gazetteer
235 Index

List of Maps

14 The political and physical geography of the Islamic world today
24 Expansion of the Islamic world to 1500
29 Regions in which the various Sunni schools of law were dominant c. 1500
32 The international world of Islamic scholarship 1200–1500
36 Leading sufi orders c. 1500
45 The Safavid empire in the 16th and 17th centuries
59 The Mughal empire 1526–1707
73 The Ottoman empire 1512–1683
88 Long-distance trade routes across the Islamic world c. 1500
89 The spread of Islam in southeast Asia 1500–1800
91 The sultanates of the Malacca straits and Java in the 16th and 17th centuries
95 Islam in Africa beyond the Ottoman empire 1500 to the 18th century
97 Desert, savanna and forest in Africa
101 The northern Islamic lands in the 16th century
103 Central Asia in the 17th and 18th centuries
112 The break-up of Muslim power in 18th-century Iran
113 The decline of Mughal and Muslim power in 18th-century India
114 The decline of Ottoman power in the 18th century
115 The decline of Muslim power in southeast Asia
118 The Islamic revival of the 18th and 19th centuries
121 The rise of Saudi-Wahhabi power in Arabia 1744–1818
124 Distribution of Muslims in China, excluding the Tarim Basin, c. 1900
126 The Mahdist movement in the Sudan 1881–98
126 The spread of Sanusi sufi lodges in the Sahara
128 The holy war of Usuman dan Fodio and the foundation of the caliphate of Sokoto
128 The traditionalist revival in the Maghrib
130 Russia conquers the northern Islamic lands
131 Europe advances into Africa
132 Europe envelops the Ottoman empire 1812–1923
134 European imperialism and the Muslim world c. 1920
139 Egyptian power under Muhammad Ali 1805–48
141 The Husain-McMahon understanding 1915
141 The Sykes-Picot agreement 1916 and the Balfour Declaration 1917
141 The new arrangements in the Arab lands 1920–21
142 The emergence of the Saudi Arabian state
143 Russian and British imperialism in Iran 1800–1946
145 The Muslim press in Russia 1917
150 Muslim separatism in India and the foundation of Pakistan
152 The Malay states in the first half of the 20th century
155 The advance of Islam in Africa south of the Sahara since 1800
157 European settlement on the southern and eastern shores of the Mediterranean in the 19th and 20th centuries
158 The achievement of independence in the Muslim world
161 The expansion of the Israeli state
172 The reassertion of Islam in the 1960s and 1970s
173 The Muslim world and oil
174 Muslim population of the world by country
176 Muslims in Europe
194 Pilgrimage to Mecca in 1977
206 Centers of carpet production
212 Nomadic peoples

CHRONOLOGICAL TABLE

	SAFAVID/IRAN	MUGHAL/SOUTH ASIA	OTTOMAN/WEST ASIA AND NORTH AFRICA
1500	1501–10 Shah Ismail conquers Iran and establishes a Shia state 1514 Iran defeated at Chaldiran: loss of Diyarbakir and Iraq 1524–33, 1579–88 Qizilbash tribes in power Uzbegs invade Khurasan Ottomans invade Azarbaijan 1588–1629 Iran defeats Uzbegs and Ottomans, recaptures lost territory, and establishes strong central government Finest flowering of Iranian art New capital built at Isfahan A young man. Safavid, 1630.	1526 Babur victorious at Panipat and establishes Mughal rule in India 1556–1605 Akbar extends empire throughout northern India Policy of religious tolerance Arts flourish under imperial patronage 1569–85 New capital built at Fatehpur Sikri 1598 Capital moved to Agra Taj Mahal. Mughal, 1648.	1500–70 empire expands to east and south: Azarbaijan (1514), Syria and Palestine (1516), Egypt (1517); Hijaz, Yemen and Iraq by 1534 1520–66 Sulaiman the Magnificent advances into Europe: Belgrade (1521), Mohacs (1526), Vienna (1529), Greece (1540s); and North Africa to Morocco (1551) and Malta (1565) 1571 defeated at Lepanto Arts flourish, especially ceramics and architecture Iznik pottery: 1490–1525 blue and white; 1525–50 Damascus and Golden Horn ware; 1550–1700 Rhodian ware 1491–1588 Sinan, architect of Shehzade (1544–48), Sulaimaniye (1550–57) and Selimiye (1569–75) mosques Sulaiman the Magnificent, 1520–66.
1600	Weakening of the dynasty and its religious legitimacy	1624 Death of Sirhindi 1632–54 Taj Mahal built at Agra by Shah Jahan 1638– New capital built at Delhi (Shahjahanabad) 1658–1707 Awrangzeb captures Bijapur (1686) and Golkonda (1687): empire now at greatest extent, but arts cease to flourish and Marathas establish state in the Deccan	Crete taken (1669), Ukraine (1670s), Vienna attacked (1683) 1699 Ottomans surrender Hungary, Transylvania and Podolia
1700	1722 Mahmud of Qandahar takes Isfahan and destroys the empire 1736–48 Nadir Shah reestablishes Safavid rule and 1739 sacks Delhi Return to tribal rule after his death.	Weakening of Muslim power in primarily Hindu environment 1761 Delhi sacked by Ahmad Abdali of Afghanistan By 1800 Marathas rule subcontinent from Rajasthan to the Deccan, Sikhs control Punjab, and Gangetic plain in British hands	Weakening of central authority 1718 Ottomans surrender Serbia and Wallachia but regained in Austrian war of 1735–39 1740 Muhammad al-Wahhab campaigns for renewal in Arabia 1774–1812 Loss of Black Sea north coast, Crimea and Bessarabia to Russia 1798 French invade Egypt
1800	Continual pressure from Britain and Russia Growth of Western education	1803 Delhi falls to British Mujahidin and Faraizi movements preach reform 1818 British rule established throughout India 1857 Indian Mutiny: holy war declared against British 1877 Aligarh College founded to offer Western education	1802–05 Wahhabi revolt in Iraq, Syria and Arabia 1818 Muhammad Ali of Egypt checks Wahhabis and restores sultan Wahhabis retain influence in Arabia 1830 French invade Algeria; 1881 Tunisia 1869 Suez Canal opened 1882 British occupy Egypt Ottomans move towards Western-style secular government
1900	1908 Anglo-Iranian Oil Company strikes oil 1921 Compulsory state education introduced 1935 University of Teheran founded Gradual Europeanization and secularization of society 1953 Western-led coup deposes Musaddeq 1978–79 Revolution led by Ayatullah Khomeini establishes an Islamic republic	1906 All-India Muslim League founded 1947 Formation of Muslim state of Pakistan; Indian independence 1971 Pakistani civil war ends in secession of Bangladesh	1908 Young Turks come to power By 1920 Ottomans confined to Anatolia 1920 French given mandates for Lebanon and Syria; British for Iraq, Transjordan and Palestine 1922 Ataturk expels Greeks 1923 sultanate abolished; 1924 caliphate abolished; European-style rule imposed 1925 Abd al-Aziz Ibn Saud conquers Hijaz and 1938 founds Saudi Arabia 1951 Libya independent under King Idris 1956 Tunisia independent under President Bourguiba Nasser nationalizes Suez Canal 1962 Algeria independent under President Ben Bella 1981 President Sadat assassinated

AFRICA	SOUTHEAST ASIA	CENTRAL ASIA AND CHINA
New empires in Morocco and Niger Basin 1506–43 Ahmad Gran challenges Christian Ethiopia In Upper Egypt Muslim Arabs conquer Nubia Mid-16th century–18th century Muslim sultanate of the Funj 1570–1619 King Idris Aloma makes Kanem-Bornu a power in the central Sahara Songhai empire of Gao weakened by antipathy between Muslims and followers of traditional religions Morocco: strongly Islamic but weakened by succession struggles; cultural life dominated by maraboutic sufis	Muslim sultanates replace Hindu regimes in Sumatra and Java	Uzbegs threaten to dominate from Bukhara Muslim strength declines as trade along the Old Silk route falls into European hands Tatar khanates on the Asian border with Europe subdued by Russia

Friday mosque at Mopti, Mali.

Javanese dancer.

Yomud prayer rug (detail).

AFRICA	SOUTHEAST ASIA	CENTRAL ASIA AND CHINA
1680 First Fulani war culminates in establishment of Islamic state in Bondu	1608–37 Sultan Iskander Muda makes Aceh a focus for trade in the southern seas; also center of scholarship in SE Asia 1613–46 Sultan Agung controls almost all Java from Mataram Islamization indicated by spread of Malay language, stylization of batik patterns and greater modesty of women's dance 1631–70 Hasan al-Din extends Macassar empire, yielding to the Dutch in 1667 1641 Dutch conquer Malacca	1644 Manchu dynasty alienates Chinese Muslims Decline in arts except coinage and carpet weaving
Niger states lost to heathen Bambara Fulani extend Islamic influence in west 1725 Second Fulani war establishes Muslim dynasty in Futa Jallon 1776 Third Fulani war establishes Islam in Futa Toro	By 1800 Islamic sultanates on Java and Sumatra lose power to Dutch	Nomads subdued by Russian advance Attempt to assimilate Chinese Muslims to Confucianism 1758–60 China dominates Tarim Basin
Khalwatiya and Idrisiya lead reformist movements 1804 Usuman dan Fodio, supported by Fulani and Hausa, forms sultanate of Sokoto 1863–93 Tijani empire from Niger to Senegal 1885–98 Mahdist state established in Sudan	1803–37 Padri movement extends Islamic influence in Sumatra 1825–30 Reformist movement in Java boosts Islamization 1873–1910 Aceh war opposes Dutch expansion in north Sumatra Dutch authority now complete throughout archipelago	Naqshbandi sufis wage holy war against Russia and Chinese Manchus and preach reform "New Sect" encourages Muslim revival throughout China Russia imposes direct rule on Central Asia
1900 Britain colonizes Nigeria (inc. Sokoto) 1912 French capture Morocco and the Sahara 1912 Italy conquers Libya European rule stimulates growth of Muslim institutions 1956 Morocco independent	1912 Formation of Islamic league 1938 Formation of *Partai Islam Indonesia* 1942–45 Japanese occupation strengthens Islam 1949 Indonesia independent	1917 Russian Revolution brings cultural disaster to Muslims

RULERS OF THE ISLAMIC WORLD

MOROCCO

Saadians
1511 Muhammad al-Mahdi (in Sus)
1517 Ahmad al-Araj (in Marrakesh till 1540)
1517 Muhammad al-Shaikh al-Mahdi (at first in Sus, later in Fez)
1557 Abd Allah al-Ghalib
1574 Muhammad al-Mutawakkil al-Maslukh
1576 Abd al-Malik
1578 Ahmad al-Mansur
1603–08 Muhammad al-Shaikh al-Mamun
1603–08 Abd Allah al-Wathiq (in Marrakesh)
1603–28 Zaidan an-Nasir (at first in Fez only)
sons of Ahmad in rivalry for the succession
1623 Abd al-Malik
1631 al-Walid
1636 Muhammad al-Asghar
1654–59 Ahmad al-Abbas *in Marrakesh only*

Filalis
1631 Muhammad I al-Sharif (in Tafilalt)
1635 Muhammad II
1664 al-Rashid
1672 Ismail al-Samin
1727 Ahmad al-Dhahabi
1729 Abd Allah (1735–45 power contested by various usurpers and pretenders)
1757 Muhammad III
1790 Yazid
1792 Hisham
1793 Sulaiman
1822 Abd al-Rahman
1859 Muhammad IV
1873 al-Hasan I
1895 Abd al-Aziz
1907 al-Hafiz
1912 Yusuf
1927 Muhammad V (first reign)
1953 Muhammad
1955 Muhammad V (second reign)
1962 al-Hasan II

NIGERIA

Sokoto caliphate
1754 Usuman dan Fodio
1817 Muhammad Bello
1837 Abu Bakr Atiku
1842 Ali
1859 Ahmad
1866 Ali
1867 Ahmad Rufai
1873 Abu Bakr
1877 Muadh
1881 Umar
1891 Abd al-Rahman
1902 Muhammad Attahiru I
1903 Muhammad Attahiru II
1915 Muhammad Maiturare
1924 Muhammad
1931 Hassan
1938 Abu Bakr

EGYPT

Muhammad Ali's line
1805 Muhammad Ali Pasha
1848 Ibrahim Pasha
1848 Abbas I Pasha
1854 Said Pasha
1863 Ismail (khedive from 1867)
1879 Tawfiq
1892 Abbas II Hilmi
1914 Husain Kamil (sultan)
1917 Ahmad Fuad I (king from 1922)
1936 Faruq
1952 Fuad II
1953 republic

Presidents
1953–54 Neguib
1956 Nasser
1970 Sadat
1981 Mubarak

OTTOMAN EMPIRE

Ottomans
1481 Bayazid II
1512 Selim I Yaviz ("the Grim")
1520 Sulaiman II Qanuni ("the law giver" or "the Magnificent")
1566 Selim II
1574 Murad III
1594 Muhammad III
1603 Ahmad I
1617 Mustafa I (first reign)
1618 Uthman II
1622 Mustafa I (second reign)
1623 Murad IV
1640 Ibrahim
1648 Muhammad IV
1687 Sulaiman III
1691 Ahmad II
1695 Mustafa II
1703 Ahmad III
1730 Mahmud I
1754 Uthman III
1757 Mustafa III
1774 Abd al-Hamid I
1789 Selim III
1807 Mustafa IV
1808 Mahmud II
1839 Abd al-Majid I
1861 Abd al-Aziz
1876 Murad V
1876 Abd al-Hamid II
1909 Muhammad V Rashad
1918 Muhammad VI Wahid al-Din
1922–24 Abd al-Majid II (as caliph only)

TURKEY
1923 Mustafa Kemal (Ataturk)
1938 Ismet Inonu
1950 Celal Bayar
1961 General Gursel
1966 Senator Cevdet Sunay
1973 Senator Fahri Koroturk
1980 General Kenan Evren

LEBANON
1920 French mandate
1926 republic

Presidents
1926 Charles Dabbas
1934 Habib Saad
1936 Emile Edde
1941 independent
1941 Alfred Naccache
1943 al-Khuri
1952 Camille Chamoun
1958 Fuad Chehab
1964 Charles Helou
1970 Sulaiman Franjiya
1976 Elias Sarkis

SYRIA
1918 Faisal (son of Amir Husain) heads autonomous government in Damascus
1920 French mandate
1941 independent
1943 republic

Presidents
1943 Shukri al-Quwatli
1949 Hashim al-Atassi
1951 General Fawzi Selo
1953–54 General Shishakli
1955 Shukri al-Quwatli
1958 Nasser (United Arab Republic)
1961 Nazim Qudsi
1963 Major General Amin al-Hafiz
1966 Nur al-Din Atassi
1970 Ahmad Khatib
1971 General Assad

HIJAZ

Hashimites
1908 Amir Husain (sharif of Mecca)
1916 takes the title of king
1924 Ali
1925 Hijaz conquered by Saudis

TRANSJORDAN
1920 British mandate

Hashimites
1921 Amir Abd Allah
1946 Abd Allah takes the title of king (of Jordan from 1949)
1951 Talal
1952 Husain

IRAQ
1920 British mandate

Hashimites
1921 Faisal I Ibn Husain
1933 Ghazi
1939 Faisal II
1958 republic

Presidents
1958 Major General Najib al-Rubai
1963 Field Marshal Abd al-Salam Muhammad Arif
1966 Lt-General Abd al-Rahman Muhammad Arif
1968 Major General Ahmad Hassan Bakr
1979 Saddam Husain al-Takriti

YEMEN

Zaidi imams: Qasimid line
c. 1592 al-Qasim al-Mansur
1620 Muhammad al-Muayyad I
1654 Ismail al-Mutawakkil
1676 Muhammad al-Muayyad II
1681 Muhammad al-Hadi
1686 Muhammad al-Mahdi
1716 al-Qasim al-Mutawakkil
1726 al-Husain al-Mansur (first reign)
1726 Muhammad al-Hadi al-Majid (?)
1728 al-Husain al-Mansur (second reign)
1747 al-Abbas al-Mahdi (?)
c. 1776 Ali al-Mansur
1806 Ahmad al-Mahdi (?)
? Ali al-Mansur (second reign?)
1841 al-Qasim al-Mahdi
1845 Muhammad Yahya
1872 Ottoman occupation
1890 Hamid al-Din Yahya
1904 Yahya Mahmud al-Mutawakkil
1948 Saif al-Islam Ahmad
1962 Muhammad Badr
1962 republic

Presidents
1962 Colonel Abd Allah Sallal
1968 Abd al-Rahman al-Iriani
1974 constitution suspended
1977 Lt-Col Ahmad Ibn Husain al-Ghashmi
1978 Lt-Col Ali Abd Allah Saleh
1980 Ali Nasser Muhammad

ARABIA

Saudis
1746 Muhammad b. Saud
1765 Abd al-Aziz
1803 Saud b. Abd al-Aziz
1814 Abd Allah I b. Saud
1818–22 Ottoman occupation
1823 Turki
1834 Faisal I (first reign)
1837 Khalid b. Saud
1841 Abd Allah II (as a vassal of Muhammad Ali of Egypt)
1843 Faisal I (second reign)
1865 Abd Allah III b. Faisal (first reign)
1871 Saud b. Faisal
1874 Abd Allah III (second reign)
1887 conquest by Rashidis of Hail, Abd Allah remains as governor of Riyadh till 1889
1889 Abd al-Rahman b. Faisal, vassal governor
1891 Muhammad b. Faisal, vassal governor
1902 Abd al-Aziz II
1953 Saud
1964 Faisal II
1975 Khalid
1982 Fahd

OMAN AND ZANZIBAR

United Sultanate
1741 Ahmad b. Said
1783 Said b. Ahmad
?1786 Hamid b. Said
1792 Sultan b. Ahmad
1806 Salim b. Sultan
1806 Said b. Sultan (division of the sultanate on Said's death)

Zanzibar
1856 Majid b. Said
1870 Barghash b. Said
1888 Khalifa b. Barghash
1890 Ali b. Said
1893 Hamid
1896 Hammud
1902 Ali b. Hammud
1911 Khalifa
1960 Abd Allah b. Khalifa
1963 Jamshid
1964 revolution and incorporation in the Republic of Tanzania

Oman
1856 Thuwaini b. Said
1866 Salim b. Thuwaini
1868 Azzan b. Qais
1870 Turki b. Said
1888 Faisal b. Turki
1913 Taimur b. Faisal
1932 Said b. Taimur
1970 Qabus b. Said

IRAN

Safavids
1501 Ismail I
1524 Tahmasp I
1576 Ismail II
1578 Muhammad Khudabanda
1588 Abbas I
1629 Safi I
1642 Abbas II
1666 Sulaiman I (Safi II)
1694 Sultan Husain I
1722 Tahmasp II
1732 Abbas III
1749 Sulaiman II
1750 Ismail III
1753 Husain II
1786 Muhammad
nominal rulers

Afsharids
1736 Nadir Shah
1747 Adil Shah
1748 Ibrahim
1748–95 Shah Rukh (in Khurasan)

Zands
1750 Muhammad Karim Khan
1779 Abul Fath Muhammad Ali *conjointly*
1779–81 Sadiq (in Shiraz)
1779–85 Ali Murad (in Isfahan)
1785 Jafar
1789–94 Lutf Ali

Qajars
1779 Agha Muhammad
1797 Fath Ali Shah
1834 Muhammad
1848 Nasir al-Din
1896 Muzaffar al-Din
1907 Muhammad Ali
1909–24 Ahmad

Pahlavis
1925 Riza Shah
1941 Muhammad Riza Shah
1979 Islamic republic

Presidents
1980 Abol Hassan Bani-Sadr
1981 Hojjatolislam Sayad Ali Khamenei

INDIA

Mughal Emperors
1526 Babur
1530 Humayun (first reign)
1540–55 Suri sultans of Delhi
1555 Humayun (second reign)
1556 Akbar I
1605 Jahangir
1627 Dawar Baksh
1628 Shah Jahan I
1657 Murad Bakhsh (in Gujarat)
1657 Shah Shuja (in Bengal till 1660)
1658 Awrangzeb Alamgir I
1707 Azam Shah

1707	Kam Bakhsh (in the Deccan)
1707	Shah Alam I
1712	Azim al-Shan
1712	Muiz al-Din Jahandar
1713	Farrukh-siyar
1719	Shams al-Din Rafi al-Darajat
1719	Rafi al-Dawla Shah Jahan II
1719	Niku-siyar
1719	Nasir al-Din Muhammad
1748	Ahmad Shah Bahadur
1754	Aziz al-Din Alamgir II
1760	Shah Jahan III
1760	Shah Alam II (first reign)
1788	Bidar-bakht
1788	Shah Alam II (second reign)
1806	Muin al-Din Akbar II
1837	Siraj al-Din Bahadur Shah II
1858	under British crown
1947	dominion

Governors-general

1947	Earl Mountbatten of Burma
1948	Chakravarti Rajagopalachari
1950	republic

Presidents

1950	Rajendra Prasad
1962	Savepalli Radhakrishnan
1967	Zakir Husain
1969	Varanagrii Venkata Giri
1974	Fakhruddin Ali Ahmed
1977	Neelam Sanjiva Reddy

PAKISTAN

Governors-general

1947	Muhammad Ali Jinnah
1948	Khwaja Nazimuddin
1951	Ghulam Muhammad
1955	Major General Iskander Mirza
1956	Islamic republic

Presidents

1956	Major General Iskander Mirza
1958	Field Marshal Ayub Khan
1969	Major General Yahya Khan
1971	Zulfiqar Ali Bhutto
1973	Fazl Elahi Chaudhry
1978	General Zia ul-Haq

BANGLADESH

1971	republic

Presidents

1972	Abu Sayeed Chowdhury
1973	Mohammadullah
1975	Shaikh Mujibur Rahman
1975	Mushtaq Ahmad
1975	Abusadat Muhammad Sayem
1977	Major General Ziaur Rahman
1981	Abdus Sattar
1982	General Muhammad Hossain Ershad

AFGHANISTAN

Durranis

1747	Ahmad Shah Durrani
1773	Timur Shah
1793	Zaman Shah
1800	Mahmud Shah (first reign)
1803	Shah Shuja (first reign in Kabul, from 1800 ruler in Peshawar)
1809	Mahmud (second reign in Kabul till 1818, in Herat till 1829)
1818	Ali Shah
1839	Shuja (second reign)
1842	Fath Jang

Barakzais

1819	Dost Muhammad
1863	Shir Ali (first reign)
1866	Afzal
1867	Shir Ali (second reign)
1879	Muhammad Yaqub Khan
1880	Abd al-Rahman Khan
1901	Habib Allah
1919	Aman Allah (Amanullah)
1929	Nadir Shah
1933	Muhammad Zahir Shah
1973	republic

Presidents

1973	Sardar Muhammad Daud
1978	Nur Muhammad Taraqqi
1979	Hafiz Allah Amin
1979	Babrak Karmal

THE CRIMEA

Girai Khans

1478	Mengli (third reign)
1514	Muhammad I
1523	Ghazi I
1524	Saadat I
1532	Islam I
1532	Sahib I
1551	Dawlat I
1577	Muhammad II
1584	Islam II
1588	Ghazi II (first reign)
1596	Fath I
1606	Ghazi II (second reign)
1608	Toqtamish
1608	Salamat I
1610	Muhammad III (first reign)
1610	Janbeg (first reign)
1623	Muhammad III (second reign)
1627	Janbeg (second reign)
1635	Inayat
1637	Bahadur I
1641	Muhammad IV (first reign)
1644	Islam III
1654	Muhammad IV (second reign)
1666	Adil
1671	Selim I (first reign)
1678	Murad
1683	Hajji II
1684	Selim I (second reign)
1691	Saadat II
1691	Safa
1692	Selim I (third reign)
1699	Dawlat II (first reign)
1702	Selim I (fourth reign)
1704	Ghazi III
1707	Qaplan I (first reign)
1708	Dawlat II (second reign)
1713	Qaplan I (second reign)
1716	Dawlat III
1717	Saadat III
1724	Mengli II (first reign)
1730	Qaplan I (third reign)
1736	Fath II
1737	Mengli II (second reign)
1740	Salamat II
1743	Selim II
1748	Arslan (first reign)
1756	Halim
1758	Qirim (first reign)
1764	Selim III (first reign)
1767	Arslan (second reign)
1767	Maqsud (first reign)
1768	Qirim (second reign)
1769	Dawlat IV (first reign)
1770	Qaplan II
1770	Selim III (second reign)
1771	Maqsud (second reign)
1772	Sahib II
1775	Dawlat IV (second reign)
1777	Shahin (first reign)
1783	Russian annexation of the Crimea
[1784	Bahadur II
[1785	Shahin (second reign)
	as Russian vassals

CENTRAL ASIA

Samarqand (Shaibanids)

1500	Muhammad Shaibani
1510	Kochkunji
1530	Abu Said
1533	Ubaid Allah
1539	Abd Allah I
1540	Abd al-Latif
1551	Nuruz Ahmad
1555	Pir Muhammad I
1560	Iskandar

Bukhara (Shaibanids)

1583	Abd Allah II
1598	Abd al-Mumin
1599	Pir Muhammad II

(Janids)

1599	Baqi Muhammad
1605	Wali Muhammad
1608	Imam Quli
1640	Nazir Muhammad
1647	Abd al-Aziz
1680	Subhan Quli
1702	Ubaid Allah
1705	Abul Faiz
1747	Abd al-Mumin
1751	Ubaid Allah II
1753	Muhammad Rahim (Mangit)
1758	Abul Ghazi

(Mangits)

1785	Mir Masum Shah Murad
1800	Haidar Tora
1826	Husain
1826	Umar
1827	Nasr-Allah
1860	Muzaffar al-Din
1868	Russian protectorate

Khiva

c. 1515	Ilbars I
c. 1525	Sultan Hajji
	Hasan Quli
	Sufyan
	Bujugha
	Avanak
	Kal
c. 1540	Akatai
1546	Dost
1558	Hajji Muhammad I
1602	Arab Muhammad I
1623	Isfandiyar
1643	Abul Ghazi I
1663	Anusha
c. 1674	Muhammad Arank
1687	Ishaq Aqa Shah Niyaz
1702	Arab Muhammad II
	Hajji Muhammad II
1714	Yadighar
1714	Arank
1715	Shir Ghazi
c. 1730	Ilbars II
1740	annexation by Nadir Shah
1741	Tagir, Persian governor
1741	Abu Muhammad
1741	Abul Ghazi II
1745	Kaip
c. 1770	Abul Ghazi III
1804	Iltazar
1806	Muhammad Rahim
1825	Allah Quli
1842	Rahim Quli
1845	Muhammad Amin
1855	Abd Allah
1855	Qutlugh Muhammad
?1856	Saiyid Muhammad
1865	Saiyid Muhammad Rahim
1873	Russian protectorate

Khokand

c. 1700	Shah Rukh Beg Rahim
	Abd al-Qarim
	Erdeni
1770	Sulaiman
1770	Shah Rukh II
?1770	Narbuta
1800	Alim
1809	Muhammad Umar
1822	Muhammad Ali
1840	Shir Ali
1841	Murad
1845	Khudayar (first reign)
1857	Malla
1859	Shah Murad
1861	Khudayar (second reign)
1864	Saiyid Sultan
1871	Khudayar (third reign)
1875	Nasir al-Din
1876	annexed by Russia

INDONESIA

Sultans of Mataram

1575	Mas Ngabehi Suta Wijaya (Senapati)
1601	Panembahan Seda Krapyak (Raden Jolang)
1613	Sultan Agung (Mas Rangsang)
1649	Mangkurat I (Seda Tegal Arum)
1677	Mangkurat II (Kartasura)
1703	Mangkurat III
1708	Pakubuwana I (Puger)
1719	Mangkurat IV (Jawa)
1727	Pakubuwana II (Kombul)
1749	Pakabuwana III (Swarga)

Surakarta

1788	Pakubuwana IV (Bagus)
1820	Pakubuwana V (Sugih)
1823	Pakubuwana VI (Bangun)
1830	Pakubuwana VII (Purbaya)
1858	Pakubuwana VIII (Angabehi)
1861	Pakubuwana IX (Bangun Kadaton)
1893	Pakubuwana X (Wicaksana)
1939	Pukubuwana XI
1944	Pakubuwana XII

Jogjakarta

1755	Mangkubuwana I (Swarga)
1792–1810	Mangkubuwana II (Sepuh) (first reign)
1810–11	Mangkubuwana III (Raja) (first reign)
1811–12	Mangkubuwana II (second reign)
1812–14	Mangkubuwana III (second reign)
1814–22	Mangkubuwana IV (Seda Pesiyar)
1822–26	Mangkubuwana V (Menol) (first reign)
1826–28	Mangkubuwana II (third reign)
1828–55	Mangkubuwana V (second reign)
1855	Mangkubuwana VI
1877	Mangkubuwana VII (Angabehi)
1921	Mangkubuwana VIII
1939	Mangkubuwana IX

Aceh

1496	Ali Maghayat Shah
1528	Salah al-Din Ibn Ali
1537	Ala al-Din al-Zahar Ibn Ali
1568	Husain
1575	Sultan Muda
1575	Sultan Sri Alam
1576	Zainal Abidin
1577	Ala al-Din of Perak (Mansur Shah)
?1589	Sultan Boyong
1596	Ala al-Din Riayat Shah
1604	Ali Riayat Shah
1607	Iskandar Muda (Meukuta Alam)
1636	Iskandar Thani
1641	Safiyat al-Din Taj al-Alam bint Iskandar Muda (widow of Iskandar Thani)
1675	Naqiyat al-Din Nur al-Alam
1678	Zaqiyat al-Din Inayat Shah
1688	Kamalat Shah Zinat al-Din
1699	Badr al-Alam Sharif Haslim Jamal al-Din
1702	Perkara Alam Sharif Lamtui
1703	Jamal al-Alam Badr al-Munir
1726	Jauhan al-Alam Amir al-Din
1726	Shams al-Alam
1727	Ala al-Din Ahmad Shah
1735	Ala al-Din Johan Shah
1760	Mahmud Shah (first reign)
1764	Badr al-Din Johan Shah
1765	Mahmud Shah (second reign)
1773	Sulaiman Shah (Udahna Lela)
1773	Mahmud Shah (third reign)
1781	Ala al-Din Muhammad Shah
1795	Ala al-Din Jauhar al-Alam (1815–23 contested by Sharif Saif al-Alam)
1823	Muhammad Shah
1838	Sulaiman (1850–57 contested by Ali Ala al-Din Mansur Shah)
1857	Ali Ala al-Din Mansur Shah (Ibrahim)
1870	Mahmud Shah
1874	Muhammad Daud Shah
1874	Dutch occupation
1945–49	War of independence
1949	republic

Presidents

1950	Muhammad Ahmad Sukarno
1966	Presidium
1968	General Suharto

PREFACE

The rise of Islam and the interaction of Muslims with other peoples on our planet over the past 14 centuries is one of the great stories of world history. The pattern for existence laid down by Islam is one of the main ways men have had of living life. The purpose for life established by Islam is one of the main ways men have had of giving meaning to existence. These facts alone mean that Islam should command our attention. Today one-fifth of the world's population are Muslims who live almost entirely in its developing regions; the growing political and economic interdependence of global life means that movements among them have increasing repercussions in the world beyond, while significant Muslim communities have come to be established by migration in major societies of the West. It is important, as never before, that the dynamics of Muslim history and the values of Muslim peoples should be widely comprehended.

One purpose of this Atlas is to provide a framework within which the last 500 years of Muslim history can be understood. It is particularly concerned to demonstrate how Islamic society has been maintained, how it has been transmitted from generation to generation, and how it has been spread throughout the world. Chapter 1 offers a brief overview of the first nine centuries of Islamic history and then examines the institutions which were established during the period to mold Islamic society and to transmit its forms and values, down the ages and into new regions. Chapters 2 and 3 examine six main areas of the Muslim world between 1500 and the 18th century: the Safavid, Mughal, and Ottoman empires, southeast Asia, Africa, and Central Asia and China. Particular attention has been paid to the transmitters of Islamic culture, their interactions with the wielders of political power and with the pagan or partially Islamized peoples among which they often moved. Chapter 4 shows how Muslim power began to crumble in the 18th century and how throughout the Islamic world the transmitters of Islamic culture led movements of revival and reform. Chapter 5 shows how in the 19th and 20th centuries many Muslim elites responded to the threat of being swamped by European power by striving to fashion their societies after a European model. Chapter 6 suggests why in recent years the attraction of this model might have seemed to fade and how Muslims have begun to assert their own Islamic vision of progress with greater confidence.

A second purpose has been to introduce the reader to the lives which Muslims live. Wherever possible, Muslims have spoken for themselves, so we hear how they call on God, or dream of the pleasures of the pilgrimage, or assert their way forward as against that of the West. Part Two, in particular, examines aspects of religious life, the artistic expressions of Islamic values, and the various types of Muslim society and their interactions with the modern world. Taking Parts One and Two together, readers should be able to acquire a clear idea of what Muslims believe and the manifold ways in which their faith molds their lives.

A third purpose has been to provide a basis for a broader vision of the Islamic world. Established understandings of Islam have been to some considerable extent formed by the experience of the central Islamic lands. Our concern has been to present in addition the often very different experience of the further Islamic lands, in southeast Asia, in Africa, and in Central Asia and China, where Islam has faced powerful cultures, sometimes on a less than equal footing. These parts of the Muslim world, where almost as many Muslims live as in the central Islamic lands, are relatively little studied. Knowledge of them adds both to our appreciation of the Muslim achievement and to our understanding of the many ways there are of being Muslim.

Important parts of the story have been told in maps, many of which are new in what they show. Most have been drawn on a Mercator projection, unless otherwise stated. This means that the correct shape can be maintained in spite of the exaggeration in scale which occurs increasingly with distance from the equator and as one moves from west to east. Indeed, as many of the maps deal with large areas of the world at one time, the projection is particularly useful. Scale bars have not been included on the maps, but a representative fraction is given, calculated at the equator.

Transliteration, the correct representation of the sounds of the different Islamic languages in the roman script, is a perennially thorny question. There is the solution adopted by the *Encyclopaedia of Islam*, which reduces all the sounds of the various Islamic languages to one system which favors Arabic. Its problem is that it makes many words, which non-Arabic speakers are used to seeing in other transliterated forms, unrecognizable. There is the solution adopted by Marshall Hodgson of using different systems for different languages, but this has the opposite effect of reducing the apparent relationships between words in different languages which do exist. The problem is of moment to the professional scholar but of little significance to the general reader. Our prime concern has been ease of communication, and with this in mind we have adopted the following policy. The system of the *Encyclopaedia of Islam* (1st edition) has been made the basis with the qualifications that: all diacritical marks have been omitted, *j* has been used for *dj* and *q* for *ḳ*, and wherever a name or a term has acquired an acknowledged form in English this has been retained, inevitably introducing some inconsistencies: for instance, we write Rashid Rida for the Arab thinker but Riza Shah for the Pahlavi ruler of Iran. This policy will probably cause dissatisfaction among some professional scholars. They, however, know what the forms should be and do not need to be told. Our concern is to offer as many points of contact as possible for the general reader.

Translations of the Quran also present difficulties, as one might expect in the case of a book which is widely held to be untranslatable. Translations can differ; so can even the numbering of verses. Throughout we have used the translation of Muhammad Ali of Lahore (6th edition, Lahore, 1973) with one change and an exception. The change is that whenever Muhammad Ali has used ''Allah'' we have used ''God,'' which should enable quotations to speak more directly to the Christian reader. The exception is that in the special feature devoted to the Quran we have used translations by Kenneth Cragg which seemed especially able to convey the power and beauty of the original.

This Atlas grows out of 15 years' work on aspects of Islamic history in which period I have incurred, as every scholar does, many debts both personal and intellectual. I would like to acknowledge in particular the inspiration of Marshall G.S. Hodgson's *Venture of Islam: Conscience and History in a World Civilization*. No one who dares to embrace the length and breadth of Islamic history can afford to ignore his many insights and lofty vision. Friends and colleagues have, as always, been generous with their time and with their knowledge. I thank Anthony Atmore, Peter Carey, Michael Crowder, Anthony Stockwell and Rita Townsend. I thank especially Ralph Leigh and Peter Brown for their warm encouragement and wise counsel. My greatest debt, however, is to the learned and holy men of the Firangi Mahal family at Lucknow, India, who for over a decade, and particularly over the last six years, have been generous hosts, patient guides, firm and yet kindly critics. All that I have written is my responsibility, but that it should have been done at all is in large part due to them.

Enjoy this book. For those who like to begin at the beginning and work through to the end there is an argument about the development of Islamic history to be assessed. But the book is equally to be savored in parts. Whatever approach you choose, I hope that you will come to share in my pleasure in Islamic civilization and its history.

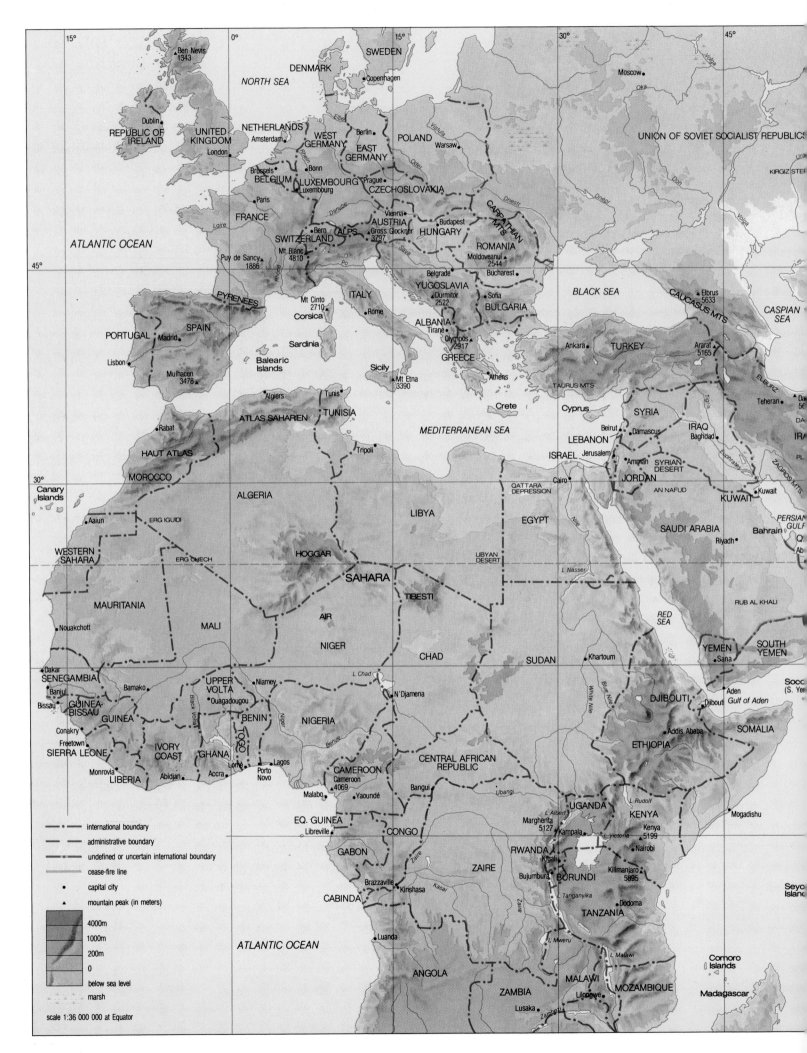

15°   0°   15°   30°   45°

▲ Ben Nevis
1343

SWEDEN

DENMARK
• Copenhagen

NORTH SEA

Moscow •

UNION OF SOVIET SOCIALIST REPUBLICS

Oka

Volga

Dublin •
REPUBLIC OF
IRELAND

UNITED
KINGDOM

NETHERLANDS
Amsterdam •

WEST
GERMANY

Berlin •
EAST
GERMANY

POLAND
Warsaw •

KIRGIZ STEP

London •

Brussels •
BELGIUM

Bonn •

LUXEMBOURG
Luxembourg

Prague •
CZECHOSLOVAKIA

Vistula

Don

Volga

Paris •

FRANCE

Danube

Vienna •
AUSTRIA

Budapest •

CARPATHIAN MTS

Dnestr

Dnepr

ATLANTIC OCEAN

45°

Loire

Puy de Sancy ▲
1886

SWITZERLAND
ALPS
Bern •

Gross Glockner
3797

HUNGARY

ROMANIA
Moldoveanul ▲
2544

Mt Blanc
4810

Po

Sava

Bucharest •

BLACK SEA

CAUCASUS MTS

▲ Elbrus
5633

CASPIAN
SEA

PYRENEES

Mt Cinto
2710 ▲
Corsica

ITALY
Rome •

YUGOSLAVIA
Belgrade •

Durmitor
2522

Sofia •
BULGARIA

TURKEY
Ankara •

Ararat
5165

ELBURZ

Da
5(

PORTUGAL

SPAIN
Madrid •

Sardinia

ALBANIA
Tirane •

Olympos
2917
GREECE

Da
5

Lisbon •

Balearic
Islands

Mulhacen
3478

Sicily

Mt Etna
3390

Athens •

Crete

Cyprus

Teheran •

Algiers •

Tunis •

MEDITERRANEAN SEA

SYRIA
Damascus •

IRAQ
Baghdad •

IRA

ATLAS SAHARIEN

TUNISIA

LEBANON
Beirut •

ZAGROS MTS

PL

Rabat •

Tripoli •

ISRAEL
Jerusalem •

Amman •
JORDAN

SYRIAN
DESERT

Euphrates

HAUT ATLAS

TAURUS MTS

Tigris

• Kuwait

MOROCCO

Canary
Islands

30°

QATTARA
DEPRESSION

Cairo •

AN NAFUD

KUWAIT

WESTERN
SAHARA

Aaiun •

ERG IGUIDI

ALGERIA

LIBYA

EGYPT

Nile

SAUDI ARABIA

Riyadh •

PERSIAN
GULF

Bahrain •

Q
A

ERG CHECH

HOGGAR

SAHARA

TIBESTI

LIBYAN
DESERT

L Nasser

RUB AL KHALI

RED
SEA

MAURITANIA

MALI

AIR

NIGER

CHAD

SUDAN

Khartoum •

YEMEN
Sana •

SOUTH
YEMEN

Nouakchott •

Dakar •
SENEGAMBIA

L Chad

Niamey •

N'Djamena •

White Nile

Blue Nile

DJIBOUTI
Djibouti •

Aden •
Gulf of Aden

Soco
(S. Yeı

Banjul •
Bissau •
GUINEA-
BISSAU

UPPER
VOLTA
Bamako •
Ouagadougou •

Black Volta

GUINEA

BENIN

Niger

NIGERIA

Benue

CENTRAL AFRICAN
REPUBLIC

Addis Ababa •

SOMALIA

Conakry •

Freetown •
SIERRA LEONE

IVORY
COAST

TOGO
GHANA

Lagos •
Lomé •
Porto
Novo

CAMEROON
Cameroon
▲ 4069

Bangui •

ETHIOPIA

Monrovia •

LIBERIA

Abidjan •

Accra •

Malabo •

Yaoundé •

Ubangi

L Rudolf

Mogadishu •

EQ. GUINEA
Libreville •

CONGO

GABON

ZAIRE

Zaire

Kasai

UGANDA
Margherita
5127

Kampala •

L Albert

L Victoria

RWANDA
Kigali •

Bujumbura •
BURUNDI

KENYA

Kenya
5199 ▲

Nairobi •

Kilimanjaro
5895 ▲

Brazzaville •
Kinshasa •

CABINDA

Tanganyika

Dodoma •

TANZANIA

Seyc
Islaı

Luanda •

ATLANTIC OCEAN

ANGOLA

ZAMBIA

Lusaka •

L Mweru

MALAWI

L Malawi

Lilongwe •

Zambezi

MOZAMBIQUE

Comoro
Islands

Madagascar

• international boundary
• administrative boundary
• undefined or uncertain international boundary
• cease-fire line
• capital city
▲ mountain peak (in meters)

4000m
1000m
200m
0
below sea level
marsh

scale 1:36 000 000 at Equator

14

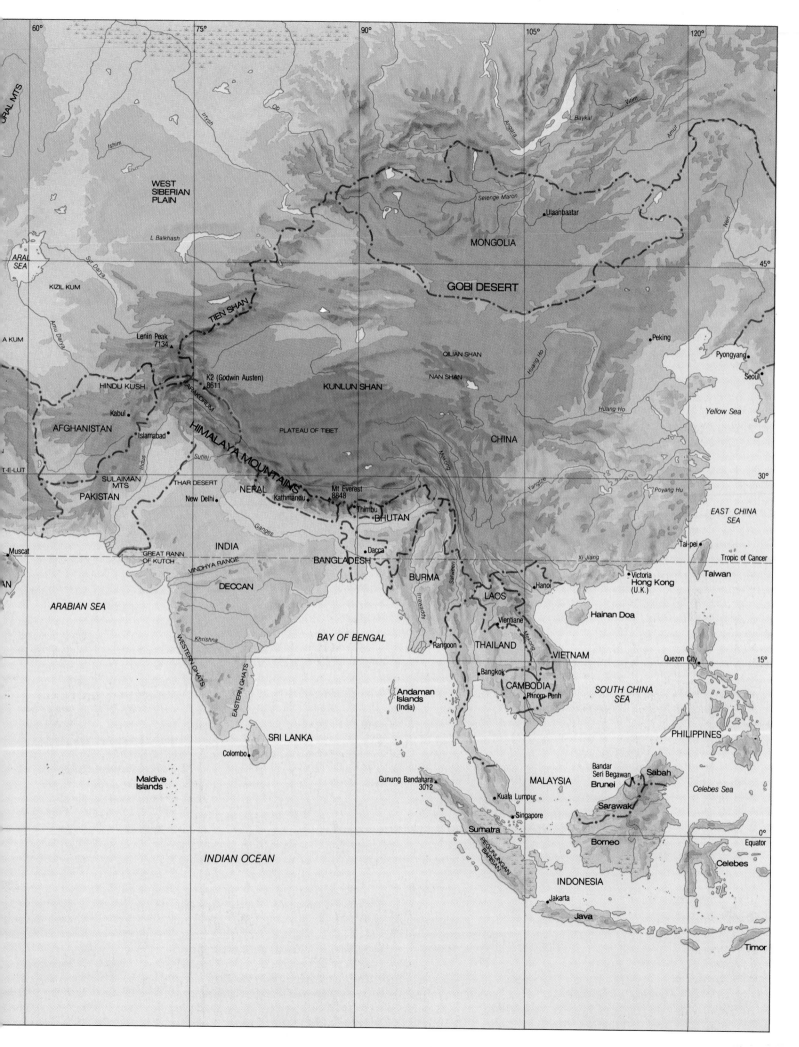

URAL MTS

WEST
SIBERIAN
PLAIN

Ishim

Irtysh

Ob

Selenge Maron

L. Baykal

Vitim

Angara

Amur

ARAL
SEA

L. Balkhash

•Ulaanbaatar

MONGOLIA

Nen

A KUM

Syr Darya

KIZIL KUM

TIEN SHAN

GOBI DESERT

45°

Amu Darya

Lenin Peak
7134

HINDU KUSH

Kabul•

AFGHANISTAN

•Islamabad

K2 (Godwin Austen)
8611

KARAKORUM

KUNLUN SHAN

QILIAN SHAN

NAN SHAN

Huang Ho

•Peking

•Pyongyang

•Seoul

Yellow Sea

T-E-LUT

Indus

HIMALAYA MOUNTAINS

PLATEAU OF TIBET

Huang Ho

CHINA

Mekong

Yangtze

Poyang Hu

30°

SULAIMAN
MTS

Sutlej

THAR DESERT

NEPAL

•New Delhi

•Kathmandu

Mt Everest
8848

•Thimbu

BHUTAN

EAST CHINA
SEA

PAKISTAN

Muscat•

GREAT RANN
OF KUTCH

INDIA

Ganges

•Dacca

BANGLADESH

BURMA

Salween

•Hanoi

Xi Jiang

•Tai-pei

Tropic of Cancer

VINDHYA RANGE

DECCAN

LAOS

•Victoria
Hong Kong
(U.K.)

Taiwan

ARABIAN SEA

Khrishna

Irrawaddy

Hainan Doa

•Vientiane

BAY OF BENGAL

•Rangoon

THAILAND

Mekong

VIETNAM

•Quezon City

15°

WESTERN GHATS

EASTERN GHATS

•Bangkok

CAMBODIA

SOUTH CHINA
SEA

Andaman
Islands
(India)

•Phnom Penh

SRI LANKA

•Colombo

PHILIPPINES

Maldive
Islands

Gunung Bandahara
3012

MALAYSIA

Bandar
Seri Begawan

•Sabah

Brunei

Celebes Sea

•Kuala Lumpur

Sarawak

•Singapore

Sumatra

Borneo

0°

INDIAN OCEAN

PEGUNUNGAN
BARISAN

Equator

Celebes

INDONESIA

•Jakarta

Java

Timor

15

INTRODUCTION
WESTERN ATTITUDES TO ISLAM

For much of the past 1300 years Europeans have regarded Islam as a menace. Devout Christians have felt challenged by a faith which acknowledged one God as creator of the universe but denied the doctrine of the Trinity; which accepted that Christ was a prophet and was born of a virgin but denied that he was divine or that he was crucified; which believed in a day of judgment and heaven and hell, but appeared to make sex the chief of heaven's rewards; which regarded the Christian Bible as the word of God but gave supreme authority to a book which seemed in great part to deny its teachings. Christian states have felt threatened by the success of Muslim power which penetrated to the heart of France in the 8th century, probed the depths of central Europe in the 16th and 17th centuries, and for nearly a thousand years patrolled the southern and eastern flanks of Christendom. Even in the 18th and 19th centuries, when the tables were turned and European power was spread throughout the world, Muslims were still seen to be a danger, this time to the security of European empire. Facts such as these have fashioned European attitudes to the Islamic world, fostering among many an enduring antagonism and an unwillingness to sympathize with the Islamic vision of life and of the way it should be lived; while the distinctive civilization which has been formed by this vision has been valued less for its own sake than as a foil against which the European identity could be discerned and the European achievement measured.

From the beginning, European attitudes were fundamentally hostile. Early Europeans, cut off from the main centers of Muslim civilization by the Byzantine empire, built a vague and fantastic picture of Islam from Byzantine sources: it was a heresy derived from the Christian teachings which the monk, Bahira, had been forced to reveal to Muhammad; the Quran had been borne to the people on the horns of a white bull; the Prophet was a sorcerer whose success owed much to his proclaimed revelation of divine approval for sexual license. From the beginning of the 12th century and the time of the First Crusade, however, a rather more serious appreciation developed, marked by the translation of the Quran into Latin by the English scholar, Robert of Ketton, in 1143. In the 13th and 14th centuries Europeans came to emphasize two elements in their more knowledgeable picture of Islam. The first was the extent to which the Quran could be made to corroborate the Gospel. The second – which is of dubious logic when combined with the first – was an attack on the status of Muhammad as a prophet. How could a man who performed no miracles and who, according to Christian legend, lied and wallowed in debauch, be a prophet of God? And two particular aspects of his message were singled out as targets for Christian polemic: the support Islam was believed to give to the use of force (although Christians too waged holy wars), and the sexual freedom Muslims were supposed to enjoy in this life combined with the sensual ecstasy they were promised in the next. Dante contrived a horrible fate for Muhammad, the false prophet. In the *Inferno* a few Muslims, the philosophers Avicenna and Averroes, and Saladin, the great hero of medieval chivalry, were numbered among the virtuous heathen who, like Hector, Socrates and Aristotle, were allowed to suffer only moderate punishment in the first circle of hell. But the Prophet of Islam was consigned to the ninth of the 10 gloomy ditches surrounding Satan's stronghold, where, branded a spreader of scandal and discord, he was condemned to being split continually from his chin to his anus as the staves of a cask are ripped apart.

The great mass of the medieval polemic against Islam continued to be deployed throughout the Renaissance and the Reformation into the 18th century. Polydore Vergil, quintessence of Renaissance historical scholarship, merely repeated the medieval accusations: Muhammad was a magician, he had been taught by a Christian monk, his heresy had been spread by violence and by the promise of divine approval for sexual indulgence, and so on ... Prominent among the accusations was that Muhammad was an impostor. A notorious 17th-century biography by a dean of Norwich cathedral was subtitled *The True Nature of Imposture Fully Display'd*, and Barthélemy d'Herbelot's influential *Bibliothèque Orientale*, an encyclopedia published in 1697, began its entry on the Prophet: "He is the notorious impostor Muhammad, author and founder of a heresy, which has taken the name of religion." Even the superbly rational and judicious Edward Gibbon, who wrote admiringly of Muhammad in *The Decline and Fall of the Roman Empire*, could not decide whether he was an enthusiast or merely a charlatan. So damning was the image of the Prophet that it was a powerful metaphor to brandish in European polemic. Thus Luther bracketed the Roman Catholic Church with Muhammad's heresy, as the work of the devil in Christendom, and Voltaire, attacking all revealed religion through the example of Islam, brought down the curtain on his tragedy, *Le Fanatisme, ou Mahomet le prophète*, with the dying Muhammad bidding his successor hide his evil from the Muslims lest it destroy their faith.

From the 18th century onwards, however, the basis of a broader understanding of Islam was beginning to be fashioned. Within Europe Christian revelation was losing its comprehensive hold over men, and although the old Christian prejudices still survived in secularized minds, the change enabled Europeans increasingly to perceive other ways of understanding the world and even to sympathize with them. Simultaneously, the attitude of European powers to those of the Muslim world evolved from a real fear of the Ottoman threat to confident equality as not just the Ottoman but the Safavid and the Mughal empires too declined. By the end of the 18th century Europeans were sure of themselves in

The French invasion of Egypt in 1798 marked dramatically a major change in European attitudes to the Muslim world. For the first time since the crusades Europeans walked as conquerors in the lands of the eastern Mediterranean. Although the old Christian prejudices still survived, as they do today, Europeans now began to explore new attitudes ranging from a confident sense of superiority to a genuine desire to understand the motive force and achievement of Islamic civilization. In this picture, Napoleon, triumphant amid the fallen enemy, commands his army at the battle of the Pyramids in July 1798.

their relations with Muslim powers, a change symbolized by the dramatic French invasion and occupation of Egypt in 1798, and the British conquest of Mysore, the last actively hostile Indian Muslim stronghold, in 1799. This confidence, moreover, continued to grow throughout the 19th century as the Russians and the Dutch joined the British and the French in bringing Muslim peoples beneath their control, till by the treaty of San Remo in 1920 more than three-quarters of the Muslim world was under European sway. As Europeans began to liberate themselves from the medieval Christian vision, and met more Muslims and came to know their civilization better, a deeper understanding of Islam became possible.

Nevertheless, among the attitudes which flourished from the 18th century, the old uncompromising approach remained prominent. Seizing the opportunities made available by empire, Christian missionaries moved among Muslim peoples as never before; and although some like Bishop Heber and Dr Livingstone had a certain sympathy with Muslims, others slipped all too readily into the traditional pattern of Christian prejudice. Much of the medieval polemic was repeated in a *Life of Muhammad*, published in 1851 by the Bombay Tract and Book Society, while Sir William Muir, a senior Indian administrator, translated for missionary use the *Risalah*, the Arabic work which had furnished medieval churchmen with plentiful ammunition concerning the Prophet's sexual indulgence, alleged murders and forcible conversions. But it was not just missionaries who kept alive the old association of Islam with sex and violence. Two mid-19th-century visitors to Egypt as different from each other as the influential Arabic scholar, Edward Lane, and the novelist, Gustave Flaubert, were impressed by the place of sex and sensuality in an Islamic environment, the former hinting at an

excessive "freedom of intercourse," while the latter's visit was a fundamentally sexual experience which left a distinct imprint on his work. Not surprisingly the colonial administrator was struck by the violent aspects of Islam, being exercised by the holy wars which Muslims always seemed likely to wage against European rule. Indeed, the terms "Muslim" and "fanatic" became almost synonymous for Europeans confronting Muslim resistance in places as far apart as Algeria, India and Indonesia, and during the great European expansion of the 19th century the image of Islam as a religion of violence gained fresh currency as Muslims put up the strongest resistance to European dominion over the earth: "the sword of Muhammad, and the Kor'an," declared Sir William Muir, "are the most stubborn enemies of Civilisation, Liberty, and the Truth which the world has yet known."

There was no greater contrast to the attitude of Christian antagonism than the way in which Napoleon, child of the Enlightenment, assumed a Muslim persona and manipulated Muslim institutions as part of his imperial purpose in Egypt. "I respect God, his Prophet and the Quran," he declared on landing in 1798, and then proceeded to act the Muslim ruler, publicly honoring the Prophet, beginning his letters to the Muslim potentates of the area with the Islamic *basmala*, and winning the religious and social leaders of the land to his side. Thus Napoleon, who according to Victor Hugo "appeared to the dazzled tribes like a Muhammad from the West," expressed a pragmatism in the face of Islam of which Europeans had hitherto been largely incapable. Others, as they strove to rule Muslim peoples in the years to come, were to follow his example, though never so conspicuously.

Undoubtedly there was also a tinge of Romanticism in Napoleon's attitude to Islam, symbol though he was of the newly triumphant classical age. In courting an Islamic identity he was striving, as Romantics did, to reach beyond the classical limits of 18th-century civilization just as his advance to Egypt and the East challenged those of the European power system. In doing so he was exploring the possibilities of an increasingly important element in the European attitude to the Islamic world: its position as a richly laid table at which the European imagination could feed. For a hundred years or so European appetites had already been whetted by the growing number of travelers' tales, and especially by the *Arabian Nights*, first translated by Galland in 1704. This offered that sumptuous array of caliphs, viziers, slaves, genies, lamps and fabulous happenings which has furnished a large part of the store of words and images Europeans use to embrace the Islamic world. Indeed, for some this world now became an exotic realm in which they could explore new possibilities, as did Montesquieu in his *Persian Letters*, or Mozart in the *Abduction from the Seraglio*, or Goethe in his *West-Easterly Diwan*; but it also became a world in which Europeans traveled in search of themselves, masquerading in outlandish dress — great has been the love of flowing robes and Arab attentions among the British from Lady Hester Stanhope, who gloried in entering Palmyra through a triumphal arch and pitching her tent amid thousands of Bedouin, to T. E. Lawrence, who never seemed to get over the excitement of Arabs, camels, sand and war in the desert. But whether these Europeans journeyed in person or only in the imagination, they were concerned more to impose their vision on this world than to savor its reality, more to make it serve their purpose than to value it for its own sake. Certainly their romantic attitude brought some advances in knowledge and sympathy but in the end a new barrier of the imagination was being created to replace a significant part of the old one of prejudice.

A further attitude which both fed off the others and helped shore them up was the profound sense of superiority which grew together with European empire. Abu Taleb Khan, an Indian Muslim who visited London in 1800, had to tolerate a stream of unsympathetic criticism of Muslim customs from the practice of eating with the hands to the ceremonies performed by pilgrims at Mecca. This assumption that European ways were better was echoed by those who viewed Muslim societies for themselves. French diplomats in Teheran a few years later, sure that they understood native ways, complained of the lack of honor or shame among Persians and of their tendency to exaggerate. In India nearly three decades afterwards, Macaulay asserted in his notorious minute on education that "by universal confession there are no books," of Muslim, or for that matter Hindu, learning, "which deserve to be compared with our own." Not surprisingly such overweening confidence persuaded the government of India for a time to forget the fragile basis of British rule and to give moral support to efforts to convert the population to Christianity: Europeans were sure that they were both different from and better than Muslims. Europeans, in fact, ruled Muslims by divine right, while Muslims, in the words of the British prime minister, Gladstone, were "radically incapable of

Sex, violence and fanaticism have traditionally filled a large part of the European image of the Islamic world. *Above* Sensuality and sex ooze from this languorous Algerian odalisque by Renoir. The harem and its delights were a frequent resort for the imagination of 19th-century painters and writers. Renoir painted this lady in 1870, nine years before he visited Algiers. *Left* As to violence, this brilliant but shocking painting by Henri Regnault, entitled *Summary Execution under the Moorish Kings of Granada*, says all. *Right* The terms "Muslim" and "fanatic" have often been synonymous in the European mind. Moreover, *dhikrs*, or the various techniques developed by mystics to help in their remembrance and glorification of God, although often objects of great curiosity, have also seemed alien. This unsympathetic lithograph of 1880, which depicts a *dhikr* in Cairo, speaks more of religious fanaticism than of religious ecstasy.

establishing good or tolerable government over civilized and Christian races."

Side by side with this broadening range of attitudes there developed the scholarly study of the faith and of Islamic societies. This began with more accurate translations of the Quran: that of Maracci into Latin in 1698 and of Sale into English in 1734. Sale's Quran also featured a preliminary discourse in which he both spoke of Muslim achievements with admiration and used Muslim sources to write their history. In doing so he followed a trail blazed not long before by two Oxford professors of Arabic, Edward Pococke and his pupil Simon Ockley, who, after collecting and studying manuscripts, wrote Islamic history not as polemic but as history. Towards the end of the 18th century, large numbers of texts, both literary and religious, began to be translated into European languages, work in which Sir William Jones, founder of the Asiatic Society of Bengal in 1783, and Silvestre de Sacy, first president of the French Asiatic Society in 1822, were prominent. During the 19th century the range of study continued to broaden as students of those intrinsically 19th-century subjects, the science of religion, biblical criticism and comparative philology, brought Islam and the languages Muslims spoke within their purview. At the beginning of the 20th century, the study of Islam emerged from the shadow of these subjects to become an independent discipline. Men like the Hungarian Jew, Ignaz Goldziher, the Dutch scholar-administrator, Snouck Hurgronje, the Scottish-American, D. B. McDonald, and the Russian, V. V. Barthold, began to think of themselves as Islamic specialists concerned to bring the highest standards of scholarship and interpretation to bear on their subjects. They founded a scholastic tradition which has reached its highest peak so far in the work of the Frenchman, Louis Massignon, who greatly enlarged understanding of the spiritual dimensions of Islam, and the Englishman, Hamilton Gibb, who strove to provide a frame within which the historical development of Islam could be comprehended. Since World War II, Islamic studies have steadily expanded as the subject has grown in the USA and as scholars have begun to apply the insights of the social sciences, in particular those of anthropology. Consequently, Islamic studies have gained new dimensions, in part because the anthropologist has extended the search for knowledge from the antique and citied communities of the central Islamic lands to tribes and villages in Africa and south and southeast Asia, and in part because by being able to see the many compromises Islam has made and is making with local cultures, we have come to learn of the many different ways there are of being Muslim.

As we would expect, the scholarly study of Islam reflected the attitudes of the society in which it was pursued. Simon Ockley, for instance, although he was concerned to present the facts of the development of Islamic civilization and its relation to Europe, nevertheless shared the common view of early 18th-century Europe that Islam was an outrageous heresy. Ernest Renan, the comparative philologist and biblical exegete, considered that Islam with its emphasis on the overwhelming authority of God's word was characteristically Semitic, opposed to the scientific spirit, and a barrier to progress: its civilization was inferior to Aryan civilization which had produced science and philosophy. Indeed, confidence in the superiority of Western civilization, and of Western ways of looking at things over the Islamic, has been instinct in much Western scholarship. There is a tendency to produce studies which seem more concerned with debates going on among Western intellectuals than with an imaginative understanding of Muslim societies. It appears, moreover, particularly difficult for scholars raised in a fundamentally agnostic and materialistic environment to understand the power of faith. This may explain why some of the best and most sensitive research has been done by devout Christians: at a time when they are increasingly burdened by worldly pressures, Christians have found a new affinity with those who also worship the one God. Massignon was renowned for his saintliness; while Gibb declared, "the metaphors in which Christian doctrine is traditionally enshrined satisfy me intellectually as expressing the highest range of spiritual truth."

We are left with the singular paradox that, although traditional sources of hostility to Islam derived from the medieval Christian polemic still flourish in secular form, it is devout Christians who seem to come closest to understanding Islam. The old objection which focused on the enjoyment of sex and sensuality has become a new objection to the position of women. The concern about violence has become disapproval of the inhumane punishments and bloodthirsty politics of some Muslim societies. The fear of Muslim power, which gave way after the expansion of the West to a sense of superiority, rises again as oil brings Muslims the ability to influence Western life and a new assertiveness brings them the will to do so. Moreover, if Westerners are no longer perturbed by the thought of Muhammad's imposture, they are worried by what now seems heresy in their eyes: the desire of many Muslims to subordinate the life of their society and the workings of the modern state to the holy law. Indeed, a disapproval of Islam, which sometimes amounts to outright hostility, seems ingrained in the secular culture of the West. Christian leaders, on the other hand, are no longer hostile, they no longer wish to emphasize what divides them from their great rival monotheistic faith. Thus the Second Vatican Council, while not pronouncing upon whether the Quran is the word of God or not, asks Christians to look upon Islam with understanding in their hearts. It declared

Upon the Muslims, too, the Church looks with esteem. They adore one God, living and enduring, merciful and all-powerful, maker of heaven and earth and Speaker to men. They strive to submit wholeheartedly even to His inscrutable decrees, just as did Abraham, with whom the Islamic faith is pleased to associate itself. Though they do not acknowledge Jesus as God, they revere Him as a prophet. They also honor Mary, His virgin mother; at times they call on her, too, with devotion. In addition they await the day of judgement when God will give each man his due after raising him up. Consequently, they prize moral life, and give worship to God especially through prayer, almsgiving, and fasting.

PART ONE
REVELATION AND MUSLIM HISTORY

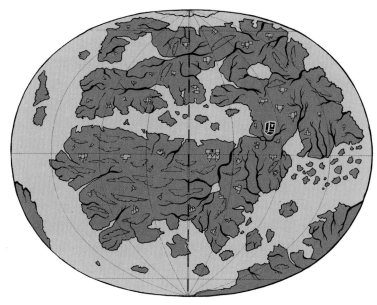

THE FIRST NINE CENTURIES FROM 622 TO 1500

The spread of Islam 622–1000

By 1500 Muslims ruled, or lived in, most of those areas of the world where men had flourished from ancient times. Baghdad and Cairo had been great centers of Muslim civilization, Athens and Benares lay beneath Muslim sway, while the limits of Muslim expansion lay far beyond. In the west they guarded the Atlantic shores of Morocco and patrolled the savanna lands which lie between the Sahara and the rain forests of tropical Africa. In the east they flourished in communities scattered throughout Ming China and found fertile ground for the faith on the Malaysian peninsula, the northern shores of Sumatra and Java, and Philippine Mindanao. In the north Islam had claimed the souls of the Mongol hordes' nomadic followers from the Tarim Basin to the great bend in the Volga at Kazan, while in the south Muslims held their own against a revivalist Hindu Vijayanagar empire on the edge of India's Deccan plateau and filtered down Africa's eastern shore as far as Kilwa and Madagascar's northern tip. Moreover Islamic civilization was still gaining ground at the expense of others, replacing China's influence on the steppes of the northeast, challenging Hinduism in south and southeast Asia, and winning on points against Christianity in the west. Only in Sicily and the Iberian peninsula had Muslims given ground, and most notably in 1492 when eight centuries of Muslim rule came to an end with the fall of the kingdom of Granada. But this loss was more than matched by Ottoman gains in southeastern Europe

where they were pressing into the central Balkans and along the northern shores of the Black Sea towards the Crimea, an advance crowned in 1453 by the capture of Constantinople, capital of eastern Christendom. Although there was at this time no one great political center at which the power of these far-flung Muslim peoples could be drawn together and displayed, if we survey their situation in the perspective of world history it is at this time that they begin to stand forth most strongly against their competitors.

The faith of Islam began around 610 AD when Muhammad (born 570 AD), son of Abd Allah, a Meccan merchant given to religious contemplation, had a vision. While he was asleep in his solitary cave on Mount Hira some miles from the city, the Angel Gabriel came to him and said: "Read." Muhammad hesitated and the angel clasped him tightly, almost smothering him, till Muhammad asked, "What shall I read?" Then the angel said: "Read in the name of thy Lord who creates – creates man from a clot. Read and thy Lord is most Generous, who taught by the pen, taught man what he knew not." This was the first of many messages from God which Muhammad was to receive. They form the Quran, which in Arabic means "reading" or "recitation." Inspired by these messages Muhammad began to preach to the people of Mecca exhorting them to give up the many idols they worshiped and to submit to the one and indivisible God. Muhammad found few followers and provoked much hostility. So, when in 622 he and his supporters were invited to the oasis town of Medina some 340 kilometers northeast of Mecca, they went.

That the emigration to Medina was the decisive moment in Muhammad's mission was recognized by the first generation of Muslims who made 622 AD the first year of the Islamic era. In Mecca Muhammad had preached his new faith as a private citizen. In Medina he quickly became a ruler wielding political and military as well as religious authority. The change is manifest in the revelations Muhammad transmitted; the Meccan chapters of the Quran were concerned primarily with doctrine and ethics, but those revealed at Medina relate to the political and legal problems which emerged as the religious community grew into a Muslim state. By the time Muhammad died on 8 June 632 his achievement had been extraordinary: he had given the nomads and townsmen of this out-of-the-way corner of the ancient world a faith in one God and a book of revelations which pointed the way to a life which was vastly superior to the paganism which it replaced; he had also by means of warfare and of wise alliance led the expansion of his community from Medina until it formed the state which dominated western Arabia.

Muslims believe that Muhammad was the last of God's prophets. He is seen as completing the work begun by the great Hebrew prophets, Abraham, Moses and Christ, in showing the way to a true

monotheism. Muhammad finally called the faith he preached Islam, meaning "submitting" to God; Muslims were those who submitted, and the community of Muslims were those who accepted God's final revelation to mankind through Muhammad. In this community sovereignty rested with God alone. There was no distinction between the religious and the secular spheres, between the things which were God's and the things which were Caesar's; all things were subject to God's will revealed in the Quran. The function of the leader of the community, after Muhammad the caliph or successor, was to administer God's will. What he should administer he was told by the community of Muslims whose duty it was to uphold God's will and to bring the benefit of his guidance to the rest of mankind.

Fired by their new faith the Muslims exploded out of western Arabia and within a few years had rearranged the long-established political geography of the Mediterranean and west Asian world. By 634 the rest of Arabia was conquered and they were advancing into Palestine. Eight years later they had defeated the great Byzantine and Sassanian empires which lay to the north and had taken control of Syria, Iraq, western Iran and Egypt. By the death of the third caliph, Uthman, in 656, Muslim armies had advanced through Cyrenaica in the west, the Caucasus in the north, and to the Oxus and the Hindu Kush in the east. Subsequently expansion slowed a little, but by 711 Muslims had set about the occupation of Sind in the east and by 712 they had reached Tashkent and begun to secure Central Asia for Islam, an achievement which was consolidated when Chinese forces were defeated at the battle of the river Talas in 751. In the west they finished their conquest of North Africa in 709 and advanced through Spain into France where their northward expansion was finally halted by the Franks at Poitiers in 732. By the mid-8th century the Muslim caliphs ruled from their capital Damascus a vast empire stretching from the Indus valley and Tashkent in the east to the Atlas mountains and the Pyrenees in the west. The Muslims had expanded most marvelously, a triumph which seemed to confirm that Muhammad was the seal of the prophets and which has left an enduring mark on their thinking down the centuries. They felt they had taken command of history.

Despite the community's victories over other peoples, during the first 120 years it endured three great civil wars. A continuing element in the strife was the opposition of the party of the Prophet's cousin and son-in-law, Ali, that is the *Shia* (party) of Ali, often just known as the Shias to those who occupied the caliphate. They believed that rightful leadership belonged with the descendants of the Prophet. Their opposition came out in the open during the reign of the third caliph, Uthman, and war broke out when Uthman was assassinated and Ali succeeded to the caliphate in compromising circumstances. It ended only after Ali himself was assassinated at his headquarters in Kufa in 661 and his eldest son resigned his claims to the office. Shia opposition, however, did not end here; indeed it was stimulated further by the fact that the caliphate, originally an elected office and always so ideally, now became the dynastic possession of the Umaiyads, an aristocratic Meccan clan. In 680 the second civil war began when Husain, the younger son of Ali, led a revolt against the Umaiyad caliph Yazid and was massacred with most of his small force at Karbala. Thus the grandson and the nearest relatives of the Prophet were destroyed and the young Muslim world was horrified. "Gently," cried a voice from the crowd as the Umaiyad viceroy turned over Husain's head with his stick, "on that face I have seen the lips of the Apostle of God." Immediately there was a fresh surge of Shia resistance which was not quelled till 692. In the long run it transformed the party into a religious sect whose distinctive belief was to replace the caliph with an imam from whom they received in each generation the original light of Muhammad's revelation and whose most hallowed rites mourned the slaughter of the purest sources of that light at Karbala. Thus the Shias continued to oppose the Umaiyad caliphate and joined other groups to fight a third civil war which culminated in the destruction of the dynasty in 750 and the enthronement of the descendants of the Prophet's uncle, al-Abbas, in their stead.

The establishment of the Abbasid caliphate marked the end of the first phase of Muslim expansion: for some hundreds of years there was little progress beyond the frontiers won by the Umaiyads. Instead there was a period of internal expansion and consolidation. Now a great Muslim civilization was created. The Arabs brought to it Muhammad's revelation and the tools they had developed for its everyday use – the study of the traditions relating to the Prophet's life, philology and the law. These interacted with the deep-rooted cultures and civilizations the Arabs ruled, slowly fashioning a Muslim life. The conquered peoples, on the other hand, met and mingled as never before in the great *Pax Islamica* carved out by Arab arms, and a brilliant civilization was created. Trade grew as men and goods moved from China to Egypt, from Spain to western India. Towns burgeoned and Baghdad, the Abbasid capital founded in 762, was a major entrepôt larger than Seleucia and Ctesiphon, its Greek and Sassanian predecessors. Persians, Iraqis, Syrians, Egyptians, all made their contribution to an extraordinary creative achievement in architecture and the arts. The great mosques of Samarra in Iraq, Kairouan in Tunisia, and Ahmad Ibn Tulun in Cairo stand witness to the power and confidence of the new Muslim civilization. The tales of the *Thousand and One Nights*, which are drawn from Egypt, India, China, Greece and elsewhere, reveal the far-flung horizons of the Baghdad of Caliph Harun al-Rashid (786–809) and the magnificence of its life.

Intellectual activity also flourished. Religious studies multiplied in towns from Samarqand to Spain, and the pursuit of knowledge broadened to embrace history, literature, Greek medicine, Greek mathematics, which was developed to include algebra and trigonometry, and geography, whose variety and scope as a subject reflected the spreading vision of the age. It was at this time that Greek logic and philosophy, which were based on pure reason and implied that the human mind was superior to the divine, came seriously to challenge the religious culture. At the same time the Muslim master science, the law, was given decisive form. Based on the Quran and the traditions, four great codes were produced, not differing from each other in any important respect and comprehensive in their range. Indeed, there was no aspect of human life for which Muslim law did not legislate, which was why it was the crucial agent in molding Muslim lives and why it was, and remains, a crucial means of fashioning a growing likeness of form and of mind among the Muslims of the world. Arabic was, of course, the language of the law and of religious culture wherever Muslim communities grew up, and so by and large it was to remain.

The shift of the caliphate from Damascus to Baghdad signaled more than just a change of dynasty; it also signaled a shifting of the focus of Muslim civilization from the eastern Mediterranean to the borderlands of Asia. Baghdad, only 56 kilometers from the old Sassanian capital of Ctesiphon, was as open to influence from China or India as it was from Spain or North Africa. Now, too, Arab political power began rapidly to decline as the subject peoples of the empire, particularly the Persians, asserted themselves; the authority of the caliphate came to be represented less by the explosive verve of the Bedouin armies than by a

Expansion of the Islamic world to 1500
This map demonstrates how the first nine centuries of Islamic history were a period of almost continual expansion, with the exceptions of the losses of Spain, Portugal and Sicily and the temporary irritation of the crusades in the eastern Mediterranean. The greatest threat to Islam came from the Mongol invasions. But, by

extent of the Islamic world at the death of Muhammad 632
extent of the Islamic world at the death of Uthman 656
extent of the Islamic world at the end of the Umayyad dynasty 750
limit of the Islamic world at the end of the Umayyad dynasty 750
extent of the Islamic world 1250
limit of the Islamic world 1250
extent of the Islamic world 1500
area reconquered by Christians 1250
area reconquered by Christians 1500
extent of Christian crusading principalities in 12th century
site and date of important battle
scale 1:40 000 000

converting the Mongols to Islam, the Muslims transformed this major reverse into an opportunity for further expansion in Russia, Central Asia and China. Into Africa south of the Sahara and around the Indian Ocean shore to southeast Asia, Islam was carried to pagan peoples mainly along trade routes. Sufis, Muslim mystics, were usually the first bearers of the faith.

slow-moving imperial bureaucracy which owed much to a Sassanian past.

Then, although Arab culture continued to grow as a unifying force throughout the Muslim world, the power of the caliphate itself declined. The Abbasids, in fact, never ruled the Muslim world as the Umaiyads had done; their very accession had in 756 AD led to the establishment of an independent amirate in Spain by a fleeing Umaiyad prince. In the late 8th and 9th centuries other independent regimes were established: the Idrisids, Aghlabids and Tulunids in the Maghrib and Egypt, the

Tahirids, Saffarids and Samanids in the eastern lands. These dynasties, while effectively independent, recognized the Abbasid caliph as the head of all Islam. In the 10th century, however, this titular supremacy was challenged by Shia Fatimids, rising first in Tunisia and later in Egypt, which they conquered in 969 and where they established their own caliphate which at its height ruled much of North Africa, Syria and south and west Arabia. In self-protection the Spanish Umaiyads promptly declared their own caliphate at Cordoba, and for a time there were three caliphs in the Muslim world. The legitimacy of the Abbasid caliphs was the most widely recognized, although from the mid-10th century they were no more than puppets of the Buyids, a family of Shia brigands who carved out a state in Mesopotamia and the Iranian highlands.

The 9th and 10th centuries saw the emergence of an increasingly well-defined Persian identity within the Muslim world. The independent kingdoms which arose in the eastern lands of the Abbasid caliphate were Persian kingdoms; it was thus that the Persians who had been swallowed whole when the Arabs devoured the Sassanian empire and had been made Muslim, began to express themselves again politically. These courts, particularly that of the Samanids (819–1005), became patrons of a new evolving Persian culture. Of course, Persians played a distinguished part in the flowering of the great international Muslim literature in Arabic, as they have continued to do in the religious sciences down the ages. But they also preserved their own pre-Islamic language, which, padded now with Arabic loan words and written in the Arabic script, reappeared as a powerful cultural vehicle in its own right; it grew into the most potent bearer of the Persian ethnic identity, especially after Firdawsi (935–1020) composed his *Shahnama* which drew on the richly stocked Persian folk memory and so perfectly captured the Persian ideal of heroism. Persian thus rose to become the second language of Islam, dominant in the Muslim land empires of Asia, the medium of polite culture, and in its literary wealth both a source of education and a model of excellence.

The nomad invasions

By the end of the 10th century, Islam bounded a world which was rich in trade, brilliant in intellectual endeavor, considerable in artistic achievement, but which had lost the political unity and the military strength which marked its early years. For the next five centuries its heartlands were to suffer invasions of nomads, most particularly nomads from Central Asia who pressed into the Islamic lands as other nomads pressed into southern Russia and eastern Europe. The first were Turkish tribesmen who began to infiltrate during the 9th century, coming either as captured slaves or soldiers of fortune. In 977 one of the latter seized control of Ghazna in the Samanid dominions and established a dynasty which in 17 great campaigns from 1000 to 1030 conquered north India. Then in the middle of the 11th century Turkish tribesmen began to flood in. Already Muslims (they had been converted by the Samanids a century before), these Turks, known as Seljuqs, quickly brought most of western Asia beneath their control and carried the flag of Islam into Asia Minor where no Arab had been able to

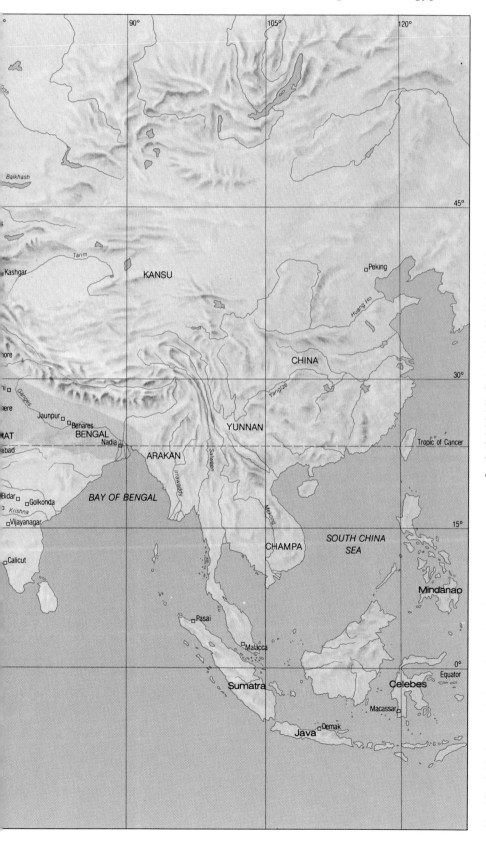

bear it. In Africa, too, nomads were on the move: Arab tribesmen were raiding and destroying centers of civilization which the early Arabs had built on the continent's northern shore, while in the far west Berber nomads were carrying Islam into the Senegal and Niger basins. Our prime concern at this stage, however, is with the central Islamic lands where by 1100 Turks controlled the caliphate but shared dominant power in the Islamic community with the Fatimids of Egypt.

The coming of the Turks was an event of great importance in the development of Islam. A third race was added to the leading races of Islam, bringing fresh blood and new energy. The caliphate was given another lease of life as the Turks freed the Abbasids from their Buyid thralldom and created a new institution, the universal sultanate. Henceforth the caliph bestowed legitimacy on the effective holders of power as he did when he crowned the first Seljuq sultan in 1058, while it was now the sultan's duty to impose his authority on the Islamic community, defending it against attacks from outside and denials of God's word within. In the east the Ghaznavid Turks firmly established Muslim power in northern India, effectively beginning the expansion in the subcontinent where Islamic civilization was to flower most abundantly. In the west the Seljuq invasion of Asia Minor began the process which was to make it the modern land of the Turks and the base from which the greatest Islamic empire of the past 600 years would expand into southeast Europe.

The great Seljuq victory over the forces of Byzantine Christendom at Manzikert northwest of Lake Van in 1071 led to the preaching of the First Crusade some 25 years later, and a stream of Frankish crusaders over the following 200 years. The crusading activities in Palestine, though they bulk large in Western memory, were no more than a minor irritant to the Muslims, and in the long run, more than anything else, important for the boost they gave to Muslim–Christian trade in the Mediterranean and the severe deterioration which they brought to the conditions of Christians under Muslim rule. Outside Palestine, however, the Muslims suffered some permanent defeats. In 1091 the Normans completed the reconquest of Sicily, in 1147 Lisbon was recaptured by the Second Crusade, and by 1212 the Spanish Christians had reconquered most of Spain leaving just a small enclave at Granada in the south.

Even more important than the coming of the Turks was the coming of the Mongols, the last great nomadic invasion of the settled world. The first wave was led by Gengis Khan who between 1220 and 1225 brought Transoxania, Khurasan and the Caucasus beneath his control. The second wave left Central Asia under the command of his grandson Hulagu in 1255. By 1258 Baghdad had been sacked and the last Abbasid caliph and his family destroyed, trampled to death beneath carpets. By 1260 most of the Muslim world, except Egypt, Arabia, Syria and the lands to the west, acknowledged the supremacy of the pagan Mongol. These areas, moreover, survived the Mongol scourge more by luck than by anything else; it was only the chance of the Great Khan Mongke's death in 1259 which turned Hulagu's eyes eastward and left the Egyptian Mamluks only a fraction of his army to

defeat at Ain Jalut, near Nazareth, in 1260. This victory, however, which was won by Turkish and Kipchak military slaves, enabled the Mamluks to reestablish the caliphate in Cairo, and the Nile valley to sustain the old Arab Muslim civilization till the Ottoman conquest in 1517. Muslims under Mongol suzerainty found themselves for a while ruled from the Mongol capital in Peking, although by 1258 they were divided between three great Mongol states, that of the Chaghatai Mongols in Central Asia, the Golden Horde in the Volga Basin, and the Il-Khans, descendants of Hulagu, in Iraq and Iran. And when these states declined and Mongol prestige sank, it was restored by Timur Lang, the lame, better known in English as Tamerlaine, who commanded the last great wave of invaders from the steppes of Central Asia. Between 1370 and 1405 he won a vast empire which stretched from Tashkent to Mesopotamia, and he went one better than his Mongol forbears (though in blood more Turk than Mongol) by conquering Delhi and frightening Cairo into a respectful submission.

The impact of the Mongol invasion was immense, though not quite as disastrous as historians both Muslim and non-Muslim once used to suggest. Admittedly, it was the first time that pagans had conquered the heartlands of Islamic civilization but by the beginning of the 14th century they had accepted Islam, which must be accounted one of the greatest of Muslim achievements as it ensured that Central Asia to the Altaic mountains would continue to be Muslim. The actual process of Mongol conquest wrought hideous destruction among the urban communities which filled the area from Samarqand to Baghdad to Delhi. They delighted in devastating the higher cultures of the settled peoples for its own sake: it seemed not to matter that economies contracted and tax revenues declined as irrigation systems were wrecked, city populations slaughtered to a man, and gruesome towers of skulls built whose ghastly fluorescence at night as they decayed warned subject peoples of the terrible risks run by the defiant. On the other hand, the Mongol Khans and their successors patronized Islamic learning, the arts and sciences, as they had never been patronized before. In Tabriz Rashid al-Din the world historian flourished; in Tamerlaine's Samarqand Saad al-Din Taftazani wrote books which were to be at the heart of Islamic learning to the present day; Nasir al-Din Tusi and Ulugh Beg fostered astronomy; Saadi, Hafiz and Jami brought Persian poetry to its highest pitch; miniature painting, fertilized by Chinese influences, blossomed to bring forth its finest fruit in the work of Bihzad at the court of Herat; architecture reached new heights as the Mongols rebuilt some at least of the cities they had destroyed. The overall effect, moreover, was that Persian culture was so developed and spread so widely as to become the dominant culture of the eastern Islamic world. Then finally the Mongols were Turkicized as they had been Islamized. Although they came to power by crushing Turkish regimes, they were themselves but an elite which led Turkish tribesmen, and the outcome of their conquest was to confirm the political dominance of the Turkish peoples from Asia Minor to northern India. From these peoples were to emerge the founders of the three great empires which dominated the early modern period.

Above The 14th-century tomb tower of Halim Hatun in Gevas, Lake Van, Turkey. The spread of tomb towers is often associated with the coming of the Turks, and they remain a characteristic building of these nomadic people, even though there was an established Persian tradition of such towers two centuries before they arrived. It has been suggested that the Turks brought with them the funeral customs of their Central Asian ancestors, on the grounds that their tombs greatly resemble their ceremonial *yourts* or tents.

The Mongol soldier, whose horsemanship was the most effective in military history, enabled his khans to conquer the greatest land empire in world history, from Java and Korea in the east to Poland in the west, from the Arctic in the north to Turkey and Iran in the south. Mongol armies were remarkable for their strategy, mobility, endurance, discipline and coordinated tactics. They even had organization resembling a modern general staff.

The widening Islamic world

As Islam fought its great contest with the Mongols, it was also expanding on the margins. The growth of trade played a leading role in its spread along the shores of the Indian Ocean and in sub-Saharan Africa. Thus Muslim communities were established on the east coast of Africa, on India's southwestern shore and in the ports of China. By 1200 they were also established in Gujarat and Bengal, and were soon to be established along Burma's Arakan coast. Then in the 13th century there came the Islamization of the entrepôt communities on either side of the Malay straits, a crucial event which prepared the way for the steady spread of Islam in island southeast Asia. By 1500 Islam was established around the coasts of the Malay peninsula and the northern coasts of Sumatra and Java and was pressing into the Moluccas and the southern Philippines. To Africa south of the Sahara Islam was brought not by ships but by camels as Muslim traders exchanged gold and slaves from the Guinea coast for handicrafts and salt from the north. Great states grew in the western Sudan: Ghana, athwart the Senegal and Niger rivers, which in the 11th century the missionary Almoravids brought within their Berber empire; Mali, which from the 12th to the 14th centuries stretched from the Atlantic to the great bend in the Niger and whose vast wealth was fabled in Europe; Songhai, which dominated the central Sudan from the 14th to the 16th centuries. Great cities also grew where traders from many lands mingled with scholars and with poets: Gao, capital of the Songhai empire; Jenne, center of learning in southern Mali; Timbuktu, intellectual, cultural and economic capital of the Sudan.

Elsewhere the expansion of the area where Muslims lived owed more to arms than to trade. In India the Turkish Khaljis and Tughluqs extended the sway of the Delhi sultanate to the south for a time, and when the tide of conquest receded, there emerged successor states in most of which Muslims ruled predominantly Hindu populations. In Asia Minor the Ottoman Turks established a small *ghazi*, or holy warrior, principality on the borders between Christendom and Islam. Founded in the mid-13th century, it had by the mid-14th century conquered northwestern Asia Minor and entered Rumelia. Then surviving the heavy defeat of Ankara at the hands of Tamerlane, the Ottomans took the eastern Christian bastion of Constantinople in 1453, annexed Greece and Herzegovina, and began to exercise their sway over Bosnia and the states of the northern Black Sea shore. In China the Mongol Yuan dynasty (1279–1368) imported Muslims from the west as civil servants; these helped to form Muslim communities throughout the land, the most numerous of which have always been in Kansu at the eastern end of the Islamized Tarim Basin and in Yunnan on the southwestern frontier.

By 1500 all hope of political unity in the Islamic world had long since passed. The universal caliphate was a subject for political thinkers and dreamers alone. Two main centers of power stood out: Egypt, where the Mamluk sultanate of Turks and Circassians still fostered high Arab culture, and the Ottoman empire, which now bridged the Bosphorus and was to claim to be the universal Islamic monarchy. Elsewhere power was divided among many sultans. Moreover the dispersion of

Right A page from a Quran written in the eastern Kufic style in Iraq or Iran during the late 11th century. Kufic script, named for the early center of Islamic learning at Kufa in Iraq, is distinguished by the static form of its letters, a form which seems to emphasize the air of command which runs through every sentence of the holy book. Many early Qurans are in Kufic, which was also widely used for monumental inscriptions. Copying out the Quran in calligraphy has always been an important act of devotion for Muslims.

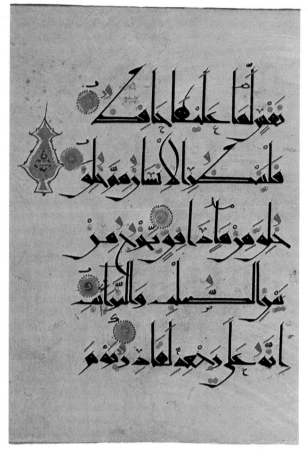

political power was coming to be matched by cultural diversification. Two great high cultures divided the Muslims: the Arab in Egypt, Africa and among the traders of the southern seas, and the Persian which had spread in the great land empires created by the Turkish peoples. Then, as Islam continued to expand, increasing numbers joined the faith in Africa, in India, or in southeast Asia, whose prime means of cultural or religious expression owed little or nothing to Arab or Persian forms. Nevertheless there remained a level at which matters of central importance were shared: the Quran, the traditions and the law, and the skills needed to make them a social force, which meant a mastery of Arabic. Thus between 1325 and 1354 the Moroccan scholar Ibn Battuta had been able to travel 120 000 kilometers throughout the Muslim world from Tangier and Timbuktu to China and Sumatra, being received with honor almost wherever he went, and wherever he decided to rest a while taking employment as a judge.

The shaping of Islamic life: the law

The main influences which shaped the beliefs and behavior of the ever-growing community of Muslims were the holy law which told the Muslim how he should behave towards God and towards his fellow men and sufi mysticism which taught him how to know God in his heart. Both institutions were based on the Quran and the traditions.

The Quran was the first and the most profound guide to the living of Muslim life. The size of an average book, it is divided into 114 chapters, called *suras*. These are arranged, not according to when they were revealed, but roughly, except for the brief opening chapter, according to length, chapter 2 having 286 verses and chapter 114 six short verses. Consequently many of the earlier chapters deal with the Muslim community's political and legal problems at Medina, while the later chapters convey Muhammad's ethical message in the urgent and estatic form of the early revelations. It is not known if the Quran was written down in full in Muhammad's lifetime and it is generally thought to have been compiled a few years after his death from "scraps of parchment and leather, tablets of stone, ribs of palm branches, camels' shoulder-blades and ribs, pieces of board and the breasts of men." For a while there were several differing versions but by the end of the Umaiyad caliphate the text had been established in all but a few details.

The Quran, Muslims believe, is the word of God; and truly it speaks to men in terms of awesome command which contrast markedly with the quiet counsel of the Christian New Testament. It is the perfect book; it explains all that man needs to know to live a normal and spiritual life and, as verse succeeds verse, it presents to him a massive challenge. God is one – indivisible. Nothing stands between man and God; there is no one to intercede for him. God is all-powerful. He created man who is ever in danger of incurring his wrath. Forgiveness cannot be won by merit; it flows only from God's grace, although a man may make himself worthy of forgiveness by a life devoted to God's service. A stark choice is offered. There is the right path which man, submitting to God, must follow if he hopes to reach paradise. Should he turn away from this path he will surely suffer on the day of judgment. "I, God, am the best knower," begins the first verse of the second chapter of the Quran:

> This Book, there is no doubt in it, is a guide to
>   those who keep their duty.
> Who believe in the Unseen and keep up
>   prayer and spend out of what we have given
>   them.
> And who believe in that which has been
>   revealed before thee, and of the Hereafter
>   they are sure.
> These are on a right course from their Lord
>   and these it is that are successful.
> Those who disbelieve – it being alike to them
>   whether thou warn them or warn them not –
>   they will not believe.
> God has sealed their hearts and their hearing;
>   and there is a covering on their eyes, and for
>   them is a grievous chastisement.

Westerners have usually found the Quran confused, obscure and wearisome to read, in part because they usually read it in translation and miss its rhymes and rhythmic language, that majestic Arabic which in the Prophet's mouth reached its highest peak, and in part because they tend to treat it merely as a source of information about what Muslims should believe and how they should behave. But for Muslims it has always been much more than this. It is to be recited as an act of commitment in worship. Quran means "recitation" and Muslims recite it whenever they pray. Indeed, Muslims worship by means of it, and in reaffirming it they renew the event of revelation. It is the unfathomable well-spring of the community. "There is no end to its miracle," wrote al-Ghazzali, giant among the scholars of the Islamic Middle Ages; "it is ever fresh and new to the reciters." And

as Islam expanded, its ever fresh challenge was brought to peoples who knew no Arabic. Yet translations were not made, not into the languages of southeast Asia or West Africa, not even into Persian. It was held to be untranslatable, and although translations have been attempted in recent centuries, Muslims still feel so today. Thus many came to affirm their faith in a language they did not understand; there was just the ineffable power of giving voice to the very words of God. Some of course had to understand. They learned Arabic which remained the lingua franca of Muslim scholarship, and so the Quran continually contributed to the unity of the community.

The second source of guidance were the *Hadiths*, the traditions relating to the life of Muhammad who is believed to have been divinely inspired in all that he said and did. In the early years, writing being an unusual accomplishment, these were handed down by word of mouth. But then, as sects and rivalries

A 16th-century Ottoman tile depicting the praying stations of the four main schools of Islamic law around the Kaaba, the sanctuary in the great mosque at Mecca which Muslims believe was first built by Abraham. To the right, there is the station of the Hanafis, at the top that of the Malikis, to the left that of the Hanbalis, and at the bottom, with the well of Zamzam to the left and the pulpit to the right, that of the Shafiis. At prayer times Muslims of the different schools stand behind their respective imams in the appropriate part of the mosque.

sprang up, *Hadiths* began to be manufactured to support partisan interests. Scholars began to study them to distinguish the genuine from the forged. They were concerned to give currency only to those traditions with a reliable chain of narration going back to the person who first witnessed the Prophet's action or heard him speak. A typical *Hadith* runs thus: "Anas reported that the Messenger of God said: I shall be the foremost of the prophets in respect of followers on the Resurrection day, and I shall be the first of those who will knock at the door of paradise." By the end of the third century of the Islamic era, six great critical collections had been compiled, two of which, those of Muslim and Bukhari, had acquired special authority. Bukhari, for instance, quotes 2762 authenticated traditions which are arranged in 97 books under headings dealing with many aspects of faith and works and which were sifted, according to Muslim tradition, from over 200 000. Bukhari's compilation is venerated by Muslims second only to the Quran.

The law is usually referred to as the *Sharia*, meaning originally in Arabic "the path leading to the water," that is, the way to the source of life. It grew from the attempts of early Muslims, as they confronted immediate social and political problems, to derive systematic codes of Muslim behavior from the Quran and the *Hadiths*. During the Muslim community's first 200 years four main schools of legal interpretation developed: the Hanafi school, which grew up in the Abbasid capital of Baghdad and which is said to have been founded by Abu Hanifa (died 767); the Maliki school, which grew out of the practice of the Medinan judge Malik Bin Anas (died 795); the Shafii school, developed by a disciple of Malik, al-Shafii (died 820); and the Hanbalite school, founded by Ahmad Ibn Hanbal (died 855) in Baghdad. The first three schools all had formal differences of emphasis and technique. Hanafis, for instance, allowed more room for personal reasoning than the others, while the Shafiis

were concerned to distinguish their use of the *Hadiths* from the more limited use of the Malikis. All agreed, however, on important matters; all recognized each other's systems as equally orthodox. The Hanbalite school, on the other hand, developed as a traditionalist reaction against what it felt to be the speculative innovations of the earlier established schools. Although recognized as the fourth orthodox school by the other three, Hanbalites were less willing to return the compliment. At the beginning of our period they were a declining force in Iraq and Syria. The Hanafites, however, were strong throughout mainland Asia, the Shafiis prevailed in Lower Egypt, the Hijaz, southeast Asia and East Africa, and the Malikis dominated the rest of Muslim Africa.

Scholars developed these systems roughly in this way: they treated the Quran as containing the general principles by which all matters should be regulated, and where the Quran was unclear they sought clarification from the *Hadiths*. The foundations of the *Sharia*, then, were the clear and unambiguous commands and prohibitions to be found in these sources. When points of law arose on which the Quran or the *Hadiths* offered no firm guidance, most scholars turned to *qiyas*, which meant arguing by analogy and applying to the new problem the principles underlying a decision which had already been reached on a comparable problem. As the years passed, scholars increasingly came to agree on points of law, and the principle of *ijma*, or consensus of the community, came into play. "My community," went a very important *Hadith*, "will never agree upon an error," so if the community embodied in its legal experts came to agree on a point, that agreement gained the authority of revelation itself and the development of new ideas on the subject was forbidden. Steadily more and more of the law was underpinned by *ijma*, and the right of *ijtihad*, or individual interpretation, became confined to the decreasing area on which no general agreement had been reached. By the mid-10th

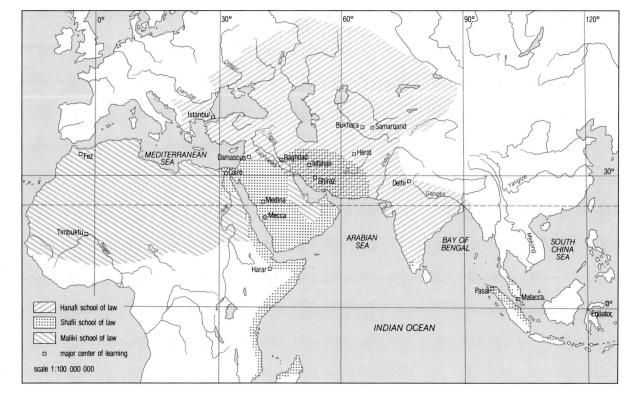

Regions in which the various Sunni schools of law were dominant c. 1500
By this time the Hanbali school had few followers, although it was to have a new lease of life as a result of the Wahhabi revival in the 18th century. The various areas of influence represent different, although certainly not exclusive, cultural worlds: that of Maliki scholarship in Africa, which usually looked to Cairo; that of Shafii scholarship in southeast Asia, which usually looked to Arabian centers of learning; and the areas of Turko-Mongol rule and Persian culture, which stretched from the Ottoman lands through Central Asia and into India. All schools except the Hanbali regarded each other as equally orthodox.

Hanafi school of law
Shafii school of law
Maliki school of law
□ major center of learning
scale 1:100 000 000

century most Muslim scholars had declared the "gate of *ijtihad*" finally shut. Henceforth, if a man questioned the meaning of a text in such a way as to challenge the interpretation supported by *ijma*, he committed *bida*, an act of innovation, which is as near as Islam came to the Christian idea of heresy.

The *Sharia* grew slowly during the first three Islamic centuries into a unified system and in the process, as Western historians have revealed, drew on much customary practice which had become embodied in the *Hadiths*. But most Muslims since then have believed that it was fashioned quite independently of historical or social influences. Flowing from revelation it was the embodiment of the Divine Will: those who disobeyed sinned, and had to expect God's retribution. As this was the last occasion on which God would speak to man, the law could not be changed, and man was limited to development within the divine framework. Westerners know that their law has grown out of and been molded by society, but for Muslims, writes a leading legal historian, "law precedes and molds society"; it is a practical elaboration of the eternal standards which God has set for man.

The *Sharia* is comprehensive; it embraces all human activities defining both man's relations with God and his relations with his fellow men. In the first role it prescribes what a man should believe and how by ritual acts he should express his belief (see below, pp. 40–43); in the second it covers those areas which in Western codes would come under the heading of civil, commercial, penal, private law and so on. No formal legal code was ever created, the *Sharia* being more a discussion of how Muslims ought to behave. Indeed, as one might expect from a system which is concerned to lay down absolute standards of good and evil, human actions are classified on a five-point scale: obligatory, meritorious, indifferent, reprehensible, forbidden. The object of the *Sharia* was to establish the sure path, to show man what he must do to live righteously in this world and prepare himself for the next.

It would be a mistake to imagine that in the years up to 1500, or indeed at any time in Islamic history, this comprehensive system had ever been enforced in its entirety. It was impossible to enforce a system which included moral obligations as well as hard-and-fast rules. Moreover, the realities of power were not to be avoided. Theoretically it was the task of scholars, appointed as *qadi* or judge, to interpret the law, and that of the holders of political power to administer it. But few rulers could afford to allow the interpreters of the law of God to be completely out of their control. Even the Abbasids, who presided over the formulation of the *Sharia* and declared themselves its servants, could not permit the courts to be independent. Equally, Muslim rulers could not afford to antagonize their partially Islamized peoples by trying at one stroke to abolish social and legal traditions which owed nothing to Islam. When the traveler Ibn Battuta, appointed *qadi* of the Maldives, strove his "utmost to establish the prescriptions of the sacred law," beating those who did not pray and trying to make the women wear clothes, he found himself at loggerheads with the sultan and needing to escape as quickly as he could. Thus the *Sharia* had to coexist with other laws, as under the Mongols it had lived side by side with their *yasa* or dynastic law, or as among many

Muslim peoples it rubbed shoulders with the local *adah* or customary law. Some parts of the *Sharia* have never been put into practice, for instance those relating to the constitution of the Muslim state, international relations and war. Others, for instance those dealing with personal relations such as marriage, divorce and inheritance, were widely enforced. Yet even here there were many exceptions, such as the Berber peoples of North Africa who refused to allow the *Sharia* to overturn their tribal customs which, for example, did not permit women to possess property.

The *Sharia*, however, remained a potent ideal. All who accepted Islam, accepted in principle its authority and the fact that it should supplant other laws. Some scholars would always be striving, as Ibn Battuta did, to bring local usages up to the Islamic standard. As far as they succeeded in doing so, they brought unity to the Islamic world.

The shaping of Islamic life: mysticism

The second great formative influence on the development of Islamic civilization was mysticism, or sufism as it is generally called. Whereas the *Sharia* dictates the formal relations of the Muslim towards God and his fellow men, sufism cultivates the inner attitude with which the believer performs his outward obligations. The Muslim is frequently reminded by the Quran and the *Hadiths* that he should live his life as if always in the sight of God, which does not mean merely that he should pray regularly and remember God in his heart as he does so, but also that he should remember God in every other action of the day, before eating, before working, before making love. Among the "seven whom God will give shade under his shade on the day on which there will be no shade except his shade," Muhammad is reported to have said, will be "a man whom a young girl of accomplishment and beauty calls and who says [before he joins her to make love]: 'Certainly I fear God'."

Although instinct in the Quran and the *Hadiths*, sufism grew as a distinct strand of Muslim devotion, in part as the Arab Muslims came into contact with the Christian and other mystic traditions of the lands they conquered, and in part in reaction to the moral laxness and worldliness of the Umaiyad court at Damascus. The term "sufi" is probably derived from the Arabic *suf*, meaning wool, which referred to the simple woolen clothes worn by the mystics in contrast to the rich apparel of the worldly.

In the beginning the basis of sufi feeling was fear of God and of judgment, but by the second Islamic century the doctrine of love had become prominent. "Love of God hath so absorbed me," declared the woman saint Rabia (died 801), "that neither love nor hate of any other thing remains in my heart." And of her approach to God she wrote:

I love Thee with two loves, love of my happiness,
And perfect love, to love Thee as is Thy due.
My selfish love is that I do nought
But think on Thee, excluding all beside;
But that purest love, which is Thy due,
Is that the veils which hide Thee fall, and I gaze on
Thee,
No praise to me in either this or that,
Nay, Thine the praise for both that love and this.

(trans. R. A. Nicholson)

Sufism, Islamic mysticism, was the second great formative influence on the development of Muslim civilization. Sufis were concerned to cultivate the inner attitude with which the Muslim performed his outward obligations; they were concerned with spiritual development, with the ways in which a man might come to know God in his heart. Many sought God in ascetic living and withdrawal from the world. Some were mendicants, like this Qalandar, whose worldly possessions of stick, animal skin and begging bowl are portrayed around him.

Sufis, however, did not remain satisfied with this intense gospel of love. By the third Islamic century they had begun to develop the doctrine of the "inner way" or the spiritual journey towards God. There were different stages of the way corresponding to different levels of sufi experience. The mystic was first a seeker, then a traveler, and then an initiate. He progressed along the way through processes of self-abnegation and enhanced awareness of God. The nearer he came to God, the more God spoke with his lips, controlled his limbs and moved the desires of his heart, until he reached the final stage when self was annihilated and totally absorbed in God.

Sufi claims to be able to achieve knowledge of God through direct personal experience brought them into conflict with the *ulama* (plural of the Arabic *alim*, learned man), men learned in the Islamic sciences. As far as the *ulama* were concerned, knowledge of God came through the study of the Quran, the *Hadiths*, the *Sharia* and theology, with the aid of the weighty tools of Islamic scholarship which they had developed. The sufi claim was both provocative and dangerous for Islam as they understood it. Moreover, the *ulama* were uneasy about the growing popular support for the sufi way and feared for their role as protectors of the faith and sole arbiters of Islamic doctrine. They tried to silence the sufis, but incidents of repression such as the brutal execution in 922 of al-Hallaj of Baghdad, who following the sufi path to its limit had declared "I am the Truth," could not prevent the continued growth of a movement which was deeply rooted in the Quran and satisfied the religious hunger of many ordinary men and women. In the third and fourth Islamic centuries the two sides continued to grow apart.

That the division did not become unbridgeable is largely due to one man, the greatest figure in medieval Islam, indeed the most influential Muslim after Muhammad, al-Ghazzali (died 1111), who in religious insight and intellectual vigor has been compared with St Augustine and Martin Luther. Al-Ghazzali, as he reveals most illuminatingly in his autobiography *The Deliverer from Error*, traveled long in search of God. Finding, like growing numbers of his learned contemporaries, that the hyper-rationalism of the theologians could not satisfy the longings of his soul, he eventually "turned with set purpose to the method of mysticism . . . I knew that the complete mystic 'way' includes both intellectual belief and practical activity; the latter consists in getting rid of the obstacles in the self and in stripping off its base characteristics and vicious morals, so that the heart may attain to freedom from what is not God and to constant recollection of Him." Al-Ghazzali found God. From this achievement flowed work in which he was able to combine scholastic and mystical systems of ideas and find a place for the emotional religious life within Islam, a place which the consensus of the community was willing to support. This is not to say that the way of the *ulama* and the way of the sufis became completely fused, but that what had been diverging paths were now linked, though distinct. Moreover, it was possible for the two paths to come together in one man.

After al-Ghazzali sufism spread rapidly throughout the Islamic world. It attracted many in western Asia and North Africa who up to this point had not been moved; it seems to have won over many Shias; while in the lands of Africa and Asia, where Islam was rapidly expanding, it was mainly sufi missionaries who went among the infidel peoples, revealed by their example the quality of the Islamic life and slowly drew converts to their side. In many areas sufis were the typical Muslims, and so great was their popular appeal, and such was the support that they received from secular rulers, that there was little the *ulama* could do to limit their influence.

At the same time new elements, which were quite alien to early Islamic ideas, became fixed in sufi thought. One of the more important was the veneration of the sufi shaikh (*pir* in Persian), or master, by his disciples in his lifetime, which led to the worship of the shaikh after he died. Such practices challenged the central tenet of Islam, the Muslim's belief in the unity of God. Nevertheless they spread widely and with them spread another potentially dangerous doctrine, the belief in the *qutb*, the pole of the world, who with his saintly followers governs the earth. Most noted of all the sufi *qutbs* was Mawlana Jalal al-Din Rumi (died 1273), whose long religious poem, the *Mathnawi*, is the supreme work of Persian sufism, sometimes referred to as the Persian Quran, and treasured as a source of spiritual guidance down the centuries wherever Persian has been spoken.

A second new element was the spread of pantheistic thought. This was elaborated most effectively by the Spanish sufi scholar Ibn al-Arabi (died 1240 at Damascus), who in his master work, *The Meccan Revelations*, argued that all phenomena are manifestations of a single being which is one with God and produced a mystical interpretation of Islamic doctrine which he claimed had been revealed to him as the "seal of the saints." These pretensions which challenged the status of the Prophet were too preposterous to be taken seriously, but the doctrine of the "unity of being" was another matter; the wide popularity it gained threatened the *Sharia*. Sufis who claimed that "everything is God," however pious they may have been, would have found the absolute standards of human behavior laid down in the *Sharia* hard to take seriously. Indeed some claimed that those who achieved mystic truth, who discovered the *haqiqa* or "inner meaning," no longer had need of the *Sharia*; the tendency of Ibn al-Arabi's thought was to deny all that Islam stood for.

To many *ulama* Ibn al-Arabi was hardly a Muslim, and from time to time down to the present day his works have been proscribed, but they were extremely influential, especially in the Persian and Turkish areas of the eastern Islamic world. The doctrine of the "unity of being" had obvious uses when Islam was establishing itself among large numbers of shamanistic, Hindu and animist peoples, as it made possible the compromises essential if the faith was to spread rapidly in regions with no traditions of ethical monotheism. The doctrine, however, also benefited from being embodied in the brilliant flowering of Persian

poetry from 1200 to 1500. It was there in the odes of Hafiz who, following Ibn al-Arabi, uses the language of human love to express spiritual communion with God. It is most completely expressed in the *Mathnawi* of Rumi and the mystical poetry of Jami, men whose art placed Arabi's esoteric doctrine on the lips of all who used the second language of the Islamic world. So Jami in beginning his idyll "Salaman and Absal" declares:

I would be
Thy Lover, and thine only-I, mine eyes
Seal'd in the light of Thee to all but Thee,
Yea, in the revelation of Thyself
Lost to Myself, and all that Self is not
Within the Double world that is but One.
Thou lurkest under all the forms of Thought,
Under the form of all Created things;
Look where I may, still nothing I discern
But Thee throughout this Universe, wherein
Thyself Thou dost reflect, and through those eyes
Of him whom MAN thou madest, scrutinize.

(trans. Edward FitzGerald)

By 1500 most Muslims approached God as sufis. The *Sharia* had in no way managed to keep up with the rapid spread of sufi influence. Indeed, often

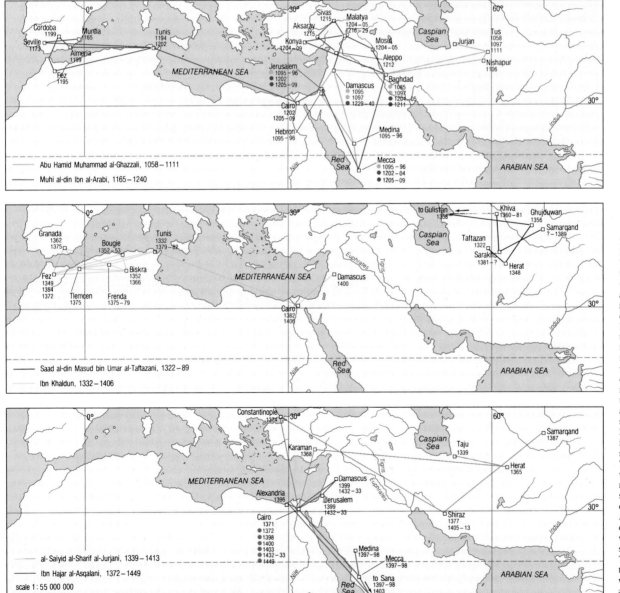

The international world of Islamic scholarship 1200–1500 "Seek ye knowledge," declared the Prophet, "even if it be in China"; and so *ulama* were always ready to travel to learn more. There was, for instance, constant traffic through medieval Damascus, and half the *ulama* in the city at any one time came from outside: during the first nine centuries the Islamic world was knit together by a community of scholarship. The maps on the *left* set out the travels of six leading figures among the *ulama*: al-Ghazzali, supreme scholar of medieval Islam; Ibn al-Arabi, dominant influence on the development of sufism; al-Taftazani of Tamerlaine's court at Samarqand, whose works still figure in the madrasa syllabus; Ibn Khaldun, sociologist, philosopher and outstanding historian; al-Asqalani, who brought the study of *Hadith* to its zenith; al-Jurjani, whose works also still live in the syllabus. After capturing Shiraz, Tamerlaine carried al-Jurjani off to Samarqand where he debated with al-Taftazani: opinions differ as to who won.

Map legends:

— Abu Hamid Muhammad al-Ghazzali, 1058–1111
— Muhi al-din Ibn al-Arabi, 1165–1240

— Saad al-din Masud bin Umar al-Taftazani, 1322–89
— Ibn Khaldun, 1332–1406

— al-Saiyid al-Sharif al-Jurjani, 1339–1413
— Ibn Hajar al-Asqalani, 1372–1449
scale 1 : 55 000 000

The life of Jalal al-Din Rumi, long regarded as the greatest mystic poet of Islam, was transformed when he met a wandering sufi called Shams al-Din, in whom he found the "perfect image of the Divine Beloved." He changed from being a sober man of God into an ecstatic from whom poetry flowed in torrents. After Shams al-Din disappeared, he invented the whirling dance of his Mawlawiya order to symbolize, so it is said, his search for the lost Beloved. Above we see an incident in the life of Rumi when, passing by some gold beaters, he falls into an ecstasy at the chinking rhythm of the hammers and begins to dance. Another sufi, who has studied alongside Rumi but has been forced by poverty to become a gold beater, sees the holy man and dashes from the shop to embrace his feet. Later he becomes a disciple.

being associated with the state and with aristocratic and intellectual education, the *Sharia* was at a disadvantage as it sought to shape the lives of the masses in the classical Islamic mold. Through sufism many popular religious observances had entered Islam. There was singing, dancing and mystic feats such as the eating of glass and walking on fire. Belief in the miracle-working power of saints was widespread and the Islamic countryside was dotted with their tombs, which were places of worship. Sufism made a myriad compromises with local rites and superstitions, and as sufi thought came to be dominated by the belief that God was immanent rather than transcendent so the body of Islam tended to reflect more the beliefs and structure of the societies it embraced than those enshrined in the *Sharia*. There were great dangers. It still had to be decided whether the sufis, by making compromises which enabled them to attract millions of souls which the *ulama* had never been able to touch, had hopelessly degraded Islam, or whether they had merely created the circumstances in which down the centuries converts, while still comforted by their homely superstitions, might slowly absorb the doctrines of the Quran.

Scholars, mystics and the transmission of Islamic culture

Central to the historical development of Islam were the *ulama* and the sufis who preserved and transmitted the shaping forces of law and mysticism

down the ages. They were not priests in any Christian sense; Islam needed no ordained priests to administer sacraments and in theory tolerated no individuals who placed themselves between man and God. Nevertheless, these bearers and administrators of the knowledge which both fashioned Islamic society and nourished its spirit were no less important.

The first *ulama* were the religious specialists of the early Islamic era, the reciters of the Quran and the memorizers of the *Hadiths*. When under the Abbasid caliphate the essence of these primary sources was distilled into the *Sharia*, the *ulama* were transformed into men whose activities focused on the application of the *Sharia* and the teaching of the skills to enable others to do so; by the 12th and 13th centuries they had become, in Damascus for instance, an almost professional body, highly qualified and with many state appointments open to them. By 1500, although their situation varied in different parts of the Islamic world, being much stronger in Egypt, for example, than in the newly Islamized lands of southeast Asia, they were generally a powerful and respected body of men. Some were supported by land grants or salaries from the state, but most lived off endowments established by the pious or the proceeds of the crafts and trades in which they were engaged. Among their duties were the administration of mosques, schools, hospitals and orphanages, in which functions they might control great corporate wealth. But their first task remained the preservation and transmission of the great shaping force of the *Sharia*. As scholars they defended the orthodox understanding of the *Sharia*, as *qadis* they administered it on behalf of the state, as *muftis* they expounded it on behalf of the community for whom they issued *fatwas* (legal decisions) free of charge, they warned the people of their obligations under it in their sermons, and instructed Muslims of all ages in it in their schools.

Our prime concern here is with the process of transmission, that is with the *ulama* as teachers of other *ulama*. They taught most frequently in their homes, or in the compounds of mosques and shrines. They also taught in madrasas, formal schools, which sprang up in much of the Islamic world in the 11th century as secular authorities strove to bring the religious institution beneath their control: among the most important of these were the Nizamiya madrasa at Baghdad, where al-Ghazzali taught, and the al-Azhar madrasa, founded in Cairo in 972, which became the most important teaching institution in the Muslim world.

The subjects taught were: Arabic grammar and literature – which was necessary throughout the Islamic world because the classical Arabic of the Quran and the *Hadiths* was almost as strange to the speakers of demotic Arabic as it was to those who spoke other tongues – the *Hadiths*, Quran commentary, the law including jurisprudence, and theology, although this was often ignored as containing too many dangers for a Muslim's faith. Occasionally there was a little arithmetic, which *ulama* needed if they were to give a *fatwa* on inheritance, or medicine or some sufi works, but the religious sciences were the dominant subjects, while the philosophic and scientific disciplines in which the Muslims so excelled over the Europeans at this time were barred from the madrasas and the normal teaching of the *ulama*. Textbooks in different subjects, like *Hidaya*, Shaikh Burhan al-Din's basic work on the Hanafi law, or Baizawi's Quran commentary, slowly became established. By 1500 standard works existed for most subjects and were used widely throughout the Islamic world, as they have continued to be during the past five centuries.

The tendency of the educational system developed by *ulama* to train their successors was conservative. It was understandable. They knew that they had received the most precious favor from God in the Quran and the life of Muhammad; they also knew that up to the day of judgment there would be no further guidance for man. It was their foremost duty to strive to pass on this gift in as pure a form as possible along with the skills to interpret it for the benefit of the community. The further they got from the time of the Prophet the greater was the chance that parts of God's precious favor would be corrupted or lost. There was no chance of Muslims discovering more of the truth, only a danger that they might preserve less. Education was learning as many fixed statements as possible in as sound a form as possible without necessarily understanding them; it was also normative, learning how things ought to be in the light of divine revelation rather than drawing conclusions from what happened in the parlous present. There was much rote learning, indeed some texts were written in rhyme to help memorization. Classical texts, moreover, tended to gain in authority; as time passed, few new texts were written, *ulama* confining themselves to writing commentaries and supercommentaries on the classical version till it was all but overwhelmed by layers of annotation.

When a teacher finished teaching a book he gave his pupil an *ijaza*, or certificate, permitting him to teach the book which listed the teacher's teacher and followed the chain of transmission back to the original writer and first teacher of the book. It was a highly personalized system which thought in terms of teachers and books rather than schools and subjects. The pupil in his turn knew that he was receiving something infinitely precious, and that he was now a carrier of part of the central traditions of his faith. His respect for his teacher as well as his gratitude were boundless. "Know that [your] teacher is the begetter of your soul," exhorted one 13th-century educational manual, "and the cause of its creation and the essence of its life, in the same way as your father is the begetter of your body and its existence."

Veneration, however, was not bestowed on just one teacher; most *ulama* had several in different places. From the beginning when men had scoured the world in search of information concerning the life of the Prophet, *ulama* had traveled great distances to sit at the feet of famous teachers, and for the dedicated student only the guidance of the most intelligent and sound scholars of his day would do. Al-Ghazzali studied in Tus, Jurjan and Nishapur, and traveled as a scholar to Baghdad, Mecca, Damascus, Jerusalem, Egypt and back to his native Tus. Ibn al-Arabi studied in Seville, Ceuta and Tunis, and traveled to Mecca, Baghdad, Mosul, Asia Minor and finally Damascus. Ibn Battuta went everywhere. The Islamic world was criss-crossed by a network of pupil–teacher loyalties, which formed the basis of a worldwide community of Islamic

feeling and learning, and which was more deeply rooted and far stronger than the ephemeral conquerors and courts which sprang up within its frame. No common cultural artifact better illustrates this phenomenon than the dictionaries of the lives of the *ulama*; they tell of their learning and their travels, their teachers and their pupils, all the details in fact which reveal their contribution to the transmission of the law and of Muslim values.

The sufis developed an equally clear and all-embracing system for the transmission of mystical knowledge. From the 9th century disciples had begun to gather around outstanding spiritual personalities in hope of learning their *tariqat*, or "way" of approaching God. They would follow him as he traveled, or settle down with him in the monasteries which began to be endowed by the pious. The shaikh or master initiated his disciples in his mystic practices according to their abilities. Each shaikh would normally have his established pattern of devotional practice called *dhikr*. In the beginning just one way of remembering God by reciting phrases and perhaps controlling breathing to intensify concentration, it grew into a fully developed collective ritual in which adepts often sought estatic religious experience by chanting, by dancing or by listening to music. Once a disciple had placed himself in the hands of a shaikh, he had to obey him at all costs, even if it meant going against

Collective rituals in which sufis sought through ecstatic experience to come closer to God have always been for outsiders the most striking sufi activities. The picture on the *right*, from the brush of Sultan-Muhammad, master painter of the Safavid court in the early 16th century, illustrates the works of Hafiz, beloved sufi poet of Iran. This witty composition demonstrates well the intentional oscillation between mystical and profane ecstasy which is the feature of Hafiz's poetry. Is it in spiritual or alcoholic ecstasy that the sufis dance and sing? Is the scholar, who approaches the taproom with his bottle, exchanging his book for a new path to God, or just for wine? We cannot even be sure whether the glazed-eyed poet, who presides over the revels, is in a spiritual or earthly stupor.

Left In this charming early 16th-century Mughal painting, a learned man teaches, perhaps in the garden of his house, perhaps in the compound of a shrine. Books are scattered about; the attention of one pupil has been lost and he meditates, rosary in hand. Prayer goes on in the midst of study as the most natural of activities. The man in front performs his ritual ablutions before he prays; the man behind places his forehead on the ground in the course of a *rakat* of prayer.

کرشمه سلطز عشرت فرشته ارحمت زجره بر یخ حور و پری کلاب زد

the *Sharia*; he was to be, as the saying went, "like a corpse in the hands of the washer of the dead."

The veneration of the disciple for his shaikh was the key to the transmission of mystical knowledge down the centuries. Shaikhs normally had two kinds of disciples: *khalifas*, or successors, gifted mystics who were equipped to pass on the shaikh's teaching and have disciples of their own, and those, less gifted, who remained just disciples. *Khalifas* broadcast their shaikh's teaching to the world and usually became saints in their turn. The sequence of successors of a saint was called a *silsila*, or chain of transmission, of which sufis kept a close record in much the same way as the *ulama* kept records of the transmission of the religious sciences. By the 12th and 13th centuries, most sufis traced their particular "way" back to a founding saint from whom their "way" took its name, and then from him through one or more of the great mystics of the early Abbasid period to a companion of the Prophet, usually Ali. Thus the spiritual training which the Prophet had given his followers was seen to have been handed down to the present through a series of holy men.

The shrine of the founding saint was the focal point for the followers of a particular "way" or order. It was usually controlled by the saint's physical descendants, sometimes more ceremonial than genuine spiritual successors. These men also controlled the saint's endowments, sometimes considerable sums, and although they rarely used them for personal benefit, the charity they dispensed in the community could bring considerable influence. If the shrine held the bones of the founder of a major order, it was at the head of a hierarchy of thousands of lesser shrines and the center of international pilgrimage. The lesser shrines in their turn were the focus of a local or regional cult. But whether of local or international importance, the stones of a Christian church perhaps, or a Hindu temple, incorporated in the shrine, or the rites practiced by those who attended it, would hint at how an Islamic sanction had been given to devotions at what the people had long believed to be a sacred place.

Hundreds of sufi orders grew up. The map indicates merely some of the more important which had become established by 1500. Their differences stemmed in part from the extent to which they were

Leading sufi orders c. 1500
The most important development in Islam from the 12th century onwards was the growth of institutional sufism. The map shows the spread of the main traditions of sufi teaching, marks the shrines of the founding saints of the most important orders, and indicates where some of the more important orders established by 1500 were most prominent.

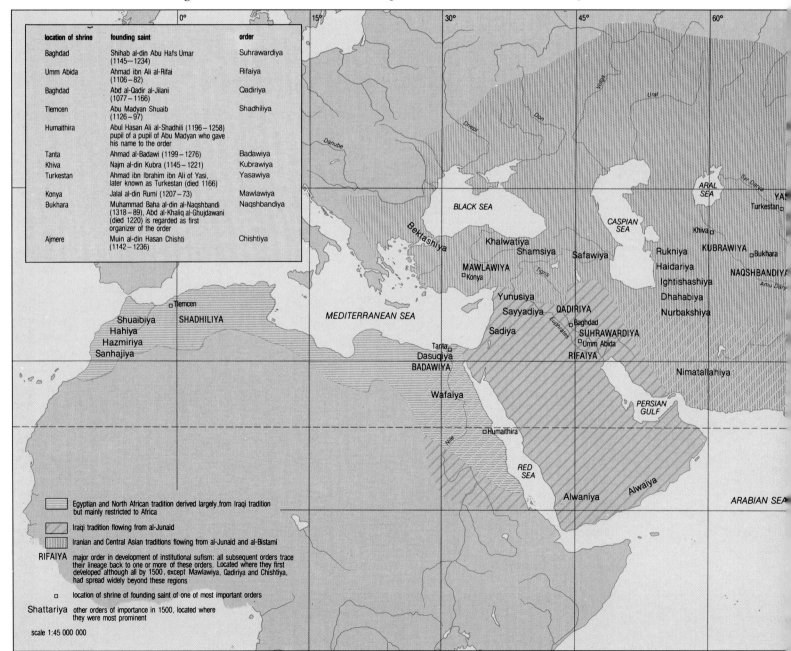

location of shrine	founding saint	order
Baghdad	Shihab al-din Abu Hafs Umar (1145–1234)	Suhrawardiya
Umm Abida	Ahmad ibn Ali al-Rifai (1106–82)	Rifaiya
Baghdad	Abd al-Qadir al-Jilani (1077–1166)	Qadiriya
Tlemcen	Abu Madyan Shuaib (1126–97)	Shadhiliya
Humaithira	Abul Hasan Ali al-Shadhili (1196–1258) pupil of a pupil of Abu Madyan who gave his name to the order	
Tanta	Ahmad al-Badawi (1199–1276)	Badawiya
Khiva	Najm al-din Kubra (1145–1221)	Kubrawiya
Turkestan	Ahmad ibn Ibrahim ibn Ali of Yasi, later known as Turkestan (died 1166)	Yasawiya
Konya	Jalal al-din Rumi (1207–73)	Mawlawiya
Bukhara	Muhammad Baha al-din al-Naqshbandi (1318–89), Abd al-Khaliq al-Ghujdawani (died 1220) is regarded as first organizer of the order	Naqshbandiya
Ajmere	Muin al-din Hasan Chishti (1142–1236)	Chishtiya

Egyptian and North African tradition derived largely from Iraqi tradition but mainly restricted to Africa

Iraqi tradition flowing from al-Junaid

Iranian and Central Asian traditions flowing from al-Junaid and al-Bistami

RIFAIYA   major order in development of institutional sufism: all subsequent orders trace their lineage back to one or more of these orders. Located where they first developed although all by 1500, except Mawlawiya, Qadiriya and Chishtiya, had spread widely beyond these regions

▫   location of shrine of founding saint of one of most important orders

Shattariya   other orders of importance in 1500, located where they were most prominent

scale 1:45 000 000

organized but primarily from variations in their rituals and ways of remembering God, and the extent to which they followed the *Sharia* closely or tolerated deviations from it. This last difference in the main followed the boundary between the urban orders, whose members lived cheek by jowl with the *ulama* and the educated, and the rural orders who did not. Some orders had considerable social and political importance, especially in Africa.

Most prominent, and eventually most widespread, of all the orders were the Qadiriya, named for Abd al-Qadir of Gilan (1077–1166), on the Caspian coast. A strict Hanbali scholar, but also a mystic, Abd al-Qadir's preaching, after he returned from 25 years of ascetic wandering in the Iraqi desert, so impressed the people of Baghdad that they built a monastery for him outside the city walls. His teaching was orthodox, as the following *dhikr* used by the order shows: "I ask pardon of thee mighty God; Glorified be God; May God bless our Master Muhammad and his household and Companions; There is no God but God." Although there is no evidence that Abd al-Qadir intended that his "way" should be continued, a great order did develop around the memory of his personality, and a large number of miracles, which he would most certainly have denied, were attributed to his spiritual powers. He is said, for instance, to have woken up a sleepy audience by making the lights move, and to have taken 13 steps in the air off his pulpit. All of which went to support the old Persian tag that "it is not the masters who fly, but their disciples who make them fly."

Of the other leading orders the Chishtiya should be noted as the most influential Indian order, although the subcontinent is also notable for a large number of irregular orders of which the best known were the Qalandars whose practices were strongly influenced by indigenous beliefs and not bound by the *Sharia*. The Bektashis of Anatolia behaved with like freedom, ignoring many of the outward rites of

Right The transmission of mystical knowledge from the Prophet to the emergence of the early mystical traditions.

Bottom right Many sufis would withdraw to the wilderness to meditate; here a holy man sits on a bearskin beneath a tree, surrounded by disciples and pupils. Such groups, like this one drawn in Isfahan in the mid-17th century, were popular subjects for artists.

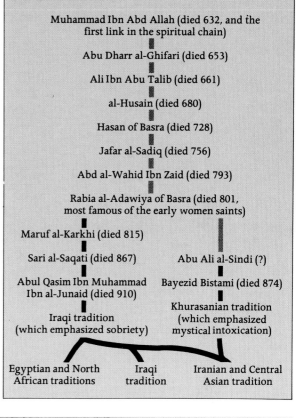

The Transmission of Mystical Knowledge

There is no chain in the transmission of mystical knowledge from the Prophet as firm as that for the transmission of the reliable *Hadiths*. The classic chain of transmission, which the main religious orders all came to adopt, was not established until the 13th century, and since then Muslim scholars have shown that some of its links are false. The chart, therefore, names some of the leading mystics who lie between the Prophet and the emergence of the early mystical traditions. But it should be noted that there is no intention to indicate any direct line of transmission from the Prophet to Maruf al-Karkhi and Abu Ali al-Sindi.

Muhammad Ibn Abd Allah (died 632, and the first link in the spiritual chain)

Abu Dharr al-Ghifari (died 653)

Ali Ibn Abu Talib (died 661)

al-Husain (died 680)

Hasan of Basra (died 728)

Jafar al-Sadiq (died 756)

Abd al-Wahid Ibn Zaid (died 793)

Rabia al-Adawiya of Basra (died 801, most famous of the early women saints)

Maruf al-Karkhi (died 815)

Sari al-Saqati (died 867)

Abu Ali al-Sindi (?)

Abul Qasim Ibn Muhammad Ibn al-Junaid (died 910)

Bayezid Bistami (died 874)

Iraqi tradition (which emphasized sobriety)

Khurasanian tradition (which emphasized mystical intoxication)

Egyptian and North African traditions

Iraqi tradition

Iranian and Central Asian tradition

The mother convent of the Mawlawiya order at Konya. The founder, Jalal al-Din Rumi, lies beneath the blue-tiled Seljuq mausoleum on which the famous lines are written: "Come back, come back, even if you have broken your repentance a thousand times." In the immediate foreground by the weeping willow there is the beginning of a cloister of 18 cells wherein celibate sufis reside. Behind the tree, under the first large dome, is the mosque, and under the second large dome, the dancing floor.

Left Learned and holy men, ideally, submitted to God alone. To emphasize this, many made a point of never visiting princes, so that princes were forced to visit them. Such visits were, like the groups of sufis on page 35, a popular subject for Persian and Indian painting. In this mid-16th-century Safavid picture to illustrate Jami's *Haft Awrang*, a king visits a holy man, whose disciple he has become. He has done so many times before with rich gifts which were spurned. This time he offers a simple gift of a brace of duck. This, too, is rejected. The holy man meant that the only gift he valued was the king's lifelong devotion to his way; only thus could he be sure of reaching heaven.

helped men reach out across the seas and deserts. Although many traveled along their networks, and the pious were automatically drawn to the shrines of the holy, one senses that no less important was the unity of feeling which sufism was slowly fashioning. The orders, by making a myriad compromises, had offered a home to a rich variety of believers from scholars to ascetics to superstitious peasants. All were being offered a sense of spiritual unity as they took their place at the foot of a hierarchy of saints which led to the Prophet. They were becoming part of a second principle of unity in the Islamic world which paradoxically sacrificed the *Sharia*'s unity of outward form to enable millions to share in a common piety.

It would be a mistake, however, to imagine that the transmitters of the two great shaping influences of the Islamic world lined up on sharply opposing sides. Many sufis were deeply learned in the *Sharia* while many *ulama* were also sufis; indeed it was often said that the best sufis and the best *ulama* were those like al-Ghazzali who combined the insights of both traditions. Yet there was a potent source of tension; *ulama* and the stricter sufi orders could not stand by while many sufis ignored the *Sharia*. They would feel compelled to strive to persuade those who had been drawn to the saints' tombs to give up their local customs in favor of the *Sharia* and the central cultural traditions of Islam. They were bound to try to make their own the trail which the sufis had blazed.

There was a second and potentially greater source of tension, this time between the transmitters of the two great Islamic traditions and those who wielded political power. In theory it was the duty of the caliph or his representative to execute the *Sharia* as interpreted by the *ulama*. The realities of power, of course, rarely made such action possible. Nevertheless, rulers were always keen to have the legitimizing force of the men of God on their side, not to mention the popular followings they often led, and with this aim in mind they sought to control them through jobs in government service and grants of land. *Ulama* and sufis could not, ideally, approve a situation in which they became subject to mortal rulers; they must manifest their knowledge in their own lives, which meant submitting only to God. They deplored association with earthly powers. "My room has two doors," declared the great Chishti saint, Nizam al-Din Awliya, whose order laid especial emphasis on avoiding princes; "if the sultan comes through one door, I will leave by the other." Indeed, the only way in which a king might meet a sufi shaikh was to go to the holy man's dwelling and approach him in all humility, a theme which formed a popular genre of Indian Muslim painting. The ideal was the same for the *ulama*. "The worst of scholars is he who visits princes," went an oft quoted *Hadith*, "and the best of princes is he who visits scholars." And biographies of *ulama* would list, as evidence of their virtue, the number of times they had refused state employment. In fact, for much of the time of course, rulers and men of God found a *modus vivendi*, and many *ulama* in particular served their princes. But the ideal of the relationship between the transmitters of Islamic knowledge and the wielders of power was always there to be resurrected, when the *modus vivendi* broke down or Islam seemed to face new dangers.

Islam, observing what seem remarkably like a Christian ritual of communion with bread, wine and cheese, making confessions to their shaikhs, and believing in a quasi-Trinity of God, Muhammad and Ali. Other important Turkish orders were the Mawlawiya founded by the poet Jalal al-Din Rumi and famous for their whirling dance, the Naqshbandiya who were prominent in Central Asia, and the Safaviya who adopted Shiism and fostered the dynasty which founded the modern Iran. The growth of sufism in North Africa was closely associated with the rise of the Almohad dynasty in opposition to Almoravid rule. One of the sufis engaged in the Almohad cause was Abu Madyan (died 1197) from whom most of the "ways" of the region stem, including the Shadhiliya who came to be very influential throughout northern Africa and beyond. Towards the end of the 15th century the characteristic feature of Berber Islam, maraboutism, or the cult of the living holy man endowed with magical powers, had begun to emerge.

When a disciple was accepted by a shaikh he received a certificate which set out the stages by which mystical knowledge had come down from the founder of the order to his new spiritual guide. When he attended the celebrations of the day of his local saint's death the odds were that the rituals would celebrate the stages by which knowledge had come down from the Prophet to the dead holy man. Sufis were as alive as the *ulama* to the process of transmission from the original source of revelation. Moreover, their links, like those of the *ulama*, helped to create a vision of unity in the Islamic world not only in time but also in space. Already by 1500 the Shadhiliya order had adherents from Morocco to southeast Asia. In due course other orders like the Qadiriya and the Naqshbandiya were to spread as widely. But it would be wrong to lay too great an emphasis on how the orders themselves

Belief and Practice

There is no systematic exposition in the Quran of what Muslims should believe and do, yet, taken as a whole, it expresses a consistent body of doctrine and duties. These are contained in the "five pillars," or fundamental observances, of Islam: (1) the observance of the creed, which demands belief in God, his angels, his books, his prophets and the last day on which men will be judged; (2) the performance of prayer; (3) the giving of alms; (4) the observance of fasting; (5) the performance of pilgrimage. There was nearly a sixth pillar, *jihad* or "striving in the way of God." The Quran frequently urges Muslims to "fight in the way of God against those who fight you but be not aggressive . . . and fight them until there is no persecution, and religion is only for God" (Quran 2: 190 and 193). Devout Muslims are constantly aware of the exhortation to "strive in the way of God," although they have come to see it not just as holy war against the unbeliever but also as holy war against the enemy within, man's baser instincts.

"Verily there are 99 names of God," declares one *Hadith*, "and whoever recites them shall enter into Paradise." The names tell Muslims what God is like: "the one," "the creator," "the knower," "the hearer," "the forgiver," "the protector," "the provider," "the merciful," "the compassionate," and so on. Devout Muslims learn the names by heart and recite them in spare moments or as a form of *dhikr*. Rosaries, with either 33 or 99 beads, are used by many Muslims as they recite these most excellent names of God.

God

The one God, the Arabic *Allah*, is but a shortened version of *al-ilah*, "the God," who has no partners, is utterly transcendent, creator of all things, judge of all men, all-knowing, all-powerful. He exists from eternity to eternity, beyond the reach of men's minds. He is the ultimate reality to whom Muslims give their total allegiance.

Angels

As God was beyond all physical perception, angels were needed to bring his messages to man. It was Gabriel who communicated the Quran to Muhammad, and it was Gabriel who announced the birth of Jesus to the Virgin Mary. Along with the angels there were also devils, evil spirits or jinns, the chief among whom is known as Iblis.

The Creed

It is widely agreed that anyone who utters the *shahada*, or testimony, "There is no God but God and Muhammad is the Prophet of God," may be regarded as Muslim. This formula comprises the irreducible minimum of Muslim belief. Many Muslims, however, would most probably point to the Quran chapter 4 verse 136 as providing the basic outline of what they should believe: "Oh you who believe, believe in God and his messenger and the book which he has revealed to his messenger and the book which he revealed before. And whoever disbelieves in God and his angels and his books and his messengers and the last day, he indeed strays far away."

Right Recording angels from a manuscript of al-Qazwini's *The Wonders of Creation and Their Singularities*, painted at Wasit, Iraq, in 1280. Muslims believe that they are attended by two recording angels, one to take note of their good deeds, the other to note their bad ones. All Muslims have guardian angels, while eight angels support the throne of God and 19 have charge of hell. Angels are said to be inferior to the prophets because all of them were commanded to prostrate themselves before Adam (Quran 2:34).

Right Muslims share many prophets with the Jews and the Christians. In this miniature from the *History* of Hafiz-i Abru, painted in Herat c. 1425, Moses and the Israelites watch Pharaoh and his host drown in the Red Sea.

Prophets

The men who received God's messages from the angels were the prophets, men of piety and models of good behavior. They did not work miracles except when God enabled them to do so as a sign. The Quran mentions 28, of whom 21 also appear in the Bible, and of these Adam, Noah, Abraham, David, Jacob, Joseph, Job, Moses and Jesus are given especial honor. Particular stress is laid upon Jesus's immaculate conception and his miracles, although his claim to divinity is denied. Muhammad is, of course, the seal of the prophets; his message is for all men.

Books

The messages transmitted by the prophets are harmonious in fundamentals and represent a steady progress towards the perfect revelation of Muhammad. The Quran names and recognizes the scriptures of Abraham, the Torah of Moses, the Psalms of David and the Gospel of Jesus as books revealed by God.

The Archangel Asrafil will sound the last trump on the day of judgment. Muslims believe in three other archangels: Gabriel, angel of revelations, Michael, patron of the Israelites, and Azrail, angel of death. This vibrant miniature was probably painted in Iraq c. 1370–80.

The last day

The trumpet will sound the last judgment when men will be raised from the dead and called to account. Those who have believed the messages of the prophets and have struggled to follow God's path will be summoned to enter paradise where they will live for ever in a garden with cool streams, beautiful and spotless women, couches adorned with silk, flowing cups and luscious fruit, although all these will be as nothing compared with the ultimate reward, the sight of God. Those who have ignored the messages, and have followed other gods, will be cast into hell where they will be burned by fire, drink boiling water, eat of the vile zaqqum tree and endure other torments without hope of release through death. Only God can save men, believers or not, from further torment and in the Quran he often reassures men of his merciful intent.

Prayer

Prayer, the remembrance of the absolute sovereignty of God on earth, is prescribed to be performed five times a day: on rising, and the Muslim should rise early, early in the afternoon, late in the afternoon, at sunset, and at night before going to bed. Spontaneous extra prayers are encouraged, for instance prayer in the last quarter of the night after the Prophet's custom is thought particularly meritorious. So too is ritual prayer in the company of other Muslims; indeed it is prescribed that the early afternoon prayer each Friday should be in congregation and should be led by the chief Muslim of the locality who also delivers a sermon.

The ritual of prayer symbolizes the humility of men in the presence of God. First the Muslim ritually purifies himself by washing, and then orientates himself towards Mecca, the direction of which is indicated in a mosque by the *mihrab* or niche in the wall facing Mecca. Then he performs the number of *rakats* or "bowings" prescribed for the prayer time, each "bowing" consisting of a sequence of seven movements accompanied by recitations. He begins by placing his hands on each side of his face and reciting "God is most great"; continuing to stand upright he recitates the opening chapter of the Quran, which may be followed by other passages; he bows from the hips; he straightens up; he moves to his knees and prostrates himself face to the ground – continued contact with the ground over the years develops a distinctive callus or mark of prayer on the foreheads of some Muslims; he sits back on his haunches; and finally he makes a second prostration. Thus the Muslim, the submitter, by word of mouth and graphic gesture demonstrates the meaning of the word Islam – "submitting."

Below right A charming Muslim vision of heaven where the blessed are seen in a beautiful garden, visiting one another and exchanging nosegays of flowers. This illustrates a manuscript of the *Miraj Namah*, the Miraculous Journey of Muhammad, painted at Herat in the 15th century.

Below center Hellfire burns no less fiercely for Muslims than it does for Christians. This miniature from the same Herat *Miraj Namah* depicts the fate of adulterous women.

Below right Pilgrim caravans were joyous occasions; pilgrims were going to present themselves to God. This scene from the *Maqamat* of al-Hariri, painted in Baghdad in 1237, shows a pilgrim caravan accompanied by the music of trumpets and kettledrums.

Fasting

The Muslim is required to observe the ninth month of the lunar year, Ramadan, as a period of fasting in which he abstains from eating, drinking, smoking and sexual relations during daylight hours. The purpose is to subjugate the body to the spirit and to fortify the will through discipline to enable the believer to come closer to God, and in harmony with this purpose the devout will offer extra prayers during the month and make recitations of the Quran. This shared physical privation and spiritual discipline foster each year a renewed sense of community.

Pilgrimage

The final pillar is the pilgrimage to Mecca, where Muslims believe Abraham rebuilt the house of Adam, which all Muslims must perform at least once in a lifetime providing they have the means. The pilgrimage takes place each year. Before entering Mecca, the pilgrim puts off his ordinary clothes and dons two plain white sheets, symbolizing his abandonment of ordinary life and his will to annihilate self as he presents himself to God. Then, with thousands of fellow pilgrims, he walks seven times around the central sanctuary in the great mosque of Mecca, runs seven times from Mecca towards Marwa and back, recalling the desperate search for water for her son Ishmael by Hagar, Abraham's wife, stands on the plain of Arafat outside Mecca in remembrance of the standing of Abraham against idolatry, stones the pillars at Mina in remembrance of Abraham, Hagar and Ishmael's rejection of the temptation of Satan, and finally sacrifices an animal and shaves his head. No rite has done more to foster the solidarity of the Muslim community. It is described in greater detail on pages 192–97 below.

Alms

"Keep up prayer and pay the poor rate" (58:13) is one of many reminders in the Quran that benevolence is one of the chief virtues of the true believer; indeed prayer and the giving of alms (*zakat*) are often linked. The amount which the Muslim should pay was fixed at one-fortieth of his revenue for the year in cash or kind. The object of giving alms was two-fold: on the one hand to purify or legitimize the gaining of private property by devoting a proportion of what was gained to the common need, the word *zakat* being derived from the root *zaka*, to be pure; and on the other hand as a manifestation of the believer's sense of social responsibility, of his will to help cement the community. The revenue from alms is to be spent on the poor, the needy, the collectors of alms, those who might become Muslims, the freeing of prisoners of war, debtors, travelers and those who strive in the "way of God."

THE EMPIRES OF THE HEARTLANDS IN THE 16th AND 17th CENTURIES

In the century after 1500 Muslim power reached its peak. From West Africa, where new empires rose in Morocco and the Niger Basin, to Central Asia, where an energetic Uzbeg house threatened to dominate from Bukhara, to southeast Asia, where the first Muslim sultanates were coming to replace Hindu regimes in Sumatra and Java, Muslims were becoming more powerful; they did not see the growing activities of the European, whether those of the Russians in Asia or the Portuguese in the southern seas, as a major threat. Most powerful by far were the Safavid, Mughal and Ottoman empires which came to straddle the central Islamic lands. Here strong political institutions and centralized bureaucratic systems, which were to leave lingering traces in the 20th century, replaced the tribal confederations, the shortlived sultanates and the generally weak regimes which had emerged as the Mongol tide receded. There was a marvelous flowering of the arts as rulers of genius spent the wealth raised by their efficient state machines. There was also a new threat to the cosmopolitanism of Muslim life and culture, which stemmed in part from the great boost the Safavids gave to Shiism by making it the official faith of their empire, but in the main from the very strength of the new regimes which enabled them to foster increasingly distinctive cultural worlds.

It is hard to be sure about the new sources of strength which made these three great empires possible. Certainly their dynasties had deeply rooted power bases reaching back to the 14th century: the Ottomans already ruled much territory, the Safavids led a powerful sufi order, while the awesome blood of Tamerlaine flowed in the veins of the Mughals. They may also have benefited from a new interest in agriculture: much attention was paid to irrigation works in Safavid Iran while Western visitors to the Ottoman empire often remarked on the new prosperity which had been brought to former Christian lands. Probably what was most important, as in contemporary Europe, was the emergence of gunpowder as the dominant force in war. By 1450 artillery was as crucial a factor in siege warfare as it was soon to become in open battle, and only 50 years later the handgun gained a similar importance. In general only a powerful ruler could pay for the growing rate of technological innovation that the increasingly sophisticated use of gunpowder involved, and having done so he had a decisive advantage both against subjects who wished to assert their independence from behind walled forts and against the nomads who in previous centuries had poured in from the steppes.

All three empires had some roots in the vision of world empire created by the Mongols and the political institutions they had developed. Indeed, these empires were the culmination of what has been termed the "military patronage state" in which government organized like a great military family strove to protect and promote the best in city culture. Typical of this form of government was the absorption of all state functions into a royal military household in which bureaucrats, and sometimes *ulama* responsible as *qadis* for the administration of the holy law, would be ranked and paid in the same way as the military elite. The royal household regarded all economic and cultural resources as its own, and assumed with equal ease the right to take control of the private endowments off which *ulama* lived or to resettle large segments of the population to suit its purpose. Dynastic law, which represented the sum of royal decrees down the ages, ran side by side with the holy law and the customary law. In fact a carefully defined sphere had usually been found for the holy law which did not conflict with these other more flexible legal traditions, and the idea had formed that any ruler who enforced the holy law within these limits was a legitimate caliph. Nevertheless, should dynasties even at the height of their power pay too scant a respect to the holy law, or should they weaken and lose some of the legitimacy which seemed to come to them through power alone, there were always some among the pious who would use the opportunity to attempt to carve out a wider role for God's law in the lives of mortal men, than royal power allowed.

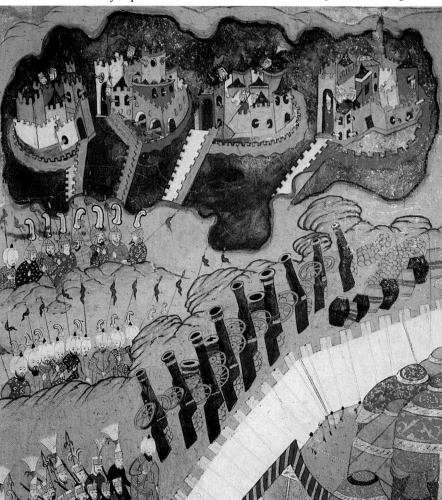

Gunpowder played a crucial role in the growth of strong central governments which made the Ottoman, Safavid and Mughal empires possible. By the mid-15th century artillery had become the dominant factor in siege warfare, as in the 16th and 17th centuries the fieldgun and handgun were to become in open battle. *Below* the Ottoman artillery at the siege of the Hungarian town of Szigetvar.

The Safavid Empire

The rise of the Safavids

The first Safavids were sufi shaikhs whose disciples provided the platform on which they established themselves as rulers of Iran. The Safavid order was founded by Safi al-Din (1252/3–1334) whose ancestors had during the previous three centuries acquired a reputation for piety in the east Azarbaijani mountain town of Ardabil. Safi al-Din was the spiritual successor of Shaikh Zahid of Gilan and his achievement was to turn a sufi order of purely local importance into one with disciples throughout eastern Antolia, Syria, Iran, the Caucasus and even among the Mongol nobility. During the 15th century the order was transformed into a revolutionary movement as its beliefs became increasingly Shiite and acquired political importance as the Safavid shaikhs commanded their disciples to fight for these beliefs – Safavid soldiers were dubbed Qizilbash (Redheads) by the Turks on account of their distinctive red turbans with 12 folds commemorating the 12 Shiite imams. Between 1459 and 1494 three heads of the order died violently, but so effective was the organization of their order and so fast the loyalty of their disciples that in 1501 the 14-year-old Shah Ismail was able to defeat the Turkoman rulers of northern Iran at Sharur and have himself proclaimed Shah Ismail I (1501–24) in Tabriz.

In 1501 Ismail ruled only Azarbaijan; by 1510, after conquering the remainder of Iran and the eastern Fertile Crescent, he had achieved what were to be the furthest limits of Safavid dominion. But immediately he was confronted by the danger which stalked the dynasty throughout the 16th century, that of having to fight on two fronts. In the

east he was up against the Uzbegs who must have resented his attack on Samarqand no less than the gold he poured into the skull of their dead leader, Muhammad Shaibani Khan, so that it should serve as his drinking cup. As soon as he had met this threat, the Ottomans were on the march in the west. This conflict was always likely because the very emergence of the Safavid Shia state and the activities of its militant supporters in eastern Anatolia threatened the Ottoman empire. The outcome was the crushing defeat of the Safavids at Chaldiran (1514), which happened mainly because they refused to use firearms, and the loss of Diyarbakir and the Shia sacred cities in Iraq.

The failure at Chaldiran brought into the open the problem which was to dog the Safavids for the rest of the century, the competition for power with the Qizilbash. Before Chaldiran the Qizilbash regarded Shah Ismail not just as the head of their order and their spiritual director but as a manifestation of God himself. Now the spell was broken; the Qizilbash reverted from being disciples obedient unto death to being tribal leaders in need of discipline. For two periods (1524–33, 1579–88) the Qizilbash were in complete control; for much of the period in between, however, Ismail's son, Shah Tahmasp (1524–76), ruled with some effect by holding the ring between the Turkoman Qizilbash and the Persians, the main groupings in the state. Tahmasp has had a bad press, probably because his mild nature and ascetic habits did not inspire those Westerners who met him; nevertheless his achievement should be measured by the fact that, although he lost further territory, he brought the Safavid state through five Uzbeg invasions of Khurasan and four Ottoman invasions of Azarbaijan.

Safavid fortunes were rescued and then brought to their peak by Tahmasp's grandson, Shah Abbas

Below: **The Safavid empire in the 16th and 17th centuries** Shah Ismail needed only nine years to conquer what was to be the furthest extent of Safavid territory. For more than 100 years afterwards his heirs fought, often desperately, to defend these gains against the Ottomans in the west and the Uzbegs in the northeast; later they also had to defend them against the Mughals in the east.

empire of Shah Ismail c.1512

area contested with Mughals in 17th century

Ottoman empire

1516   area and date conquered by Ottomans

(1603)   date of reconquest by Safavids

Uzbeg lands

area contested by Uzbegs in 16th century

Mughal empire

khanate of Jaghatai

■   Safavid capital

○   Shia shrine

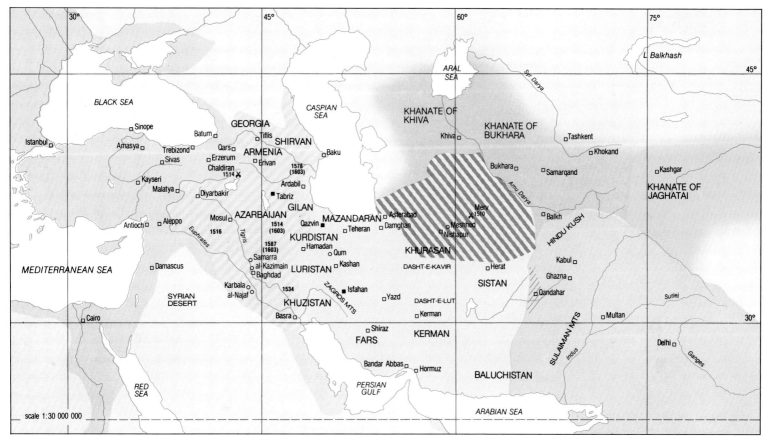

Left This mural from Isfahan's Chihil Sutun depicts Shah Ismail killing an Ottoman cavalryman at Chaldiran (1514); his sword was famed for its capacity to cleave a man to the saddle. The shah's deeds apart, the battle was a disaster for the Safavids who were defeated by Ottoman cannon and handguns. As a result they were forced to surrender much territory and to go on the defensive in the west for nearly three-quarters of a century.

Shah Abbas I, by Bishn Das, whom the Mughal emperor Jahangir sent to the Safavid court in 1613 with the embassy of Khan Alam to paint the shah's portrait, was the greatest of the Safavid shahs; he made central government strong, the frontiers secure, and his reign produced one of the finest flowerings of Persian art. A charismatic general, he also had the common touch, often walking incognito through the bazars of Isfahan and chatting with his people in teahouses. "When this great prince ceased to live," declared a European traveler some 80 years after his death, "Persia ceased to prosper."

the Great (1588–1629). Coming to the throne aged 17, his first move was to rein in the Qizilbash and to place the state on a new basis. Taking up an idea pioneered by Tahmasp, he turned to the large numbers of Georgian, Circassian and Armenian prisoners of war and their descendants who had become Muslims and had been Persianized. These he formed into a personal force, known as the "slaves of the royal household," and paid directly from the royal treasury. They were then made to supplant the Qizilbash tribal levies in the field, to oust the Qizilbash chiefs from the major offices of government, and to act as a powerful counterweight to the tribal forces in the state. Loyalty to the Shah, not membership of the Qizilbash tribal elite, was now the key to advancement. By 1598 Abbas evidently felt that his reshaping of the basis of the Safavid state had gone far enough to be able to go on the offensive against the empire's old enemies to whom he had been forced, as a holding operation, to surrender territory at the beginning of his reign. By 1606 he had administered decisive defeats to both the Uzbegs and the Ottomans, recaptured much lost territory, and greatly reduced the threat of attack from east and west.

The achievement of Shah Abbas was not limited to the political and military fields. He brought peace to the countryside, he fostered industry, especially the manufacture of carpets and silk, he encouraged traders and ambassadors from much of Europe and Asia to throng his court, and he patronized one of the finest flowerings of the Persian artistic genius. He compares well with his great contemporaries, Akbar of India and Elizabeth of England. But his greatest achievement was the fashioning of a basis for the state which was strong enough to carry it

through nearly a century of weak rule. Admittedly the price of this achievement was a rapid increase in crown lands to pay for the hugely expanded royal household, which in the long run weakened the empire. For a time, however, it solved the problem of establishing strong institutions of central government in a largely tribal society.

Shiism and the Safavid state

Shah Ismail's most important act on achieving power was to declare that the official religion of the Safavid state would be Twelver (Ithna Ashari) Shiism. Shiism, it will be recalled, began as a movement of political opposition to the early caliphs, which justified itself doctrinally by claiming that the only legitimate successors of Muhammad were the descendants of his cousin and son-in-law Ali. The belief developed that, along with the exoteric interpretation of the Quran, there was a secret interpretation which had been transmitted from Muhammad to Ali and from Ali to his heir; hence the only authoritative source of guidance were those successors of Ali to whom this secret knowledge had been transmitted, and who had thus been designated imam, or leader of the community. Gradually the imams were raised to a superhuman status which was expressed in the belief that they were incarnations of Divine Light which had descended to them through the prophets from Adam. It followed that they were infallible and without sin. The Twelvers, the most important Shia sect, recognized twelve imams, the last being Muhammad al-Muntazar, who disappeared down a well, or so it is said, around the year 873 and whose return is expected. There were many other Shia sects of whom the most important were the Zaidis,

Shiism was the rock on which the Safavid state was built: the shahs claimed to be the Twelfth Imam incarnate. Shias believe that the only legitimate successors of Muhammad were the descendants of his cousin and son-in-law, Ali, in whom the primal light, which had descended through the prophets from Adam, still shone. These men were the only authoritative guides for Muslims, hence their title, imam, or leader of the community. Iranian Shias recognize 12 imams. Their shrines, and the shrines of those associated with them, have become great places of pilgrimage. Most are in Iraq; only two exist in Iran proper, both of which were restored by Shah Abbas I. *Above* the shrine of Fatima, sister of the Eighth Imam, at Qum; *overleaf* the shrine of the Eighth Imam himself, Imam Riza, at Meshhed.

dominant in the Yemen, who recognized only the first four imams and ascribed to them no supernatural attributes, and the Ismailis who recognized the first seven imams and were represented by the Qarmatian revolutionary movement which flourished in eastern Arabia in the 10th century, the Fatimid caliphs who ruled Egypt from 969 to 1171, and the infamous order of Assassins.

The Shias are most clearly distinguished from the orthodox or Sunni community by where they locate religious authority. For Sunnis it lies in the consensus of the community which underpins the holy law; for Shias it lies in the infallible imams, belief in whom is the third article of the Shia creed after God and his Prophet. Sunnis have all the guidance they are going to receive in the Quran, the traditions and the holy law: ideally they must strive to live according to a pattern of perfection formed finally in the middle of the 10th century. Shias, on the other hand, through their imams and those who claim to represent them, have the possibility of a renewed source of guidance in succeeding generations. Shah Ismail and his heirs presented themselves as incarnations of the Twelfth Imam.

Later in the development of the Safavid state Shia *ulama* were to claim to be *mujtahids*, men with the right in the absence of the Imam to establish rulings in holy law, something which Sunni *ulama* no longer considered possible. So Shiism offered much greater opportunity for legal development and adaptation to changing circumstances. The Shias also evolved markedly different emphases in their rites. If Sunni religious energy is absorbed in the remembrance of God, that of the Shias is absorbed to a great extent in the remembrance of the martyrdom of Husain in particular and of the imams in general, all of whom are supposed to have been murdered by Sunnis. Muharram is the month of mourning, and 10 Muharram (Ashura), the day on which Husain was killed at Karbala, is the high point of the religious year, celebrated by processions bearing models of Husain's tomb, self-flagellation in repentance for disloyalty to the house of Ali, the retelling of the story of Karbala in a state of high emotion and the cursing of the Sunnis. As one would expect, pilgrimage to Karbala and the tombs of the other imams has come to be as important as pilgrimage to Mecca.

Twelver Shiism was the rock on which the early Safavid state was built. It was a theocratic state, Shah Ismail being the Twelfth Imam made flesh. His family further bolstered their claim for respect by asserting a spurious descent from the Seventh Imam, Musa al-Kazim. There were, moreover, aspects of Iranian belief and of Shiism which contributed to the process. From at least the 13th century Iranian sufis had expressed a strong loyalty to Ali, while Shias had long claimed that Husain married the daughter of Yazdigird III, the last Sassanian king, thus linking the house of Ali to the deeply rooted Iranian monarchical tradition. On coming to power Ismail set about imposing Shiism on what was, outwardly, a predominantly Sunni population. He threatened force and the people succumbed; Sunni *ulama* resisted and were faced with the alternatives of flight or death. Being a Shia now became the test of loyalty to the state. After a similar fashion the loyalties of the Safavi sufi order cemented the early state machine; Shah Ismail was the perfect sufi master, and the Qizilbash, who filled the principal offices, were his disciples. Thus people and government were united in a common religious devotion to their king.

The Safavid shahs claimed throughout the 16th and 17th centuries that they were incarnations of the Twelfth Imam, but the value of this claim as a source of authority began to weaken even in Shah Ismail's reign. We have seen how the Qizilbash lost faith in Ismail's spiritual leadership after the defeat of Chaldiran. Then around the same time the theocratic quality of the regime was further diminished by the separation of religious and political powers as a distinction came to be made between the state religious institution and the state bureaucracy. This was the first hint of the crucial change which was to take place in the relations between the *ulama* and the state in the coming 200 years. At the beginning the *ulama* were an instrument of state power. Large numbers had had to be imported from Syria and Bahrain as there were few Shia *ulama* in Iran; consequently they owed everything – endowments, functions, titles – to the state. Moreover, although it is unlikely that they

would have endorsed Safavid claims to be imams incarnate, they do seem to have been willing to accept a theory of the divine right of kings, based on the concept that the shah was the shadow of God (*zill-allah*) on earth. Furthermore, *ulama* did not begin openly to question this theory until the time of Shah Abbas, when Mulla Ahmad Ardabili told the shah that he did not rule by divine right but held his power as a trust on behalf of the imam and that it was for the *ulama* to decide whether that trust was being honored or not. After the death of Shah Abbas the *ulama* challenged the legitimacy of royal government more vigorously and cut further into it by asserting that the only proper representative of The Imam was a genuinely learned and competent *mujtahid*. They were now bidding to take control of the Shia people whom the Safavids had created.

Thus the Safavids laid the basis of the modern Iranian state, roughly marking out its borders, establishing a monarchical ideal, and through Twelver Shiism giving it a sharply defined identity. On the other hand, by being harnessed to the most powerful state form of the time, Twelver Shiism also had great opportunity for growth and development. Hitherto the faith of a minority, it now acquired forms through which it could embrace a whole people. Institutions grew strong on state patronage in lands and taxes; theology and jurisprudence were further refined; while from its interplay with the Safavid state there emerged doctrines which threatened the legitimacy of all future Iranian government which was not in the hands of the *mujtahids*. The outcome was a great Shia edifice erected in the midst of the international Sunni community. Fruitful interaction did still happen, but significant cultural, political and intellectual barriers had been raised which had not previously existed.

The blossoming of Iranian art
The Safavids presided over the finest flowering of Iranian art. Like the princes of Renaissance Europe they were often artists themselves. Shah Ismail was a poet and Shah Tahmasp a painter, but most important they were great patrons, men of highly refined taste who fostered the gifts of talented men and developed close relationships with them; Shah Abbas would hold the candle while his favorite calligrapher, Ali Riza, was at work. Miniature painting was the field in which the fruits of patronage were first and most brilliantly revealed. After defeating the Uzbegs Shah Ismail carried back with him Bihzad, the master painter who brought the high refinement of the Herat school to combine with that of Tabriz. Later Bihzad was appointed director of the royal library, which was not so much a library as we would understand the term as a workshop in which all the arts of making a book were practiced. Here, under the expert patronage of Shah Tahmasp, Safavid painting was brought to its peak in a jeweled style of taut perfection, and breathtaking harmony of color and rhythm in design, which was used to illustrate great works of Iranian literature like Firdawsi's *Shahnama* and Jami's *Haft Awrang*. By the time of Shah Abbas manuscript illustration was giving way to single page painting, and the depiction of a legendary past to the idealized portrayal of beautiful people in coy embrace or offering wine with youthful charm. By

the mid-17th century new trends had emerged of blatant eroticism and a concern for harsh reality. There had been a marked transition which doubtless owed something to the freshening air of secularism in a society once dominated by a triumphant theocracy. Certainly there was decadence as the marvelously controlled set-pieces of early Safavid art gave way to svelte youths sniffing languidly at flowers, and masterly technique to a coarsening of skill, yet there was also the opening vista of a whole new way of seeing life as artists came to paint the real world about them.

As far as other arts are concerned, the elaborate and ornate Safavid poetry did not match that of Saadi, Hafiz and Jami, although it is not now considered to be as inferior as it was formerly. Metalwork was excellent, though not quite approaching the standard of the Seljuq and Mongol periods. On the other hand, carpets, textiles and ceramics reached unprecedented heights of perfection. Leading painters from the royal workshops often had a hand in design, and all benefited from royal encouragement, most especially from Shah Abbas who was determined to make the nation's artistic talents serve the export trade. He raised the cottage industry of carpet weaving into a national industry with factories in different parts of the country. Textile factories wove an amazing range of silks, brocades, damasks, velvets and the like of unrivaled quality, color and design, and so considerable was the enterprise that in Isfahan alone employment was available for 25 000 people. Potteries also produced a wide range of colors, styles and glazes, and to improve Iran's chances in the European market 300 Chinese potters were imported to impart their skills. The supreme achievement of the Safavid potters, however, was the tiles they fired to decorate the great buildings of their time. Such was their mastery over mineral pigments and glazing that the tiles still gleam in the torrid Iranian sun as brightly as they did 400 years ago.

Nothing represented the artistic achievement and the prosperity of the Safavid period as fittingly as Isfahan. In this town, 1600 meters above sea level on the central Iranian plateau and girdled by mountains, Shah Abbas established his capital. He made it one of the world's beautiful cities, and also one of the largest of its time, boasting 162 mosques, 48 madrasas, 1801 caravanserais, 273 public baths, about one million people, with water, trees and parks everywhere. There was the Chahar Bagh, a magnificent avenue four kilometers long lined by gardens and court residences. There was also the great bazar covering 30 square kilometers, which was, according to one visitor, "the surprisingest piece of Greatness in Honour of Commerce the world can boast of." This bazar, moreover, led into a huge central maidan carrying the theme of commerce into the heart of the new royal city, and around this rectangular open space marched two tiers of shops whose progress was broken only by the principal buildings, the unpretentious Ali Qapu palace – the shahs did not build to set themselves apart from their people – the beautiful Lutf Allah mosque and the majestic royal mosque. These houses of prayer were masterpieces of Iranian architecture, although the greatest masterpiece of all was the vision which created the city.

The Safavid World

Painting: From Formality to Sensuality

We can enter the world of the Safavids most readily, by looking at their paintings. Primarily, these were designed to illustrate manuscripts or to fill albums collected by connoisseurs. The early Safavids were bibliophiles. Heirs to a world in which men lived mainly in tents, they disdained cumbersome possessions. It is easy to understand the popularity of the portable book and to sense how the miniature world of dazzling color and delicacy, which so often featured gardens decked with flowers and cooled by chattering streams, appealed to men who lived ruggedly in a bleak and barren landscape.

The Safavids developed the brilliant artistic traditions fostered by the descendants of Tamerlaine at Herat. When Shah Ismail captured the city in 1510 he carried Bihzad, the leading painter, back to Tabriz. His son, Shah Tahmasp, spent most of his early years in Herat where he studied painting to the extent that he was able to follow his artists' work as closely as if it was his own. He numbered leading painters among his bosom companions, although this did not prevent him from cutting off the nose of the painter who ran off with his favorite page boy.

Young painters had to learn the essential social graces from literature to etiquette; they had to master the preparation of the basic tools of the craft from making brushes out of kitten or baby squirrel hairs to grading and pulverizing pigments. There was constant practice at drawing trees and dragons, horses and warriors; there was the slow attuning of the eye to the properties of each color both separately and together with others. In time the apprentice might be allowed to color in a minor part of a master's work. If he showed outstanding talent, the odds were that he would eventually be employed in the royal library. This was not just a library as we would understand it, but also a workshop in which all the arts of making a book were practiced from the manufacture of paper and the binding of folios to filling pages with calligraphy and with pictures. The products of the royal library in Tabriz, of which we illustrate three pictures, the *Court of Gayumarth* (*opposite*), *Worldly and Other-worldly Drunkenness* (p. 35) and *Another Inadequate Gift* (p. 38), brought the art of the book to perfection.

Safavid painting did not remain devoted to illustrating great works of literature. By the 17th century single-page painting had supplanted manuscript illustration. The subjects favored came to be idealized visions of beautiful people, and then there developed strands of sensuality, eroticism and realism. Artists, now patronized by the nobility as much as by the shahs, deserted the grand style to explore people and emotions. They now presented an altogether more human world.

The idealized portrayal of beautiful people was one of the strands in later Safavid painting: some may have been "pin-up boys" for homosexuals. *Below* A typical youth on silk cloth designed by the painter Riza Abbasi. It was common for leading artists to place their designs at the disposal of the textile industry.

The greatest product of the royal library at Tabriz was a *Shahnama* of Firdawsi, commissioned by Shah Ismail for his son, Tahmasp. Most of the outstanding court painters of the time contributed, and the scale of the project can be appreciated from the fact that it contained 250 miniatures, whereas no extant contemporary manuscript contains more than 14. *Right* A detail of the *Court of Gayumarth*, the legendary first shah of Iran, which is held to be the supreme masterpiece of the *Shahnama*, if not of all Iranian painting. Though unsigned, the painter is thought to be Sultan-Muhammad; the rocks are alive with hidden people and animals, which is characteristic of Sultan-Muhammad's work.

Left Another painting by Riza Abbasi illustrates the 17th-century exploration of realism. Here we have Muhammad Ali, a gilder of Shiraz, who had come from India. This fat old man with his hooked nose is surely painted just as he was.

Below Sensuality became increasingly prominent in late Safavid painting and eroticism more blatant. These two lovers embracing were painted by Afzal al-Husaini at Isfahan (1646).

Isfahan is sited on an oasis in an arid plain surrounded by mountains. *Below* We look over the dome of the Lutf Allah mosque, across one end of the Maidan, to the royal mosque, before which we can just see the old marble goalposts for polo, to the "Punch's hump" of the Kuh-i-Sufi beyond.

Right The majestic entrance to the royal mosque: it is 27 meters high. Note the cascade of stalactites, which form a typically Islamic method of marking the transition from a square base to a circular dome, and the calligraphic frieze, which proclaims the glory of God and of Shah Abbas.

Isfahan: City of Shah Abbas

If painting offers the easiest route into the Safavid world, the city of Isfahan offers the best measure of its wealth and artistic achievement. In 1597–98 Shah Abbas I made this town his capital and planned a great city worthy to be the focus of his empire; he was assisted by a veritable Iranian Leonardo da Vinci, Shaikh Baha al-Din Muhammad Amili, an eminent theologian, philosopher, Quran commentator, jurisprudent, astronomer, teacher, poet and engineer, the very exemplar of his age. The outcome was one of the largest cities of the time, 38 kilometers in circumference and housing about one million people; it was also one of the most beautiful of all time, with a great number of "spacious caravanserais, very fine bazars and canals and streets lined with plane trees," according to one French visitor; "from whatever direction one looks at the city it looks like a wood."

There were two main features, the Chahar Bagh, a magnificent avenue 4 kilometers long lined by gardens and court residences, and the Maidan, a rectangle 507 meters long and 158 meters wide, around which Shah Abbas raised two tiers of shops broken only by the principal buildings, the Ali Qapu palace and the Lutf Allah and royal mosques. The Maidan was the focus of the city's life, both a marketplace and a sportsfield. Here the shah might play polo or just mingle with his people.

"The beauty of Isfahan steals on the mind unawares," recorded the English scholar and traveler, Robert Byron, in 1934:

You drive about, under avenues of white tree-trunks and canopies of shining twigs; past domes or turquoise and spring yellow in a sky of liquid violet-blue; along the river patched with twisting shoals, catching that blue in its muddy silver, and lined with feathery groves where the sap calls, across bridges of pale toffee brick, tier on tier of arches breaking into piled pavilions; overlooked by lilac mountains, by the Kuh-i-Sufi shaped like Punch's hump and by other ranges receding to a line of snowy surf; and before you know how, Isfahan has become indelible, has insinuated its image into that gallery of places which everyone privately treasures.

Isfahan: The Bazar

Isfahan was more than a place of beauty and royal magnificence; it was also an industrial and commercial center. Shah Abbas was determined that his realm should prosper, and cities throughout the land were encouraged to increase and improve their production of carpets, textiles, ceramics and metalwork. Isfahan was the center of the enterprise. Merchants from throughout the world thronged its bazar, which began at the far end of the Maidan, opposite the royal mosque, and stretched across the city as a warren of shops, factories, mosques, madrasas, baths, caravanserais and warehouses.

Previous page Trade and industry were the source of Isfahan's prosperity; the bazar was the center of activity. The line of domes snaking its way through the city, covering 2½ kilometers from the Maidan to the ancient Friday mosque, is the main thoroughfare of the bazar.

Up to 25 000 people were employed in Isfahan's textile industry and visitors marveled at the range of designs, colors and weaves, which were sought after in Europe. *Below left* A length of woven polychrome velvet, manufactured in the early 17th century.

Safavid metalwork was of high standard. *Below* The helmet of Shah Abbas I, dated 1625/6, and decorated with verses from the *Bustan* of Saadi.

Shah Abbas introduced Chinese potters to teach Iranians the skills which would enable them to take advantage of the European vogue for Chinese porcelain. Many settled in Isfahan. *Bottom left* A hookah base in the Iranian style which aimed to imitate the Chinese blue-and-white porcelain of the Ming period.

ⓜ mosque
ⓐ madrasa
ⓑ baths
ⓒ caravanserai

Qaysariya gate

Maidan

Lutf Allah mosque

Ali Qapu palace

royal mosque

Friday mosque

main bazar
thoroughfare

Right Textile manufacture was a major activity in the bazar, and block-printed cottons (*qalam-kar*) were an important item in Safavid trade, as they still are in handicraft production today.

Below right This is what it is like inside the bazar, underneath the snaking line of domes. The vaulted streets are lit by openings in the center of each dome which create a cool well-ventilated space.

The plan gives a graphic idea of the way in which the bazar joined the Maidan, the focal point of Shah Abbas's new city, to the Friday mosque, the focal point of the old town. Note how all the mosques are orientated in the same direction, towards Mecca.

Above The work of the potter still continues in the bazar, although the product bears scant relation to the blue-and-white porcelain for the European market or the magnificent tiles which clothed the buildings of the city. Here pots and tiles are painted before firing.

The Mughal Empire

Muslim government in a Hindu society

The empire of the Mughals, unlike that of the Safavids, was founded in a society where Islam was less deeply rooted; indeed, where the majority of the people were Hindus. The Mughals, moreover, not only brought beneath their sway the classical centers of Hindu civilization in the north, like Benares and Ajudhia, but almost all the subcontinent in which the Hindus lived. Their response to the challenge of ruling a still vital civilization of unbelievers was to leave indelible marks on their achievement.

Babur (1483–1530), the founder of the Mughal empire, had good qualifications for such a task, being descended through his father from Tamerlaine, and through his mother from Gengis Khan. He spent his youth trying to recapture Samarqand as a prelude to rebuilding his ancestor's vast empire, but by the time he was 30 he had done no more than establish a realm in Afghanistan based on Kabul, Qandahar and Badakshan. Despairing of success in his homeland, he turned his gaze towards India which was divided among many rulers. In the south there was the Hindu Vijayanagar empire and a string of Muslim commercial principalities down the southwest coast. In the center there was a covey of small Muslim sultanates. In the north there were two significant powers, the warrior Rajput princes of Rajasthan and the Lodi Afghans who ruled the Indo-Gangetic heartland from the banks of the Indus to the borders of Bengal. Babur saw many divisions and little stability and seized his opportunity, defeating the Lodi army in 1526 at the hotly disputed field of Panipat, where his Turkish artillery were decisive.

Babur, a man of sensibility, taste and humor whose memoirs glitter with intelligence, brought the Mongol vision of empire to India. But, as he died in 1530, he did not enjoy it for long. He was succeeded by Humayun, his able though wayward son, who held sway for a shaky 10 years after which he was overthrown by his vassal, Sher Khan Sur, who ruled Bihar, and he was forced to take refuge at the court of the Safavid Shah Tahmasp. The Suris quickly took a firm grip, reforming land revenue assessments and creating a vigorous centralized bureaucracy. It seemed that the Mughal era was no sooner begun than ended. Only a lingering claim to Indian empire remained.

Humayun, however, was able to restore Mughal fortunes. The Suri dynasty succumbed to faction, and Humayun, helped by Shah Tahmasp, regained his patrimony in 1555. Within six months he was dead; he fell down his library stairs, which was an appropriate end for a man of learning and culture. Nevertheless, the period of Mughal greatness now began. In 1556 Humayun's son Akbar, most gifted of the remarkable Mughal line, succeeded at the age of 14. Within 10 years he began to absorb the petty regimes on his borders. By 1569 all Rajputana was subdued, except Mewar whose proud prince was still a fugitive in the jungle, or so the legend goes, when Akbar died; by 1572 he had overrun fertile Gujarat and by 1576 Bengal, richest province of the north; then followed Kashmir (1586), Orissa (1592), Baluchistan (1595), and a little later the Deccan

Left The Emperor Babur, founder of the Mughal dynasty, who strove for over 30 years to win an empire which would match the achievements of his ancestors, Tamerlaine and Gengis Khan. His memoirs reveal a life of extraordinary endurance and a mind of unusual sophistication. His opinion of his Indian subjects was not high: "the people are not handsome. They have no idea of the charms of friendly society, of frankly mixing together, or of familiar intercourse. They have no genius, no comprehension of mind, no politeness of manner, no kindness or fellow-feeling . . . they have no good horses, no good flesh, no good grapes or musk-melons, no good fruits, no ice or cold water, no good food or bread . . ."

Right: the Mughal empire 1526–1707
This map illustrates the expansion of Mughal rule from 1526 to the beginning of the 18th century when it reached its greatest extent. By this time, however, signs of decay were already evident; Hindu Maratha power was growing in western India.

kingdoms of Berar and Khandesh. By Akbar's death in 1605 his empire stretched from the Hindu Kush to the Bay of Bengal, and from the Himalayas to the Arabian Sea and the center of the Deccan plateau. There remained two unstable frontiers: that in the northwest which Jahangir (1605–27) and Shah Jahan (1627–58) contested with the Safavids and which was preserved with the loss of Qandahar (1649) into the 18th century, and that in the south where the Mughals slowly advanced at the expense of the Muslim sultanates of the Deccan. When Awrangzeb (1658–1707) captured Bijapur (1686) and Golkonda (1687) he expanded the empire to its greatest extent, although by this time it was being weakened by rebellions from within.

Akbar created the administrative and political system which brought the empire strength and durability. Following a pattern sketched by the Suris, he built a government machine which took royal power right down to the villages where officials collected the revenue. Central to the success of the Mughals was their generally fair and accurate system of revenue assessment. Admittedly they demanded a high rate, normally one-third of the annual produce, although this was not unusual in agrarian empires. On the other hand, peasants had revenue remitted in bad years, were allowed to keep the profits of good years, and were encouraged by the system to bring more land into cultivation. Much of this achievement was due to Akbar's revenue minister, the Hindu Todar Mal. The proceeds filled the imperial treasury, paid for the dynasty's great building projects and supported the imperial service, the heart of the government machine. This service, the forerunner of the British Indian Civil Service, was organized as one great military household answerable to the emperor alone. The officers, called *mansabdars*, holders of commands, were arranged in 33 grades from a commander of 10 to a commander of 5000. They did not inherit their positions, progressing only by imperial favor; they were the pool of talent from

Below The Koh-i-Nur (Mountain of Light) diamond, which Humayun gave to Babur after the capture of Agra; Babur returned it to his son after calculating that it would provide "two and a half days' food for the whole world." Humayun gave to Shah Tahmasp of Iran, who sent it to Nizam Shah in the Deccan, from where it found its way back to the Mughal treasury in the 17th century. Seized by Nadir Shah at the Iranian sack of Delhi in 1739, it later passed to the kings of Afghanistan and then to Ranjit Singh of the Punjab. After the British annexed the Sikh kingdom in 1849, it was sent to Britain to become a prize exhibit in the Great Exhibition of 1851 and was included among the crown jewels of Queen Victoria.

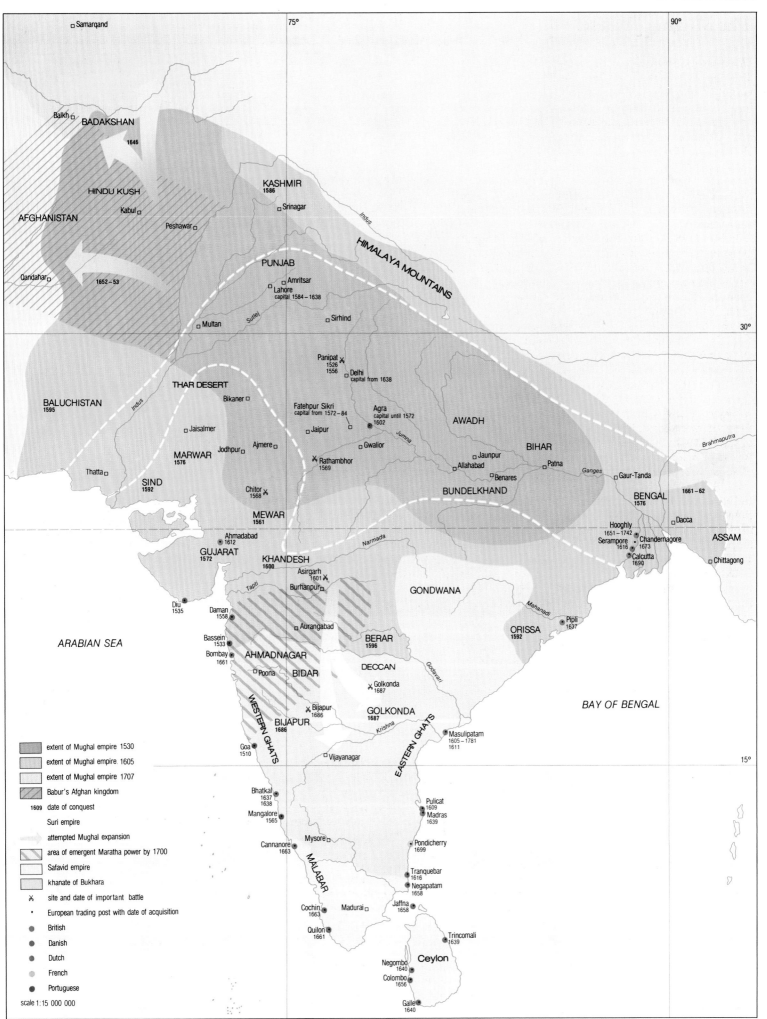

□ Samarqand

□ Balkh BADAKSHAN
1646

HINDU KUSH

AFGHANISTAN

Kabul □

□ Peshawar

Qandahar □   1652–53

KASHMIR
1586

□ Srinagar

PUNJAB

□ Amritsar
□ Lahore
capital 1584–1638

□ Multan   Sutlej   □ Sirhind

HIMALAYA MOUNTAINS

Indus

30°

BALUCHISTAN
1595

THAR DESERT

Indus

□ Bikaner

□ Jaisalmer

MARWAR
1576

Jodhpur □   Ajmere □

Panipat ✗
1526
1556   □ Delhi
capital from 1638

Fatehpur Sikri
capital from 1572–84
□ Jaipur

Agra
capital until 1572
● 1602

AWADH

Jumna

✗ Rathambhor
1569

□ Gwalior

□ Jaunpur
□ Allahabad

BIHAR

□ Patna   Ganges   □ Gaur-Tanda

Brahmaputra

Thatta □

SIND
1592

Chitor ✗
1568

MEWAR
1561

● Ahmadabad
1612

□ Benares

BUNDELKHAND

BENGAL
1576

1661–62

□ Dacca

ASSAM

GUJARAT
1572

KHANDESH
1600

Narmada

Hooghly
1651–1742
Serampore ● Chandernagore
1616 ● 1673
● Calcutta
1690

□ Chittagong

Diu ●
1535

Daman ●
1558

Asirgarh ✗
1601
Burhanpur □

Tapti

GONDWANA

Mahanadi

Pipli ●
1637

ARABIAN SEA

Bassein ●
1533

Bombay ●
1661

● Aurangabad

AHMADNAGAR

□ Poona

BIDAR

BERAR
1596

DECCAN

Godavari

ORISSA
1592

BAY OF BENGAL

✗ Golkonda
1687

GOLKONDA
1687

Bijapur ✗
1686
BIJAPUR
1686

Krishna

WESTERN GHATS

EASTERN GHATS

Goa ●
1510

● Masulipatam
1605–1781
1611

□ Vijayanagar

15°

Bhatkal ●
1637
1638

Pulicat ●
1609
● Madras
1639

Mangalore ●
1565

Mysore ●

● Pondicherry
1699

MALABAR

Cannanore ●
1663

Tranquebar ●
1616
Negapatam ●
1658

Cochin ●
1663   Madurai □

Jaffna ●
1658

Quilon ●
1661

Trincomali ●
1639

Negombo ●
1640   Ceylon

Colombo ●
1656

Galle ●
1640

▨	extent of Mughal empire 1530
▨	extent of Mughal empire 1605
□	extent of Mughal empire 1707
▨	Babur's Afghan kingdom
1609	date of conquest
	Suri empire
⟹	attempted Mughal expansion
▨	area of emergent Maratha power by 1700
□	Safavid empire
▨	khanate of Bukhara
✗	site and date of important battle
·	European trading post with date of acquisition
●	British
●	Danish
●	Dutch
●	French
●	Portuguese

scale 1:15 000 000

which the emperor drew his civil and military officers. Two points should be noted about them in Akbar's time: first that they were mainly foreigners, only about one-third being born in India, and second that, although they were assigned the revenues of specific lands and were encouraged to visit them, they were actually paid by the royal treasury.

The whole framework of government depended on Hindu cooperation. Half of the *mansabdars* born in India were Hindus and their faith did not prevent them from rising high in what was a career open to talent. Most of the lesser officials, those in fact responsible for day-to-day administration, were also Hindus, as they were to be under the British. The dependence on Hindus in the administration was mirrored in politics in relations with the Rajput chiefs who had been the Mughals' major Hindu competitors for power in northern India. Once defeated, they were drawn into the service of the empire as military commanders, provincial governors and counselors of the emperor. They ruled their own chiefdoms and shared the same privileges at court as Muslim nobles. Indeed, their partnership in empire reached into the royal bed; Akbar married a princess from Jaipur, and so the mother of his heir, Jahangir, was a Hindu.

The pious strive to defend Islam

The natural accompaniment of such reliance on Hindus was the policy of religious toleration which Akbar adopted, as had other Muslim rulers of Hindu peoples before. Soon after his reign began he abolished first the tax on Hindu pilgrims, and then the *jizya*, the tax levied by holy law on unbelievers in Muslim territory. He took steps to avoid giving offense to other faiths, replacing the Islamic lunar calendar with the solar calendar and forbidding Muslims to kill or eat the cow which Hindus revered. Concerned that no penalties should attach to any particular religion, he set aside the death penalty prescribed by the holy law for apostasy, and financed the places of worship of all faiths. That he valued justice and human dignity above the provisions of any particular faith was demonstrated by his opposition to the Muslim practice of slavery no less than to the high-caste Hindu practice of burning a widow along with her dead husband. Obviously such a liberal policy required firm control of the Muslim religious establishment. Like the early Safavids, Akbar strove to make the *ulama* dependent on the state and resumed many of their grants. He demanded that they attend court if they wished to benefit from royal funds. Intolerance was forbidden. When in the 1570s the official leaders of the *ulama* tried to persecute Akbar's freethinking friends, the family of Abul Fazl, they were irrevocably disgraced.

Akbar's public religious tolerance was matched by a private religious eclecticism; it is this side of the great man which fascinated Westerners at the time and has done so ever since. He sought all kinds of religious knowledge with extraordinary zeal. At first he was devoted to sufi saints, traveling almost every year to the shrine of Muin al-Din Chishti at Ajmere and ensuring that two of his sons were born at the house of Shaikh Salim Chishti at Fatehpur Sikri. Then, in the mid-1570s, he seems to have had a mystical experience which led to whole days and nights being spent in prayer; encouraged by the rationalist Abul Fazl, he opened a "House of Worship." Here he presided over religious discussions in which Sunni *ulama*, sufis, Hindus, Zoroastrians, Jews, Jains and Jesuits from Goa all participated. The *ulama* did not acquit themselves well, calling each other "fools and heretics" until they became, as the historian Budauni recorded, "very Jews and Egyptians for hatred of each other." In 1582 Akbar founded the "Divine Faith" (*Din-i-Ilahi*) which was his own eclectic cult, much influenced by Zoroastrianism and focused on himself. But too much should not be made of the

emperor's religious games; even at court there were only 18 followers, and the cult was not enforced throughout the empire.

Akbar's public policy was continued by Jahangir and Shah Jahan; and his tolerant and syncretic approach to Islam in India culminated in Shah Jahan's favorite son, Dara Shikoh (1615–59). This ill-fated prince, who was to be executed for apostasy by his younger brother Awrangzeb, began as a straightforward sufi of the Qadri order, writing irreproachable mystical works which were much influenced by Jami. Then he sought the company of Hindu mystics, translated their scriptures and came to build a structure of syncretic thought in which he identified the essence of Hinduism with the essence of Islam. Not surprisingly, behind much of his thinking lay the pantheistic sufism of Ibn al-Arabi, long influential in India. His aim, however, was less to move from Islam towards Hinduism than to find the ground they shared. But in the process he demonstrated the great danger in the combination of sufi and Hindu pantheism, how in fact they might combine to undermine Islamic orthodoxy.

The pious felt bound to resist such developments. They were led by followers of the Naqshbandi order, and their resistance gained momentum after Khwaja Baqi-billah came to India in the last years of Akbar's reign. One of his disciples, Abd al-Haqq of Delhi (1551–1642), influenced the response of the *ulama*. At first he had tried to escape from the freethinking atmosphere of Akbar's court by retiring to Mecca, but he was persuaded to return and proceeded to lay down the lines of a learned counter-offensive, especially in the study of the traditions. Even more important was Baqi-billah's favorite disciple, Shaikh Ahmad Sirhindi, who through sufism itself redirected Muslim attention to the Quran, the traditions and the holy law. He refuted the pantheists who said "all is He," and through an elaboration of sufi thought upheld the transcendence of God and the need for man to be guided by his revelation. Few followed Sirhindi at the time, and when he presumed on Jahangir's succession to delight in the death of Akbar, in whose reign "the sun of guidance was hidden behind the veil of error," and to urge the new

Below Dara Shikoh, eldest son of Shah Jahan, converses with holy men. In this prince the syncretic tendencies in Mughal civilization, which Akbar fostered, were brought to their zenith. He loved to debate with Hindu mystics and was concerned to reveal the ground they shared with Muslims. Although his father's favorite, he failed in the military struggle for the succession. Awrangzeb, who won, paraded Dara in rags through Delhi and summarily tried him for his religious views, after which his head was hacked from his body.

Above Awrangzeb at prayer soon after he came to the throne in 1659: fittingly, several paintings exist of this austere, even bigoted, man at his devotions. Some of the instructions in Awrangzeb's will illuminate the man: four and a half rupees recently earned from the sale of caps which he himself had sewn were to go towards the expenses of his funeral; 305 rupees from the sale of Qurans he had copied out were to be distributed to holy men; his grave was to be of the simplest kind, in sharp contrast to the mighty mausoleums built by his forebears. Awrangzeb's long reign brought a decisive shift towards Islamic orthodoxy; it also saw the last moments of Mughal glory.

emperor to mold the state on the basis of the holy law, he was made to cool his heels in prison.

The tide began to turn when Awrangzeb came to the throne. He was friendly with *ulama* and with followers of Sirhindi, and had an orthodox, even bigoted, temperament. As his reign unfolded, he slowly withdrew from the eclectic rule of his forebears into a distinctly communal style. Religious disabilities were imposed on Hindus; many temples were destroyed after 1669; and from 1679 the *jizya* was levied again, even on those who served in the army. The emphasis on the emperor as the ruler of a multi-confessional society was cut down. He attended fewer Hindu festivals and gave up making the dawn appearance to the people on a balcony. Simultaneously he strove to cast Indian society into an orthodox mold, reintroducing the lunar calendar, discouraging the study of pantheistic thought, enforcing the holy law in matters from the drinking of wine to the roofing of mausoleums, and commissioning the compilation of a comprehensive digest of Hanafi jurisprudence, the *Fatawa-i Alamgiri*, on the basis of which the empire would become an Islamic theocracy.

With the reign of Awrangzeb following on the work of Abd al-Haqq and Ahmad Sirhindi, a new strand develops in Indian Islam. In subsequent centuries members of the Mujaddidi branch of the Naqshbandi order, which Sirhindi founded, were to extend this strand not just through India but throughout much of the Islamic world. It was to be an extraordinary source of vitality both before and during the European onslaught. Not without prescience, Sirhindi's followers bestowed on him the title ''*Mujaddid-e Alf-e Sani*,'' the ''renovator of the second thousand years'' of Islam.

The cultural expression of synthesis

Mughal art expressed both the power of the empire and the compromises on which it was based. The arts flourished under all the emperors to the end of the 17th century except Awrangzeb, under whom patronage ran dry and inspiration withered. One typical area was music where a syncretic tradition which dated back to the 13th century was sustained by men like Faqir Allah, whose analysis of the principles of musical composition, *Rag Darpan* (1666), was derived in part from Sanskrit sources. Another was language. The court, of course, spoke Persian and patronized the finest Persian poets of the day, but in the interaction between the court and the world in which it moved the new Urdu language was growing up – a northern Indian dialect in grammar but largely Persian in vocabulary and metaphor, an expressive tongue which was to become the favorite language of Indo-Muslim civilization.

The most striking expressions of power and synthesis lay in painting and architecture. Akbar was the founder of Mughal painting. In exile in Kabul he and his father had both taken lessons from two leading Safavid court painters, Mir Saiyid Ali and Abdus Samad, who were persuaded to join them in India when they reconquered the empire. Akbar placed them in charge of the royal studios in which over a hundred painters, mainly Hindus from Gujarat, Rajasthan and Kashmir, learned to blend the formal and richly jeweled style inherited from Bihzad to their own lively and colorful traditions.

When Akbar died, there were 24000 illustrated manuscripts in his library. Although he could not read, he loved to have others read to him. Reflecting, no doubt, the emperor's restless curiosity, the range of subjects painted, as compared with the productions of Safavid artists, broadened significantly. The Persian literary classics favored by the Iranian and Central Asian courts were still illustrated, and into this category falls the first great project of the royal studio, the famed *Hamzanama*, which contains 1400 paintings on cloth. But Hindu epics like the *Ramayana* and the *Mahabharata* were also illustrated, as were the great sagas of the Mughal house, the *Timurnama*, the *Baburnama* and the *Akbarnama*, the last being a quite unparalleled pictorial record of the reign.

Jahangir was, if anything, an even more enthusiastic patron than his father and took pride in his connoisseurship, claiming to be able to recognize at a glance the work of artists alive and dead. In his time Mughal painting achieved its widest range of mood and most distinctive forms. The drama of the work from Akbar's studios is still there, so is the vitality, although without the crowded bustle, and so are the great state occasions, although by now they seem more grand. But there is in addition a new concern to reveal human character, a remarkable genre of political allegory, a strain of sensuousness which fortunately is not taken to the erotic lengths of late Safavid art, and above all a realism in which Mughal painters went much further than their Iranian contemporaries. This is seen in Mansur's paintings of plants, birds and animals; it is also seen vividly and disturbingly in the clinical portrayal of the dying Inayat Khan.

Architecture expresses even better than painting both the marriage of Islamic and Indian modes and the vaunting power of the empire. Nowhere is synthesis more clearly achieved than in Akbar's temporary capital of Fatehpur Sikri, a few kilometers from Agra, which has been preserved almost intact to the present day. Built between 1569 and 1585 on the hillock where Shaikh Salim Chishti, whose spiritual powers Akbar believed had brought him two sons, had lived, its architecture combines the Muslim tradition of arches, domes and spacious courts with the Hindu tradition of flat stone beams, ornate decoration and solidity. Power flows from the work of Shah Jahan, builder of builders, who restored the imperial capital to Delhi and constructed yet another city at this ancient focus of Indian government – Shahjahanabad. Around it ran a great red sandstone wall; on a plinth at the center stood the largest congregational mosque in India, commanding the city in every direction; overlooking the river Jumna stood a vast palace fortress, the Red Fort, in which the visitor who penetrated to its heart found superb white marble pavilions decorated with gold and precious stones. ''If on earth there be an Eden of Bliss,'' ran the legend in the hall of private audience, ''it is this! It is this! It is this!'' Shah Jahan would have been esteemed for these buildings and others elsewhere, but then he also raised at Agra a wondrous masterpiece, the incomparable Taj Mahal, built to hold the body of Mumtaz Mahal, the queen he loved, and defying, as a contemporary chronicler so aptly said, ''an ocean of descriptions.'' Here to synthesis and power was added perfection.

The Mughal World

Mughal Moods

The Mughals, like the Safavids, were great bibliophiles. They went one better, however, than their Iranian contemporaries. They not only collected books and commissioned illustrated editions, they also wrote them. We have already noted Babur's memoirs, one of the world's great autobiographical works, whose vigor and directness threaten to sweep the reader along no less than his aesthetic sensibility and sheer intelligence demand that he linger to savor the page. Jahangir also wrote memoirs which, somewhat undeservedly, are less well known, although remarkable for the immediacy of the picture they give of court life as well as of the emperor's consuming interest in painting and in the world about him.

Painting, in fact, is as good a route into the world of the Mughals as it is into that of the Safavids. It sets out most clearly, along with architecture, the synthesis between Islamic culture and Hindu India on which the Mughal empire rested. So Akbar's studios not only illustrated Turkish and Arabic as well as Persian classics, they also produced editions of the Hindu epics, the *Ramayana* and the *Mahabharata*. If the first masters in the studios were leading Safavid painters, the 150 or so painters'

names, that are known from their signatures, are those of Hindus, mainly from western India. In such hands the formal and highly decorated style of Iran and Central Asia with its mosaics of brilliant color was given an increasingly distinctive Indian impress, of life, humanity, more literal depiction of human and animal forms, and new color preferences, for dark greens, olives and grays.

The art reached its height under Jahangir. "As regards myself," he confided in his memoirs, "my liking for painting and my practice in judging it have arrived at such a point that when any work is brought before me . . . I say on the spur of the moment that it is the work of such and such a man. And if there be a picture containing many portraits, and each face be the work of a different master, I can discover which face is the work of each of them. If any other person has put in the eye and the eyebrow of a face, I can perceive whose work the original face is, and who has painted the eye and the eyebrows." Under the patronage of this connoisseur, Mughal painting began to display its full range of mood: allegorical, realistic, formal, sensual, the interest in character, the fascination for nature.

Above Realism is taken to distressing lengths in this drawing, attributed to Bishn Das, of Jahangir's attendant, Inayat Khan, dying in 1618 of addiction to wine and opium. Jahangir had ordered that he be brought to him. "He appeared so low and weak that I was astonished," he recorded in his memoirs. " He was skin drawn over bones. Or rather his bones too had dissolved. Though painters have striven much in drawing an emaciated face, yet I have never seen anything like this, nor even approaching to it. Good God, can a son of man come to such a shape and fashion? . . . As it was a very extraordinary case I directed my painters to take his portrait . . . Next day he traveled the road of nonexistence."

Right Some of the finest paintings of Jahangir's reign plumb a rich vein of allegory. Painted by Abul Hassan c. 1620, this work proclaims a new friendship with the Safavid emperor Shah Abbas, although the Mughal lion seems to be taking advantage of the situation by nudging the Iranian lamb into the Mediterranean. We can see too the influence of the European paintings with which Jahangir, who craved exotica, filled his palace. Cherubs bear up the crescent and a halo surrounds the emperor's head. The latter was borrowed from paintings the Jesuits had brought and was used subsequently in Mughal painting to signify the person of the emperor.

Below Under Shah Jahan painting took on a more formal character with an emphasis on court occasions and official portraits. In this scene, painted by Bichitr c. 1650, Shah Jahan receives his sons. The emperor is truly enthroned on high while his officials and courtiers stand below at precisely measured distances from the throne according to their importance. So much care has been taken to depict individual likenesses that we feel we are examining an offical "court photograph." Indeed, close inspection reveals that each courtier has been named.

This arresting miniature of a noblewoman of mature age, painted in the mid-17th century, reveals the Mughal artist's interest in character. Traces of her beauty remain; she bears her years with dignity tinged with sadness, perhaps a little bitterness. The portrait is probably imaginary as no painter would have been allowed to see a woman of her standing. She makes an interesting contrast with the girl, *bottom*, who in the full bloom of youth combs her hair after a bath. Also painted in the mid-17th century, this projects a note of restrained sensuality.

The Fascination for Nature

Jahangir loved nature. Listen to his rhapsodizing on his visit to Kashmir. It "is a garden of eternal spring ... a delightful flowerbed ... Wherever the eye reaches there is verdure and running water. The red rose, the violet and the narcissus grow of themselves ..." His descriptions of birds, moreover, reveal the talents of an ornithologist. Mansur was ordered to paint the fowl (see *bottom right*), as he painted hundreds of birds, animals and flowers for the emperor. "Ustad [master] Mansur has become such a master in painting," Jahangir records, "that he has the title Nadir al-Asr [Wonder of the Age]."

Himalayan wild goat by Inayat.

Himalayan cheer pheasant by Mansur.

Zebra by Mansur.

Indian black buck by Manohar.

Poppies.

Turkey cock by Mansur.

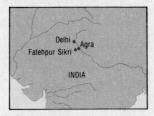

Mughal Cities

Fatehpur Sikri

Nowhere is the synthesis between Islamic culture and Hindu India more clearly achieved than in Akbar's ceremonial capital, known as Fatehpur (Town of Victory) Sikri. Here light and airy structures, reminiscent of Muslim pavilions and tents, combine with the flat stone beams and massiveness of traditional Hindu buildings. Constructed between 1569 and 1584, the city was occupied by the court for only 14 years. It seems that Akbar in his enthusiasm to build his new capital on the hillock of the holy man, Shaikh Salim Chishti, forgot to check on whether the water supply would be sufficient. The red sandstone buildings which have survived down four centuries, almost perfectly preserved, are often called a city, although in fact they were no more than a huge palace complex. The real town, which clustered around the foot of the hillock, has long since disappeared.

Agra

Agra was the Mughal capital for much of the time until Shah Jahan founded a new capital city at Delhi. Akbar seems to have had little liking for Delhi, which from the 13th century had come to be the natural capital of northern India, perhaps because it was where his father had died by misadventure, perhaps because it reminded him of the usurping Afghan Suri dynasty, or perhaps simply because it was full of Afghans who had little love for the Mughals. So Akbar built his first capital in the small town of Agra, at the heart of which was an immensely strong fortress on the banks of the river Jumna. Jahangir preferred Lahore, but Shah Jahan returned in his early years to Agra, where he built the greatest of Mughal monuments.

Delhi

Shah Jahan restored the capital of Indo-Muslim empire to Delhi, which dominates the broad strip of cultivated land linking the valley of the Indus to that of the Ganges and separating the desert of Rajasthan from the foothills of the Himalayas. In 1638 he began to build the seventh of Delhi's eight cities, Shahjahanabad. Around it he threw a noble red sandstone wall; through it he drove a magnificent boulevard, Chandni Chowk, shaded by trees and cooled by a stream running down the centre, which must have rivaled Isfahan's Chahar Bagh. At the highest point he raised the Juma Masjid, or Friday mosque, which commands the city on every side. Then, overlooking the river Jumna, he built the Red Fort, which was not only the emperor's palace but also the home of the central administrative machinery of the empire, of the imperial treasury, of a garrison, of an arsenal and even of factories for luxury goods. Every Mughal emperor held court here until Delhi fell to the British during the suppression of the Mutiny uprising of 1857–58, and the last of the Mughals, pathetic relic of the house of Tamerlane, was transported to die in Rangoon. The British then razed much of the Mughal city; in 1912 it became the "old city" when the British constructed their own imperial capital of New Delhi.

The inspiration for Fatehpur Sikri's architecture stems from a small palace built by the Hindu Raja, Man Singh, in his fort at Gwalior. Most of the masons too were probably Hindu. They hewed all the shapes they needed from stone in the way a European carpenter might have carved them from wood. They were then fitted together without pegs, precisely finished stone and gravity alone holding the construction together. *Far left* We can see the top three stories of the Panch Mahal, a five-story palace for the harem, which was originally fitted with stone screens through which the ladies could see and not be seen. It must have been marvelously cool at night during the hot weather.

Left The fort built by Akbar at Agra in the 1560s projects the power of the now firmly established Mughal regime. Most of Akbar's buildings inside were replaced by Shah Jahan.

Below Delhi's Juma Masjid, built 1644–58. Constructed of red sandstone, relieved only by decoration of white marble, it is a most imposing building.

From 1638 the Red Fort at Delhi was the heart of Mughal government; it was also a palace of extraordinary luxury. "I assert," declared Niccolo Manucci, artilleryman and physician at the Mughal court c. 1656–86, "that in the Mughal kingdom the nobles, and above all the king, live with such ostentation that the most sumptuous of European courts cannot compare in richness and magnificence with the luster beheld in the Indian court." The visitor entered the palace through a mighty main gate in the red sandstone walls (*bottom*) and progressed through bazars to a long garden, at the back of which was the hall of public audience. Beyond were more gardens, fringed by airy white marble pavilions, like the Rang Mahal (*below*), overlooking the river Jumna.

Right Marble inlaid with precious stones in the hall of private audience in the Red Fort, Delhi. Similar fine work can be found in the tomb of Itimad-ud-daula and the Taj Mahal at Agra. The technique, known as *pietra dura*, was developed in 16th-century Florence, although it seems that this Indian work is an independent development. *Below* The plan shows the walls, gates and main buildings of Shah Jahan's Delhi.

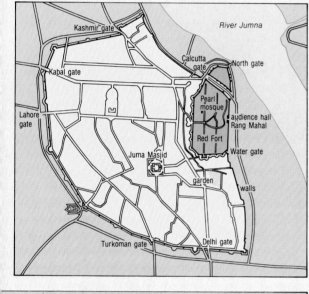

Garden Tombs

"These are the Gardens of Eden," declared the inscription over the gateway of Akbar's garden tomb at Sikandra; "enter them to dwell therein eternally." The word "paradise" is simply a transliteration of the old Persian word *pairidaeza*, meaning a walled garden, which traveled through Greek and Latin into English. The Mughals brought the vision alive on earth by burying their celebrated dead in garden tombs. The mausoleum was the focal point of a walled garden which was designed, as was the building itself, to represent basic cosmological ideas. It also asserted the power of the dynasty, not least in the scale of the architecture. The four greatest tombs, those of Humayun, Akbar, Jahangir and Shah Jahan, rank with the Pyramids as the world's finest funerary monuments. "I have never seen the vision lovelier," the English novelist E. M. Forster wrote of Shah Jahan's Taj Mahal. "I went up the left hand further minaret and saw all the magnificent buildings glowing beneath me and all the country [it was September] steaming beneath a dim red and grey sky, and just as I thought nothing could be more beautiful a muezzin with a most glorious voice gave the evening call to prayer from a Mosque. 'There is no God but God.'"

The idea of the tomb in an enclosure did not begin with the Mughals. See, for instance, that of Sher Shah Suri, c. 1540, *below*, which rises majestically from an artificial lake at Sasaram, Bihar. The tomb of Humayun, *below center*, is the first garden tomb. Close to the river Jumna in Delhi, it was begun in 1564 and took nine years to build. The tomb of Akbar (1604–13) at Sikandra, *bottom*, develops the theme, but is unique in taking the form of a tiered and domeless pyramid. It also expresses, like the architecture of nearby Fatehpur Sikri, the synthesis of Islamic culture and Hindu tradition.

The increasing use of white marble with *pietra dura* work in geometric or delicate floral patterns was a feature of the architecture of Shah Jahan's time. *Below* One of the four minarets of Jahangir's tomb (1627) at Lahore. *Bottom* One of the four minarets of the tomb of Itimad-ud-daulah (1628) at Agra. Erected by Jahangir's powerful queen, Nur Jahan, for her father, the mausoleum as a whole as well as in the detail shown here presages the Taj Mahal.

Left The Taj Mahal (1632–54) at Agra, supreme example of the garden tomb. Shah Jahan, who probably played a considerable part in the design, built the mausoleum for his dearly beloved wife, Mumtaz Mahal, who died trying to bear him their fifteenth child in 1631. Shah Jahan rests there beside her.

The Ottoman Empire

The expanding military state

The Ottoman empire was the mightiest and most enduring of the three great empires which straddled the central Islamic lands. By the beginning of the 16th century the Ottoman emperors had constructed a state system of unusual strength, which was organized as a single army with the emperor at the head, and in which soldiers and administrators of all kinds held military ranks and were paid by land grant or by salary. Central government was wherever the emperor and his army happened to be, all chief officials being expected to join the army on campaign and all state revenues being devoted to it. Here are the clear lineaments of the military patronage state which in its Ottoman form combines distinct strands from both the Safavid and the Mughal forms. There is, moreover, a particular comparison to be made with the Mughals because the Ottomans ruled a large non-Muslim population. They did not embrace almost all the followers of an alien religious tradition, as the Mughals did, ruling only the eastern Christian world at a time when the cultural initiative had passed to the West. Nevertheless, like the Mughals, much of the long-term development of their empire was to depend on how they confronted the challenges represented by the alien religious tradition in their midst.

In 1500 the Ottoman state was rapidly becoming one of the most powerful in the world, and the next 70 years were to see a tremendous expansive thrust. The greatest area of expansion was to the east and south. Azarbaijan was conquered in 1514, Syria and Palestine in 1516, Egypt in 1517. The holy cities of Mecca and Medina soon followed, and later the Yemen, and the very important province of Iraq in 1534. The Ottomans were drawn to the south by the need to ward off the Portuguese who, after their circumnavigation of Africa, were threatening Muslim trade and pilgrimage routes. Initially they had tried to meet the problem by propping up the Mamluk regime in Egypt, but soon found it inept and so annexed that wealthy province to the empire. The Ottomans were drawn to the east by the rise of the Safavids whose militant Shiism threatened their hold on the tribes of eastern Anatolia. The victory of Selim I (reigned 1512–20) over Shah Ismail at Chaldiran removed the threat to the Ottoman heartland. Nevertheless, for the next two centuries the empire was much absorbed, indeed far more so than is usually conceded by European historians, in long and debilitating wars with the Safavids over religion, trade and territory.

The traditional direction of expansion was to the northwest. It was mainly in this direction that, right from the foundation of the holy warrior state by Osman I (reigned 1281–1324) in northwestern Anatolia, the Ottomans had striven to subject infidel territory to Muslim rule and the holy law. After Selim I's great victories in the east and south, his successor, Sulaiman the Magnificent (reigned 1520–66), directed Ottoman energies into traditional paths of aggression. He began his reign in typical holy warrior style with a major victory, capturing Belgrade, the southern stronghold of the Hungarians, in 1521. This was followed by the destruction of the Hungarian army at Mohacs in

1526 and the siege of the Habsburg capital of Vienna in 1529, which was lifted just as the city was about to capitulate only because Sulaiman's army wanted to get home before winter set in. For a while the Ottomans accepted the Hungarians as vassals, but by the 1540s they had taken formal control of a vast swathe of territory whose frontier stretched in a great crescent which extended from Trieste to within sight of the walls of Vienna and eastwards to the Crimea.

The Ottomans advanced in no less marked fashion in a new area, the Mediterranean. From the late 15th century they had controlled the Black Sea, an achievement which followed from the command of the Bosphorus won by the conquest of Constantinople. Now they took control of the Aegean, expelling the Knights of St John from Rhodes in 1522 and the Venetians from their outposts on the Aegean mainland by the 1540s. At the same time, using Moorish pirates as proxy forces to begin with, they annexed the North African coast as far as Morocco and then defended it against Habsburg counter-attacks, an overall strategy which sometimes benefited from French aid. The star of this Mediterranean expansion was Khairuddin, known as Barbarossa to the Christians, who rose from being a pirate based on Tunis in 1502 to become grand admiral of the Ottoman fleet in 1533. This expansion reached its peak as twice, in 1551 and in 1565, the Ottomans attempted to seize Malta, the key to the western Mediterranean. After the second attempt failed, they annexed Cyprus in 1570 and concentrated on consolidating their hold on the eastern Mediterranean, a hold which was only temporarily shaken by their overwhelming defeat at Lepanto in 1571.

By the reign of Selim II (1566–74), known to his subjects as "Selim the Yellow" and to Europeans as "Selim the Sot," the great expansion was drawing to a close, and for the next hundred years the Ottomans concentrated on defending the frontiers they had or on recapturing territory they had lost. Then there was a brief flurry of further expansion: Crete was taken in 1669, the Ukraine in the 1670s and in 1683 the Ottoman army was once more beneath the walls of Vienna. It was, however, beaten back and henceforth the empire was always on the defensive.

Ottoman administrative institutions achieved their classic form under Sulaiman the Magnificent. Society was divided into the large mass of subjects, Muslim and non-Muslim, who produced the wealth which supported society's other class, the military, who manned the state apparatus. A late 17th-century Ottoman chronicler, Mustafa Naima, saw the relationship between the two as a "cycle of equity": 1. there could be no rule or state without the military; 2. maintaining the military required wealth; 3. wealth was raised from the subjects; 4. the subjects could only prosper through justice; 5. without rule and state there could be no justice.

To be a member of the ruling military class a man had to be a Muslim, in heart and soul, be loyal to the sultan, and follow all the complex culture which formed the Ottoman way. Men who did not possess these attributes were considered part of the subject class, whatever their fathers may have been. In Sulaiman's time the class was recruited in part from the old Turkoman families who had ruled much of

The Ottoman empire 1512–1683
The empire was born as a crusading state on the Islamic world's frontier with Christianity. By 1512 it had acquired a strong position in the Balkans and Anatolia; Istanbul, the old Constantinople, was its strategically placed capital on the Bosphorus. In the half-century which followed, there was to be an extraordinary expansion:

ATLANTIC OCEAN

Madrid

SPAIN

Fez

MOROCCO

SAHARA

Tlemcen

☐ Ottoman lands 1512

☐ conquests of Selim I 1512–20

☐ conquests of Sulaiman the Magnificent

☐ conquests of 1566–1683

▨ area temporarily held by Ottomans, later reconquered by Safavids

Spalato Venetian possession

1578 date of conquest

(1603) date of loss

✕ site and date of important battle

scale 1:28 000 000

Syria was conquered, Mesopotamia, the Arabian coastline, Egypt, North Africa and Hungary. Moreover, these areas were held, with a few more gains, until at least the end of the 17th century. For a time, as rulers of the most powerful state in the western world, the Ottomans pushed the cause of Islam further into Europe than ever before.

Anatolia after the decline of the Seljuqs, many of whom were granted *timars* or lands in exchange for which they performed government service, and in part from slaves who emerged from a careful system of recruitment and training known as the *devshirme*, meaning to collect or assemble. This was a levy on the sultan's Christian subjects which became a firmly established Ottoman practice in the mid-15th century. At regular intervals agents did a sweep through the provinces selecting Christian youths fit for the sultan's service. The most gifted, about 10 per cent of the levy, were sent to the palace school where they would be trained for service in the highest positions of the empire. They learned to read and write Arabic, Persian and Ottoman Turkish; they were converted to Islam and were instructed in the religious sciences; they learned to wrestle, shoot and ride; and finally they were trained for a particular branch of the administration. The remainder of the *devshirme* levy were sent to work for Turkish farmers in Anatolia, where they too were converted to Islam, became physically hardened, and absorbed the Ottoman way of life so that they were fitted for their destiny, which was usually to serve in the elite corps of the army. All alike had no connections with established Ottoman society except through the sultan. Understandably, sultans came increasingly to appreciate

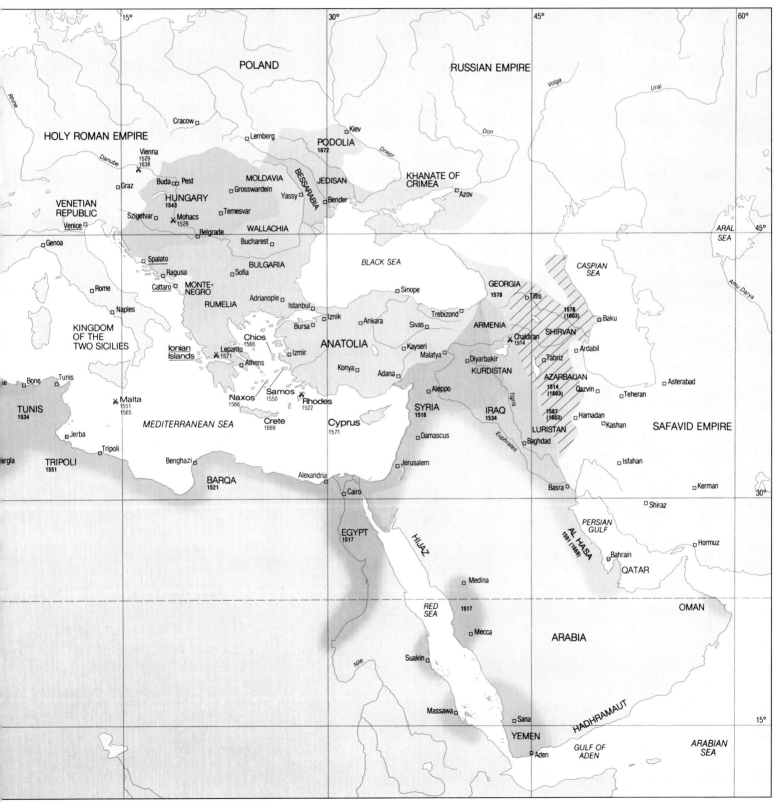

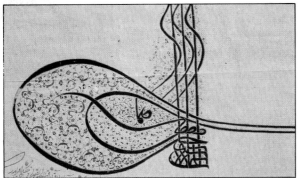

the value of a well-indoctrinated and completely loyal body of slaves, and from the reign of Mehmet II (1444–46, 1451–81) they came to play an increasingly large part in the state service. By the time of Sulaiman the Magnificent they dominated the service, having to a large extent displaced the old Turkoman aristocracy from the key positions. Indeed, they had come to play a part in the Ottoman state which resembled that of the "slaves of the royal household" in the Safavid state under Shah Abbas the Great.

The state service divided into four functional sections. At the head there was the palace, containing the harem which was at times very influential, and those who served the sultan both within the palace and in his relations with the outside world. Then there was the bureaucracy which embraced the Imperial Council, the central organ of Ottoman administration headed by the grand vizier, and the Imperial Treasury which controlled finance. Next were the armed forces, the most important part of which was the slave army, the standing army of the sultan, in which the Janissary infantry, a highly trained force numbering 30 000 men, were the elite corps. Finally there was the learned institution, which was staffed by *ulama* who enforced the *Sharia* and transmitted their Islamic knowledge to the next generation, and which was the one area of the state's activities in which members of old Ottoman families in touch with society continued to predominate. One typically successful administrative career of the early 16th century was that of Lutfi Pasha who began his service in the palace, moved to a crack regiment, went on to high posts in the provincial administration, and eventually crowned his achievement by becoming grand vizier (1539–41).

Top left Sulaiman the Magnificent, gaunt with age, walks in a garden. This sensitive portrayal by Nigari, the outstanding painter of Sulaiman's reign, leaves us in no doubt as to the considerable presence of the old monarch: note how respectfully, almost timorously, the pages stand.

Center left Sulaiman's seal, a typical example of imperial calligraphy.

Bottom left Khairuddin, or Barbarossa, the admiral who led Ottoman expansion in the Mediterranean. Nigari, who was once administrator-general of the imperial dockyards, is again the painter.

Right A stunning picture by Nigari of Selim II, son of Sulaiman the Magnificent, shooting an arrow. Selim II is often remembered for his love of Cypriot wine, but he is best remembered for making possible Sinan's masterpiece, the Selimiye mosque at Edirne.

Below Part of the Ottoman fleet, which commanded the eastern Mediterranean for much of the 16th century and received no severe check till the battle of Lepanto in 1571.

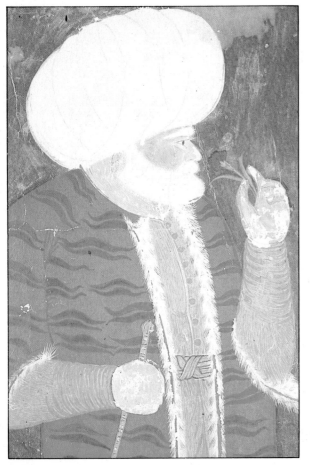

The focal point of the system was the sultan. He was the master of the ruling class, while they were his slaves and their lives and property were at his disposal; even members of the old Turkoman families had to accept slave status, which legally no free-born Muslim could do, if they wanted to enter the state service. On the other hand, the sultan was the protector of the ruled whose traditions and religions, Muslim and non-Muslim, as well as whose lives and property he made it his business to safeguard. In theory he had absolute power over all men through the authority he wielded over the ruling class. But in fact his power was greatly circumscribed. The sultan was often as much a tool of as master of the complex administrative structure, which showed itself well able to function whether he was active in government, or retired, as sultans did increasingly from the late 16th century onwards, to the delights of the harem.

This powerful system was one of the strongest pre-modern forms of government. The basic framework of administration, moreover, was able to sustain the empire as a great power into the mid-19th century. Yet it is clear that at this very time the Ottoman advance grinds to a halt, remains stationary for a hundred years or more, bar the hiccup of the late 17th century, and then begins the long retreat which culminates in the total collapse of World War I. We are left to explain why, at the height of its power, it starts on its long, slow decline.

One explanation which makes a contribution, though not the decisive contribution which has been claimed for it, sees the key problem in the military system. There was a single grand army in which the sultan had to be present and it operated from Istanbul where the great state bureaucracy was centered. Vienna and Mosul were as far as it could reach in a campaigning year, and more distant provinces could not be held against serious opposition. The army, however, depended on victorious campaigns and new territory for its morale and its rewards, so once the geographical limits of the military system were reached, victories and annexations decreased, the army deteriorated, and the state system which was founded upon it decayed.

To this contribution should be added the impact of external forces on the empire. Rival powers, especially in Europe, were growing stronger, which made further expansion increasingly difficult. Economic developments in the world at large, moreover, were undermining the empire as a base. Ottoman policy had always been one of self-sufficiency, the different areas of the empire being developed to complement each other, but it was quite unable to resist the high demand for raw materials stimulated in Europe by vast inputs of silver from the New World, the economic growth which followed, and the general rise of European capitalism and European-dominated trade. Ottoman merchants could not compete with European prices for raw materials. Then, adding insult to injury, raw materials returned as cheap finished goods which undercut the products of the Ottoman craft industries. The problems were exacerbated by a doubling of the population in the 16th century. Prices, moreover, quadrupled in the 200 years after 1570, which tended to make land more valuable as a

source of investment than as the basis on which the *timar* holders could realize their obligations to the state as soldiers or as administrators.

The limitations of the military system might not have mattered so much and the external economic pressures might not have been so damaging, had there not been a weakening at the heart of the state's strength, the administrative system. Paradoxically, the very victory of the slaves over the Turkoman aristocracy, which sultans had fostered to bring strength to the central government, was ultimately to be a source of weakness. Discipline slackened. The slave household no longer had to be mindful of the rivalry of the Turkoman military aristocracy. Corruption set in and competence was undermined as offices began to be sold. At the same time the sultans' grip of the system loosened, in part because the freak of heredity that brought to the Ottoman line a succession of rulers of genius down to the mid-16th century came to an end, and in part because the slaves themselves worked to prevent the emergence of a strong monarch. No longer did the sultan come forward as the victor in a military contest among the claimants to the succession but as the consequence of a political contest between slave factions allied to family interests within the harem, all of which wanted the elevation of a pliable ruler. In these circumstances it was the grand vizier rather than the sultan who was usually the strong man in the state. Further signs of the slackening discipline appeared in the early 17th century as the *devshirme* was abandoned and the character of the slave household changed. From being a regularly re-cruited, socially isolated elite corps in which promotion was by merit, it became a privileged hereditary group concerned to hasten the progress of their sons through bribery. This indiscipline at the center, moreover, was transmitted to the provinces, as is revealed by the many rebellions which broke out in the 16th and early 17th centuries, sometimes under the leadership of the displaced Turkoman aristocracy.

That the reasons for the halting of the Ottoman advance flow in large part from the weakening of central government is suggested by the brief resurgence of the Koprulu vizierate. Mehmed Koprulu was appointed grand vizier (1656–61) at a time of great crisis; many rebels were defying the government in eastern Anatolia, and the Venetians had just destroyed the fleet at the mouth of the Dardanelles. Reputedly one of the last members of the slave household to be recruited through the *devshirme*, he used an almost arbitrary terror to remove the abuses which had infected the system. His son, Ahmed (vizier 1661–76), followed his example, although he did not spill so much blood, and so did his foster-son, Kara Mustafa (vizier 1676–83). The result was to restore both military efficiency and military power, and to enable the Ottomans once again to threaten the Habsburg capital.

The pious in harmony with the state

The Ottoman *ulama* were in harmony with the Ottoman state. The contrast with the *ulama* of Safavid Iran, who worked themselves free of state control to challenge the legitimacy of royal government, and the *ulama* of Mughal India, some of whom attacked the compromises with Hinduism on which the state rested, is marked. This is due in part to the missionary fervor of the early Ottoman holy warrior principality: it bred a sense of communal solidarity and responsibility which influenced the development of Ottoman culture and the Ottoman state down the ages. The gradual growth of the Ottoman empire also helps to account for the difference. Unlike the Safavid and Mughal empires, as it spread into new territories and its institutions took a grip on society, it established slowly an identity of interests with the *ulama* and with sufis hallowed by custom and by faith.

The *Sharia* was at the center of the life of the Ottoman state. By the time of Selim I the Hanafi form of the *Sharia* had become the law of the empire, although it did not apply in the Maghrib where the Maliki form was dominant, or in Egypt and the holy cities of Mecca and Medina where the Shafii form was dominant. Concern for orthodoxy was emphasized by large-scale massacres of Shias. Under Sulaiman the Magnificent the principles on which the *Sharia* was accommodated within the state were elaborated; hence he was known to the Ottomans as the "Lawgiver." The work was done by Khoja Chelebi (1490–1574), the greatest legal mind of the empire and Shaikh al-Islam (head of the religious institution) from 1545 to his death. In practice there were two large areas of orthodox Muslim life in which the *Sharia* did not run. One was in matters relating to state organization and administration where the *Sharia* offered no more than principles, leaving much room for interpretation. Here the sultan, acting on precedent, made regulations, which was regarded as a legitimate proceeding by most *ulama*, who nevertheless found their role restricted to ensuring that the new regulations were consistent with the *Sharia*. The second area was at the local level, where a myriad Muslim villages, guilds and town quarters had their own internal means of government and of reconciling strife. But still the *Sharia* and the values it generated furnished the criteria by which action was judged, and in the Ottoman empire the holy law was more fully carried into effect than in any other major state in Islamic history.

As the *Sharia* was at the center of the state, so were its guardians, the *ulama*. They had great prestige. By the time of Sulaiman the Magnificent there was an extended hierarchy of learning. Budding *ulama* began by attending elementary mosque schools, which gave the rudiments of religious instruction to the masses, and worked their way up through four grades of madrasas. There they were given a very thorough training in the Islamic sciences, until they reached the topmost grade, that of the *semaniye* madrasas, which were built in the mid-16th century adjoining the Sulaimaniye mosque in Istanbul. Students who failed to complete the full curriculum either entered the bureaucracy or became minor *qadis*; those who completed the full course often became teachers, beginning in the elementary mosque schools and working their way up by merit. Teachers were allowed to apply for posts as *qadis*, and the higher they had risen in the madrasa hierarchy, the more senior the posts for which they might apply. Only teachers in the advanced and *semaniye* madrasas might become *qadis* of major cities like Damascus, Cairo or Jerusalem, while only teachers in the

semaniye madrasas might become Shaikh al-Islam. Royal authority was felt throughout the system. In administering the law, *qadis* had to obey the edicts of the sultan; the opinions of *muftis* had merely to be "respected." Posts were filled by the sultan and the grand vizier on the advice of the Shaikh al-Islam, and they were held at the sultan's pleasure.

It is remarkable that the *ulama* as a whole should have seemed to succumb so completely to the authority of the state. They were ordered, graded and controlled as nowhere else in the Islamic world. Some, of course, had always been prepared to find a way of getting on with the state, but that all should surrender, and should sense no conflict between God's law and the will of mortal monarchs, was unusual. Evidently they were satisfied that the state supported the *Sharia* so strongly and that their authority was so great that there was in practice no conflict. Nevertheless, the feeling that *ulama* should keep their distance from princes still lingered. "There was in him," declared a contemporary biographer of the great Khoja Chelebi, "an excess of complaisance and softness toward men of government."

The mark of the integration of the *Sharia* with the workings of the state was the position of religious minorities. Sufis who went too far were persecuted, and so were Shias, although those in the Shia stronghold of Iraq were not troubled. The Coptic, Greek, Armenian, Syrian Christian and Jewish communities, who were *dhimmis* and therefore tolerated minorities according to the *Sharia*, were allowed to organize themselves as separate communities, or *millets*, under their own religious leaders and subject to discriminatory taxation. Initially, Christians shared in some of the activities of state and society, providing, for instance, contingents for the army and participating in the life of the guilds. By the 17th century, however, their contingents were no longer welcome, while the guilds were splitting into Christian and Muslim sections. Indeed, there was a tendency as the empire grew older for the barriers between Muslim and non-Muslim to grow. It was a process no less significant than the repudiation of the alliance between the Mughal empire and the Hindus in India, and as in India it presaged weakness as Ottoman Muslims turned inwards to the Islamic community and Ottoman Christians came increasingly to look to the Christian West.

The cultural face of the *Sharia* state

Ottoman culture seems significantly different from that of its contemporaries. There is, for instance, little of the glitter of Safavid Iran or the vibrant humanity of Mughal India. The creation of the ruling elite who made their way up through the state madrasas and palace schools, it is much concerned with the needs of government, mindful of the restrictions of the *Sharia*, and reflects a world in which order and hierarchy were strong.

There was a solid literary and scholarly culture as one would expect in a state which went to great lengths to train its bureaucracy. Poetry flourished as it did in most Muslim societies. Two of the leading poets of the 16th century were Sulaiman Fuzuli (1480–1556), who was influenced by Persian styles, and Abdul Baki (1526–1600), who developed a distinctive Turkish style which came in the 17th

century to supplant Persian influence. More distinctive products of this highly accomplished Ottoman world, however, were its scientific and prose literature. Ottoman science was given a major boost by the opening of the *semaniye* madrasas adjoining the Sulaimaniye mosque, which produced outstanding work in mathematics, astronomy and medicine. There was also geographical writing which was stimulated by the expansion of the empire on land and sea, and historical writing which stemmed from the desire to record it. Really good historians, like Mustafa Naima, went further, seeking to draw conclusions from their studies and to analyze the causes behind events. Biography, which to a large extent meant recording the lives of the transmitters of Islamic culture, flourished as never before, the encyclopedist, Katib Chelebi (1609–57), producing a masterwork, which drew together the achievement of Islamic culture at the time in Arabic, Persian and Turkish, and described the lives of those who had contributed to it. Finally, travel writing at last improved on the high standard set by Ibn Battuta. Euliya Chelebi (1614–82) spent 40 years journeying in the Ottoman dominions and in Europe, and then devoted the last three years of his life to marshaling his impressions in a *Book of Travels* in 10 volumes.

Ottoman painting has been less highly regarded than that of the Safavid and Mughal courts, in part because it was thought to be derived from Persian models and in part because until recently much of the best work lay hidden in Topkapi museum in Istanbul. But now the low estimate seems unmerited. No one who glances for a moment at the drawings of nomadic life by Mehmet of the black pen or the portraits painted by Nigari (1484–1574), a retired administrator-general of the imperial shipyards, would doubt that there were artists of great originality and expressive power. Admittedly the classical style which began to form under the patronage of Sulaiman the Magnificent betrayed signs of Persian influence; this was to be expected as there were several Persian painters in the royal studios, some of whom had been brought back after the conquest of Tabriz in 1514. As the style developed, however, it acquired its own distinctive quality. Persian love of poetic fantasy gave way to Ottoman practicality, compositions instinct with the spirit of the arabesque to ones more angular and formal, a palette replete with pastels intricately employed to stronger shades and a more limited range.

Looking across the waters of the Golden Horn between the Galata and Ataturk bridges to the confident bulk of the Sulaimaniye in Istanbul. Set on an especially high site, it dominates the city and proclaims the triumph of Islam in this former Christian stronghold. Over 400 lesser domes swarm around the main dome creating a complex of colossal proportions, which embraced, among other things, the four *semaniye* madrasas, the apex of the Ottoman educational system.

This style, moreover, was used to illustrate works which had no parallel in the Persian canon, the histories of the sultans and their campaigns. The first of these books was the *Selimnama*, completed between 1521 and 1524. It was followed by many others, for instance, the *Sulaimannama*, illustrated by the mathematician Nasuh, with 32 miniatures depicting cities, castles and harbors connected with the sultan's Hungarian campaign and Khairuddin's Mediterranean campaign of 1543, or the *Hunernama* with 140 miniatures illustrating the achievements of the Ottoman sultans up to the death of Sulaiman the Magnificent, or the *Surnama* with 437 miniatures depicting the guilds of Istanbul progressing through the old Byzantine hippodrome to celebrate the circumcision of Mehmet, the son of Sultan Murad III (1574–95). In the 17th century the style deteriorated. Then, as sultans no longer campaigned in person and the campaigns themselves were no longer glorious advances into infidel territory but suppressions of rebellions and defenses of the empire, these works which eulogized the expanding state and its conquering rulers were abandoned for genre scenes, portraits of harem beauties and erotica. At its height, however, court painting had reflected distinctive features of the Ottoman state – the sense of order, for instance, revealed in paintings of the army, the importance of hierarchy displayed in those of the court, and the administrative competence suggested by the concern for the accurate depiction of detail.

The 16th century was also a period of high achievement in carpets, textiles and ceramics. "Ottoman Palace" carpets began to be made to add a court style to the vigorous Anatolian peasant traditions. Silks, velvets and other luxury textiles were woven in Bursa and elsewhere and, as the costumes of the sultans preserved in Topkapi reveal, they were of the highest quality in design and execution. The highest achievement, however, was in ceramics. Iznik, the old Byzantine Nicaea, was the center of production where in the mid-16th century craftsmen adopted underglaze painting and developed the capacity to produce seven different colors in this form (deep blue, green, lilac, aubergine, white, black and a bright coral red) which was an unparalleled technical achievement. At the same time they produced a host of rich but naturalistic designs based on plum and cherry blossom, hyacinths, carnations, peonies, but most of all tulips; 41 different tulip designs are to be seen, for instance, in the tiles of the mosque of Rustam Pasha in Istanbul. Iznik pottery reveals the rapid development of technical skills from 1490 to 1525 when decoration was simply blue and white, to a second phase (1525–50) known as Damascus and Golden Horn ware when more shades of blue and a sage green appear, and then a third phase (1550–1700) known as Rhodian ware when the full range of color and design is employed. By this time, however, the prime effort of the Iznik potters had been directed to tiles, and here their most glorious achievement was in the decoration of great Ottoman buildings: the mausoleum of Sulaiman the Magnificent, for example, or the private rooms of the Topkapi palace, or the mosque of Sultan Ahmed, the interior of which is covered by over 20 000 tiles in 70 different designs.

Architecture, which reached its height at the zenith of imperial power in the 16th century, best symbolizes the Ottoman spirit. Over this achievement one man presided – Sinan (1491–1588), royal architect for 50 years, whose genius was matched by a personality which enabled him to turn his post into a powerful office of state. He designed over 300 buildings, fountains and tombs, caravanserais and kiosks, baths and bridges, madrasas and mosques, scattered throughout the empire. Fittingly, Sinan was a typical product of the Ottoman system. Born around 1491, probably into a Greek family of the Kayseri region, he was recruited by the *devshirme* in 1512. After receiving the rigorous training of the *devshirme* recruits who did not enter the palace school, he became a Janissary, fighting in the great campaigns of the 1520s and 1530s, and steadily rising to royal notice as a military engineer by feats such as floating artillery across Lake Van and throwing a bridge across the Danube. In 1538, aged 47, he was appointed royal architect by Sulaiman the Magnificent.

Sinan probed the limits of the domed structure, the dominant feature of Ottoman architecture. Such a man could not live in Istanbul and fail to respond both to the inspiration and to the challenge of the cathedral of St Sophia, whose dome spanned a space greater than Ottoman architects had been able to achieve. He strove to excel the wondrous achievement of Justinian's architects. He also strove to adapt the dome structure to the liturgical requirements of Islam, which meant shifting the emphasis from length to breadth, from the ascending hierarchy of sanctity which culminated in the altar, to the open space in which every place, as the worshiper faced Mecca, was equal. He experimented with features of St Sophia in many of the mosques he designed. Three great buildings mark his development: the Shehzade mosque, built in Istanbul between 1544 and 1548, in which he rearranged the four half-domes which feature in St Sophia so that they buttressed the main dome; the Sulaimaniye mosque, built in Istanbul between 1550 and 1557, in which he achieved almost the same proportions as his Christian model but emphasized the breadth of the building as much as the length; and the Selimiye mosque, built at Edirne between 1569 and 1575, in which he raised a dome which surpassed that of St Sophia. The first Sinan regarded as the work of his apprenticeship, the second as that of his maturity, and the third, built when he was in his eighties, as his masterpiece. "Christians," he wrote in his memoirs,

> say that they have defeated the Muslims
> because no dome has been built in the Islamic
> world which can rival the dome of St Sophia.
> It greatly grieved my heart that they should
> say that to build so large a dome was so
> difficult a task. I determined to erect such a
> mosque, and with the help of God, in the
> reign of Sultan Selim Khan, I made the dome
> of this mosque six cubits wider and four
> cubits deeper than the dome of St Sophia.

But Sinan had done more than assert the superiority of his faith. He had brought Ottoman architecture to its climax and expressed most completely the imperial achievement, the sturdiness, the might, the splendor and the devotion to Islam.

79

The Ottoman World

The Crusading State at War

The Ottoman state began in the 13th century as a crusading principality on the Islamic community's frontiers with Christendom. The crusading ideal informed the state's expansion, particularly into Europe, carrying the Ottoman army to the walls of Vienna in 1529 and 1683. Sultans, when they came to the throne, liked to establish their credentials by major new conquests in the crusading tradition, so Mehmet II took Constantinople in 1453 and Sulaiman the Magnificent took Belgrade in 1521. For over 300 years the Ottoman army was the most efficient fighting machine in the world. "I tremble when I think of what the future must bring when I compare the Turkish system with our own," wrote the Habsburg ambassador to Istanbul in the mid-16th century: "one army must prevail and the other be destroyed . . . On their side are the resources of a mighty empire . . . On our side is public poverty . . . Can we doubt what the result will be?"

At the heart of the Ottoman army were the standing units maintained by the central regime: the Janissaries, the elite infantry corps, armed with guns and numbering 12 000–15 000 men in the time of Sulaiman the Magnificent; the six mounted regiments of the imperial household who were expert in particular weapons; and the specialist technical services, armorers, gunners, sappers and the transport corps. Then there was the feudal cavalry, the *sipahis*, who held grants of land (*timars*), from the revenue of which they had to maintain themselves as effective soldiers and to support retainers when summoned to war. In the 15th and 16th centuries the prowess of the Janissaries and the various specialist units gained an awesome reputation among Christians, although the weight of the army came from the *sipahis* who greatly outnumbered the state's standing forces. In battle the Janissaries and the other specialist units were usually placed at the center of the Ottoman formation in a kind of laager defended by trenches, wagons and guns. On the two wings the *sipahi* cavalry swarmed, waiting for the moment when the enemy line began to waver.

Central to the military success of the Ottomans was the willingness of the infantry and the specialists to adopt firearms. During the 15th century they began to make excellent use of siege artillery; then the harquebus became established among the Janissaries; and by the beginning of the 16th century they knew how to employ field artillery with effect, as the Safavids discovered to their cost at Chaldiran in 1514. Generally, new skills in this field were not developed by Turks, but were supplied by Christians – Serbians, Bosnians, Hungarians, Germans, Italians and French. A Hungarian called Urban cast the guns used against Constantinople in 1453. The resort of the 19th-century Ottomans, and later the Turks, to acquiring the skills of the West in order to beat, or at least to defend the state against, the West, has a long pedigree.

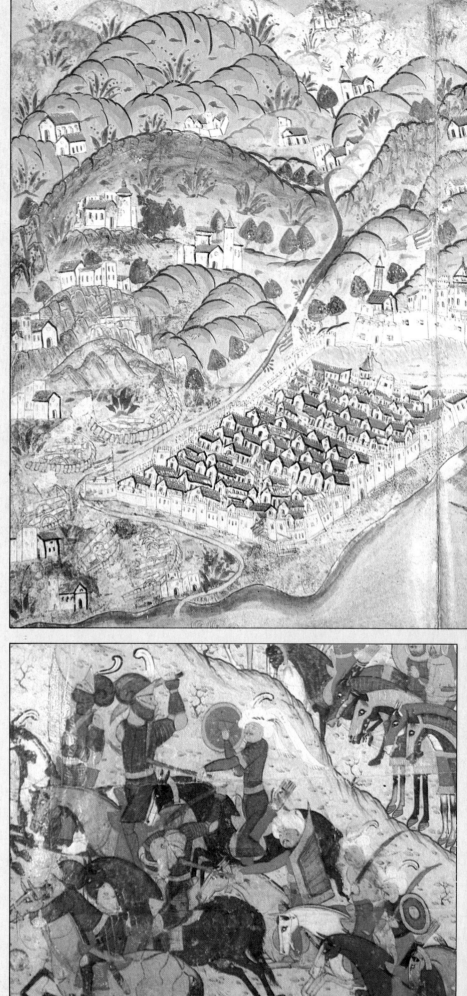

The greatest glory for the Ottomans lay in fighting the Christian regimes of Europe. *Below* The army of Sulaiman the Magnificent before Vienna in 1529. The Ottoman assault was so effective that the city was about to surrender when the impatience of the Janissaries to withdraw before winter set in forced Sulaiman to raise the siege to the amazement of the Viennese. *Left* Members of the famed Janissary corps who lived a life of rigorous discipline and were forbidden to marry until their active service ceased. *Bottom left* The sultan usually accompanied the army on campaign. Here Sulaiman the Magnificent directs mining operations at the siege of Rhodes in 1522. *Opposite below* Although infantry quickly adopted firearms, there was strong resistance to them among the cavalry. Here the Ottoman cavalry demonstrate at the battle of Mohacs, 1526, how they preferred to deal with Christian knights. *Opposite above* Constant campaigning led to a development in cartography, including many maps of cities and ports, like this one of Nice, drawn in the 16th century.

The Sultan's Palace

The feature which distinguishes Muslim palaces from those of non-Muslims, as it distinguishes the houses of ordinary Muslims from those of Europeans, is that they do not aim to present an imposing face to the outside world. Topkapi Sarai, the palace of the Ottoman sultans from the 15th century to the end of the 19th century, perfectly demonstrates the argument. Mehmet II chose a marvelous position, Seraglio Point where the Golden Horn meets the Bosphorus, for the building; but the uninformed visitor to Istanbul, looking from a distance, would be hard put to it to realize that the site contained anything unusual. In fact, Topkapi is not a palace at all in the European sense, but a series of pavilions, courts, gardens, reception halls, treasuries, baths, kitchens and so on, built down the centuries according to the needs of ceremony and practicality. There was no master plan. Thus almost every part of the palace should be considered as a separate monument, often a separate work of art.

Much of Topkapi was built in the 16th and 17th centuries, and many of its interiors were clothed with the rich color glazes and swirling, twining, sometimes wild, designs of the Iznik potters at the height of their powers. During the first half of the 16th century their skills developed rapidly; from being able to produce a simple blue-and-white ware they became able to paint under glaze a gorgeous mixture of deep blue, green, lilac, aubergine, white, black and a bright coral red.

We can grasp an idea of the achievement of the Iznik potters in the 16th century by placing examples of their work in sequence. *Below* Chinese-influenced blue-and-white ware of the period 1490–1525. *Below right* The second phase of Iznik ware, dated 1525–50, known as Damascus ware (there is another style known as Golden Horn ware), in which sage green and more shades of blue appear. Note too the vigor and confidence of the design, and how tulips, carnations and peonies have been naturalistically drawn. *Below far right* The third phase, dated 1550–1700, known as Rhodian ware, in which the full range of color and design was achieved. Most remarkable was the coral red (Armenian bole), the secret of which the Iznik potters knew for a century, then lost. *Above* We see how rooms were clothed in tiles, in this case the bedroom of Murad III, built in the late 16th century. *Opposite below left* Common themes of tile design, tulips and carnations, also appear in this piece of 16th-century Turkish fabric. The former Ottoman capital of Bursa was the center of the textile industry.

Above Looking across the roofs of the harem, or women's quarters, to the mouth of the Golden Horn beyond. It was a world of small rooms and passages, cut off from the rest of the palace.

Left The Baghdad kiosk, built by Murad IV to celebrate the recapture of Baghdad from the Safavids in 1638, is typical of the many buildings in Topkapi which should be considered as separate monuments. The exterior, elegant though it is, gives little idea of the "cool, yet radiant" interior, which is covered with floral tiles and lit by broad windows. The serenity of the building is in jarring contrast with the horrors of the campaign it commemorates. When Murad IV eventually captured Baghdad, he massacred many of its citizens: one of his pastimes was practicing archery on living targets.

The Mosques of Sinan

Architecture best symbolizes the Ottoman spirit. In the 16th century there emerged an architect of superhuman powers, Sinan Pasha, who expressed in his buildings the discipline, the might, the splendor and the devotion to Islam which marked the empire. He became royal architect in 1538 and held the post for 50 years. Although known officially as the "Architect of the Abode of Felicity," i.e. Topkapi Sarai, he designed over 300 buildings throughout the empire. Such prolific production required more than energy and genius; it also needed the skills of the administrator and the manager of men.

Sinan's notable work in Istanbul commemorates the great figures of his day. There are the tombs of Sulaiman the Magnificent, of his powerful and much-loved Russian queen, Roxelana, and of the brilliant admiral, Khairuddin, aptly placed by the seashore. There are the mosques of the grand viziers, Sokullu Mehmed Pasha and Rustam Pasha, and that of the Princess Mihrimah who was married to Rustam Pasha. Most notable, however, are the two mosque complexes he built for Sulaiman the Magnificent and the one for Selim II at Edirne.

Sinan was both irked and inspired by the 1000-year-old cathedral church of St Sophia in Istanbul. He felt that it was an affront to Islam that the emperor Justinian's architects had been able to span with a dome a greater area than Ottoman architects had been able to achieve. He determined to do better. The three great mosque complexes, the Shehzade, the Sulaimaniye and the Selimiye, mark major stages in his approach to the problem. With the span of the dome of the Selimiye he succeeded. Islam could not have triumphed with a more magnificent building.

Sinan (1491–1588) was a typical product of the Ottoman system. Born probably into a Greek family of the Kayseri region, he was recruited by the *devshirme* in 1512. He became a Janissary, fought in the great campaigns of the 1520s and 1530s, and came to royal notice through his feats as a military engineer. *Above* He is commemorated in a statue outside Ankara university. Sinan regarded the emperor Justinian's cathedral church of St Sophia, *below*, as his great challenge. Under Ottoman rule the church was converted into a mosque with the addition of minarets.

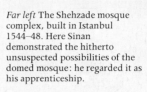

Far left The Shehzade mosque complex, built in Istanbul 1544–48. Here Sinan demonstrated the hitherto unsuspected possibilities of the domed mosque: he regarded it as his apprenticeship.

Left The Sulaimaniye mosque complex, built in Istanbul 1550–57: Sinan regarded it as the work of his maturity.

Below The Selimiye mosque complex, built at Edirne 1569–75. Sinan was in his eighties; he regarded it as his masterpiece.

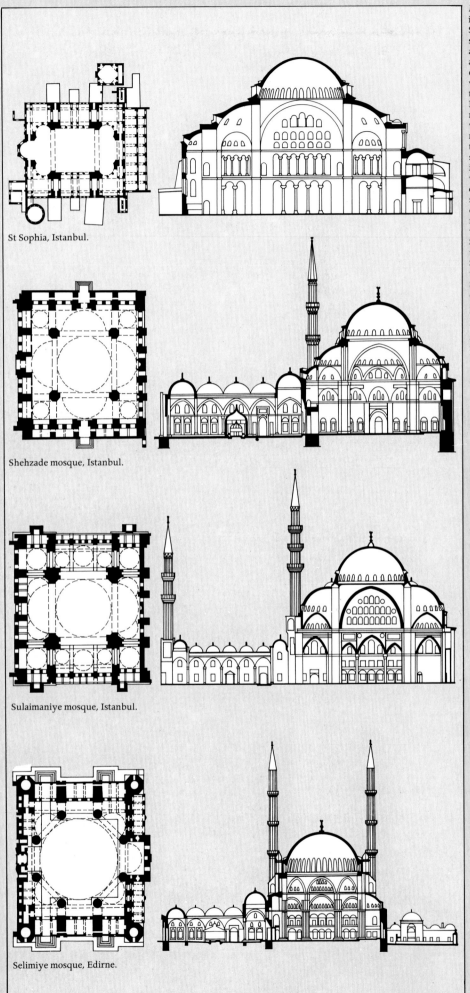

St Sophia, Istanbul.

Shehzade mosque, Istanbul.

Sulaimaniye mosque, Istanbul.

Selimiye mosque, Edirne.

Left The plans and sections illustrate three major stages in Sinan's attempts to design a structure which would outdo the achievement of Justinian's architects. This endeavor was combined with a second which was to adapt such a building to the liturgical requirements of Islam. Sinan was concerned to reduce the emphasis on length, which derived from the sense of movement in a church towards the sanctuary and altar, and to stress instead the idea of a space in which any place, as the worshiper faced Mecca, was equal. At the top there is Sinan's starting point, St Sophia. In his early design, the Shehzade, he rearranged the four half-domes, which featured at either end of St Sophia, so that they buttressed the main dome. In the Sulaimaniye he achieved almost the same proportions as those of St Sophia but strove to emphasize the breadth of the structure as much as its length. In the Selimiye, by returning to the elegant and tried formula of an octagon to make the transition from square base to domed roof, he not only succeeded in spanning a wider area than Justinian's architects but also in creating a perfect Islamic space.

Far right top The interior of St Sophia, converted for use as a mosque. Nevertheless, the design still performs its old Christian purpose; the eye is drawn to the former sanctuary in the distance. *Above right* Looking towards the *mihrab* in the Sulaimaniye, we see how this effect has been reduced; and looking in the same direction in the Selimiye (*below right*), we see how it has been eliminated. "Spaciousness and a sea of sparkling pinkish light wash through the clear shape of the building with irresistible effect," writes the English art historian, Michael Levey. "One is borne up on an exhilarating wave contained within what on first encounter seems a circular area, so totally does the high floating dome appear to govern the whole interior. This effect is increased by the withdrawal of the ring of grooved supporting piers into the surrounding skeletal fabric, leaving unimpeded the great central space beyond which gleams the recessed, richly tiled, radiant apse of the mihrab. Though it is there that the eye inevitably focuses ... there is little urge to advance beyond that serene spherical envelope of atmosphere which virtually *is* the interior." Sinan's aim is achieved.

In every mosque he designed Sinan tried new ideas. In the second he built for Princess Mihrimah (*far right center*) he created a space marked out by light-filled walls, and in consequence the dome seems weightless, almost like a balloon straining at its earthly moorings. In the first he built for the grand vizier, Sokollu Mehmed Pasha (1570–71) (*far right bottom*), which was ingeniously sited on a steep hillside below where Ahmed I's Blue Mosque now stands, a sheet of tiling sweeps up the *mihrab* wall to the very foot of the dome.

THE FURTHER ISLAMIC LANDS FROM 1500 TO THE 18th CENTURY

We now turn to lands beyond the control of the great Muslim empires, to southeast Asia, to Africa, and to Central Asia and China, where in 1500, North Africa and Central Asia apart, large numbers of Muslims had appeared but recently. They tended to have a firm foothold in particular areas rather than in the region as a whole. In southeast Asia they were established in northern Sumatra, around the Malayan coast and on Java's northern shore, and in Africa down the east coast as far as Kilwa and in a series of kingdoms on the savanna lands south of the Sahara. They were often a minority and faced great and powerful cultures like the Confucian in China or the Hindu-Buddhist in Java. They had, moreover, no overwhelming military predominance. Islam was not borne into these regions on the spears of nomadic hordes, nor was it blasted in by the superior fire power of an Ottoman or a Mughal military machine. Instead Islam slowly seeped in, mingling with local cultures and drawing men to the worship of the one God. Occasionally progress was checked, but generally it seemed to advance inexorably, and in peace. The evidence for these processes is not rich, and certainly not as rich as it is for the history of the great empires of the heartlands. Nevertheless, it is important that it should be studied, for here we witness the extraordinary capacity of Islam to adapt itself to different cultural circumstances and to express itself in forms so much more varied than those derived from the study of the central Islamic lands. We also witness how, at a time when Christians were beginning to place their impress on the continent of America, Muslims were coming to give an Islamic complexion to much of Africa and southeast Asia.

Commerce had carried Islam to these lands. Muslim traders, making good use of the fortunate geographical position of the Islamic heartlands, came in the years before 1500 to control much of the international traffic along the trade routes of the world: the routes of the southern seas which linked the east coast of Africa, the Red Sea and the Gulf to the rich ports of India, of southeast Asia and of China; the routes across the Sahara, and especially from the wealthy cities of the Magrib, into the western Sudan and the Niger Basin; and the great Asian land route, the Old Silk route, from the eastern Mediterranean, through Iran, Turkestan, and along the Tarim Basin into China. These arteries of world economy formed natural channels along which Islamic influences flowed; as Muslims came to dominate key areas of the system, their non-Muslim trading partners often came to embrace Islam as well, in part because business was so much smoother if men shared a common culture and a common law, although we should not forget the

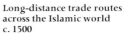

Long-distance trade routes across the Islamic world c. 1500
The central Islamic lands lay athwart the international trade routes of the late medieval world, of which the greatest was the Old Silk route from the eastern Mediterranean to China. Islam spread steadily along these commercial arteries into southeast Asia, Africa, Central Asia and China.

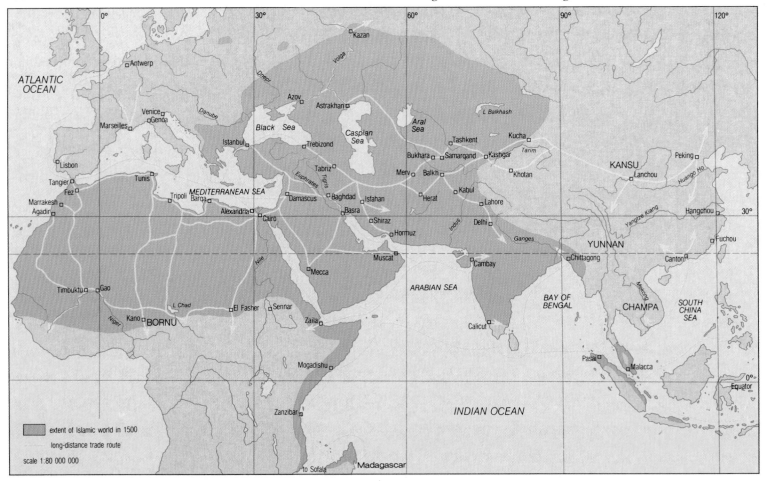

extent of Islamic world in 1500

long-distance trade route

scale 1:80 000 000

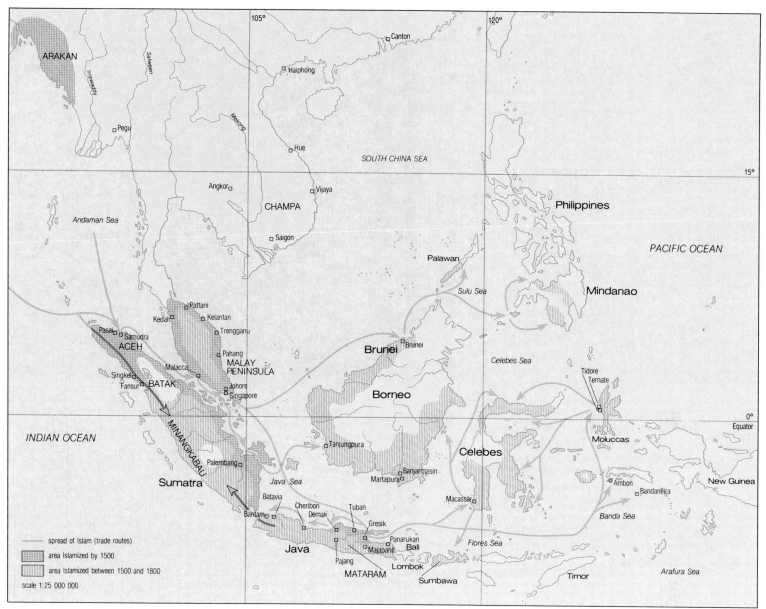

The spread of Islam in southeast Asia 1500–1800
This was a crucial phase in the expansion of Islam in the region. In 1500 the faith had a footing on a few coastlines; by 1800 it had spread through much of island southeast Asia and had established itself in the rich and populous Javan hinterland. Islam was brought to the region by Arab and Indian traders, and trading connections continued to nourish it down to the 20th century. In assessing the message of this map it should be remembered that the process of Islamization, the process by which peoples were drawn into an Islamic cultural milieu and brought to conform to the *Sharia*, was long and slow. For hundreds of years Islamic and pre-Islamic religious practices would mingle freely: sometimes Islam would be checked and the process of religious change reversed.

openness of trading communities to new ideas and new experience. It was thus that Arab and Indian traders carried Islam into southeast Asia; it was thus that Arab and Berber traders carried Islam south of the Sahara. After 1500, where Islam had already gained a foothold, traders provided the channel along which cultural reinforcements flowed to enable consolidation to take place. The importance of this process, moreover, should not be underestimated because when trade declined, as it did in China, the Muslim foothold in the Confucian world came under threat. Where, on the other hand, Islam had yet to penetrate, as in the east of the Indonesian archipelago or in the lands of the upper Niger, traders continued to perform their pioneering role.

The actual work of spreading the faith is usually attributed to saints and sufis. According to Javanese tradition Islam was introduced to the island by nine saints, while in the Upper Volta region of West Africa its arrival is normally traced back to wandering holy men. Some of these founding fathers were very possibly involved in trade themselves; from the Prophet himself Muslim men of religion have often been traders, valuing the freedom from state control trade could bring, not to mention the opportunities for meeting the religious injunction to travel in search of knowledge. Many,

however, would merely have accompanied traders on their boats and in their caravans, hoping to render religious services to their fellow travelers and to the communities with which they traded. Thus the celebrated Malay chronicle, *Hikayat Raja Pasai*, describes how a sufi traveling on a ship sent by the "king of Mecca" brought Islam to northern Sumatra. Doubtless some of these sufis were also deeply learned in the Islamic sciences, but it would have been unwise for them to insist on a strict application of the *Sharia*; the power to support such a stand was unlikely to be forthcoming; moreover, the conflict between the demands of the holy law and local religious practice was likely to be too great. Rather, bolstered on occasion by the apparently latitudinarian mystical thought of Ibn al-Arabi, they sought points of contact and social roles within the host society. They shared their knowledge of religious experience with mystics of other faiths. They helped propitiate the supernatural forces which hemmed in and seemed ever to threaten the lives of common folk. They interpreted dreams, brought rain, healed the sick and made the barren fruitful. They mediated between rulers and ruled, natives and newcomers, weak and strong. In fact, by accommodating themselves to local needs and customs, they gradually built a position from which to begin the long process of Islamization, by which the people were drawn into an Islamic cultural milieu and brought to conform to the *Sharia*.

It should be clear that rapid conversion was rare. Sufis intent on gaining acceptance in new areas did not present Islam in all its exclusiveness and its demands for unqualified commitment; and for most individuals the cost of conversion, of breaking away from their society and of achieving a total reorientation of the soul, were too great to bear. The normal process was one of gradual adhesion in which, for instance, individuals might begin to include visits to saints' tombs among their religious practices or communities might, like the Bedouin Arabs of the Prophet's time, come nominally to accept Islam after their chiefs or kings had been converted. Occasionally a ruler might make a symbolic gesture but in general, if significant boundaries were crossed, the event was barely perceptible, as was the slow transformation of the inner life. Islamic and pre-Islamic practices mingled freely in the religious activities of the people, who sometimes came to believe that their particular mixture was the "true" Islam. Such was the first main stage in Islamization in which Islam displayed flexibility and sympathy as it interacted with non-Islamic cultures. The second main stage followed as the new Muslims now began to interact with the culture of the older Islamic lands, traveling to sit at the feet of learned *ulama* in Mecca or Medina or Cairo, or welcoming them in their midst as models of behavior; such processes could lead eventually to reform movements aimed at removing pre-Islamic practices. This will be the subject of a later chapter. For the moment we are concerned with the main stage, with the countless compromises that Muslims made between doctrine and local conditions in spreading their faith in the further Islamic lands.

Southeast Asia

The information for southeast Asia, as has been said, is relatively scarce. There was no great focus of Muslim power in which intellectual and material resources could be so concentrated as to bestow rich artifacts on the present, while the tropical climate was always hostile to paper records and to wooden buildings. Indeed, it is often hard to know when fact ends and speculation begins. Moreover, we must try not to think of the area as a coherent region—after all, the concept was invented only in World War II—and we should be wary of sweeping generalization. The history of Islam in the region is not one of ever triumphant expansion. There are halts before barriers of paganism; there are even reverses where Christianity gained the upper hand. This said, we are nonetheless witnessing a crucial stage in the process by which the Indo-Malay race came to be one of the most numerous of the Muslim peoples of the world.

In 1500 Muslims were established in many parts of the region. They dwelt in many small trading communities down the Burmese coast, and especially in Arakan whose kings were subject to the sultan of Bengal. There was a distinct community of Muslim Chams in Indo-China who had but recently been conquered by the Vietnamese. Moving south to island southeast Asia we find important Muslim states at the western gateway to the archipelago:

Right: **The sultanates of the Malacca straits and Java in the 16th and 17th centuries**
This map shows how by 1650 Aceh had come to dominate much of Sumatra and the Malay peninsula, while Mataram had come to control almost the whole of Java. Note too the centers of the Javanese holy men who dominated the island's politics for much of the 16th century.

Left The minaret of Kudus whose holy men ruled the heartland of Demak. This early 16th-century structure shows how the form of the traditional Javanese temple was bent to Islamic purposes.

Below The tomb of Hasan al-Din at Gowa. This sultan of Macassar fought long and hard against the Dutch for Islam and for control of the spice trade.

Pasai in northern Sumatra, which had been the first Muslim stronghold in the region, and Malacca on Malaya's southern shore, which in the 15th century had come to dominate the straits. From Malacca Muslims had gained a footing along the northerly trade route which ran by northwest Borneo to the Sulu islands and the southern Philippines. They had also spread their influence down the southerly trade route which ran along Java's northern shore and southern Borneo till it reached the Moluccan spice islands of Ternate and Ambon. In some places the Muslims were still just a community of foreigners, in others they had brought natives and rulers to share in their beliefs. They had, however, rarely been established for long enough, particularly in the east, to make a serious impression on the hinterland, although they do seem to have gained a foothold at the Hindu-Buddhist court of the central Javan kingdom of Majapahit.

The 16th century began badly for Islam. Malacca was captured by the Portuguese in 1511 and Pasai in 1521. Within three years, however, the new state of Aceh drove the Portuguese out of northern Sumatra and devoted much of the following century to trying to drive them out of the Malay peninsula, on occasion with Ottoman help. Aceh became the new Muslim stronghold, attracting Muslim traders from Malacca and controlling the east and west coasts of Sumatra. The height of prosperity was reached under Sultan Iskander Muda (reigned 1608–37), when Aceh became a focus for all those who traded in the southern seas – Europeans, Indians and Chinese alike. Religious learning was patronized, great buildings were raised and Islam was brought to much of Sumatra, including Minangkabau. But soon afterwards Aceh declined. The closing of Japan, the Manchu conquest of China, the rise of Macassar to the east and the Dutch conquest of Malacca in 1641 stemmed the life-giving flow of

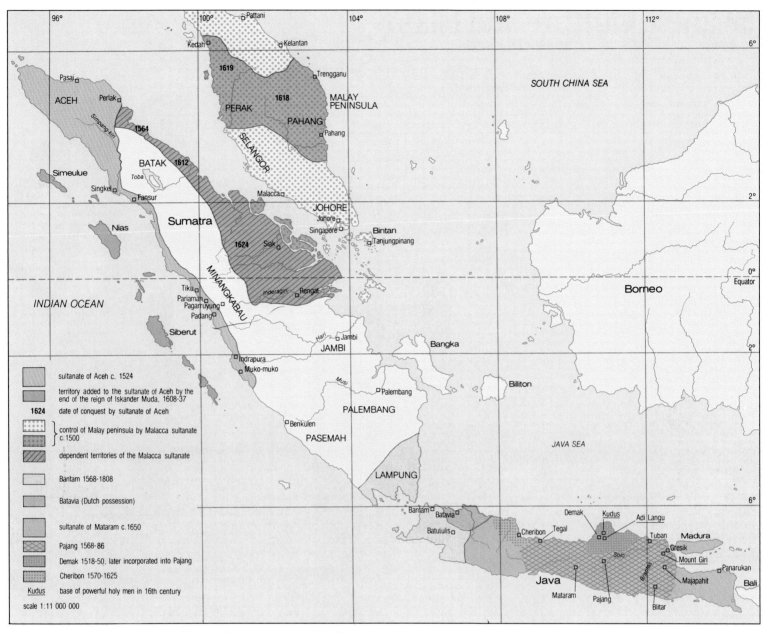

sultanate of Aceh c. 1524

territory added to the sultanate of Aceh by the end of the reign of Iskander Muda, 1608-37

1624 date of conquest by sultanate of Aceh

control of Malay peninsula by Malacca sultanate c. 1500

dependent territories of the Malacca sultanate

Bantam 1568-1808

Batavia (Dutch possession)

sultanate of Mataram c.1650

Pajang 1568-86

Demak 1518-50, later incorporated into Pajang

Cheribon 1570-1625

Kudus base of powerful holy men in 16th century

scale 1:11 000 000

trade. Yet the state remained relatively strong to the end of the century, important enough to receive a Meccan embassy and able to refuse the demands of an English one.

Macassar replaced Aceh as the standard-bearer of Islam against the European interloper. This state of the southwestern Celebes came late to Islam, and its chroniclers have left us with precise details. On 22 September 1605 the prince of Tallo embraced Islam, and on 19 November 1607 the first Friday prayer was held. Foreigners noticed the conversion because pork became scarce; neighboring states also noticed it as they became the victims of holy wars. From now on the Macassarese, noted for their devotion to the faith, fought the Dutch as Christians and as their rivals for control of the spice trade. Their greatest leader was Hasan al-Din (reigned 1631–70) whose empire at its height stretched from Borneo to New Guinea and from Lombok to the southern Philippines. Only after long and bitter fighting did he in 1667 accept Dutch terms which destroyed Macassar's dominance in the trade and politics of the region.

While Aceh and Macassar were advancing Muslim interests along the coasts, Muslims were also making gains inland, notably in Java, the richest and most populous island of the region. Demak, prominent among the Chinese-Javanese Muslim lordships of the northern coast, first spread westwards, absorbing Cheribon and carrying Islam into south Sumatra; it then advanced eastwards, destroyed the remnants of ancient Majapahit in 1527 and only failed in 1546 before the last bulwark of Hinduism in east Java. At the same time sufis became increasingly active throughout the island; many of them taught a pantheistic mysticism which found a happy home among the numerous Javanese who were still Hindu. Some sufis associated with Muslim rulers, but most kept their distance from earthly powers, gathering disciples around them and dwelling in separate communities. They helped in the rise of Demak, Shaikh Ibn Mawlana of Pasai, for instance, leading the campaign to convert pagan west Java into the Muslim state of Bantam. But after Demak declined, these sufis, whose spiritual authority also brought temporal power, came forward as the arbiters of the island's politics. Prominent among them were: the holy men of Kudus who ruled the old Demak heartland till 1588, the holy men of Giri whose disciples carried Islam to the east of the archipelago and whose fame reached as far as China, and the holy men of Adi Langu

Javanese Culture and Islam

Between 1500 and 1800 Islam came to influence to a greater or lesser extent most of the peoples of island southeast Asia. The change did not involve a total transformation of religious life. Transformation is too strong a term, as it conveys a sense of completion, for the subtle shifts in emphasis we have in mind. Certainly, there was a powerful movement towards a kind of Islamic orthodoxy in northern Sumatra, the area longest and most strongly exposed to Arab and Indian Muslim trade and culture. In Java, on the other hand, the richest and most populous part of the region, where Hindu-Buddhist civilization had once blossomed most abundantly, there was just a slow acknowledgment of new religious preferences alongside the old: sculpting of the human form was abandoned, as was cremation of the dead, while the Hindu epics were still treasured and the Goddess of the Southern Ocean still consulted. Similarly, the changing religious atmosphere modified, but did not transform, the island's distinctive art forms. Kris handles, dance, batik prints and *wayang* puppets all reveal how the Javanese began to take account of the new Islamic world in which they moved.

There are many styles of women's dance. Nevertheless, not one retains the widespread knees or raised legs of the more dynamic dancers of Hindu Barabudur or the 10th-century Shiva temple of Prambanan, *below*. Modesty and refinement dominate the art, as the court dancer from Mangkunagaran, Surakarta, suggests, *bottom*. Although there are other explanations, it seems likely that Islam's concern for feminine modesty has limited the freedom with which the dancer could use her body.

The kris, or dagger, is considered essential to complete formal dress on Java. There are many regional styles and these have been modified under Islamic influence. *Above left* A central Javanese kris of the period before 1500 in which the handle is an anthropomorphized demon; it is the *Hockerstellung* type of Majapahit kris. *Above* A classical central Javanese handle of the 18th or 19th century which developed from the *Hockerstellung* type and which reveals how under Islamic influence the demon has been stylized out of existence. *Left* A handle from the neighboring island of Bali where there has been no Islamic influence.

The Javanese *wayang* world, especially the puppet theater, lies closest to the heart of Javanese civilization. There has been no modification of the Hindu epics, nor apparently of the striking forms of the *wayang kulit* or shadow-play puppets which have traditionally performed them. Islam has left its mark in the inclusion of a new cycle in the canon, the story of Amir Hamza, uncle of the Prophet, usually performed by *wayang golek* puppets which are, paradoxically in the light of Islamic antagonism to images, most lifelike. *Left Wayang golek* puppet of Umar Maya, fellow student of Amir Hamza. *Far left* Typical *wayang kulit* puppet.

Batik is Java's notable gift to the world of textiles and the typical adornment of Javanese dress. The word in Javanese means wax painting. Wax, usually beeswax, is applied to cotton, or sometimes silk, leaving sime parts uncovered. The material is then dyed, the wax removed, with the result that a pattern is left on the cloth. Different colors and different designs are associated with various parts of the island. The designs themselves consist of natural objects in stylized form: flowers, butterflies, birds, fruits, foliage, shells, and sometimes a kris or a ship. The advent of Islam influenced design. Where

Islam was strong, living creatures were no longer portrayed, patterns became highly formalized, often geometric, and Javanese exuberance was tempered.

Above left A traditional central Javanese batik with the *garuda* motif, flowers and birds. The *garuda* (*left*) was a mythical bird and a traditional motif, favored in particular by the sultans of Jogjakarta.

Above right A silk batik from the north Javanese coast where Islamic influence has historically been strongest. The design is

highly ordered and no living creatures appear: see the detail (*above*).

whose most eminent representative, Sunan Kali Jaga, became spiritual patron of the empire of Mataram.

The rise of Mataram marked a new stage in the expansion of Islam on Java. For the first time Muslim power was based, not on the coastline, but at the traditional center of Javanese government in the hinterland. At the height of its power under Sultan Agung (reigned 1613–46) Mataram controlled almost all Java except the enclave where the Dutch held out at Batavia. Sultan Agung's regime had a decidedly Muslim face: he introduced the Islamic calendar, visited the graves of saints and received the title of sultan from Mecca. Like many Muslim princes, moreover, he found himself opposed by the guardians of the faith. How far the struggles which followed were either part of the traditional tension between the ports of the northern shore and the rice-growing hinterland, or part of the no less endemic tension between spiritual and temporal authority in Islam, we cannot know. What is clear, however, is that he and his successors came so much into conflict with the powerful holy men of the island, who led revolts and strove to influence the succession, that from the late 17th century they were forced to rely on Dutch aid to preserve their authority. The price was the steady surrender to the Europeans of their territory, which by the late 18th century had been pared down to south central Java.

The relations between the transmitters of the faith and state power varied considerably. In Mataram they were evidently bad. Indeed, in the 17th century the rulers steadily picked off the leading holy families, and on one occasion tried to wipe out all the sufis on the island. As a political force the holy men were eventually subdued, yet they survived. Usually called *Kiyayi*, they either lived in special Muslim holy villages whose peoples closely followed their example, or established themselves outside village communities in small settlements where, joined by their families and their pupils, they would scratch a living from the fields and pass on their knowledge of the Quran, the traditions, the law and mysticism. Not surprisingly, after the persecution they had endured, one of the beliefs which came to be widespread among these religious communities and schools was in the coming of a messianic *ratu adil* or just ruler.

In Aceh the situation was very different. The learned served the state which made much of scholars and religious learning. In the 17th century Aceh was the foremost center of scholarship in the archipelago. Here *ulama* and books came from India and Arabia, while the Acehnese made the pilgrimage to Mecca and studied under the leading *ulama* of the Hijaz, the Yemen and the Gulf. From Aceh too emissaries went to the Mughal and Ottoman courts. If the sultans of Mataram had to take account of the partially Hindu world over which they ruled, those of Aceh must have felt increasingly part of the mainstream Islamic world.

These differences are emphasized by the different expressions of Islamic faith which flourished. In Mataram, where Islam struggled with the ancient Hindu-Buddhist traditions, most Javanese had probably become Muslims by the end of the 18th century. The process was marked, for instance, by the abandonment of both the cremation of the dead and the sculpting of the human form. At the heart of the struggle between the two great religious traditions lay the problem of bringing an utterly transcendent God to a people who assumed that he existed in everything. Of course, the mystic thought of Ibn al-Arabi made it possible to bridge this gap. Yet, when sufis adapted their approach to the world which they wished to transform, they came dangerously close to pre-Islamic beliefs. Certainly some Javanese, when they heard the relationship of God to the world explained in terms of that between Vishnu and Krishna or listened to the story of Lebe Lontang who had achieved mystic perfection and thus could discard and mock religious ritual, saw the metaphor for what it was. But others merely heard talk of old and comfortable gods and understood that Lebe Lontang rejected every positive formulation of religious law and doctrine as the old masters of esotericism had traditionally done. If some came to comprehend the awesome prospect of the God, others, and one suspects most, continued their devotions to many gods and demigods alongside their observance of Islamic rites.

In Aceh fewer such ambiguities flourished. Here *ulama* of tender conscience had less need to feel uncomfortable. Islam was not seriously challenged; the great issues of the day lay less between an Islamic and a Hindu-Buddhist pantheism than between two schools of *ulama* struggling to advance their careers. In the early 17th century Aceh seems to have been dominated by a school of heterodox sufis and admirers of Ibn al-Arabi, some of whose writings still exist. Hamza of Fansur (died c. 1600) was the leading light and his pupil and successor Shams al-Din of Pasai was a favorite of Sultan Iskander Muda. Then, just after the sultan's death in 1637, a learned Indian, Nur al-Din al-Raniri, arrived, attacked Shams al-Din's heterodox views, burned his books and persecuted his disciples. The religious differences were not great, amounting to no more than disagreement over how strictly Ibn al-Arabi's work should be interpreted, and the fuss may well have been derived primarily from a struggle for patronage at court. Yet so close were the connections of Aceh with the intellectual centers of Islam and so great was the interest aroused by the divisions among its *ulama*, that by 1640 echoes of this dispute had reached Medina where one of the leading figures of the day, Ibrahim al-Kurani, wrote a magisterial work to resolve the points at issue. Indeed, the foremost of these learned men may well have been the equal of any in the Islamic world at the time. There is Abd al-Rauf of Singkel, for instance, who, after studying sufism and the Islamic sciences at various centers in Arabia between 1640 and 1661, returned to teach and write in Aceh for over 30 years, and to make the first translation of the Quran into Malay.

The 300 years after 1500 form a crucial phase in the progress of Islam in southeast Asia. Not all the openings for expansion were used. No progress was made in Burma or in Indo-China where international trade was sluggish; without the regular reinforcements from the heartlands which vigorous commerce brought it seems Islam could not make headway against self-confident Buddhist or Confucian civilizations. In the Philippines, moreover, from 1570 the Muslims were kept penned in to southern Mindanao by a successful Spanish occupation. In the rest of island southeast Asia, on the other hand, great progress was made. Superficially its extent might be questioned. No significant Muslim power survived to the late 18th century and the Dutch East India Company had come to occupy the greater part of Java. Indeed, the main theme in the historiography of the region used to be the rise of European power from 1500. But in recent years scholars have played down its importance. In the 18th century the Dutch had acquired no overwhelming political predominance, while commercially they were declining. Elsewhere their impact had been negligible. The people did not take to European culture and few embraced Christianity. On the contrary, it was the Dutch who had gone far towards molding their ways to the patterns of the world in which they moved. The significant influences from the West remained those which came via Muslim mouths and Muslim pens, those borne by Nur al-Din al-Raniri or Abd al-Rauf of Singkel. In this way the Indo-Malay people first encountered Western rationalist thought in the works of Plato, Plotinus and the Neo-Platonists deeply buried in the Islamic scholastic tradition, and their attachment to Hindu-Buddhist metaphysical philosophy clothed in anthropomorphic symbolism began to slacken; and in this way also they came to participate in the great monotheistic tradition and to lose their faith in the old mythologies. Of course, the depth of the change differed from place to place. If it was profound in northern Sumatra, it was still ambiguous in much of Java, and was no more than a mimicking of outward forms in Borneo. Nevertheless, by 1800 there had been a decisive shift in the orientation of Indo-Malay civilization.

We can see aspects of this shift, as well as its limitations, in the processes of cultural change. The most powerful expression of the growing influence of Islam was the spread of the Malay language as a vehicle for literature and philosophic discussion. It came to carry much writing, both popular and learned, and did so in the Arabic script. There were epics and romances and a myriad religious tales, translations of Islamic works in the Islamic canon (by al-Ghazzali or al-Taftazani, for instance) as well as influential new writing, like Hamza of Fansur's mystical poetry or al-Raniri's *Sirat al-Mustaqim*. In consequence the language was much enriched by Arabic vocabulary and technical terms, becoming widely used along the trade routes of the archipelago and displacing the dominance of Javanese. The success of Malay among the many languages of the region, however, should not lead us to imagine that Islamic culture completely enveloped all previous forms. In other spheres there was much adaptation of old systems to meet new requirements, especially in Java, but the old styles were still discernible. Batik patterns, for instance, became more stylized, mask plays after being banned from the Muslim courts became the property of strolling players, while the magical tradition of women's dance continued but with greater modesty – no longer did the dancers spread their knees wide or raise their legs high as once they had according to the sculpture of Hindu Barabudur. Pre-Islamic building styles, as elsewhere in the Islamic world, though not always so strangely, were made to serve the new religious purpose. Thus the

Islam in Africa beyond the Ottoman empire 1500 to the 18th century
Traders had brought Islam to much of Africa's east coast and to the lands south of the Sahara. From 1500 they continued to foster its expansion, and, as in southeast Asia, there was often an uneasy coexistence of Islamic and pre-Islamic religious practice. The 16th century saw *ulama* and sufis throughout the area striving to defend the faith and to promote a purer version of Islamic society. Although Europeans were beginning to be active on the Moroccan and East African shores, it was to be a long time yet before they would turn the political geography of the continent inside out. Throughout these three centuries the states along the Sahara's southern fringe looked across the desert to Morocco or to Egypt and not down to the ocean shore.

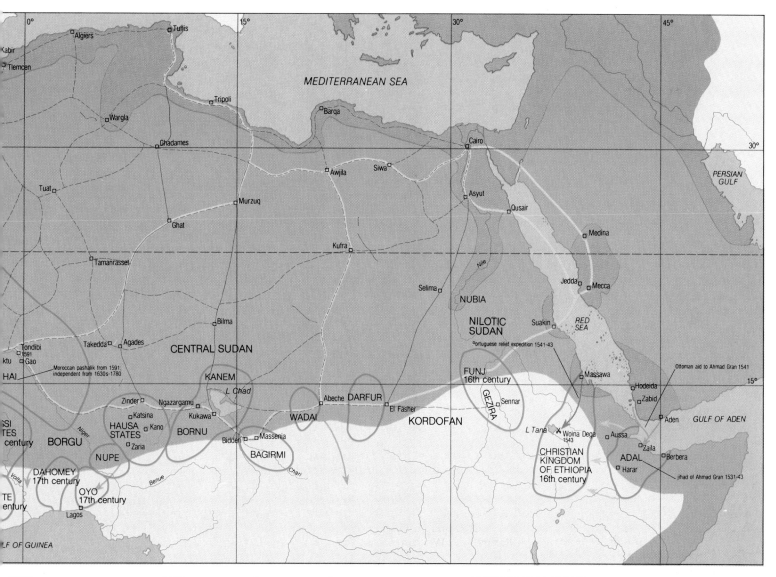

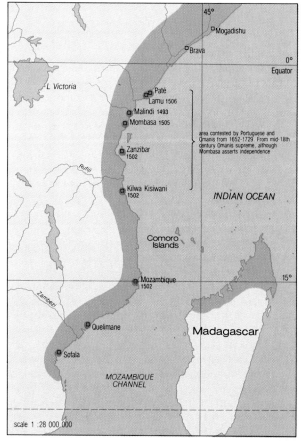

Legend (left column):

- extent of Islamic world c. 1500
- spread of Islamic world
- extent of Ottoman empire in 1683
- furthest extent of state power
- jihad of Ahmad Gran
- Portuguese possession
- 1486-1541 date of acquisition and loss
- ✕ site of important battle
- extent of Moroccan territory
- center of learning
- developing pilgrimage route
- principal caravan route
- minor caravan route

N.B. the use of caravan routes was constantly
subject to economic and political change

16th-century minaret at Kudus is Hindu-Javanese in style and the roofs of most mosques in Java and Sumatra are layered and pagoda-like. But in one sphere there was little adaptation, that of the *wayang* or shadow theater. The traditional cycles of plays, based for instance on the Hindu *Ramayana* or *Mahabharata*, persisted unchecked and conceded only the development of a new style, the *wayang golek* in which the most popular cycle of plays was based on stories about the Prophet's uncle, Amir Hamza. This apart, the ever-popular *wayang* world continued to nourish the Hindu pantheon and its values alongside the spreading message of Islam.

Africa

Here we are concerned with the areas beyond the effective reach of Ottoman power, from Morocco in the northwest to Africa's Indian Ocean shore. It was free from serious external threat save the occasional Ottoman thrust or the niggling importunity of the European trader. It was not in any way a coherent region; the histories of Morocco, of the western or the Nilotic Sudan, or of the Horn of Africa, all followed different patterns. Yet there is a linking theme. All these areas in the early 16th century saw champions of Islam striving to defend the faith or to promote a purer version of Islamic society. Throughout the three centuries from 1500, more-over, where there were states ruled by Muslim

princes, *ulama* and sufis were working to consolidate Islam, and not invariably against the royal will, while beyond the boundaries of Muslim power they continued to spread the faith, often hand in hand with trade. Indeed, the activities of the learned and the holy men stand forth with special prominence, in part because they were sometimes the crucial support of temporal power, and in part because that power itself was sometimes but precariously established.

Muslims lived in East Africa from the time of the Prophet. But, except in the Horn where they had spread to the foot of the Ethiopian highlands, they had remained penned in on the coast. There they lived in bustling port cities, for instance, Mombasa, Pate, Kilwa, Sofala, all of which fell into Portuguese hands soon after 1500. The Horn had its port cities too, notably Mogadishu and Zaila, which escaped Portuguese conquest, but it also had inland Muslim states long tributary to Ethiopia and known collectively as Adal. These rebelled frequently against their overlord, a process which culminated in the early 16th-century *jihad* of Ahmad Gran (1506–43), the leader of a militant reformist movement which challenged Christian Ethiopia and those who wanted to coexist with it. For 12 years he

ravaged the Christian land, strongly supported by the nomadic Somalis, till he was defeated by Portuguese guns and killed. This spelled the end of Adal as an area of inland Muslim states and was followed by a strengthening of the Muslim regimes on the coast. Further south, Muslims continued to strive against the Portuguese until the mid-17th century when the Omanis became strong enough to drive them out and to offer their own protection.

The Nilotic Sudan saw a decisive move in favor of Islam as well. Around the beginning of the 16th century the Muslim Arab tribes of Upper Egypt finally conquered the Christian kingdom of Nubia, only to be overwhelmed themselves soon afterwards by pagan cattle nomads, the Funj, advancing down the Nile. This defeat, however, was quickly turned into glorious victory when the Funj were converted to Islam, and Nubia and the Gezira became Muslim lands. *Ulama* and sufis played a major role in the transformation, and, supported by extensive land grants, were sometimes able to form great dynasties. Thus the land of the pagan Funj became a Muslim sultanate from the mid-16th to the late 18th century when at last it was outshone by a rival sultanate based at Dafur in the far western province of Kordofan.

From 1527 Ahmad Gran, leader of a militant reformist movement based on Harar, waged holy war against Ethiopia and its allies. From 1531 to 1543 he ravaged the Christian kingdom, destroying churches and monasteries and forcing Christians to accept Islam. To help counter these activities, the Portuguese built the castle of Gondar, *left*.

Desert, savanna and forest in Africa

Even further west there were the little-known kingdoms of Wadai and Bagirmi whose rulers became Muslims in our period. Then around Lake Chad there was the kingdom of Kanem-Bornu, for long a caravan port on the Sahara's southern fringe and trading much with Egypt and with Tripoli. In the late 15th century the kingdom entered on a new period of strength which was symbolized by the construction of a permanent walled capital at Ngazargamu on the banks of the Yo. This development reached its height under King Idris Aloma who reigned between about 1570 and 1619. For a time Kanem-Bornu was a great power in the central Sahara, cultivating the Saadids of Morocco and the Ottomans, and securing military instructions and firearms which gave it the advantage in local wars. At the same time the state was given a sharp push in an Islamic direction, the *Sharia* being widely applied and administered by *ulama*. "Truth and right came into their own," declared the royal chronicler, "evil went and hid herself and the path of righteousness was plainly established without let or hindrance, or deviation, so that all the notable people became Muslims ..." The state continued powerful to the mid-18th century, by which time its kings were known chiefly for their piety and the *ulama* had come to dominate.

From the time of King Idris Aloma Hausaland was under the influence of Kanem-Bornu. Here was a clutch of city-states on the savanna lands east of the Niger, some rising, some falling, Katsina, Kano, Gobir and Zaria being among the more important, and all embroiled in internecine conflict. The long-distance trade was the foundation on which these states were built; east–west along the savanna belt, and from the north down to the Atlantic coast, Islam accompanied this trade and the Hausa peoples came to respect Muslim susceptibilities. Thus King Muhammad Rumfa (reigned 1463–99) of Kano symbolically ceased to follow earlier superstitions by cutting down the city's sacred tree which had grown beside the congregational mosque. Yet in the 300 years which followed, while Islam strengthened its hold, earlier beliefs still flourished.

The greatest state of the west Sudan was the Songhai empire of Gao. At its height in the 16th century it embraced the great bend of the Niger from the Hausa states in the east to Borgu in the south and reached from the Atlantic coastlands in the west across the desert in the north to hold the precious salt deposits of Taghaza and Taodeni almost on the Moroccan frontier. Here too around the beginning of our period there was a shift towards Islam. In 1493 Askia Muhammad, a leading official, challenged the king, who acknowledged the claims of Islam alongside those of many spirit cults, to declare whether he was a Muslim or not. When the king refused, Askia defeated him in battle and seized the throne. He then made much of the *ulama* and set the seal on his revolution by performing the pilgrimage to Mecca between 1495 and 1497. The people of Songhai, however, were loath to accept significant changes in their religious practice, and throughout the 16th century Muhammad's successors were unable, or unwilling, to impose a rigorous Islamic administration. Indeed, the antipathy between the Muslims and those who mixed animism with their Islam formed the basis of debilitating succession struggles. These meant that,

when Morocco decided to put an end to the dangerous situation in which a Negro power controlled the two vital Saharan trade commodities of gold and salt, Songhai could not effectively resist. For 40 years from 1591 Morocco controlled the great cities of the Niger bend, and then her interest faded. Nevertheless, Songhai's might was broken, and the trans-Saharan trade which it nourished declined. A mere rump of the old empire, now based on Timbuktu, persisted into the late 18th century. It was famed more for the learning of its *ulama* than the power of its pashas.

Moroccan intervention in the affairs of the Sudan draws our attention towards this last African Muslim state beyond the reach of Ottoman power. Its people had been staunchly Muslim since the early centuries of Islam, and, with its boundaries firmly established on lines which have persisted to the present day, it had long since passed through the processes of state formation which engrossed the regimes of the Sudanic lands. The question here was not whether the state should be constructed or reconstructed but who should rule within a given territorial framework. This said, there was at the beginning of the 16th century increasing pressure from the Portuguese along the coast, which stimulated the growth in numbers and in influence of marabouts, as Moroccan sufis are called (the term being a French corruption of Arabic and meaning a man "tied" to God), devoted to their expulsion. This movement enabled one holy family, the Banu Saad, to drive the Portuguese out by 1549 and seize power from the reigning Wattasids by 1553. The Saadids then crushed a further Portuguese invasion at al-Qasr al-Kabir in 1578, set about destroying the influence of the very marabouts who had helped them to power, created a centralized administrative system which lasted into the 20th century, and established a brilliant court at Marrakesh. So mighty did the state become that the Ottomans began to scent a rival, and its greatest ruler, Ahmad al-Mansur (1578–1603), felt strong enough just before his death to plan the conquest of Spain with Elizabeth I of England. But there followed succession struggles, weakness and the resurgence of maraboutic power, until about 1660 another holy family, the Alawites, became predominant. The Saadid machine was revitalized and, as in the central Islamic lands, strengthened with loyal slaves. Henceforth the Alawites grappled with the twin problems of asserting the power of the state over sufi brotherhood and Berber tribe and protecting the integrity of the land from the encroaching European.

In Africa the role of the transmitters of Islam stands forth yet more prominently than in southeast Asia; this is in part because we know more about them, more, indeed, than for many other regions of the Islamic world, and in part because, leaving Morocco aside, state power was often even weaker than in the sultanates of island Indonesia. These transmitters were sometimes *ulama* and sometimes sufis too, although the great age of the brotherhoods was not to begin till the 18th century. They took their place in verifiable lines of transmission many centuries long, stretching back into the past and forward to the present day. These channels down which the life-giving blood of Islamic knowledge passed often seem much more clearly defined than

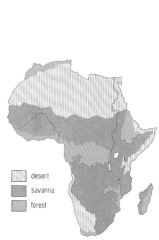

desert

savanna

forest

Left *Ulama* were influential and from time to time dominated the affairs of West African states, so it is fitting that their mosques should be the major buildings to survive to the present day. Timbuktu was the leading center of learning south of the Sahara, and the Sankore mosque, shown here, first built in the 14th–15th centuries, was an important focus of advanced teaching.

Right Religious life in Morocco, indeed most aspects of life, were dominated not by *ulama* but by marabouts, as the local sufis were called. They had risen to prominence in the 15th century as men became alarmed by Christian incursions and disenchanted by tribal leadership. So the countryside came to be dotted with shrines, great and small, like this one at Melilla, where men sought to mobilize the *barakat* or divine favor of dead saints.

the somewhat shadowy sub-Saharan states. Indeed, they seem more definitely than elsewhere to be the arteries of Islamic society, just as the record of the deeds of the transmitters seems to be the true framework of Islamic history.

Recent research has revealed how great families often stood at the heart of these lines of transmission, knowledge and blood thus mingling as they flowed down through time. In the Nilotic Sudan, before the foundation of the Funj sultanate, one Ghulam Allah from Arabia established himself on the Upper Nile and down to the late 18th century his descendants spread throughout the land as teachers. In Timbuktu the main lines of transmission passed through three families, the Aqit, the And-Agh-Muhammad and the al-Qadi al-Hajj, all of whom emerged in the 15th century and remained prominent in teaching and learning over hundreds of years. Temporal rulers, of course, would move to bring them to heel but over time the contest was rarely equal. "By contrast with the frail and unstable dynasties of the rulers," declares one historian of the Nilotic Sudan, "the holy families acquired power and prestige so that they became the true scaffolding of Sudanese society." Indeed such families could play a leading part in bearing the message of Islam far beyond the reach of Muslim princes. Most notable were the Saghananughu, a family of *ulama* whose origins had been traced to the Upper Niger region in the 14th century from where over many generations they have traveled through the savanna lands of Guinea, the Ivory

Coast, Upper Volta and Ghana establishing as they went Quran schools, some of which have continued teaching to this very day. And thus was Islam spread through much of West Africa, not just through the savanna but also into the forests further south, as *ulama* answered the needs of isolated Muslim traders for religious guidance or pagan villagers for more powerful magic.

As one would expect, important centers of Islamic learning flourished. There was Aussa and Harar in east African Adal, Ngazargamu in the center and Walata further west, but sovereign of them all was Timbuktu, from its early days an Islamic settlement, and one which had literally grown up about its mosques. Here knowledge of the Islamic sciences ran deep and broad. Budding *ulama* studied as rich a course as could be found elsewhere, reading both books and commentaries used widely throughout the Islamic world from the *Muwatta* of Malik Bin Anas to the works of al-Suyuti and the achievements of local scholarship. At the heart of the educational system lay the study of the law and jurisprudence, an emphasis reflected in the output of the city's most famous scholar, Ahmad Baba (1556–1627), whose works are still preserved in North Africa.

Contributing thus and sharing in the common fund of Islamic scholarship meant the possession of many books, and Timbuktu boasted extensive private libraries containing hundreds and even thousands of volumes. Indeed, books were the most highly prized items of 16th-century trade, scholars

Right The maraboutic movement became associated with the state after the discovery in 1437 near Fez of the tomb of Mawlay Idris I, 8th-century founder of Islamic Morocco. The Saadian and Alawite dynasties, like Mawlay Idris descended from the Prophet, drew on the maraboutic cult to underpin their rule. The shrine of Mawlay Idris I, shown here, became the most sacred site in the land.

seeking the rarest and most voluminous of tomes and being prepared to pay more for them than the average price of a slave. Such care for learning, moreover, was not restricted to an elite but seems to have been shared to some degree by the people at large. At this time the city had over 150 Quran schools which suggests that a large proportion of the city's population of 75 000 experienced the first stage of education.

Contacts with international scholarship were not limited to books. Descendants of Ghulam Allah, for instance, traveled in the 16th century to Cairo to learn from leading teachers of the time as did *ulama* from Timbuktu who also included centers of learning in western Asia as well as the Maghrib in their travels. Those who could not travel corresponded, and some of the letters still exist to show how they sought guidance from the leading scholars of the age. Nor was the traffic all one way; the great al-Suyuti (1445–1505) of Cairo and al-Maghili (died 1504) of Tlemcen, for instance, journeyed to the western Sudan where the latter left a son who founded a leading Kano family. Moreover, the learning of Timbuktu was valued highly enough in Morocco for the scholarly Sultan Ahmad al-Mansur to treat Ahmad Baba as a notable prize of his victory over Songhai and to bring him to Marrakesh where Moroccans flocked to sit at his feet. In the value placed on Ahmad Baba we have the most tangible expression of the achievement of Islamic scholarship in the Sudan.

The vigor and the success of the *ulama* should not lead us to believe that they had everything their own way. Certainly they enjoyed immense prestige under the Funj sultans and from the 17th century came to have a firm grip on Kanem-Bornu, the first manifestly Muslim state south of the Sahara. Admittedly in Timbuktu they kept their distance from the ruling military elite, and when the Askia rulers of Songhai came to the city, while everyone else attended the court, they came to the houses of the *ulama*, thus observing the ideal Islamic etiquette. Yet, although *ulama* stood up for their higher principles, more often than not they also had to stand by while their rulers compromised with pre-Islamic practices; while, for instance, the Sarkins of Kano revived pre-Islamic taboos and the Askias of Songhai observed old rituals of divine kingship. Those wrestling with problems of power had to recognize that they were ruling subjects who worshiped stones and trees and idols as well as Allah. For all the achievements of the *ulama*, many areas were still frontier territory in which the processes of Islamization had but recently begun to operate.

What remains of this distinctive Islamic civilization of the Sudan reflects the role of the *ulama* and of Islam in fashioning it. There is Arabic which Muslims brought to the region and which was the first language in which the Sudanese learned to read and write. Arabic was the language of administration, of learning, of correspondence and of record; it had, moreover, a deep impact on indigenous languages, especially Hausa. Arabic is the language in which the achievements of Sudanese scholarship have come down to us: the commentaries on texts in the madrasa curriculum, the biographies such as Ahmad Baba's famous biographical dictionary of the Maliki school, and

the chronicles such as al-Saadi's history of the Sudan or Ibn Fartuwa's history of the reign of Idris Aloma of Kanem-Bornu. More immediately accessible, however, are the clay mosques of the savanna lands, which are striking precisely because indigenous architectural forms were not completely overwhelmed by those of the central Islamic lands. Two styles developed: the Mali-Songhai style marked by buttresses, pinnacles and soaring minarets whose exposed beams give a typically hedgehog-like effect, and the Hausa-Fulani style marked by multi-domed roof systems and heavy tower minarets clearly derived from North African models. It seems an altogether proper comment on the enduring influence of the *ulama* in our period that the minarets of their mosques should still stand out so proudly while the palaces of the temporal dynasties should have crumbled.

If *ulama* figured prominently in the life of sub-Saharan states, it was sufis who did so in Morocco; indeed they came completely to embrace the state. These sufis, or marabouts, dominated all aspects of Moroccan life. Until the 15th century they had played a relatively minor part, but then they came to the fore as men became disenchanted by tribal leadership and alarmed by Christian encroachments. In fact they succeeded in so transforming the consciousness of the people that their religious life became focused on controlling the special marabou-tic attribute, *barakat* or divine favor. The country-side became dotted by shrines where the *barakat* of dead marabouts was sought, the people were organized into orders around families whose blood bore *barakat*, and religious practice became dominated by ecstatic rituals designed to mobilize *barakat*.

Prominent in this movement was a new respect for those who were *sharif*, that is descended from the Prophet. This devotion gained momentum after 1437 when the tomb of Mawlay Idris I (died 791), descendant of the Prophet and founder of the first Moroccan Islamic state, was rediscovered near Fez. Then it was given specific form by one al-Jazuli whose devotional work, *The Proofs of the Blessings*, was widely used in mystic practice, and, more important, focused intense concentration on the Prophet. To be *sharif* became a source of especial spiritual power, for such men most assuredly bore *barakat* in their veins.

It was in this context that the Saadian sharifian family led a religio-political movement, closely associated with the memory of al-Jazuli, to gain control of the land. It was thus, too, that, after the Saadians had failed to master competing brother-hoods, that the Alawite sharifian family came to establish the dynasty which has persisted to the present day. Thus the maraboutic society came to have a maraboutic government, and sufi values underpinned the state just as the sufi network transmitted them to the people. The sultan was the supreme marabout who demanded total obedience from his subjects just as thousands of lesser marabouts did in their localities. Now the educational system no longer emphasized the *Sharia* and the principles of its application but the sufi tradition of imitation and blind obedience to spiritual authority. Here the *ulama* could not hope successfully to assert the higher duty of God's law against the edicts of the sultan.

The new development in the relationship between Islam and Moroccan society is expressed in what men chose to build. Although the Saadians built the largest madrasa in the land at Marrakesh, the great age of madrasa building for which Morocco is justly famous came to an end. Instead there were vast royal palaces: the el-Badi of the Saadians, the shell of which still stands at Marrakesh, and that of the Alawite, Mawlay Ismail (reigned 1672–1727), at Meknes. Small towns in themselves and separated from their peoples by thick high walls, they proclaim the power and the distant mystery of the sharifian monarchs. But above all there were the royal mausoleums: those of Mawlay Idris I in Fez, of the Saadians in Marrakesh and of Mawlay Ismail in Meknes. These were the supreme expression of state and maraboutic cult combined.

Central Asia and China

Here were the northern marches of the Islamic world where by 1500 Muslims were widespread throughout the steppes and desert oases. In the west there were the khanates of Kazan, Astrakhan and the Crimea, successor states of the Mongol Golden Horde. In Transoxania, where Tamerlane and his descendants had presided over glittering courts, the Turkish Uzbeg tribe now ruled, and threatened Khurasan. Further east the descendants of

Above left The *mihrab* of an exquisitely decorated small mosque just outside the mausoleum in Meknes of Mawlay Ismail (1672–1727), the greatest of the Alawite rulers. Mawlay Ismail solved the problem of finding a stable basis for state authority by creating a specifically Negro army from the descendants of slaves brought to Morocco two centuries earlier. This especially trained and exclusive force, which should be compared with the Ghulams of the Safavids, the Janissaries of the Ottomans and the Mamluks of Egypt, proved effective.

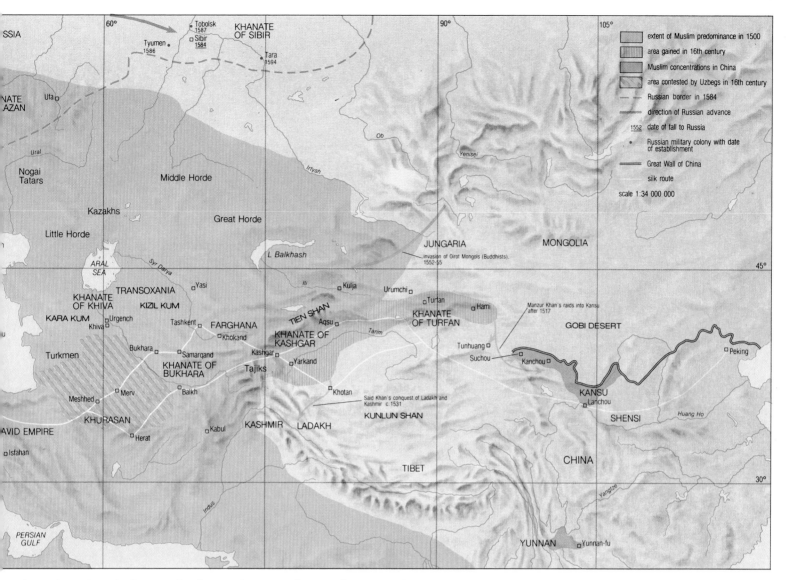

The following labels appear on the map:

Legend:
- extent of Muslim predominance in 1500
- area gained in 16th century
- Muslim concentrations in China
- area contested by Uzbegs in 16th century
- Russian border in 1584
- direction of Russian advance
- 1552 date of fall to Russia
- Russian military colony with date of establishment
- Great Wall of China
- silk route

scale 1:34 000 000

SSIA
NATE
AZAN
Ufa
Ural
Nogai Tatars
Kazakhs
Little Horde
Middle Horde
Great Horde
60°
Tobolsk 1587
Sibir 1584
Tyumen 1586
KHANATE OF SIBIR
Tara 1594
Ob
Irtysh
90°
Yenisei
JUNGARIA
invasion of Oirot Mongols (Buddhists) 1552-55
MONGOLIA
105°
45°
L Balkhash
ARAL SEA
Syr Darya
KHANATE OF KHIVA
TRANSOXANIA
KIZIL KUM
Yasi
Ili
Kulja
Urumchi
Turfan
Hami
Manzur Khan's raids into Kansu after 1517
GOBI DESERT
KARA KUM
Khiva
Urgench
Tashkent
FARGHANA
Khokand
TIEN SHAN
Aqsu
KHANATE OF KASHGAR
Tarim
KHANATE OF TURFAN
Peking
Turkmen
Bukhara
Samarqand
Kashgar
Yarkand
Tunhuang
Suchou
Kanchou
KHANATE OF BUKHARA
Tajiks
Khotan
Said Khan's conquest of Ladakh and Kashmir c.1531
KANSU
Lanchou
Huang Ho
SHENSI
Meshhed
Merv
Balkh
KUNLUN SHAN
KHURASAN
Kabul
KASHMIR
LADAKH
AVID EMPIRE
Herat
Isfahan
TIBET
CHINA
30°
PERSIAN GULF
Indus
Yangtze
YUNNAN
Yunnan-fu

The northern Islamic lands in the 16th century

The area is littered with the relatively small states which emerged after the tide of Mongol empire receded: the khanates of Kazan, Astrakhan and the Crimea, successor states of the Golden Horde; the khanates of Kashgar and Turfan, where descendants of Gengis Khan ruled; the khanates of Bukhara and Khiva, where Uzbegs, descended from the White Horde, supplanted the heirs of Tamerlaine. Elsewhere nomadic peoples, Kazakhs, Turkmen, Tajiks, roamed freely. Notable developments were: the penning of the Uzbegs in Central Asia so that for the first time for many centuries a strong Central Asian power was prevented from becoming mighty by expanding to the southwest; the few gains of Islam as compared with Africa and southeast Asia; and the ominous rise of Russia, which now began its long conquest of the Muslim peoples of Central Asia.

Chaghatai, the second son of Gengis Khan, maintained an increasingly precarious hold over Farghana, Jungaria and the oasis cities of the Tarim Basin. In the far east, in Kansu, Shensi and Yunnan, provinces of China proper, there were notable Muslim communities living under Chinese rule, the descendants of traders and of Muslim officials of the Mongol Yuan dynasty (1280–1368 AD).

Unlike southeast Asia and sub-Saharan Africa this was not, the lands north and east of the Tien Shan mountains apart, an area in which Islam was still expanding: the features of the three centuries after 1500 were increasing isolation and decline. From the time of the Seljuqs onwards, steppe peoples had poured through Khurasan into the central Islamic lands. But the Uzbegs, who disdained the use of firearms, found Safavid Iran too firm a barrier. It was, moreover, as much a religious and cultural barrier as a political and military one: while Iran had become Shia, Central Asia had remained Sunni. No longer were the Turkish peoples to be stimulated by the cultural vitality of the cities of the Iranian plateau: indeed, Persian slowly withered and Turkish came to be their favoured tongue. Simultaneously, the region was gradually isolated from its major source of wealth, the trade which flowed down the Old Silk route between China and the West. Now this fell into the hands of Europeans, both from western Europe, who developed ways to China by sea, and from the

Russian dominions, who pioneered more northerly routes by land. Furthermore, as these Muslim peoples found their wealth declining, they also found it harder to stand up to Russian and Chinese expansion. Thus some came to discover, before any other Muslims in the modern age, the weight of self-confident rule by men of other cultures, while those who still preserved their freedom became yet more confined.

The khanate of Bukhara, the focus of Uzbeg strength, was the most powerful of the Central Asian regimes, capable for much of the 16th century of contesting Khurasan with the Safavids and in the mid-17th century of throwing back a Mughal invasion. Although the great wealth which had been derived from the trans-Asian trade declined, Bukhara remained the most important entrepôt for foodstuffs, with merchants working in Siberia and the Tarim Basin. Three dynasties held sway: the Shaibanids until 1599, the Janids, 12 of them, from 1599 to 1785, and then the Mangits. Strong rulers were still able to add to their territories. Thus Abd Allah Khan, who was effective ruler for the second half of the 16th century, could annex Balkh, Tashkent and Farghana; Shah Murad (1785–1800) could make inroads into the neighboring khanates and Iran. Lands gained, however, were usually lost after a time, the authority of the Bukharan khans being reduced to Transoxania, which in this period became the land of the Uzbegs.

Two weaker Uzbeg khanates survived alongside Bukhara. To the northwest there was that of Khiva, which had been founded after 1512 by a scion of the Shaibanid family. Much less powerful than Bukhara, and protected by the black sand desert of the Kara Kum and the red sands of the Kizil Kum, it remained a bastion of Sunni orthodoxy and of mainly local importance. To the east there was the khanate of Khokand, which was founded around 1700 when another scion of the Shaibanid house, Shah Rukh (died 1722/3), declared Bukhara's fertile Farghana province independent. Throughout the 18th century this new khanate progressed, especially economically, although after the Manchu conquest of east Turkestan in 1759 it had to acknowledge Chinese suzerainty.

The three Tatar khanates which straddled the Asian border with Europe strove to play an independent role in the politics of the region, but could not long preserve their freedom. That of the Crimea came under Ottoman authority in the late 15th century; Kazan, which controlled the rich corn lands of the middle Volga, and Astrakhan, which controlled the lower Volga, followed suit in the early 16th century. Unable to influence these khanates, which were able to launch devastating expeditions into Russian territory, Tsar Ivan the Terrible annexed Kazan in 1552 and Astrakhan in 1556. The Crimea, which was much more closely attached to the Ottoman empire, suffered the same fate in 1783. The ending of Muslim independence was especially strongly resisted in Kazan. There was good reason: the Russians restructured regional society, redistributing Muslim lands to Russian nobles, reducing Muslims to a minority by importing Russian peasants, destroying mosques and

madrasas and adopting a policy of forced conversion to Christianity. Resistance continued for over 200 years until a *jihad* in 1755 and the Pugachev revolt of 1773–74 made the Russians think again. Catherine the Great ended religious persecution, established an assembly of *ulama* and rehabilitated the Tatar nobility and merchants. Now the perennial insurgents became partners in empire and wealthy enough to be the enlightened patrons of a Tatar Islamic renaissance in the 19th century.

Turning to east Turkestan, where in the early 16th century Muslim khanates reached out to the borders of China and Tibet, two Chaghatai brothers held sway. One, Manzur Khan, ruled the provinces north of the Tien Shan mountains, the Turfan and Hami oases, and was advancing towards Kansu. The other, Said Khan, ruled the south and west of the Tarim Basin and was invading Ladakh and Kashmir. From the mid-16th century, however, these expanding regimes fell into disarray. Mongol clans occupied the lands north of the Tien Shan mountains, while in the oasis cities to the south Chaghatai dominion faced increasing competition from sufi brotherhoods. The sufi leaders, known as *khojas*, were all descended from a Naqshbandi shaikh and descendant of the Prophet, Makhdum-i Azam, who was greatly venerated in Turkestan and died at the Chaghatai capital of Kashgar in 1540. His descendants split into two factions who struggled for leadership of the brotherhood. In time the oasis cities of the Tarim Basin, Kashgar, Yarkand, Khotan, Aqsu and so on, became rival city-states in the hands of the various *khoja* clans. In 1678 the last Chaghatai khan, who held Kashgar alone, was toppled by a *khoja* who depended on the aid of the Mongol Oirots (Buddhists) from the north. For the

Abd Allah Khan, last great Shaibanid khan of Bukhara, contemplates a melon with obvious relish: melons were a favorite fruit among Central Asians. School of Bukhara, late 16th century.

Central Asia in the 17th and 18th centuries
Now the relics of Mongol power become truly petty states and the area in which Muslims live freely is steadily reduced. In the north and west the Russians push their frontier forward inexorably; in the east the Muslim regimes of the Tarim Basin succumb to Mongol Buddhist and to Chinese power. Expeditions against the weakening khanates of Transoxania from Nadir Shah's Iran and Mughal India, however, meet with only temporary success.

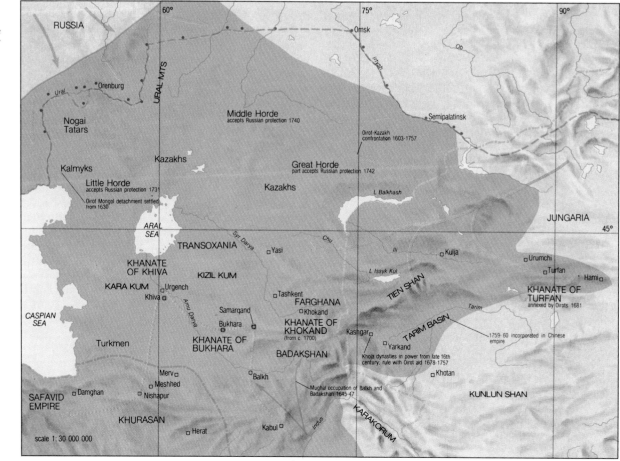

area of Muslim dominance in 1600
Russian border in 1584
Russian border in 1796
Russian fortified post
Russian advance
Oirot Mongol expansion
Chinese border c. 1760
Mughal expedition
route of Nadir Shah's raid 1738-39
boundary of Safavid empire
center of learning

following 80 years the play of Oirot power and the fate of *khoja* factions were intertwined until in 1758/9 the Manchus brought the region within the Chinese empire.

In China Muslim experiences were different from elsewhere. Scattered in small communities throughout the market centers of the land and most populous in Yunnan and Kansu, where the great trade routes from the south and the west entered China proper, they were always in a minority and without power. Nevertheless, they had a strong sense of their own identity. "Arabia, not China, is the center of the world," declared one 17th-century Muslim writer, stressing his allegiance to the community of Islam rather than to the celestial kingdom. They were conscious, moreover, of their superiority: "one Muslim equals five Chinese," the saying went. Of course, this self-awareness was enhanced by their ability to maintain their own religious and educational institutions and their dominance of particular trades like those in beef or cart transport. It was further sharpened by the almost universal Chinese contempt for a people they evidently found loud and aggressive. There was, indeed, a general feeling that the only good Muslim was a dead Muslim. In this light it may seem strange that up to the 19th century Muslims did not work to create their own religio-political community as they had done from time to time elsewhere. No doubt this is in large part explained by their scattered distribution and the fact that they were left to their own devices. Indeed, some Muslims were prepared to go to considerable lengths to smooth over the differences between Islam and Confucianism. But, after the Manchus came to power in 1644, this uneasy coexistence was harder to maintain. Under the new dynasty government became more effective and more intrusive; by the mid-18th century restrictions had been placed on worship, pilgrimage and other rites. Muslims began to feel that sense of positive alienation from Confucian society which formed the background to their rebellions in the 19th century.

In these northern Islamic lands from the Caspian Sea to the Tarim Basin the religious spirit was strong, and expressed in a strict Sunni orthodoxy which embraced all, peasants and nomads as much as *ulama* and khans. In the cities the *ulama* were dominant, supported by rich endowments, supplying state administrators from among their number and teaching in great madrasas whose fame brought students from Russia and from India. In the 1790s, according to tradition, there were as many as 30 000 students in Bukhara alone, which no doubt explains how the city came by the title "pillar of Islam." Rulers found it wiser not to quarrel with their *ulama*; indeed, they tended to reflect in their own actions the orthodox piety of their subjects. Abd Allah Khan II (reigned 1583–98) expelled students of philosophy from Samarqand and Bukhara; some of the Janid khans abdicated so as to be free to pursue a devotional life in the holy cities of Arabia.

Evidently the crucial work of maintaining and transmitting the framework and values of Islamic society was pursued with vigor and without hindrance. Over the three centuries, however, there was a shift in the nature of transmission as sufi orders came increasingly to influence the life of the people, and in places that of the state. The main orders were the Naqshbandiya, the Kubrawiya and the Qadiriya, which played and continued to play a central role in the conversion of Asia's nomadic peoples. Often shrines would be sited on the edge of the steppe within easy reach of nomadic encampments like that of Shaikh Ahmad Yasavi at Turkestan which was a major place of pilgrimage for Uzbegs and Kazakhs alike. The growing influence of the sufi orders was manifest, as elsewhere in the Islamic world at the time, by increasing emphasis on the life of the Prophet as a model, and so at the beginning of the 18th century we find Liu Chih, most famous of Chinese Muslim writers, composing his *True Annals of the Greatest Saint of Arabia*. It was also manifest in politics. Thus the affairs of the Chaghatai khanate became completely absorbed in the rivalries of two branches of the Naqshbandi order whose *khoja* leaders eventually came to replace the Chaghatai khans. Thus, too, the rulers of Bukhara came to adopt the saintly style; Shah Murad, an unusually successful general, maintained the dress and manners of a sufi, even going so far as to ride into battle on a scraggy pony.

Culturally, the impact of isolation, decline and the preferences of Sunni orthodoxy were felt more and more strongly. The Central Asian khanates, living with the memories of Tamerlaine's Samarqand and Sultan Husain Baiqara's Herat, had shining examples of artistic and scholarly achievement to follow. Moreover, in Bukhara for much of the 16th century they succeeded in approaching these high standards, largely as a result of the work of the artists and craftsmen who moved there after the destruction of Herat. There was fine painting after the style of Bihzad, which has come to be known as the Bukhara school, there was much poetry, and music. Then from the 17th century the isolation from the Iranian springs of inspiration began to tell, and, as in the Ottoman and Mughal lands, there was the steady emergence of local vernaculars to compete with and eventually to overwhelm Persian as the idiom of the courtly arts and polite intercourse. At the same time weakening resources and the narrowing focus of the patronage of intensely religious courts began to leave their mark, and, although some areas are still but lightly studied, the quality of all arts and crafts seems to have declined, except the minting of coins and the weaving of rugs.

The madrasa was the typical building of the age, embodying the profound concern of orthodox society for the maintenance and the transmission of the central traditions of the faith, a concern which was not diverted, as in Morocco, by the rise of sufi influence. Indeed here we can note a marked change, and one which contrasts sharply with contemporary developments in Morocco, from the spirit of the preceding era. Then mausoleums embraced the essence of the age, like those which glorify Tamerlaine and his family at Samarqand, the Ishrat-Khane, the Gur-i Mir and in the Shah-i Zinde. New mausoleums were still built, but as royal power came to be rivaled by that of the *ulama*, so the tombs of princes came to be overshadowed by the magnificence of the madrasas. Bukhara had three great new madrasas in the 16th century and a fourth in the 17th century, which lends some material weight to the assertion that the city entertained tens of thousands of students at one time.

A group of Chinese Muslims in Turfan. Muslims, who were descended from traders and from officials of the Mongol Yuan dynasty, lived in scattered communities throughout China in a state of uneasy coexistence with their Chinese hosts. Popular sayings give an idea of the relationship. Muslims would say: "One Muslim equals five Chinese." The Chinese would say: "Ten Peking slippery ones cannot talk down one Tien-tsin brawler; ten Tien-tsin brawlers cannot talk down one Muslim."

The orthodox ambience apart, however, we should note how the madrasa flourished naturally in the region. The very concept of the madrasa as an institution separate from the mosque had developed here, as had the *pishtaq*, or gateway, glistening with colored tiles which soared up above the roofline of the towns. Furthermore, the typical building plan, with four *iwans*, or halls, open at one end and arranged around a courtyard, belonged to Central Asia too, originating in the region's grand houses and Buddhist monasteries. The Islamic developments of the period are best expressed by the fate of Samarqand's central Registan square which slowly came to be shut in, though not entirely, by madrasas, the Ulugh Beg (1417–20), the Shir Dar (1619–36) and the Tila Kara (1660); see below, pp. 106–07.

The mosques of China tell a different story, the story of the concessions Muslims had to make to the Confucian world in which they dwelt. Here the mosques were built like pagodas, and without minarets which were forbidden by the state, the faithful being called to prayer from within the structure. The interior itself was like those of mosques throughout the Muslim world, neat and serene and with decorative verses in Arabic script and prayers offered in the Arabic tongue. Yet here again the Confucian state imposed itself; on one wall there would be the emperor's tablets which had to grace any place of prayer. Before these tablets Muslims were supposed to prostrate themselves as they did before Allah; but they did not quite, not allowing their foreheads to touch the ground as they did in Islamic prayer.

Madrasas of Central Asia

From the 16th to the 19th century Central Asian Islam came to be marked by a strict Sunni orthodoxy. The learned men of Islam, the *ulama*, gained power in relation to their secular rulers, the khans, such as would never have been dreamed of in the days when Tamerlaine ruled in Samarqand. Indeed several khans who tried to curb the power of the *ulama* found themselves in trouble. Thus the madrasas, where *ulama* learned the Islamic sciences – some to become prayer leaders or teachers themselves, others to become judges or administrators – were the typical buildings of the age. Rich endowments supported their work, and many were built in the four leading centers of Bukhara, Samarqand, Khiva and Khokand. Students came from India and Kashmir, from Russia and the cities of eastern Turkestan. Bukhara, where according to tradition there were 30 000 students in the 1790s, must have had the atmosphere of a great university city and as such can have had few equals in the world at the time.

The very concept of the madrasa as an institution separate from the mosque first developed in Central Asia. So did some of the distinguishing architectural features, for instance the typical building plan with four *iwans* or vaulted halls arranged around a courtyard, which originated in the region's grand houses and Buddhist monasteries. *Above* The courtyard of the Shir Dar madrasa in Samarqand, showing one of the *iwans*; teachers and students lived in the cells around the court as they might in an Oxford or Cambridge college. *Right* The south *iwan* of the Mir-i Arab madrasa, Bukhara, built 1530–36.

Characteristic of the Central Asian madrasas was the *pishtaq*, or monumental gateway, decorated with colored tiles. *Below* The *pishtaq* of the Shir Dar (Lion Bearer) madrasa, built between 1619 and 1636. Its name is derived from the representations of the lion and sun of Iran above the *iwan*.

Top right The positioning of three madrasas around Samarqand's central Registan square: (1) madrasa of Ulugh Beg, (2) Shir Dar madrasa, (3) Tila Kara madrasa. Arranging monumental buildings around an open square was a feature of Timurid town planning, copied later by the Uzbegs and the Safavids.

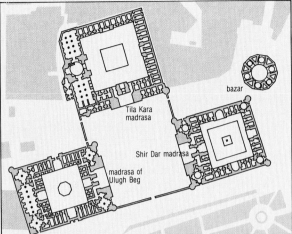

Above The Tila Kara (Gold Decorated) madrasa, built in 1660.

Center Looking across modern Samarqand to the Registan square, we see over the back of the Ulugh Beg madrasa to the Shir Dar, leaving the Tila Kara to the left. Of the Registan square Lord Curzon, the English statesman and traveler wrote: "I know of nothing in the East approaching it in massive simplicity and grandeur, and nothing in Europe, save perhaps on a humbler scale the Piazza di San Marco in Venice, which can even aspire to enter the competition." In the distance, Tamerlaine's Bibi Khanum mosque.

Mosques of the Further Islamic Lands

Below left Clay mosques are typical of the savanna lands south of the Sahara, and the Friday mosque at Kano, northern Nigeria, represents the Hausa-Fulani form with its heavy tower-minarets. Probably built in the late 15th century, the distinctive minaret was demolished in 1937–38.

A common idea of a mosque is of a building like those developed by the great Ottoman architect Sinan (1491–1588) and copied throughout much of the Ottoman empire. It is a domed structure with pencil-thin minarets, preferably four of them. But, providing simple liturgical needs are met, for instance that the direction of Mecca is clear, any building or style will do. Thus in many areas of the Islamic world vernacular styles, which have often been used for buildings of other faiths, and may even be strongly associated with them, have been adapted to Islamic purposes.

Above Many Chinese mosques are barely distinguishable from pagodas, with their elaborate systems of corbels and gabled tiled roofs characteristically sloping upwards at the corners, like this mosque in Tao-chou, Kansu. Minarets, which might have been a distinguishing feature, were forbidden, the call to prayer being made from behind the entrance.

Right The Shah Hamadan mosque in Srinagar (Kashmir), on the other hand, with its pyramid-shaped roof with finials and a steeple, reminds one more of the pagoda and stupa forms of Buddhist architecture which was once prominent in the region.

Far right This mosque in the Lake Simkarrak area of Minangkabau, Sumatra, combines the marvelously exaggerated gables typical of the region with the tiered roof found in much southeast Asian Hindu architecture.

Below This mosque in Timbuktu, Mali, with its pinnacled, buttressed and trabeated construction, is typical of another major type of clay mosque. Known as the Dyula style, it was spread widely by the Dyula trading community as they moved around West Africa.

Above A thatched Friday mosque at Namou in the Futa Jallon highlands of Guinea, where the Muslim Fulani became politically dominant from the 18th century. This design, so different from the clay mosques of the savanna region, was adopted to combat much higher rainfall.

Right It is hard to believe that this striking baroque building is not a church; one looks to find the facade crowned by a statue of the Virgin Mary. This is in fact the central mosque on Nnamdi Azikiwe Street, Lagos, Nigeria. It is one of several baroque mosques built by African slaves returning from Brazil, where they had learned their skills as architects and masons building churches.

109

DECLINE, REFORM AND REVIVAL IN THE 18th AND 19th CENTURIES

From the late 17th century there began the greatest change Muslims have experienced in their fortunes. During the previous thousand years their power and influence had spread largely unhindered throughout the world. There had been the pinpricks of the Christian crusades, the loss of Sicily and Spain to the Franks, and that of Kazan and Astrakhan to the Muscovites, but though not forgotten these were minor reverses to set against their massive achievement. There had also been the disaster of the Mongol invasions out of which had been fashioned victory as the horsemen of the steppes turned to Islam. The general pattern had been one of Muslim political and cultural domination of the heartland accompanied by a steady absorption of new territories and conversion of new peoples at the periphery. History seemed to bear out the truth of God's revelation to Muhammad; they were most assuredly the "best community raised up for mankind."

Now Muslim progress was checked; indeed, the initiative in world history seemed to be slipping from their grasp. They became poorer as they began to surrender control of the long-distance trade to the rising seafaring nations of Europe. They became weaker as the great empires strove with limited success to bend the structure of the military patronage state, with its thirst for war and expansion, to the purpose of governing peaceful territory within a static or even a contracting frontier. Muslims found themselves on the defensive. Not only were Muslim armies being pressed back and Muslims beginning to fall beneath infidel rule, but in places men of other faiths were beginning to mount cultural as well as political challenges to Islam. Muslims, in consequence, began to re-examine the fundamentals of their faith.

The ebbing of Muslim power

All three great empires which straddled the central Islamic lands declined. In the Safavid dominions the signs were there from the death of Shah Abbas I; indeed, some stemmed from the very solutions which that able ruler had found to the problem of creating strong institutions of central government in a tribal society. The personal army of "slaves of the royal household" which he introduced to check the power of the tribal forces in the state eventually led to a weakening of military competence, while the steady appropriation of state lands by the crown to pay for this new standing army led to overtaxation and the deterioration of provincial administration. The immuring of the royal princes in the female quarters of the palace to stop them plotting against the shah ensured more stable government, but meant that those who did come to the throne had little experience of the world, had been corrupted by harem life and were in the hands of powerful harem factions. All four of those who ruled from 1629 to 1722 were drunkards; of them two, Shah Safi (reigned 1629–42) and Shah Sulaiman

"Are you going to drink, or aren't you?" the shah asked Father Gabriel. "For if not, then you can go." Father Gabriel, who did not drink on principle, agreed to do so "in moderation." It was breakfast. Such were the tribulations of those Europeans who wished to push their wares at the Safavid court during its last 100 years. Indeed, a hedonistic, and sometimes debauched, court life developed in all three great empires as they declined. This lissom youth forms part of a 17th-century mural in the Chihil Sutun, Isfahan's elegant ceremonial palace, where European visitors found themselves entertained.

(reigned 1666–94), were notable largely for the slaughter they wreaked among their nobility; a third, Sultan Husain (reigned 1694–1722), was notable for his piety and his buildings; and only Abbas II (reigned 1642–60) displayed the qualities of a ruler.

As royal capacities weakened, the dynasty also began to lose the religious legitimacy which in the 16th century it had so carefully nurtured. *Ulama* began to challenge the partnership of Twelver Shiism and royal ideology which made the shah the "Shadow of God on earth," developing instead the theory that, in the absence of the Twelfth Imam, only a *mujtahid*, who was deeply learned in the *Sharia* and whose life was without blemish, could rule. In the process they were assisted by their growing material independence of the crown, and the failure of the shahs to make effective use of the machinery which existed to control the religious institution. By the reign of Sultan Husain they had gained the upper hand and the leading *mujtahid* of the time, Muhammad Baqir Majlisi, was able greatly to influence government policy, to wipe out the remnants of the Safavid sufi order which had brought the dynasty to power, and to impose his vision of orthodox Shiism on the state to the extent of having the tens of thousands of bottles of wine in the royal cellars publicly smashed.

By the end of the 17th century the empire was rotten to the core. When Sultan Husain went on pilgrimage he did not go on foot and make the journey to Meshhed in 28 days, as Abbas I had done, but took with him his harem, his court, a retinue of 60000, spent a year in the process and beggared the provinces through which he passed. When in 1697/8 a band of Baluchis raided to within 320 kilometers of the capital, Sultan Husain had no troops with which to resist them, and, supreme humiliation, was obliged to appeal to a visiting Georgian prince for help. Thus it was a simple matter in 1722 for a young Afghan adventurer, Mahmud of Qandahar, at the head of 20000 ragged tribesmen, to take Isfahan and effectively destroy the empire.

Iran, however, did not immediately cease to be a focus of Muslim strength. There was, for a brief moment, a brilliant restoration of power. Mahmud and his Afghans failed to establish a dynasty, and instead there arose a former Khurasani bandit, Nadir Khan, who reorganized the Safavid forces and in 1736 felt strong enough to set aside the dynasty and rule as Nadir Shah. Already in 1730 he had defeated the Ottomans and reannexed the Caucasus. In 1739 he invaded India, sacked Delhi and returned triumphantly with the famed peacock throne. To the north his armies occupied the Uzbeg cities of

Below: The break-up of Muslim power in 18th-century Iran
Mahmud of Qandahar, a young Afghan adventurer, was able to overthrow the Safavid dynasty in a brief campaign in 1721–22. Nevertheless, there was still enough basic strength in the Safavid system for a Khurasani bandit, Nadir Khan, to be able to reorganize it and to win victories against the Mughals, Ottomans and Uzbegs that the Safavids had never achieved at the height of their power. After his death the power of central government quickly declined and different groups – Afsharids, Safavids, Zands and Qajars – competed for power.

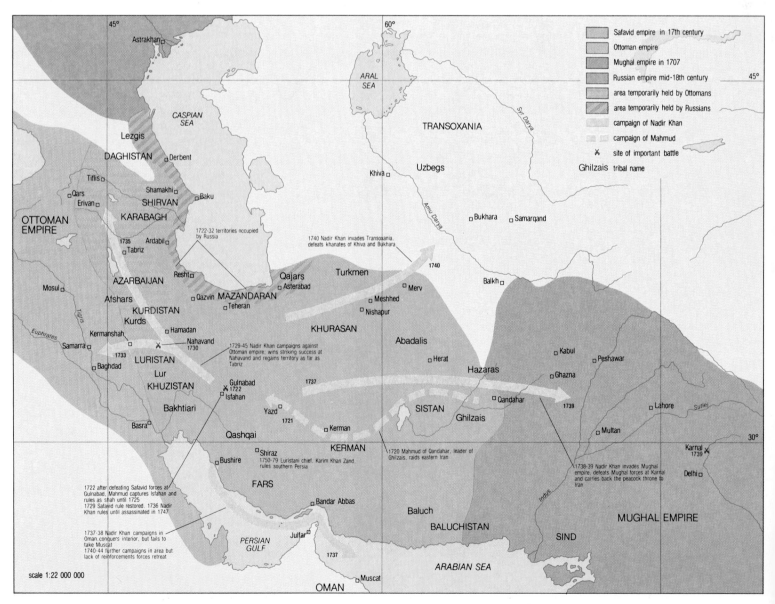

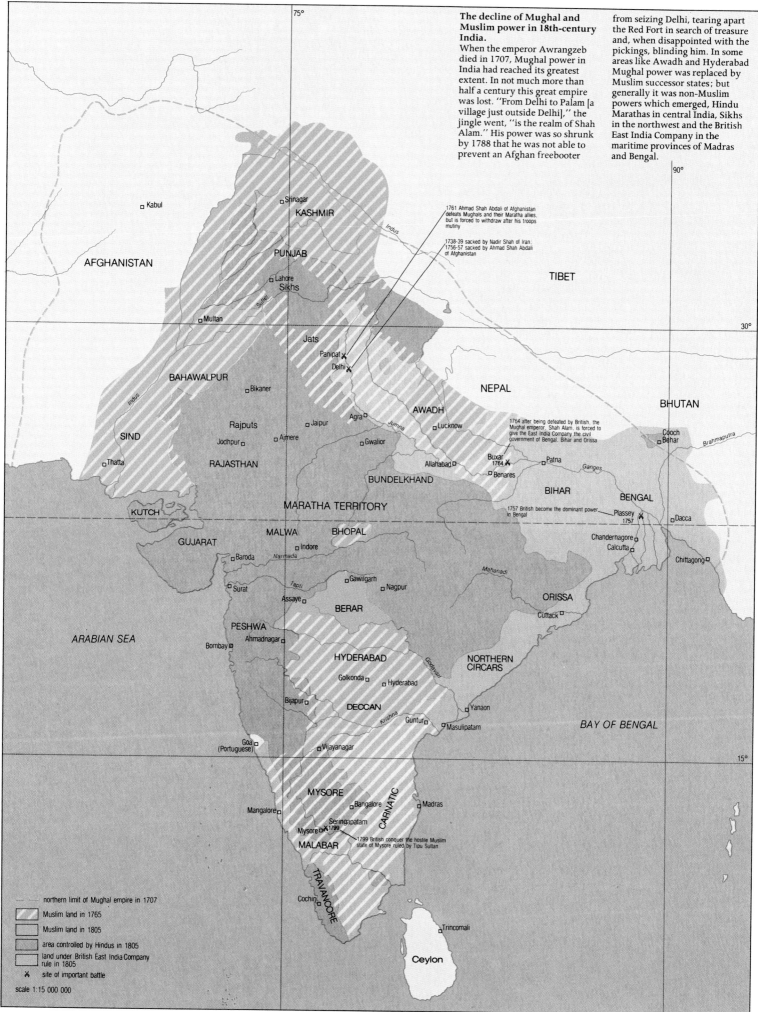

The decline of Mughal and Muslim power in 18th-century India.

When the emperor Awrangzeb died in 1707, Mughal power in India had reached its greatest extent. In not much more than half a century this great empire was lost. "From Delhi to Palam [a village just outside Delhi]," the jingle went, "is the realm of Shah Alam." His power was so shrunk by 1788 that he was not able to prevent an Afghan freebooter from seizing Delhi, tearing apart the Red Fort in search of treasure and, when disappointed with the pickings, blinding him. In some areas like Awadh and Hyderabad Mughal power was replaced by Muslim successor states; but generally it was non-Muslim powers which emerged, Hindu Marathas in central India, Sikhs in the northwest and the British East India Company in the maritime provinces of Madras and Bengal.

75°

90°

30°

15°

1761 Ahmad Shah Abdali of Afghanistan defeats Mughals and their Maratha allies, but is forced to withdraw after his troops mutiny

1738-39 sacked by Nadir Shah of Iran; 1756-57 sacked by Ahmad Shah Abdali of Afghanistan

1764 after being defeated by British, the Mughal emperor, Shah Alam, is forced to give the East India Company the civil government of Bengal, Bihar and Orissa

1757 British become the dominant power in Bengal

1799 British conquer the hostile Muslim state of Mysore ruled by Tipu Sultan

AFGHANISTAN
Kabul
Srinagar
KASHMIR
PUNJAB
Indus
TIBET
Lahore
Sikhs
Sutlej
Multan
Jats
BAHAWALPUR
Panipat
Delhi
Bikaner
NEPAL
BHUTAN
Jaipur
Agra
AWADH
Cooch Behar
Brahmaputra
Rajputs
Jumna
Lucknow
SIND
Jodhpur
Ajmere
RAJASTHAN
Gwalior
Buxar 1764
Patna
Thatta
Allahabad
Benares
Ganges
BIHAR
BENGAL
BUNDELKHAND
MARATHA TERRITORY
Plassey 1757
Dacca
KUTCH
MALWA
BHOPAL
Chandernagore
Calcutta
GUJARAT
Indore
Narmada
Chittagong
Baroda
Tapti
Gawilgarh
Nagpur
Mahanadi
Surat
Assaye
ORISSA
BERAR
Cuttack
PESHWA
Ahmadnagar
Bombay
HYDERABAD
NORTHERN CIRCARS
ARABIAN SEA
Golconda
Hyderabad
Godavari
Bijapur
DECCAN
Yanaon
Krishna
Guntur
Masulipatam
BAY OF BENGAL
Goa (Portuguese)
Vijayanagar
MYSORE
CARNATIC
Bangalore
Madras
Mangalore
Seringapatam 1799
Mysore
MALABAR
TRAVANCORE
Cochin
Trincomali
Ceylon

northern limit of Mughal empire in 1707

Muslim land in 1765

Muslim land in 1805

area controlled by Hindus in 1805

land under British East India Company rule in 1805

× site of important battle

scale 1:15 000 000

113

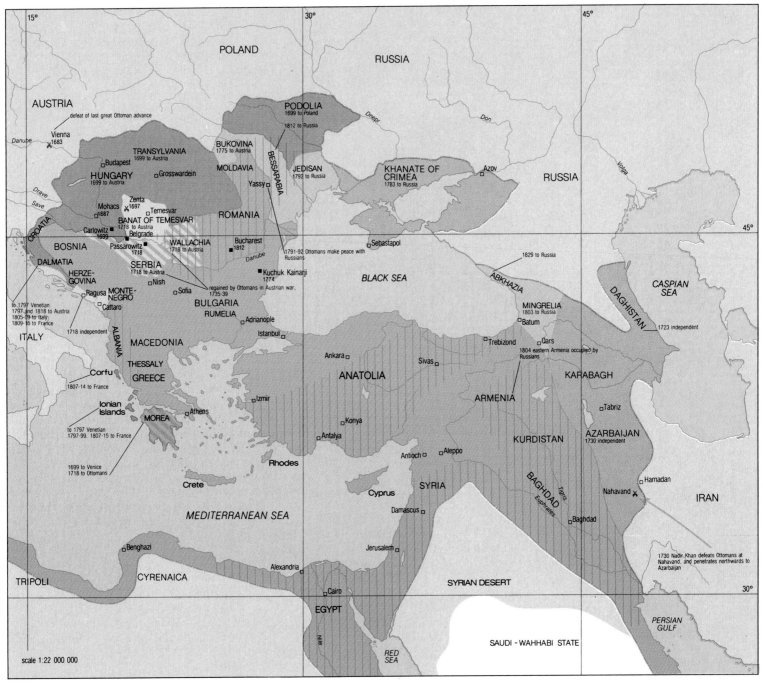

Transoxania; to the south they occupied Oman, the center of resurgent Arab merchant power. All was quickly lost, however, after his death in 1748, and Iran was delivered over to tribal power. The Luristani chief, Karim Khan Zand, kept the peace in the center and south from Shiraz until he died in 1779. Elsewhere other tribes came to the fore, notably the Qajars, who fought for two decades to succeed the Zand till by 1794 they had established a state based on Teheran in the heart of west Iran. Eventually the Qajars restored effective central government, but the years of anarchy, marked by towers of skulls, mass blindings and wanton savagery, had greatly impoverished the land. Many villages were deserted, the cities were desolate – only a quarter of late 18th-century Isfahan was occupied – and trade was much reduced.

This same period saw the extinction of Muslim power in India. Initially there was no weakening at the top as there was in Iran: Darwinian selection still prevailed among the Mughals. The emperor Awrangzeb, who presided over the beginnings of

decline, was no pampered harem-bred prince but a ruthless man of action who clambered to power over the bodies of his father, whom he jailed, and his brothers, whom he killed. Power waned as the conflicts inherent in running a Muslim empire in a primarily Hindu society and the weaknesses of the military patronage system could no longer be controlled. It was inevitable that *ulama* like Shaikh Ahmad Sirhindi and his Naqshbandi followers should come forward to challenge the religious compromises on which the Mughal state was based. Three Mughal emperors chose to ignore them, but Awrangzeb, moved by his own preferences and perhaps supremely confident in the strength of imperial power, did listen to them and abandoned the partnership with the Hindus on which the empire rested. His policies of imposing disabilities on Hindus and of moving the state in an Islamic direction excited opposition. There were revolts of Hindu landlords, of Afghan tribesmen, of Sikhs in the Punjab, of Rajput chiefs resisting Islamization and of Jat peasants resisting taxation. By far the

boundary of Ottoman empire in 1683
losses to 1699, treaty of Carlowitz
losses to 1718, treaty of Passarowitz
losses to 1774, treaty of Kuchuk Kainarji
losses to 1812, treaty of Bucharest
Ottoman empire in 1813
area under autonomous or tribal rulers c. 1800
■ 1699 site and date of treaty
✕ site of important battle

The decline of Ottoman power in the 18th century
After the Ottomans failed for a second time in 1683 to take Vienna, the frontiers of the empire from Croatia in the northwest to Azerbaijan in the southeast receded steadily. Even within the empire large areas only nominally acknowledged the sultan's suzerainty. Much of Anatolia and the Fertile Crescent was controlled by autonomous valley lords and tribal rulers; in Egypt Muhammad Ali ruled, independent in all but name.

Mughal decline was closely associated with the reassertion of Hindu power, which boded ill for the future of Islam in India. *Above* Shivaji (1627–80), leader of the Maratha forces against the Mughal empire, hero of the Hindu revival and a gifted and ruthless leader. Most famous of his deeds was the murder of the Bijapur general, Afzal Khan. They met to parley, supposedly unarmed. Shivaji came wearing a concealed breastplate and a steel tiger claw (*below*), attached to his left hand. As he greeted Afzal Khan with an embrace, he thrust the claw into the general's belly and ripped it out.

The decline of Muslim power in southeast Asia
From the mid-17th century the great sultanates of Aceh in northern Sumatra and Mataram in Java declined, and the Dutch began to assert their power throughout the region.

most serious resistance, however, came from the Marathas, who, under their Hindu chief Shivaji, carved out a state for themselves in the Deccan and refused either to be absorbed in the empire or to coexist with it. To meet this threat, and to appropriate the riches of the sultanates of Bijapur and Golkonda, Awrangzeb campaigned in the Deccan from 1680, thus shifting the focus of government from Delhi to central India. By the time he died in 1707, he had gained little. Bijapur and Golkonda were conquered, but the Marathas still raided from Gujarat to the far south.

Weaknesses in the military patronage system aggravated the effects of the ideological shift that Awrangzeb brought to the empire. Indeed, some, influenced no doubt by the secular vision of the West and the secular needs of independent India, would explain the whole process of decline primarily in these terms. Two factors stand out: the empire had established itself in India largely by incorporating provincial warrior elites into its political system, and it could only continue to win the loyalty of its *mansabdars* (that is, the imperial service elite composed of holders of commands in the military household) as long as it could reward them. These two factors were inexorable. When the Maratha warrior elite refused to come to terms with the empire, Awrangzeb had no choice but to move south to subdue them. When he failed to do so, in part it seems because the Marathas had technological advantages in musketry, he resorted to bribery, bestowing high *mansabs* on more and more of them. The result was that the empire was handing out *mansabs* without having won the fresh lands to pay for them. There was a growing number of *mansabdars* supported by a static pool of resources, which meant that the peasantry was impoverished by the growing exactions of government, the army was weakened because the *mansabdars* were unable to meet their military commitments, the *mansabdars* themselves were demoralized by their unaccustomed failure to win victories, and the emperor was increasingly less able either to impose his authority at home or to meet threats on the frontier.

After Awrangzeb's death the ruling class fell apart. The *mansabdars* divided into factions supporting rival claimants to the throne. Emperors squandered their lands in rewarding clients and favorites rather than in sustaining a body of loyal troops able to enforce their will. The countryside became increasingly disorderly as neither the *mansabdars* nor the emperor could raise sufficient force to hold it in awe. By the 1740s there had been the humiliation of Nadir Shah's invasion, the Marathas had helped themselves to Gujarat and Malwa, the governors of the Punjab, Awadh, Bengal and Hyderabad had converted these imperial provinces into their own domains, and the Mughal writ hardly ran beyond Delhi. Three more decades saw the murder of two emperors, Ahmad Shah (1748–54) and Alamgir II (1754–59), the flight of a third, Shah Alam (1759–1806), and the sacking of Delhi in 1761 by the invading forces of Ahmad Abdali, king of Afghanistan (1747–73). All the while, non-Muslims took increasing control of India. By 1800 the Marathas ruled the subcontinent from Rajasthan in the north to the Deccan in the south, and from the Arabian Sea in the west to the Bay of Bengal in the east as they had done for 60 years. In the Punjab the gifted Sikh leader, Ranjit Singh, had just secured Lahore. Throughout most of the Gangetic plain the British ruled. Only two significant Muslim states remained, Awadh and Hyderabad, and they both acknowledged British paramountcy. Never before in Islamic history had Muslims surrendered so much power to their former subjects and other infidels. Shah Abd al-Aziz, the leading scholar of Delhi, symbolically acknowledged the disaster when in 1803, the year General Lake defeated the Mughal emperor's Maratha allies under the city walls, he announced India to be no longer *dar al-Islam*, the land of Islam, but *dar al-harb*, the land of war.

The decline of the Ottoman empire took much longer than that of its Safavid and Mughal contemporaries. If the Safavid empire fell as the result of one battle, and the Mughal crumbled away over a century, the Ottoman took 300 years to die. It was, of course, much stronger, with a more deeply rooted and more highly developed version of the

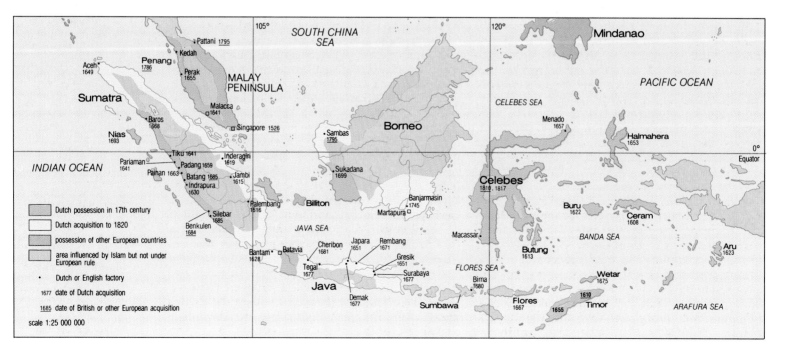

Dutch possession in 17th century
Dutch acquisition to 1820
possession of other European countries
area influenced by Islam but not under European rule
• Dutch or English factory
1677 date of Dutch acquisition
1685 date of British or other European acquisition
scale 1:25 000 000

military patronage state; it also had quite remarkable recuperative powers. Thus in 1683, after nearly a century of administrative decline, we find the empire at its point of furthest expansion, revitalized by the Koprulu viziers and threatening central Europe even more seriously than in the days of Sulaiman the Magnificent. Yet soon afterwards, though interrupted by brief moments of recovery and extensive periods of stability, the long retreat began once more. In the treaty of Carlowitz of 1699 the Ottomans surrendered Hungary, Transylvania and Podolia; this was the first time that they had signed a peace as the defeated power in a clearly decided war. In the treaty of Passarowitz of 1718 they surrendered the Banat of Temesvar, Serbia and Wallachia. In the 1720s they tried to regain former territories in northwest Iran but were humiliatingly rebuffed in 1730 by Nadir Khan. There was some respite when they managed to regain Serbia and Wallachia in the Austrian war of 1735–39; moreover the Habsburgs were able to make only one more significant gain in the 18th century, that of Bukovina in 1775.

By now a much more dangerous enemy had come forward, Russia, who after 1768 subjected Ottoman forces to massive defeats on land and sea. In the subsequent treaty of Kuchuk Kainarji in 1774 the Ottomans lost control of a large chunk of the Black Sea shore, conceded to Russia the right to intervene on behalf of the sultan's Greek Orthodox Christian subjects, but most shamefully surrendered political control for the first time over a wholly Muslim people, the Tatars of the Crimea. Then Russian control of the Black Sea's northern shore was completed by the annexation of Jedisan in 1792 and Bessarabia in 1812. By this time a curious paradox had emerged. The Ottoman empire was the only remaining Muslim great power and the sultan was coming to be seen as the *khalifa*, or successor of the Prophet, as the leader of the Muslim community. Yet the empire was no longer strong enough even to defend itself single-handed against a major power. Indeed, in the 18th century and throughout the 19th century, its capacity to survive as the standard-bearer of Islam depended on its ability to ally itself with infidel states and to play a part in the European balance of power.

Within the empire the weakening of central authority, which had been the hallmark of decline from the late 16th century, continued in the 18th century and defied all attempts to reverse the process. One manifestation was the bestowal on Christian powers of privileges within the empire, beginning in 1740 with the French, who were being repaid for diplomatic services against the Habsburgs. The most important of these was the extension of certificates of protection to non-Muslim Ottoman subjects which enabled them to gain the privileges of foreign nationals. Christians and Jews, placing themselves in droves under the protection of one or the other European power, came to control the growing trade with Europe, and to edge out their Muslim rivals. As most traders moved from Ottoman to privileged foreign jurisdiction, government lost the capacity to tax or to control much of the commerce of its territory. A second manifestation lies in the growing subordination of the ideal of service to the state to self-interest. "No business can be accomplished in this country without a bribe," declared an Indian visitor in 1802, "even the Government departments are ruined by this nefarious system. The army is without discipline, the ordnance unfit for use, the regulation of the post office totally neglected ... The persons at the head of all these departments are only anxious to procure money and deceive the Government." Indeed the interests of almost all seemed to be served by the maintenance of weak central authority: the leading *ulama*, who had formed themselves into a hereditary and closed corps, the Janissaries, who had also become hereditary and whose special privileges were enjoyed by many throughout the land, the valley lords of Anatolia and the new notables of Rumelia, who had turned government posts into semi-autonomous principalities, and the governors of distant Arab provinces, who were virtually independent. When men strove to strengthen central authority, as did the vizier Ibrahim Pasha (vizier 1718–30) and the sultan Selim III (reigned 1789–1807), they were given short shrift. Both sought to create new power bases beyond the reach of sectional interests by opening windows on Europe and by training new army units along European lines – drawing in the West, as it were, to redress the balance of the East. Both were stopped by an alliance of Janissaries and of *ulama* who were quick to see the threat to their independence and no less quick to raise the cry of Islam in danger. Nevertheless, some Ottomans were clearly coming to feel that infidel knowledge was needed to bolster the standard-bearer of Islam from within, just as infidel allies were needed in the world at large. The Turks had begun their long flirtation with the West.

In the further Islamic lands, as we began to see in the last chapter, there was a similar story of waning power, of threats from infidel culture, of Muslims actually falling under infidel rule. In Central Asia holy men ruled where once there had been mighty Mongol khans, and the former center of world empire slid into a lethargic provincialism, while all the while the Russian line crept forward and the nomad peoples of the steppe slipped into vassalage. In China Muslims suffered an energetic attempt to assimilate them to the dominant Confucian culture, while between 1758 and 1760 those of the Tarim Basin came to feel the weight of Chinese rule for the first time. In Java by 1800 the sultanate of Mataram had been all but gobbled up by the Dutch; the fragment which survived had been cut off from the Islamized north coast and formed a central state in which Hindu-Javanese culture was definitely pre-eminent and the progress of Islam was checked. In Sumatra the once great power of Aceh was restricted to the northern coastal strip and scattered ports in the southwest, while a weakening of royal authority in Minangkabau was breeding social and political discontent. In West Africa Islam was still expanding, it is true, borne forward by the spears of the Fulani holy warriors of Senegal and the acumen of the Dyula who traded through much of the region. But there were startling reverses too: the cities of the Niger bend, Jenne, Timbuktu, Gao, the heart of Muslim empire for 500 years or more, had fallen beneath the sway of the heathen Bambara. Moreover, where Muslims ruled, as they did in most places where they had in the past, they no longer challenged pagan beliefs so strongly.

Ottoman Turkey's long flirtation with European culture began in the 18th century. Twice during the century rulers sought to throw open windows on the west with the aim of strengthening both the power of central government against sectional interests within and the power of the state against the enemy without. The development of the Ottoman rococo style of architecture demonstrates the new willingness to draw on European inspiration, as does the painting of Levni, court painter to Ahmad III (1703–30), see for instance the stylish beau *above*. After Ahmad III was deposed in 1730, interest in Europe declined until Selim III (1789–1807), influenced by the French Revolution, embarked on a large-scale, though not particularly successful, process of administrative and military reform along European lines. *Right* This equestrian portrait of Selim III by Hippolyte Berteaux, which is in the heroic style beloved by European potentates, emphasizes how once again Ottoman Turkey was looking to Europe for inspiration.

Reform and revival

The unprecedented political decline in the Muslim world of the 18th century provided the context for the most important development in Islam since sufism first took widespread hold 600 years before. This was a movement of inner renewal, of reform of religious practice, of revival of religious élan, which sprang up in and spread to almost every part of the Islamic world from the mid-18th century to the beginning of the 20th century. As Muslim power waned and Muslim princes no longer seemed to command the fate of humankind, *ulama* and sufis,

guardians of the central traditions of the faith, seized the initiative and strove as they had never done before to promote a purer vision of the Islamic life and society. This led on occasion to declarations of *jihad*, and these holy wars were waged with that especial ferocity which seems reserved for the times when co-religionists fall out. Sometimes these movements collided with expanding European empires and turned to give the intruder the full force of their religious fury, adding in the process yet more lurid colors to the Western understanding of the faith.

The Islamic revival of the 18th and 19th centuries
As Muslim power waned, *ulama* and sufis, guardians of the central traditions of Islam, seized the initiative in many parts of the Muslim world and strove as never before to promote a purer vision of Islamic life and society. Often they declared holy war on those who refused to submit to their will. In general, with the exception of some instances in West Africa, the process was stimulated, sometimes initiated,

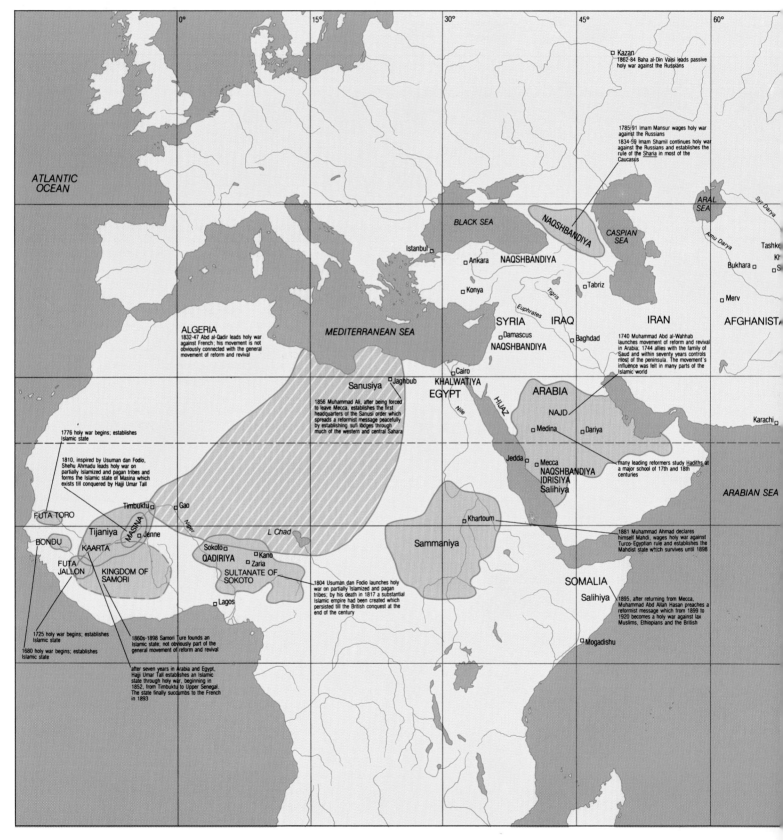

by reformist ideas traveling along the connections of the *ulama*, especially those associated with the influential school of *Hadiths* in Medina, and along those of the sufis, especially those of the Naqshbandiya, the Khalwatiya and the Idrisiya. Here, on the eve of the great European expansion, we have graphic evidence of the extent to which the Islamic world was a community of thought and feeling.

The decline of Muslim power exacerbated the crucial inner tensions of Islam, those points where visions of the ideal chafed against parlous reality, where *ulama* and sufis suffered the shifts made by Muslim rulers to accommodate pagan subjects, where they endured the countless concessions to local religious practice which compromised the pure monotheism of the faith. They responded by returning to first principles for guidance, to the word of God in the Quran and to the actions of the Prophet in the *Hadiths*, and by rejecting much of the scholastic and mystical superstructure built up

as Islam had encountered other civilizations down the centuries. Closely involved with this process was an Islamic "right wing" which had habitually suspected sufism and bitterly opposed its extravagances; it was represented by those who had always limited their sources of authority to the Quran and the *Hadiths* and by the followers of the Hanbali school of law who from the beginning had rejected the speculative innovations of the other schools. These, and those who thought like them, now attacked the widely held beliefs in the powers of saints and holy men and the practices connected with them: the worship of and at saints' tombs, prayers for the intercession of the Prophet and the saints, all aspects in fact of popular religion which challenged the unity of God. They also attacked, though not with such unanimity, Ibn al-Arabi's philosophy of the unity of being which had so long made it possible for half-Islamized peoples to be made comfortable in the faith.

Ironically, although directed against dubious sufi practices and fed by an ancient suspicion of sufism as a whole, this movement was spread throughout much of the Islamic world by sufi orders. Sufis responded to the reformist challenge by absorbing within the sufi framework the orthodox emphasis on the Quran and the *Hadiths*, and by stripping their rites of ecstatic practices and their beliefs of metaphysical tendencies. The concern of the *ulama* with Quran and the *Hadiths*, moreover, was matched by the sufis in a new emphasis on the person of the Prophet. It became a notable feature of the reformed sufism, the spread of which can be traced in the steady increase of the literary genre devoted to the life of the Prophet and in the institution of *mawlid* ceremonies to celebrate his birthday. Some orders actually gave themselves the title *Tariqa Muhammadiya* (the order of Muhammad), thus symbolizing their intention of following the path laid down by the Prophet and of forsaking the degraded practices of the past. All of this amounted to a sufi revival, an infusion of fresh vigor; old orders were revitalized and new orders founded. This purified sufism did not displace the older form, but subsisted side by side with it. It tended, however, to be less attractive to the masses.

From the movement's attention to the *Hadiths* and the example of the Prophet came a new emphasis on action. The life of the Prophet and of the early Muslim community showed how dynamic action had brought a decisive change for the better in human affairs, an example that proved an inspiration to reformist *ulama* and sufis as they surveyed the political weakness, the economic disintegration and the religious backsliding about them. Not unreasonably, they were more concerned with direct action aimed at recreating a rightly guided society than with preparation for the hereafter. Just as the Prophet had himself gone to cast out the idols from the Kaaba, so they would act to stop men worshiping false gods. Such emphasis on action could lead to violence – holy war in the way of the Lord – because at times only through force might the object be achieved. Thus several reformist orders fought for their beliefs, and some came to combine military training with their orthodox learning. Action could also lead ultimately, following the example of early Muslim history, to attempts to form a theocratic state.

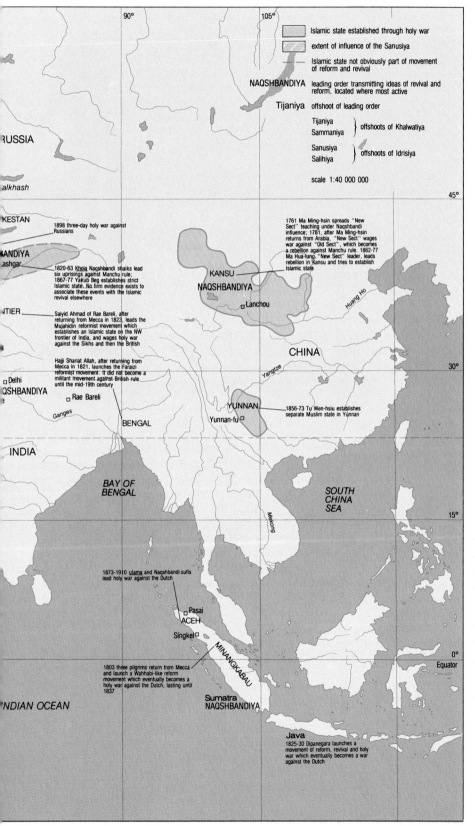

Islamic state established through holy war

extent of influence of the Sanusiya

Islamic state not obviously part of movement of reform and revival

NAQSHBANDIYA — leading order transmitting ideas of revival and reform, located where most active

Tijaniya — offshoot of leading order

Tijaniya
Sammaniya } offshoots of Khalwatiya

Sanusiya
Salihiya } offshoots of Idrisiya

scale 1:40 000 000

1898 three-day holy war against Russians

1820-63 Khoja Naqshbandi shaiks lead six uprisings against Manchu rule; 1867-77 Yakub Beg establishes strict Islamic state. No firm evidence exists to associate these events with the Islamic revival elsewhere

Saiyid Ahmad of Rae Bareli, after returning from Mecca in 1823, leads the Mujahidin reformist movement which establishes an Islamic state on the NW frontier of India, and wages holy war against the Sikhs and then the British

Hajji Shariat Allah, after returning from Mecca in 1821, launches the Faraizi reformist movement. It did not become a militant movement against British rule until the mid-19th century

1761 Ma Ming-hsin spreads "New Sect" teaching under Naqshbandi influence; 1781, after Ma Ming-hsin returns from Arabia, "New Sect" wages war against "Old Sect", which becomes a rebellion against Manchu rule. 1862-77 Ma Hua-lung. "New Sect" leader, leads rebellion in Kansu and tries to establish Islamic state

1856-73 Tu Wen-hsiu establishes separate Muslim state in Yunnan

1873-1910 ulama and Naqshbandi sufis lead holy war against the Dutch

1803 three pilgrims return from Mecca and launch a Wahhabi-like reform movement which eventually becomes a holy war against the Dutch, lasting until 1837

1825-30 Dipanegara launches a movement of reform, revival and holy war which eventually becomes a war against the Dutch

RUSSIA

alkhash

KESTAN

ANDIYA
ashgar

TIER

Delhi
QSHBANDIYA

Rae Bareli

Ganges

BENGAL

INDIA

BAY OF BENGAL

KANSU
NAQSHBANDIYA

Lanchou

Huang Ho

CHINA

Yangtze

YUNNAN

Yunnan-fu

SOUTH CHINA SEA

Mekong

Pasai
ACEH

Singkel

MINANGKABAU

Sumatra
NAQSHBANDIYA

Java

INDIAN OCEAN

This movement did not spring into existence all of a sudden in the mid-18th century. There had been a slow spiritual and scholarly preparation over many years. We have already witnessed some of its earlier manifestations. There was the reaction led by Mawlana Abd al-Haqq and Shaikh Ahmad Sirhindi in the early 17th century to the compromises Mughal rulers made with Hindus and Indian Muslims with Hinduism. There was the great debate at the court of Aceh in the mid-17th century over the interpretation of Ibn al-Arabi's thought which attracted the attention of leading scholars in Medina. There was the steady assertion of the power of the *ulama* against the shah in Safavid Iran which led by the end of the century to the almost dictatorial position of Muhammad Baqir Majlisi. In Syria Abd al-Ghani of Nablus (1641–1731), a prolific scholar and a Naqshbandi shaikh, strove to create a revitalized theology and a reformed sufism. In India Shah Wali Allah (1702–60), a Naqshbandi too and a considerable scholar of *Hadiths*, strove not only to achieve the same ends as Abd al-Ghani but also to persuade Shah Ahmad Abdali of Afghanistan to wage holy war against the Hindus in order to bring about a restoration of Muslim power. The Naqshbandi sufi order deriving from Shaikh Ahmad Sirhindi and bearing his purified sufi message, if somewhat diluted, spread from India to Mecca, Damascus, Istanbul and the Balkans. The Damascene scholar Mustafa al-Bakri (died 1749), the chief pupil of Abd al-Ghani of Nablus, revived the Khalwati sufi order, making it a vehicle for his reformist ideas. Based in Cairo, it gained great influence at the university of al-Azhar, where al-Bakri's leading pupil, Muhammad al-Hifnawi, was rector from 1758 to 1767, and was the framework within which reformist ideas developed in Egypt. But above all stands a leading group of teachers of *Hadiths* in 17th- and 18th-century Medina, strategically placed to influence those performing pilgrimage, as many reformers did. Major figures in this group, and also Naqshbandis, were Ibrahim al-Kurani, who settled the great debate at Aceh, and the Indian Muhammad Hayya al-Sindi. The pupils of the group included many leading reformers: Abd al-Rauf of Singkel, Shah Wali Allah of Delhi and Mustafa al-Bakri (see above) and Muhammad Abd al-Wahhab (1703–92) and Shaikh Muhammad Samman (1717–75) (see below, p. 126).

Muhammad Abd al-Wahhab was the first to steer the movement out of the studies of the learned and on to the field of action when in the middle of the 18th century he led a campaign for purification and renewal in Arabia. In his youth, as a sufi from the Najd in central Arabia, he had traveled widely in Iran, Iraq and the Hijaz in search of knowledge. As a result he came to be strongly influenced by the orthodox scholarship of his time, adopting the Hanbali legal position and the anti-sufi polemic of the 14th-century Hanbali scholar, Ibn Taimiya. Around 1740 he returned to the Najd and began to preach against the corruption of religion among the Bedouin, saint worship and all other sufi innovations. He was determined to put an end to practices which threatened the oneness of God, which meant that he even opposed reverence for Muhammad's tomb at Medina which was a favorite object of devotion for many pilgrims to Mecca.

In 1744 his campaign acquired explosive energy when he allied himself with Muhammad Ibn Saud, a petty chieftain of Dariya in the Najd, who accepted the reformer's religious views and significantly sealed the compact with the same oath that the Prophet and the men of Medina had sworn in making their alliance in 622 AD. During the remainder of the century the Wahhabis steadily expanded through central and western Arabia. Then in 1802 they advanced into Iraq and Syria, occupying Karbala, the burial place of Husain, and destroying much that was holy to the Shias. In 1803 they occupied Mecca, in 1805 Medina and, to the horror of the Muslim world, tried to destroy all sacred tombs, including that of the Prophet, massacred the inhabitants and imposed their unbending standards on those performing pilgrimage. A mighty challenge was delivered both to Islam, as Muslims generally had come to understand it, and to the Ottoman empire. The political gauntlet was picked up by Muhammad Ali, the viceroy of Egypt, whose European-style army and modern artillery managed by 1818 to break Wahhabi power, raze their capital at Dariya and restore the sultan's authority.

The impact of the Wahhabis, however, did not end here. For much of the 19th century they succeeded in sustaining a nucleus of power in the Najd from which in the 20th century they were able to launch a second great expansion which culminated in the foundation of the Saudi Arabian state. But there was a much more important impact on the Islamic world at large for which it came to symbolize the wider movement of reform. Many were influenced by the Wahhabis' puritanism and inspired by their religious zeal, though not all sympathized with their extremism and intolerance. Many too were attracted by the Wahhabi theological position which dismissed the medieval superstructure of Islam and sought authority in the Quran and *Hadiths* alone. Muslims could now reject blind faith and form fresh opinions: there was new opportunity for flexibility and for creative response to the time. It was a position as attractive to those who wished to reconcile Islam with the modern world as it was to those who wished to restore the pure milk of monotheism.

Ripples from these developments in Arabia mingled with the endemic conflict, now exacerbated by Muslim social and political decay, between the supporters of the Islamic ideal and the supporters of accommodation to the local milieu in southeast Asia. In the Minangkabau region of Sumatra, for instance, as royal power declined in the late 18th century, *ulama* were beginning to assert their independence. Then in 1803 three pilgrims returned from Mecca and launched a Wahhabi-like reform movement, known to the Dutch as the Padri movement ("padre" being Portuguese for "clergyman"). They attacked all moral looseness, insisted that professing Muslims should observe the duties of the faith and required in addition that women should go veiled and men wear white clothing after the Arab fashion. For 15 years the Padris steadily imposed their will on the villages of the Sumatran hinterland, but eventually they became entangled with the expansion of Dutch power and what had been a campaign of purification became a war against the interloper, which did not end till 1837. The result was a marked increase in the penetration

The Wahhabis destroyed shrines because they encouraged saint worship and threatened the oneness of God; their attentions extended to the tomb of the Prophet himself at Medina. *Bottom* Medina as Sir Richard Burton saw it nearly 50 years later. The Prophet's tomb had been restored: "And behind, in the most Easterly part of the city, remarkable from afar, is the gem of Al-Madinah, – the four tall substantial towers, and the flashing green Dome under which the Apostle's remains rest." *Below* Abd Allah Ibn Saud, defeated Wahhabi chief, a captive in Cairo, 1818.

The rise of Saudi-Wahhabi power in Arabia 1744–1818
This was the first major manifestation of the Islamic revival in the 18th century. It was felt widely throughout the Islamic world and has had a continuing influence on Islamic history to the present. By the beginning of the 19th century the Wahhabis had conquered most of Arabia and were imposing their fundamentalist values on the areas they ruled, destroying shrines in Mecca and Medina, as well as at Karbala in Iraq, and massacring the inhabitants. The growth of the Saudi-Wahhabi state was eventually halted by the European equipment and discipline of Muhammad Ali's reformed army.

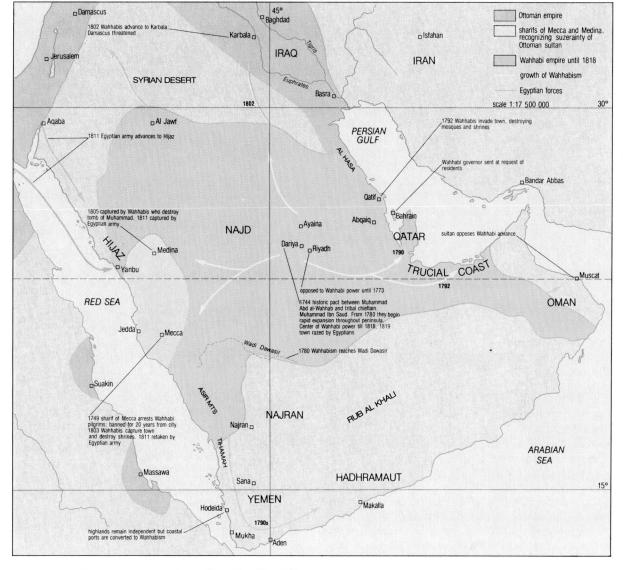

of Islam into Minangkabau society.

A second notable reformist movement broke out in Java between 1825 and 1830. This time there are no certain connections with the broader reformist stream of activity. The conflict was due to the way in which the long-standing antipathy between the Islamic orthodox and the syncretic Hindu-Javanese elite was being exacerbated by the economic and cultural impact of the Dutch, who allied with the latter. One Dipanegara, of royal blood and religious temper, was moved to attack the European ways of the aristocracy and the growing misery that European rule brought the peasantry. He took to wandering through the countryside in Arab dress and meditating in holy places. Voices told him of his mission to purify Islam and save the people; the people hailed him as the long-awaited *ratu adil* or just ruler. Holy war was declared with massive support from the *ulama*. At first the struggle was mainly against the Hindu-Javanese elite, but eventually, as in the Padri wars, it came to be a war of all against the foreigner, and although the Dutch gained the upper hand, the outcome, as in Minangkabau, gave a powerful thrust to the process of Islamization.

There was a third great holy war in the area in the 19th century, the Aceh war of 1873–1910, which would seem to have been primarily a war of resistance to Dutch expansion into northern Sumatra. Nevertheless it was stiffened by the active

involvement of the Naqshbandi sufi order as well as by pan-Islamic ideas broadcast from Istanbul. It was led by *ulama*, the most important being of Arab descent, who greatly strengthened their hold on Acehnese society, at least for the duration of the war.

Turning to India, we find two notable reformist movements in the 19th century. The first, the Mujahidin movement of Saiyid Ahmad of Rae Bareli (1786–1831), stemmed in large part from the reformist stream in Indian Islam which derived from the Naqshbandi order and Shaikh Ahmad Sirhindi. Taught by Shah Abd al-Aziz of Delhi, son of Shah Wali Allah, and followed by his descendants, Saiyid Ahmad preached the usual reformist program, and was one of those who organized his followers along sufi lines in a *Tariqa Muhammadiya*. After returning from pilgrimage to Mecca in 1823, where he was probably exposed to west Asian reformist influences, he raised support throughout India and in 1826/7, following the example of the Prophet's flight to Medina, fled pagan-dominated India to establish his ideal Islamic state on the Northwest Frontier. Although he waged holy war first against the Sikh kingdom in the Punjab, it was clear that his campaign was no less directed against British expansion. Hindustan, he said, had fallen under the rule of Christians, and he was going to strive to free it and establish the supremacy of the *Sharia*. Saiyid Ahmad died in 1831 at the battle of Balakot. Nevertheless, his followers continued to spread his message, fighting in the great uprising of 1857 and remaining active on the frontier down to World War I.

The second Indian reformist movement, the Faraizi movement of the eastern Bengal province, was more profoundly influenced by reformist ideas in the wider Islamic world, probably Wahhabi ones. The founder, Hajji Shariat Allah (1781–1840), lived in Mecca from 1799 to 1818; then after returning from his second pilgrimage in 1821 he launched a typical reformist movement, in which he urged Bengalis to observe their duties (*faraiz*) according to the Quran and the example of the Prophet, and attacked Hindu influence on Islamic practice. Shariat Allah also attacked the British presence, but did not declare holy war against the foreigner, preferring to concentrate on his mission of religious purification. After his death, however, the movement transferred its attentions to the foreign ruler, became organized as a military brotherhood and maintained an underground organization which worked quite independently of British law for most of the 19th century.

The Naqshbandiya in Asia

Many of those involved in reformist thought or action were members of the Naqshbandi sufi order, and indeed they were at the heart of Muslim activism throughout Asia. Some of the drive came from India as a result of the expansion of the order under Sirhindi's influence in the 17th and 18th centuries. In the 19th century the westward transmission of the Naqshbandi way received a second fillip from Mawlana Khalid Baghdadi (1776–1827), who, after studying in Delhi at the feet of the spiritual successors of Sirhindi, returned to western Asia where within a few years large numbers came to follow his guidance in Syria, Iraq,

Dipanegara, leader of the holy war against the Hindu-Javanese elite and later the Dutch, 1825–30, in exile. Note how he seems to be using the appurtenances of mid-19th-century Dutch life. The war, which took place in the context of growing impoverishment, brought to the Javanese countryside by European rule, gave a powerful boost to the process of Islamization on the island.

the Hijaz, Kurdistan, Anatolia and the Balkans. Later his influence spread to East Africa, Ceylon and southeast Asia. Too much, however, should not be ascribed to Indian influences. Activity also stemmed from other branches of the order in the Caucasus, Central Asia and China.

Two striking movements of reform which merged into resistance to alien rule took place in the Caucasus. The first was led by Imam Mansur (died 1794) who, though it cannot be proved he was a Naqshbandi, is regarded as one by popular tradition and in fact preached a pure Naqshbandi message. From 1785 to 1791, supported in particular by the people of Daghistan, he waged holy war against the Russians until defeated and captured. He wrote stirring letters to the Daghistanis which still survive. The second movement emerged 50 years later and was led by Imam Shamil (c. 1796–1871) who was third in a line of Naqshbandi shaikhs which derived from northeastern Turkey. In 1834 he came to lead the order of Daghistan and, continuing the work begun by Imam Mansur, spread his rule over most of the Caucasus, imposed the *Sharia* so effectively that his reign came later to be known as "the period of the *Sharia*," and for nearly 30 years resisted mighty Russian invasions. But eventually, after cutting down the forests on which Shamil's forces depended for cover, the Russians gained the upper hand, and the imam rather uncharacteristically surrendered. Still the Naqshbandis continued sporadically to resist.

In Central Asia, heartland of the Naqshbandi order, activity was by comparison feeble in the extreme. Quite exceptional was the three-day holy war against Russian rule, led, organized and financed by the Naqshbandis, which broke out in Andijan in 1898. In the Volga Basin, on the other hand, there was an unusual variation in the style of reformist action – passive holy war. It was launched in 1862 in Kazan by one Baha al-Din Vaisi (1804–93) who had just returned from Turkestan where he had entered the Naqshbandi order. Shocked by the way in which the local Islamic leadership was being absorbed into the Russian state, he preached a typically reformist program with the difference that he conducted his fight with the infidel power not with arms but by refusing to pay taxes or to perform military service. His message was so well received among the Tatars that by 1884 the government had to move; it broke up his organization, transported its leaders to Siberia and committed Baha al-Din to a mental hospital. His movement, however, did not die, reemerging 20 years later and being marked by increasing puritanism as well as by involvement with Tatar nationalism.

China, by contrast, saw extraordinary Muslim activity in the 19th century. In east Turkestan holy wars against Manchu rule were led by the *khoja* Naqshbandi shaikhs living in exile in Khokand. Their record is impressive – five uprisings in 1820–28, 1830, 1847, 1857 and 1861. Then, after the Muslim rebellions in Kansu isolated the region from the rest of China in 1862, the *khojas* were able to reoccupy the whole of east Turkestan in 1863, only to be thrust aside by their brilliant subordinate, Yakub Beg (1820–77), who imposed a strict Islamic regime on the area which he ruled from 1867 to 1877. Given the leadership of the Naqshbandi *khojas*, it is tempting to suggest that these risings are

further evidence of the reformist spirit that the Naqshbandis were disseminating throughout the Asian Islamic world. However, firm evidence is lacking, and the ambitions of the *khojas* to win back their lost lands and the machinations of Khokand against China should not be discounted.

Among the remaining Muslims scattered throughout China there was striking evidence of Naqshbandi influence, reform and revival. Chinese Muslims were becoming increasingly self-conscious as they combated the sinicizing policies of the Manchus; they adopted the Prophet's color of green, emphasized his example as the model for the rightly conducted life, and for the first time wrote on religious matters in Chinese, so important had it become to make every Muslim aware of his religious duty. Then around 1761 one Ma Ming-hsin (died 1781) returned from study in Kashgar and began to spread the teaching of what came to be called the "New Sect" (as opposed to the "Old Sect" which embraced long-accepted Chinese Muslim doctrines of accommodation to Confucian society). Much controversy surrounds the nature of the "New Sect"; indeed there may have been not one but several. Nevertheless, it is agreed that Ma Ming-hsin taught the way of the Jahriya branch of the Naqshbandi order, that the "New Sect" aimed to root out vestiges of acculturation to the Chinese environment in religious practice, and that they were behind every major Muslim rebellion down to the 20th century.

Muslims of the "New Sect" showed their first signs of real militancy after Ma Ming-hsin returned from a visit to Arabia, and in 1781 armed conflict with the "Old Sect" around Lanchou, known as the "Mecca of Chinese Islam," merged into rebellion against Chinese rule. This militancy grew in the 19th century as the "New Sect" spread throughout China and its message was probably reinforced by returning pilgrims from Arabia and reformist influences from India. Its vitality was revealed in two great rebellions led by members of the "New

Imam Shamil, a Naqshbandi shaikh, who spread his rule over the Caucasus in the 1830s and resisted Russian conquest until 1859. Russian aristocracy fought in the wars and Shamil became well known in Europe; his deputy, Hajji Murad, is the hero of a short story by Tolstoy.

Distribution of Muslims in China, excluding the Tarim Basin, c. 1900
Note that there are particular concentrations in Kansu, where the Old Silk route had once entered China, and in eastern Yunnan, where routes from the Bay of Bengal did so. Both areas saw massive uprisings led by members of the "New Sect" in the 19th century. Generally, Muslims lived scattered in small communities which formed the basis of trading networks. Towns where these communities were sizable have been marked. After Broomhall.

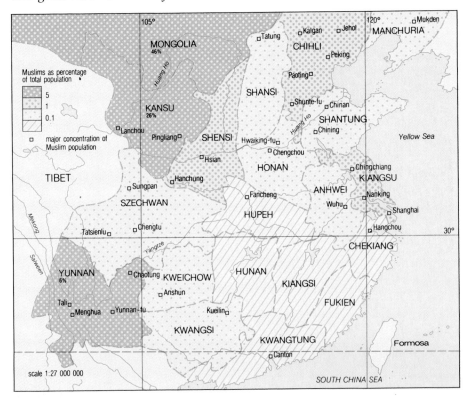

As Sultan Sulaiman, Tu Wen-hsiu ruled half the province of Yunnan from 1856 to 1873. Towards the end of his reign he sent his son to England in order to seek the help of Queen Victoria: his letter in Chinese still exists. *Above* Looking from the mountains over Sultan Sulaiman's capital of Tali to the lake beyond. *Below* The seal of Tu Wen-hsiu, which says in Chinese "Commander-in-chief of foot soldiers and cavalry, Generalissimo Tu," and in Arabic "Sultan of all the Faithful." Made of gold and weighing 2·4 kilograms, its handle was in the shape of a lion with a ruby in its jaws.

Sect." The first raged across Kansu and Shensi from 1862 to 1877, during which time its leader, Ma Hua-lung, tried to establish a Muslim state, and according to one estimate over 90 per cent of the population were killed. In the second, which racked Yunnan from 1856 to 1873, the leader, Tu Wen-hsiu, actually succeeded in establishing a separate Muslim state for 16 years in which he ruled over half the province as Sultan Sulaiman. So powerfully did this revivalist current run that for a time it even swept along with it members of the "Old Sect." The first leader of the Yunnan rebellion was Ma Te-hsin, member of the "Old Sect" and major scholar of the day. Like others brushed by the reformist spirit elsewhere – Abd al-Rauf of Singkel, translator of the Quran into Malay, Shah Wali Allah of Delhi, translator into Persian, and Shah Abd al-Qadir of Delhi, translator into Urdu – Ma Te-hsin was the first to translate the Quran into his native tongue.

The Khalwatiya and the Idrisiya in Africa
Looking now towards the western Islamic world we find the role of the Naqshbandiya as fount of reformist ideas taken up by the Khalwatiya and the Idrisiya. The former was an ancient order given new life by Mustafa al-Bakri (see above, p. 120). The latter was a new order founded by the Moroccan Ahmad Ibn Idris (1760–1837) who, after coming under Khalwati influence during a long period of study in Cairo, eventually settled as a sufi shaikh in Mecca. Here he taught a sufi way which embraced an almost Wahhabi program and emphasized the importance of following the path beaten by the

Prophet. Hence it was called, like that of Saiyid Ahmad of Rae Bareli, *Tariqa Muhammadiya*. Streams from these two founts of reformist vigor spread throughout Islamic Africa in the 19th century, having a dynamic impact on the relations between those who strove to realize the Islamic ideal and those who did not. They also helped to sustain and on occasion to satisfy the expectation, particularly strong in Africa, that at the end of each Muslim century (in this case 1199 AH /1784–85 AD and 1299 AH /1881–82 AD) a Mahdi would appear who would "fill the world with justice, as it was previously filled with injustice and oppression."

One important offshoot of the Khalwatiya was the Tijaniya, founded by the Algerian Ahmad al-Tijani (1737–1815), who had been taught by Mahmud al-Kurdi (1715–80), a leading pupil of both al-Bakri and al-Hifnawi. His order spread to Algeria and Morocco and to the Nilotic and central Sudan, but it spread most widely in West Africa. At the heart of its success in this region was Hajji Umar Tall (1794–1864), a Fulani from Futa Toro in Senegal, a state long established by holy war. On pilgrimage in the 1820s he became caught up in the reformist movement after spending three years in Medina as a pupil of the Tijani shaikh, Muhammad al-Ghali, who made him his successor in the Sudan, and four years among the Khalwatis in Egypt from whom he learned his practice of retreat into prayer (*khalwat*), which he often practiced before battle. He returned to the western Sudan and founded a theocratic state just outside Futa Jallon. In 1852 he began his holy war, fighting the pagan Bambara of Karta, and by

1863, after he had captured Timbuktu, he commanded an empire which stretched from the bend in the Niger to Upper Senegal. Indeed only the French on the coast had prevented him from "dipping the Quran in the Atlantic." The state survived to 1893 when it was absorbed by the French, but the Tijaniya continued to flourish, becoming the most popular order in West Africa.

The second important offshoot of the Khalwatiya was the Sammaniya, which was founded by Shaikh Muhammad Samman and spread in the Nilotic Sudan, Eritrea and southwest Ethiopia. Out of the spiritual tradition of this order there flowed one of the most remarkable manifestations of Muslim reform and revival, the Sudanese Mahdiya. Muhammad Ahmad (1840–85), who declared himself to be the expected Mahdi on 29 June 1881, spent his life from 1861 under the instruction of two leading Sammaniya shaikhs of the Sudan and became renowned for his asceticism and his rigor in observing the *Sharia*. His movement was nourished by a variety of local resentments against the Turko-Egyptian regime which had ruled since 1821; the Sudanese resented the *ulama* imported from Lower Egypt, the "Western" innovations of the administration and the abolition of the slave trade. So he waged a holy war against the regime which led to the capture of Khartoum in 1885 and the establishment of a separate Mahdist state in the Sudan. The ideas he promulgated and the institutions he founded were full of the reformist spirit. There was much conscious imitation of the early Islamic community. Muhammad Ahmad was the successor of the Prophet, the divinely elected Mahdi, and his followers were the successors of the companions of the Prophet, the *Ansar* – hence the name of the sufi way flowing from the Mahdi, the Ansariya. All formed the basis of an effective theocratic state which only fell in 1898 because its simple arma-

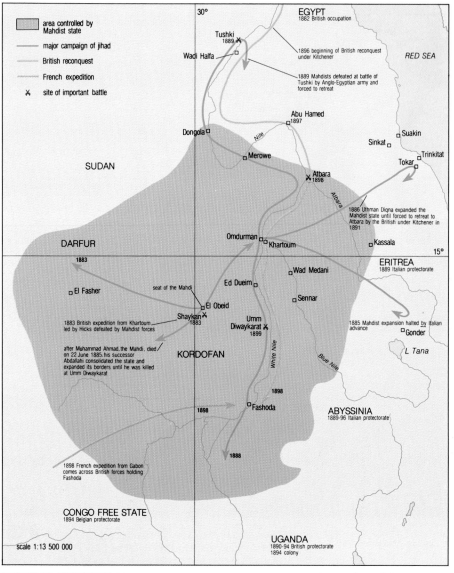

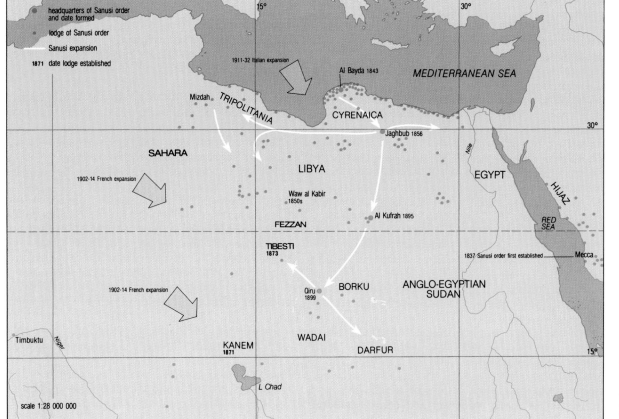

Above: The Mahdist movement in the Sudan 1881–98
One of the most striking manifestations of the general movement of reform and revival, this culminated in the establishment of an effective theocratic state from 1885 to 1898. Its natural expansive impulse curbed by European imperial powers on its borders, the state was eventually overcome by British forces led by Kitchener. Extensive records of the administration of the Mahdist state survive in Khartoum.

Right The tomb in Khartoum of Muhammad Ahmad, who declared himself the divinely elected Mahdi, or successor of the Prophet, on 29 June 1881. After his death in 1885, the state was led by his successor Abdallahi.

Left: The spread of Sanusi sufi lodges in the Sahara
This shows the expansion of the Sanusi order in the later 19th century as it came to coordinate in one organization many Saharan tribes. At the heart of its expansive techniques was its system of lodges which operated as cells of Islamic culture in the nomadic and often semipagan environment.

ments were exposed to the overwhelming power of a modern army.

The Idrisiya also produced two offshoots with notable records. Strangely enough they both stemmed from those who lost a dispute for the succession in Mecca after the death of Ahmad Ibn Idris. In fact, the winner, Muhammad Usman Mirghani, repudiated the reformist way of his master and established an order in the Nilotic Sudan which both resisted the Mahdiya and sided with the government. One of those who lost the dispute was Muhammad Ali al-Sanusi (1787–1859). He was forced to leave Mecca and eventually in 1856 came to establish his headquarters at Jaghbub deep in the Libyan desert. From here he spread a reformist message, owing much to the inspiration of his late master, which emphasized reliance on the Quran and the *Hadiths* and the need to purify sufism. In marked contrast to many reformists, moreover, he strove to create a theocratically organized society by peaceful means. His method was to establish sufi lodges (*zawiya*) which functioned as cells of Islamic culture in the nomadic and often semipagan environment of the desert. Each lodge was regarded as belonging to the tribe in whose region it was placed and from whom increasing numbers of adherents were won. Steadily in the 19th century a vast network of lodges, coordinating in one organization the once contentious tribes, spread down the Saharan trade routes till they stretched from Cyrenaica to Timbuktu and the kingdom of Wadai. They came, of course, to collide with the French as they expanded across the Sahara, and with the Italians as they invaded Libya. Nevertheless, they survived to become the basis of Libyan resistance to foreign domination, while their hereditary leaders became the first rulers of an independent Libyan state.

The second of those who failed to succeed Ahmad Ibn Idris was Ibrahim al-Rashid (died 1874). His pupil and nephew, Muhammad Ibn Salih, founded the Salihiya, based in Mecca, whose most notable product was the Somali leader Muhammad Abd Allah Hasan (1864–1920), described most inaccurately by his British opponents as the "mad mullah." A gifted scholar, he traveled widely in search of knowledge and was impressed by the attitude and success of the Sudanese Mahdiya. Like so many reformist leaders, he had his major formative experience in Mecca where he studied for five years and joined the Salihiya. On returning to Somalia in 1895 he preached a particularly puritan message: justice could only flow from the Quran and the *Hadiths*; holy war was a perpetual obligation; intercession at saints' tombs must end; those who missed their prayers risked mutilation or even death. By 1899 he was waging holy war on all sides: against the laxer Qadiri order, against the Ethiopians, against the British. For 20 years he fought, and he died unbeaten. His poetry, ringing with defiance, lives on. A British captain tried to cut off his retreat in August 1913 and suffered for it:

> O Corfield, you are a traveler who
> Will not stay long here below
> You will follow the Path were there is no rest
> You who are among the Denizens of Hell
> You will journey to the Next World.

(trans. I. M. Lewis)

Local movements in West Africa

Not all African movements received their major stimulus from the reform movement in the Islamic world at large. In West Africa, the work of Hajji Umar Tall apart, the prime reformist drive was locally generated. The main leaders came from one tribe, the Fulani, a people of Negro origin from Senegal who intermarried with Berbers drifting southwards from the Sahara; they had been converted to Islam before the 14th century, some clans developing traditions of deep learning. From the 15th century groups of Fulani began a long migration eastwards to Hausaland, spreading like an often highly Islamized fifth column among the syncretic or pagan communities from Senegambia to Bornu. Like the *ulama* of Timbuktu or the Hausa city-states, they coexisted uneasily with those who mixed pagan rites with their Islamic practice. Eventually some launched holy wars. Those who

Far right Fulani warriors who, typically of cavalry aristocracy, disdained firearms: guns were for slaves alone. The Fulani were the generators of religious reform in West Africa. In 1680 they began a series of holy wars against the pagan rulers around them lasting nearly two centuries, in which they established the theocratic states of Futa Jallon, Futa Toro, Khasso, Kaarta, Masina and Sokoto.

Right A North African *zawiya*, or sufi lodge, which would normally embrace the mausoleum of a saint, surmounted by a dome, a small mosque, a room for Quran recitation, a Quran school, and rooms for students, guests and pilgrims. Sanusi lodges spread the reformist message throughout the central and eastern Saharan desert.

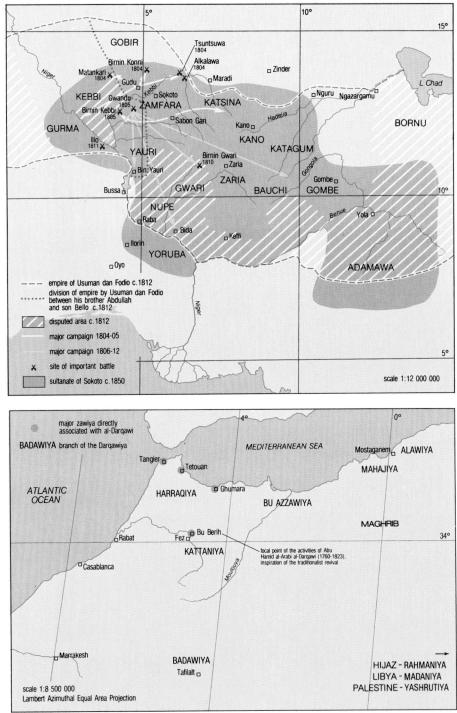

empire of Usuman dan Fodio c.1812
division of empire by Usuman dan Fodio between his brother Abdullah and son Bello c.1812
disputed area c.1812
major campaign 1804-05
major campaign 1806-12
✕ site of important battle
sultanate of Sokoto c.1850

scale 1:12 000 000

major zawiya directly associated with al-Darqawi
branch of the Darqawiya

focal point of the activities of Abu Hamid al-Arabi al-Darqawi (1760-1823), inspiration of the traditionalist revival

scale 1:8 500 000
Lambert Azimuthal Equal Area Projection

HIJAZ – RAHMANIYA
LIBYA – MADANIYA
PALESTINE – YASHRUTIYA

Left: The holy war of Usuman dan Fodio and the foundation of the caliphate of Sokoto
This was the most spectacular holy war leading in turn to the formation of the greatest state. "The government of a country is the government of its king," wrote Usuman dan Fodio in explaining the reasons for the war. "If the king is a Muslim, his land is Muslim; if he is an unbeliever, his land is a land of unbelievers ... There is no dispute that the sultans of these countries venerate certain places, certain trees, and certain rocks and offer sacrifice to them. This constitutes unbelief according to the consensus of opinion ... The above description was applicable to the condition of the Hausa peoples as we found them, before the *jihad*. Since then we have fought them and put them to flight, and killed some, and driven others from this land by the power of God (exalted be he)." The expansion of the caliphate was halted to the northeast only by Kanem-Bornu and carried a vigorous Islamic thrust into the Cameroons and the lands of the Nupe and Yoruba in central Nigeria. By the mid-19th century the fervor for religious reform was largely spent and the Fulani became a ruling class. They played a key role in giving northern Nigeria its distinctively Islamic character and in driving the faith southwards to the Atlantic shore.

Left: The traditionalist revival in the Maghrib
Not all revived religious feeling in the 18th and 19th centuries was reformist. The map illustrates the centers of activity of the major sufi ways flowing from Ahmad al-Darqawi which were the most popular in the region from the 19th century. Al-Darqawi's way owed nothing to the reformist movement.

did drew more on the long tradition of Saharan scholarship and mysticism than on the pulses of reform which beat out from 18th-century Cairo and western Asia. The most important leader, Usuman dan Fodio (1754–1817), never traveled to Cairo or to Mecca, and, although he and his followers formed part of a sufi network which reached into western Asia and although his teacher, the iconoclastic Jibril Ibn Umar of Agades, was a Khalwati, he sprang in mind and spirit from the Saharan tradition. His sufi inspiration came from the Qadiriya whom al-Maghili of Tlemcen had done much to spread in the area in the late 15th century. His writings drew on the whole range of Islamic classical and post-classical literature from al-Ghazzali to al-Suyuti. Nothing could have distinguished him more sharply from the west Asian reformers. Whereas they cast aside the medieval superstructure of Islam, Usuman, dwelling in an only partially Islamized society, found in it still a dynamic inspiration.

The Fulani holy wars themselves began in Senegambia. The first broke out in Bondu around 1680 and culminated in the founding of an Islamic state; the second, which began in 1725, led to the establishment of a Muslim dynasty in Futa Jallon; while the third, which began in 1776, brought an Islamic theocracy to Futa Toro. Then the focus switched 1600 kilometers east to Hausaland where Usuman dan Fodio's preaching excited increasing tension with local rulers. Eventually in 1804 he launched a holy war, in which Hausa as well as Fulani supported him, and which led to the formation of the sultanate of Sokoto out of the fractious gaggle of Hausa city-states. Nor did the holy war end here. After driving unsuccessfully into Bornu, Sokoto with local Fulani help was able by 1850 to draw Adamawa to the southeast, Nupe to the south and Ilorin to the southwest into its Islamic empire. Usuman's achievement was noted by Fulani elsewhere. Between 1810 and 1815 Shehu Ahmadu (1775/6–1844) led a holy war on the Upper Niger against partially Muslim chiefs and pagan Bambara which led to the creation of the Islamic state of Masina reaching down river to Timbuktu.

These were the developments prompted directly by the spirit of reform as it flowed across the face of African Islam. But the atmosphere they created was felt beyond reforming circles. It helped sufi orders expand in East Africa where, for instance, the Shadhiliya were being established in the Comoros and the Qadariya in Tanzania. It stiffened resistance against French expansion in Algeria which Abd al-Qadir (1808-83) led as a holy war from 1832 to 1847. It encouraged Samori Ture (1830–1900) to transform the kingdom he built in the Guinea highlands from the 1860s into an Islamic state. Moreover, it stimulated a revival of activity among those whose Islam was in no way touched by ideas of reform and who were on occasion no less influential than the reformers. In the Maghrib, for instance, the most popular sufi ways from the 19th century onwards were those which stemmed from the ecstatic master, Ahmad al-Darqawi (1760–1823).

This great movement of reform, and the revival it stimulated, was inspired in part by crises in the enduring tensions between the Islamic ideal and local conditions, and in part by the impact of ideas of reform as they spread throughout the Islamic world. Until recently scholars, perhaps unduly influenced by visions of the world created by 20th-century nation-states, have tended to emphasize the local origins of each manifestation of this move-ment. The present analysis on the other hand has shown just how much sufi orders, the Naqsh-bandiya and the Khalwatiya in particular, con-tributed to broadcasting the reformist outlook and élan. We have also been able to get a glimpse of the influence of a powerful tradition in the teaching of the *Hadiths* strategically placed in Medina to attract scholars and to influence those performing pil-grimage. Indeed, no development in Muslim affairs since 1500 demonstrates more effectively the central role of *ulama* and of sufis, whether in the localities or in the world at large, as the principal sustainers of the community. As Muslim power crumbled from within, they strove to restore it by promoting the Islamic ideal. As old arteries began to harden, they built new ones along which they pumped fresh vitality. As the community seemed to lose momentum and direction, they tried to place it once more on the sure base of revelation and the example of the Prophet.

THE RISE OF EUROPE AND THE RESPONSE OF ISLAM UNTIL THE MID-20th CENTURY

The advance of the Europeans

In the 19th and 20th centuries the Muslims experienced disaster. The slow erosion of power on the margins of their world during the 18th century became a rampant decay as European empire came to envelop the community. This brought a series of threats to the very heart of Islamic civilization: Christian missionaries, secular philosophies, rational learning, purely earthly visions of progress, and all supported by unprecedented material prosperity and power. Muslims were ill equipped to respond. Even the revivalist movements, products of the new vitality which surged through the Muslim world from the mid-18th century, could offer only temporary and niggling resistance. Nevertheless, their new spirit and ideas did provide some lasting basis for Muslim responses, which was important because the processes unleashed by Europe were powerful enough to make Muslims march to their tempo, as indeed all human beings were beginning to do. Muslims now faced a civilization strong enough to transform them in its own image.

The symbolic beginning of the new era came when the French invaded Egypt in 1798. The revolutionary army represented the new forces of reason, nationalism and state power; their action epitomized the new confidence of the Europeans who had not dared to violate the eastern Mediterranean shore since the crusades. Within three years the British and the Ottomans had chased the intruders away, but the great forward thrust of Europe had now begun. In island southeast Asia the Dutch government took over from its East India Company in 1800 and spread Dutch authority throughout the archipelago until the process was completed by the end of the Aceh war in 1908. In India the British were recognized as paramount by

1818 and 40 years later ruled all Indians either directly or through Indian princes. The strategic demands of this vast possession inexorably drew them into other Muslim lands. The Afghans, fortunate in their terrain, their warlike habits and their position as a buffer between the ambitions of British India and tsarist Russia, were able to maintain their independence. In the Gulf, on the other hand, British power steadily grew, as it did in southern Iran and along Arabia's Indian Ocean shore. Further west the construction of the Suez Canal in 1869 and European competition for power resulted in the government of huge Muslim territories. In 1882 the British occupied Egypt; this in turn led to the establishment in 1898 of an Anglo-Egyptian "condominion" over the Nilotic Sudan, where they held effective power. On the East African coast they shared out the considerable possessions of the sultans of Zanzibar with Germany and Italy, while far away on the other side of the Indian Ocean they had from the 1870s begun to assert their hegemony over the sultans of the various Malay states.

Tsarist Russia was one of the four European powers – together with Holland, Britain and France – to come to rule large numbers of Muslims. In the Caucasus Russia made large steps forward at the beginning of the 19th century when it conquered the Iranian territories of northern Azarbaijan and by 1864 the whole region was effectively occupied. In Central Asia the lands of the Kazakhs were secured by 1854, the khanate of Khokand by 1873, the lands of the Turkomans and the Tajiks by 1885 and 1895, while protectorates had been established over the ancient khanates of Khiva and Bukhara which were converted into direct rule after the Bolshevik revolution. The French advance in North

Russia conquers the northern Islamic lands
In the 19th century Russia pressed forward its frontiers until they met those of Iran, Afghanistan and China, and all the Muslims of the Caucasus and Turkestan came under some kind of Russian rule. In 1920 Bukhara, last fragment of the once mighty Mongol Muslim power, and a Russian protectorate since 1868, was finally absorbed within the new Soviet state.

- Russian territory 1801
- Islamic lands lost by 1825
- Islamic lands lost by 1855
- Islamic lands lost by 1881
- Islamic lands lost by 1914
- Russian protectorate prior to annexation in 1920
- boundary of Russia 1920
- 1873 date of loss
- Russian line of fortification (19th century)

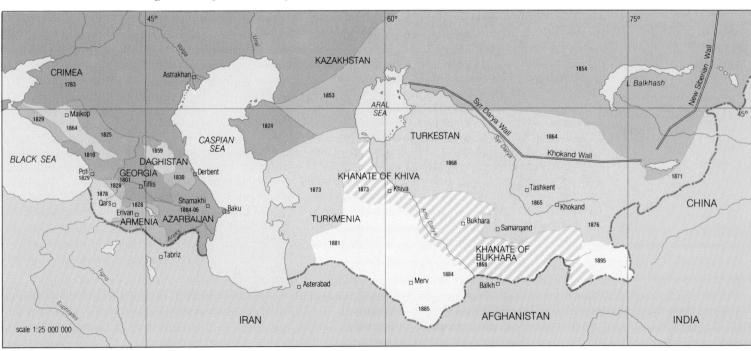

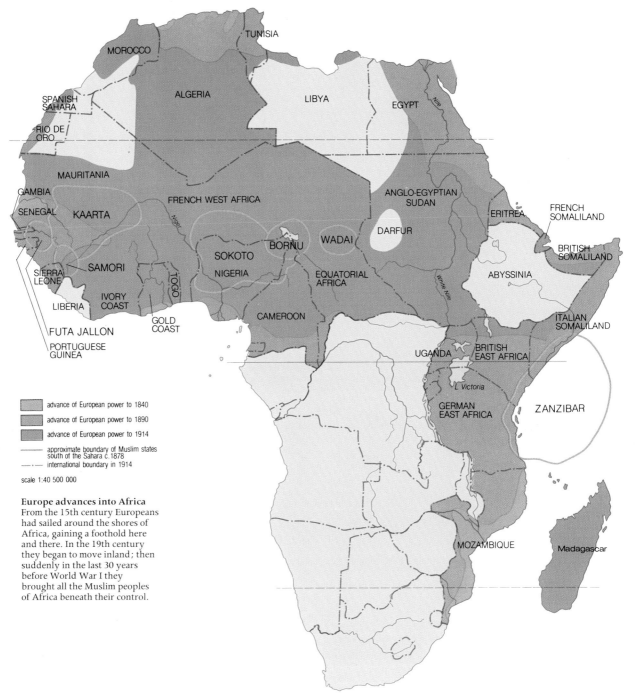

TUNISIA
MOROCCO
SPANISH SAHARA
RIO DE ORO
ALGERIA
LIBYA
EGYPT
Nile
MAURITANIA
ANGLO-EGYPTIAN SUDAN
GAMBIA
FRENCH WEST AFRICA
ERITREA
FRENCH SOMALILAND
SENEGAL
KAARTA
Niger
DARFUR
BRITISH SOMALILAND
WADAI
SIERRA LEONE
SAMORI
SOKOTO
BORNU
NIGERIA
ABYSSINIA
LIBERIA
IVORY COAST
TOGO
EQUATORIAL AFRICA
White Nile
ITALIAN SOMALILAND
FUTA JALLON
GOLD COAST
CAMEROON
PORTUGUESE GUINEA
UGANDA
BRITISH EAST AFRICA
L Victoria
GERMAN EAST AFRICA
ZANZIBAR
MOZAMBIQUE
Madagascar

advance of European power to 1840
advance of European power to 1890
advance of European power to 1914
approximate boundary of Muslim states south of the Sahara c.1878
international boundary in 1914

scale 1:40 500 000

Europe advances into Africa
From the 15th century Europeans had sailed around the shores of Africa, gaining a foothold here and there. In the 19th century they began to move inland; then suddenly in the last 30 years before World War I they brought all the Muslim peoples of Africa beneath their control.

and West Africa was, if anything, even more dramatic, and was accompanied in some areas, as the Russian had been, by a massive influx of European settlers. In 1830 they invaded Algeria; in 1881 they declared Tunisia a protectorate, and in 1912 Morocco. The first two territories were the main focus of French settlement. By 1912 they had also seized the Saharan wastes and expanded from Senegal across the savanna lands to the border of the Anglo-Egyptian Sudan, subduing in the process that string of Muslim states, many newly forged in the years of Muslim revival, which rested on the desert's southern fringe. Only the British, who absorbed the sultanate of Sokoto in their main West African colony of Nigeria, also ruled large numbers of Muslims in the region. Other European powers picked up what crumbs they could; in 1912, for instance, Spain asserted a protectorate over the northern tip of Morocco, and Italy conquered Libya. By the outbreak of World War I all the Muslims of Africa were under infidel rule.

Throughout the 19th century the Ottoman

empire remained the only significant focus of Muslim power. But even here Muslims were falling steadily into the hands of unbelievers. The European powers, determined that not one of their number should gain an advantage over the rest, used every financial, political and military device to build up influence in the empire. Direct results were that the Christian peoples of the Balkans – Greeks, Serbians, Romanians, Bulgarians – supported by one European power or the other, threw off Ottoman rule, and that the sizeable and long-established Muslim populations of the region lost their lands and sometimes their lives. By World War I only Rumelia remained of the once vast empire in Europe. The war itself saw the Arab peoples of the empire also fall under European rule as the British, with Arab help, rolled the Ottoman forces back into Anatolia and divided the spoils with their French allies. By 1920 the Ottomans, whose subjects were now mainly Turks, were fighting to hold on to their Anatolian heartland, which the Europeans according to the treaty of Sèvres proposed to dismember,

131

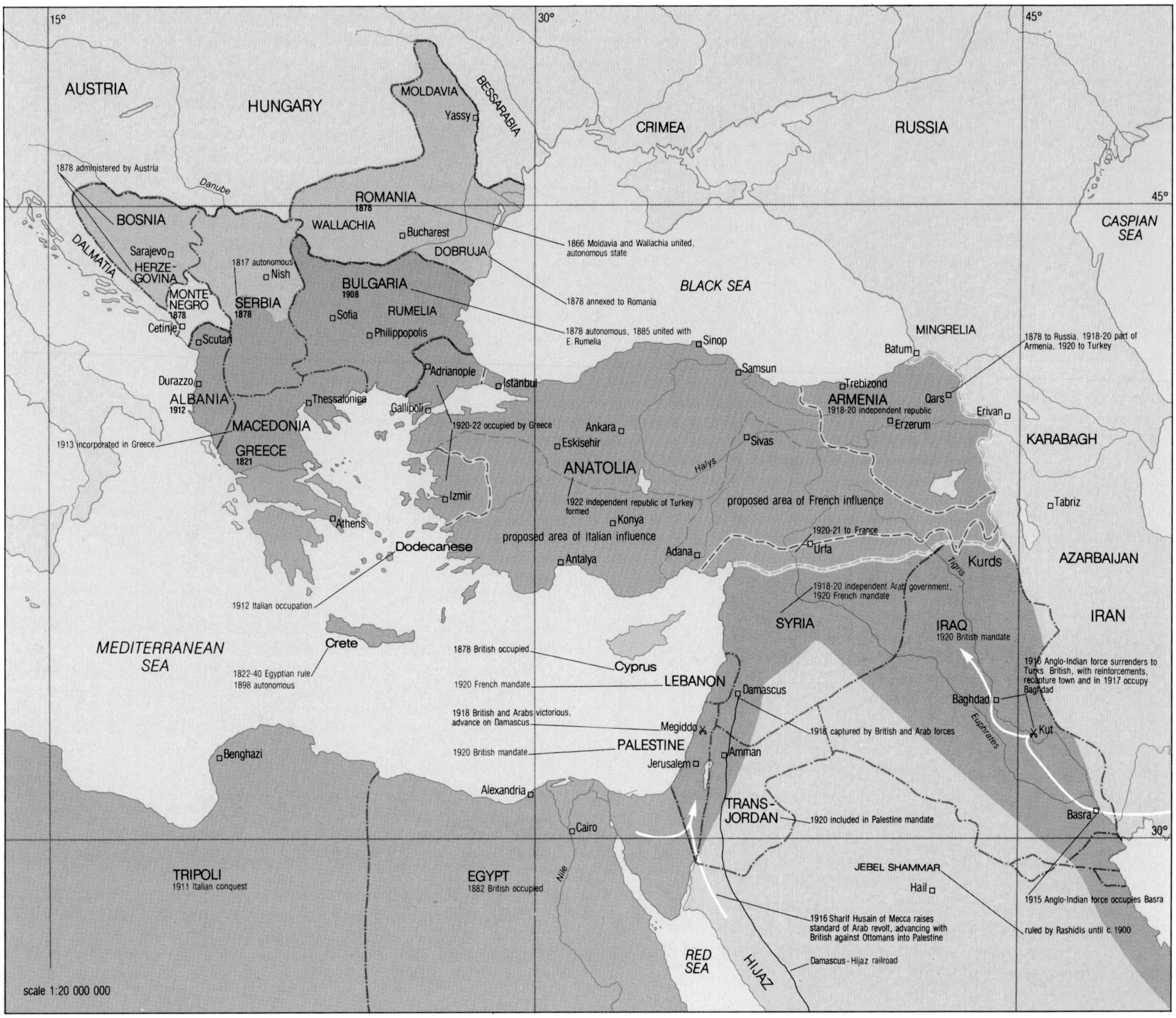
15°
30°
45°
45°
30°
AUSTRIA
HUNGARY
MOLDAVIA
Yassy
BESSARABIA
CRIMEA
RUSSIA
1878 administered by Austria
Danube
ROMANIA
1878
WALLACHIA
Bucharest
DOBRUJA
1866 Moldavia and Wallachia united, autonomous state
BOSNIA
Sarajevo
HERZE-GOVINA
DALMATIA
1817 autonomous
Nish
SERBIA
1878
MONTE-NEGRO
1878
Cetinje
Scutari
BULGARIA
1908
Sofia
RUMELIA
Philippopolis
1878 annexed to Romania
1878 autonomous, 1885 united with E. Rumelia
BLACK SEA
CASPIAN SEA
MINGRELIA
Batum
1878 to Russia, 1918-20 part of Armenia, 1920 to Turkey
Sinop
Samsun
Trebizond
Durazzo
ALBANIA
1912
Adrianople
Istanbul
Thessalonica
Gallipoli
ARMENIA
1918-20 independent republic
Qars
Erivan
Erzerum
MACEDONIA
1913 incorporated in Greece
GREECE
1821
1920-22 occupied by Greece
Ankara
Eskisehir
Sivas
KARABAGH
ANATOLIA
Halys
1922 independent republic of Turkey formed
Izmir
Konya
proposed area of French influence
Tabriz
Athens
proposed area of Italian influence
1920-21 to France
Urfa
Dodecanese
Adana
Antalya
Kurds
AZARBAIJAN
Tigris
1912 Italian occupation
1918-20 independent Arab government, 1920 French mandate
SYRIA
IRAQ
1920 British mandate
IRAN
MEDITERRANEAN SEA
Crete
1822-40 Egyptian rule
1898 autonomous
1878 British occupied
Cyprus
1916 Anglo-Indian force surrenders to Turks. British, with reinforcements, recapture town and in 1917 occupy Baghdad
1920 French mandate
LEBANON
Damascus
Baghdad
1918 British and Arabs victorious, advance on Damascus
Megiddo
1918 captured by British and Arab forces
Euphrates
Kut
1920 British mandate
PALESTINE
Benghazi
Jerusalem
Amman
Alexandria
TRANS-JORDAN
1920 included in Palestine mandate
Basra
Cairo
TRIPOLI
1911 Italian conquest
EGYPT
1882 British occupied
Nile
JEBEL SHAMMAR
Hail
1915 Anglo-Indian force occupies Basra
1916 Sharif Husain of Mecca raises standard of Arab revolt, advancing with British against Ottomans into Palestine
ruled by Rashidis until c. 1900
RED SEA
HIJAZ
Damascus-Hijaz railroad
scale 1:20 000 000

remainder of Ottoman empire in 1923
boundary of Turkey after treaty of Sèvres 1920
boundary of Turkey after treaty of Lausanne 1923
land lost from the Ottoman empire
to 1830
to 1878
to 1915
to 1923
proposed boundary for division of Anatolia between French, Italian and Turks
1878 date of independence

Europe envelops the Ottoman empire 1812–1923
Between the treaty of Bucharest in 1812 and the treaty of Lausanne in 1923 almost all the Ottoman lands fell beneath European rule. For a moment between 1921 and 1922 it seemed that even the Anatolian heartland might be dismembered. But this remnant of the 600-year-old empire was saved by the military genius of Mustafa Kemal Ataturk and became the focus of the modern Turkish state.

by seizing chunks for themselves, and by creating a Greek Christian province in the west and an Armenian Christian state in the east. This was the nadir of Muslim fortunes. No great Muslim power existed any longer to protect the community. Only Afghanistan, the Yemen and the Muslims of central Arabia could pretend to any kind of independence. The great Muslim cities so redolent of past glories – Damascus, Baghdad, Cairo, Samarqand – had all been conquered by infidel powers. Only Istanbul remained free, but was no longer willing or able to take a lead in Muslim affairs. The future, moreover, looked bleak; although the Europeans trumpeted words of freedom to the peoples of Europe, they seemed to consider only further bondage for the peoples of Islam.

The European challenge

In the beginning the rise of Europe did not seem to demand a fundamental transformation of the way in which Muslims thought and lived. All that seemed necessary for independent Muslim states, Selim III's Ottoman empire, for instance, or Muhammad Ali's Egypt, was that they should take from the Europeans what had made them strong and install it in their societies. All they had to do was to buy European weapons or European machines, and their armies would automatically be stronger and their industries more productive. No concomitant changes in the organization of society or in the nature of its aspirations were seen to be necessary. For those Muslims who were conquered there was the considerable trauma of defeat and of rule by infidel powers; there might also be the worrying attentions of Christian missionaries. It should be realized, however, that conquest rarely meant, in the 18th and the first half of the 19th centuries, any radical transformation of Muslim society. The old ruling class might have been swept away, in part at least, but underneath Muslim life continued very much as before: the schools still taught the traditional Islamic sciences, government was still served in large part by Muslims, and the law was still the *Sharia*. Indeed, in the early stages of colonial rule, Europeans often adapted themselves considerably to the societies to which they had come, learning their language, using their systems of law and even marrying their women.

In the beginning Europeans in Muslim societies often adapted themselves considerably to the environment. *Above* William Palmer, of the British East India Company's service, and his family, painted by Francesco Renaldi, at Calcutta in 1786. The woman seated with a baby on her lap is Palmer's senior wife, Begum Faiz Baksh, a princess of the Mughal royal family in Delhi. The woman whose hand rests on Palmer's knee as she gazes at him ardently is his junior wife from the Awadh royal family in Lucknow. The remaining women are servants. From the left, Faiz Baksh's children, William, the baby, Hastings, no doubt named for Warren Hastings, the governor-general to whom Palmer was aide-de-camp, and Mary.

As European power grew, however, the fundamental nature of the challenges offered to Islam was revealed. There were the challenges posed by Western philosophical and scientific theories to God, to his relationship with nature and man and to the life hereafter. There was the more general challenge as to whether faith could ever be reconciled with reason. Beyond this, moreover, there was the implicit challenge for men, who for 13 centuries had known history to be on their side, of the material and political success of societies in which Allah and his revelation played no part.

There were challenges which questioned the organization of Muslim society and Muslim values. These, furthermore, were severe because Islam, unlike other major religions, established rules of social conduct in minute detail; God had ruled very precisely on the behavior of the first Muslim community at Medina. But some of Europe's most cherished beliefs and practices seemed to clash violently with his commands. European capitalism challenged the Quranic prohibition on the taking of interest; the new European commitment to the rights of man challenged the Quranic acceptance of slavery; most important of all, the new European belief in the equality of all human souls challenged the inferior position which the Quran seemed to have designated for women: a man's right to four wives, his right to easy divorce and the injunction to keep women in seclusion.

The most obvious set of challenges, however, came at the level of the state. From 1800 the pressing problem for Muslims was one of power – power to command their own destinies. The prime instrument of the new European strength was the modern state. It was aspects of this state which Muslims introduced to make their regimes strong enough to keep the Europeans out and which Europeans introduced to exploit the resources of their colonies. The key feature of the modern state was its capacity to control available physical and human resources. There followed the increasing involvement of the people in the activities of the state and the spread of the idea of the people as the legitimizer of those activities, of popular sovereignty. The meaning of these developments should be clear. The growth of state power meant the development of machinery to direct the minds and energies of the people in the service of the state. It meant the creation of an educational system to transmit the modern knowledge the state needed, a code of law which would make it strong, and a political structure which would express in some form or other the popular will. It meant, in fact, the creation of a framework for Muslim lives and minds which need owe nothing to Quranic revelation. The spread of the idea of popular sovereignty, on the other hand, challenged the sovereignty of God. In Islam only God was sovereign, only God could make law, and the legitimacy of the state was measured according to the extent that it administered his law. The duty of man was to come up to God's standards, not to establish his own. But the struggle for power seemed to demand that the strongest aspirations of the people be expressed in terms of the state, in terms of some national state within the community, and not in terms of their relationship to God. "The country is the darling of their hearts," wrote the Indian philosopher-poet Muhammad Iqbal, "vanished is humankind; there but abide the disunited nations. Politics dethroned religion. . ."

Muslims had a choice. They could ignore the European challenge, in which case they risked conquest and, if conquered, continuing servitude. On the other hand, they could strive to seize hold of the new sources of power Europe had revealed; they could learn the new knowledge, train the new armies, build the new factories, construct the machinery of the modern state and fashion a "modern" outlook on the world. They could, moreover, work to reconcile all these things with the patterns for a Muslim life revealed in the Quran. But in doing so they ran the risk that the central institutions of Islamic society would wither away. The *Sharia* would seem redundant, *ulama* and sufis would seem irrelevant and Muslims would no longer know how to submit. They ran the risk, in trying to absorb the new forces within the Islamic frame, of being transformed themselves by what they hoped would make them strong, of being just a Muslim husk of language, memory and culture which enclosed a spirit secular, materialistic and quasi-European.

Europeanization in Ottoman lands
One theme emerges from the various strategies adopted by Muslims to answer the European challenge. Presented first and most strikingly in

European imperialism and the Muslim world c. 1920
By this time few Muslim peoples had not succumbed to European expansion. Only the Afghans of Afghanistan and the Arabs of the Hijaz, the Yemen and the Najd, all areas which the dynamics of the balance of power enabled the Europeans in large part to ignore, were truly free. Iranians, most of whose land was divided into spheres of influence between Britain and Russia, had only a qualified independence; the Turks were fighting for their lives in Anatolia.

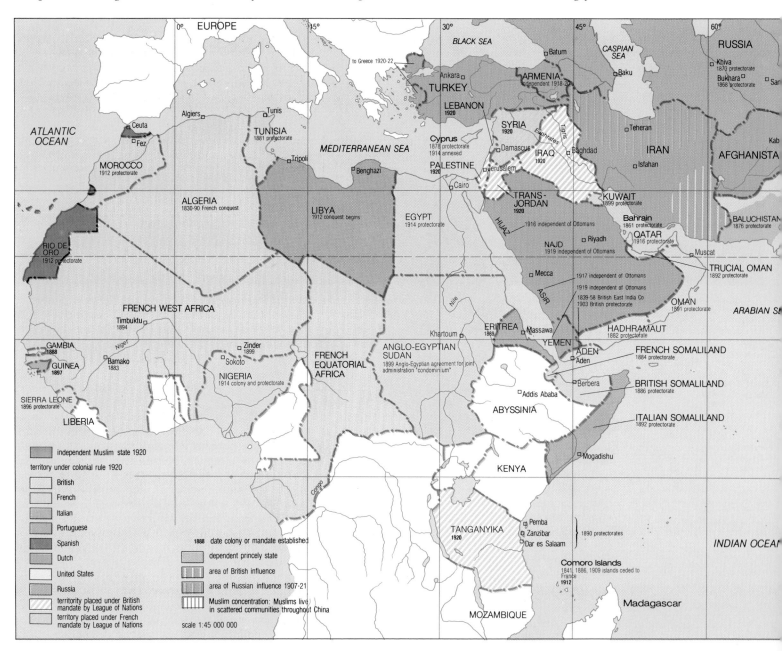

The first part of the state machine which most Muslim leaders strove to modernize, in order to keep the European out, was the army; so the army, as in many developing societies in the 20th century, occupied the vanguard of attempts to master the secrets of European power. *Right* A Janissary officer of low rank flanked by new recruits in 1825, just a year before the historic elite corps of the Ottoman army was wiped out by Mahmud II. *Far right* Ottoman soldiers fighting in the Crimean War less than 30 years later. The uniforms are barely distinguishable from those of contemporary European armies. It seems, however, that Muslim soldiers did not take kindly to European-style uniforms, because they were mocked by civilians as "the trousered ones": when off duty they would roll their trousers up above their knees.

terms of power, it was taken up by those primarily concerned with power. *Ulama* and sufis, if they played a role at all, played a minor one. The result was that in the continuing tension between the powerful and the transmitters in Muslim society there was a marked shift in favor of the former.

Ottoman leaders tried to build a system strong enough to prevent the steady encroachment of the Europeans on the empire. Work began in earnest under Sultan Mahmud II (reigned 1808–39) who from 1812 set about destroying the semiautonomous groups which had so long defied and limited the central power. He first used the Janissaries to help him bring to heel local notables, valley lords and provincial pashas, except for Muhammad Ali of Egypt, and then on 15 June 1826 used a new European-trained force to wipe out this historic elite corps of the Ottoman army turned hereditary corporation. There followed a slow, halting, but in the long run successful construction of a new state system of Western character, quite distinct from those remnants of the old order which managed to survive. There was a modern army, trained by Prussian officers, who began the close association between Germany and the Turkish people which has existed to the present day. Schools teaching European learning, often in European languages, were established to provide capable officers for this army as well as competent civil servants. By the end of the century these schools formed an empire-wide system, headed by the university of Istanbul, the first truly indigenous modern university in the Muslim world, and controlled by a ministry of education. Rather earlier, indeed by 1863, all criminal, commercial, maritime and land law was based on codes of French origin. The meaning of these changes for the *ulama* and for the transmission of the molding forces of an Islamic society should be evident. The Ottoman state which had once existed to spread Islam now treated Islamic knowledge as irrelevant to its purposes; the state, which had gone further than any other towards putting the *Sharia* into effect, was now thrusting it to one side. The

135

ulama themselves, moreover, found their endowments expropriated, and their standing, now that they were just state pensioners, much lowered in the eyes of ordinary Muslims.

The growth of this heavily centralized secular government continued throughout the century and was much helped by improved communications, by railroads and by the telegraph. It was not diluted by the espousal by Sultan Abd al-Hamid II (reigned 1876–1909) of a pan-Islamic ideology, which was as much for external as internal consumption. It was not deflected by moves to involve the people in government which led to the abortive Ottoman constitution of 1876 and the attempt of the Young Turks to restore it in 1908. By World War I the latter, who formed the Committee of Union and Progress, had shown themselves as despotic as any of their predecessors in commanding the new state machine, which was alien in spirit and out of sympathy with the mass of the people.

As we might expect, the development of the new secular Ottoman state created problems of identity. Would it be able to reconcile and to represent the aspirations of the various peoples and religions which made up the empire? The 19th-century reformers backed the idea of an Ottoman nationality. The great edicts of the time, the Noble Rescript of the Rose Chamber of 1839 and the Imperial Rescript of 1856, both declared that all the sultan's subjects, whether Muslim or not, were equal before the law. The state offered itself as the object of the affections of all, rejecting its old Islamic basis and bidding to overcome the religious divisions which had weakened it from the 17th century. Such a policy, combined as it was with the dismantling of the old Islamic fabric, was bound to antagonize Muslims. Thus Abdul Hamid II felt able to experiment with an Islamic identity, to distinguish again between Muslim and non-Muslim, to restore esteem to the *ulama*, though not their power, and to promulgate the idea that he was the caliph with spiritual authority over the whole Muslim community. The attempt was wrecked by its internal contradictions: Islam was a dangerous identity for an absolutism which fostered Western education and Western law; it was a liability for a ruler striving to cope with rebellious Christian subjects within and meddlesome Christian powers without. When the Young Turks came to power in 1908 the Islamic option was finished. There were two further possibilities: they could return to the supra-communal Ottoman identity, or they could turn to a completely new option, a Turkish identity. The theorist of Turkism was Ziya Gokalp (1876–1924) who, influenced by French sociologists, saw language as the only effective basis of nationality and argued that the genius of the Turkish speakers would be most fully expressed through the medium of Western civilization. At first the Young Turks backed the Ottoman identity; they could not find much in common with Turkish peasants and they still ruled an empire which also consisted of Greeks, Armenians and Arabs. The nature of the problem however, was changed dramatically by the final European assault which reduced the empire to its Anatolian heartland. Now only the Turkish option was left.

The man who gave life to this option was Mustafa Kemal (1881–1938), who later came to be called

Ataturk, meaning "Father Turk." The most successful Turkish general of World War I, he led his people to victory in 1922 against the Greeks who occupied Rumelia and western Anatolia. After making peace with the Allies in 1923, when they recognized the existence of a Turkish national state, he then set about bringing to fruition within this purely Turkish frame the modern secular system which the Ottomans had been building from the early 19th century and also pointing it firmly towards Western civilization. The sultanate was abolished in 1923, the caliphate in 1924, the last ruler of the august house of Osman being packed unceremoniously into the Orient Express for Paris. Religious schools and religious courts were swept away; the last vestiges of the *Sharia* were replaced by the Swiss legal code; state training of *ulama* ceased; sufi orders were abolished; their mosques and convents became museums; the Perso-Arabic script was replaced by the Roman; and the Turks were compelled to abandon their multifarious headgear in favor of the hat, which had long been a symbol of Europeanization and in which it was impossible to perform the Muslim prayer. Hence-

Above Abd al-Hamid II experimented with an Islamic identity for the modernizing Ottoman state, and strongly emphasized his claim to be caliph, or successor of the Prophet, as leader of the Muslim community. One symbol of this role was the railroad he built between 1900 and 1908 from Damascus through the Hijaz to Medina. Muslims contributed to the project from all over the world. It made life easier for pilgrims to Mecca; it also made it easier for the Ottomans to assert their authority over the peninsula. Here Principal Engineer Moukhtar Bey opens a stretch of the line.

Right The poster celebrates the emergence of the new Turkish republic after the treaty of Lausanne in 1923. Aggressively stating the modern and secular ideology of the new national state, an unveiled woman leads the victorious general of the war of independence, Ismet Inonu.

forth, Islam was to be a purely private affair, a matter of individual conscience. The whole process, moreover, was imposed by a Westernized elite. They succeeded in removing the last traces of the old high religious culture of Islam based on the *Sharia*, but among the people at large both sufi orders and a vigorous piety survived.

Egypt's divided response

Egypt also answered the European challenge by striving to modernize the army and to strengthen the state. In the beginning, moreover, the Egyptians were more vigorous than the Ottomans, which was to be expected as they had felt European military power more sharply. Their leader was Muhammad Ali, who ruled from 1805 to 1848; he was the commander of an Albanian contingent serving in the Anglo-Ottoman operations against the French invasion, who after becoming master of Cairo was appointed viceroy by the sultan. He created strong central government. By 1809 the *ulama* had submitted, and by 1811 the Mamluks, the old slave soldiery, had been massacred in a fashion which presaged the fate of the Janissaries. The endowments and tax farms of both groups were resumed, a huge system of monopolies was introduced to exploit trade and attempts were made to generate an industrial revolution. In command of new resources and new power, Muhammed Ali directed Egypt along a European road. A new conscript army was trained by foreign instructors, Egyptians were sent to study technical subjects in Europe, the rudiments of a state educational system imparting European knowledge were established, and participation in it was made the key to posts in the army and the bureaucracy.

Egypt gained in strength and wealth, but her growth was stunted by Europe. Muhammad Ali's armies spread his power to Arabia, the Sudan, Palestine, Syria and Greece, but when he threatened to advance into the Ottoman heartland, the

European powers intervened. The new enterprises of Muhammad Ali and his successors encouraged European intervention in the economy, which withered its expansion at the roots and shackled it to European finance and industry. By 1882 European involvement had led to British military occupation. They found a situation in Egypt in which there was a "modern" layer of society which had Western education, served the state and administered the law which was entirely based on French codes except in personal matters where the *Sharia* still held; there was also a "traditional" Islamic layer, trained at al-Azhar and the great network of schools attached to it, which survived Muhammed Ali's assault on the income of the *ulama* and which still taught 95 per cent of those Egyptians attending school.

The existence of these two distinct social and cultural layers was reflected in the 70 years of Egyptian history that followed. The campaign to free Egypt from British control was led by the heirs, in spirit at least, of Muhammad Ali; there was, for instance, Saad Zaghlul (1860–1927) who in 1919 founded the Wafd, the first mass nationalist party. This forced Britain to grant a limited independence in 1922. In the following decades it was Wafdists and other secular nationalists who led the fight to remove the last vestiges of British influence. At the same time they strove to extend the frontiers of the secular state into Egypt's still essentially Islamic society. The new constitution, promulgated in 1923, and based on Belgian and Ottoman models, asserted the sovereignty of the people as opposed to that of God. Vigorous measures were taken, after years of British neglect, to expand the state educational system which offered compulsory free elementary education from 1925. Active steps were also taken to bring al-Azhar, its curriculum, its *ulama* and its subject schools under government control. The *ulama*, on the other hand, played only a small role in the nationalist struggle. After participating in the mass agitations of 1919, which their countrywide network of pupils made possible, they withdrew.

Europeanization of dress was an important aspect of Ataturk's attempts to drag his people into the mainstream of Western civilization. "In some places I have seen women," he declared at Kastamonu in 1925, "who put a piece of cloth or a towel or something like it over their heads to hide their faces, and who turn their backs or huddle themselves on the ground when a man passes by. What are the meaning and sense of this behavior?... It is a spectacle that makes the nation an object of ridicule." *Left* Turkish women as Ataturk wished them to be: he dances with his adopted daughter at her wedding.

Right: Egyptian power under Muhammad Ali 1805–48 This ruler's ruthless policies of modernization along European lines brought Egypt considerable power in the eastern Mediterranean. He was able to suppress the Saudi-Wahhabi movement in Arabia, to conquer the Sudan, to campaign with success against the Greek nationalists, until the European powers intervened, and finally to conquer Syria and to advance into Anatolia itself. Nevertheless, even before this remarkable ruler (*inset*) died in 1848, the European powers were beginning to acquire the massive influence over the Egyptian economy which was to be a feature of its history in the coming century.

Below The Mamluks, the old slave soldiery, who ruled Egypt from 1260 and played a leading part in its politics after the Ottoman conquest, resisted Muhammad Ali's assertion of power. So in 1811 he invited nearly 500 Mamluk leaders to a reception. As they left on horseback down a narrow street, the gates were closed at either end and sharp shooters killed them to a man.

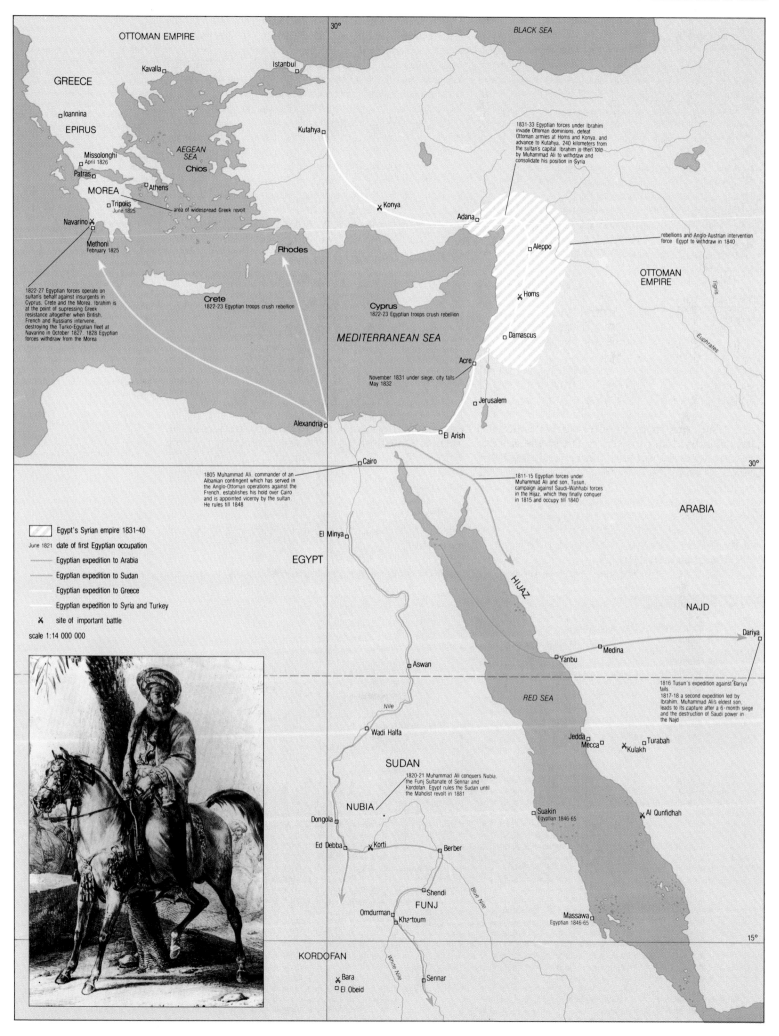

OTTOMAN EMPIRE

GREECE

Kavalla

Istanbul

Ioannina

EPIRUS

Missolonghi
April 1826

AEGEAN
SEA

Chios

Patras

MOREA

Athens

Tripolis
June 1825

Kutahya

area of widespread Greek revolt

Navarino

Methoni
February 1825

Konya

Adana

1831-33 Egyptian forces under Ibrahim
invade Ottoman dominions, defeat
Ottoman armies at Homs and Konya, and
advance to Kutahya, 240 kilometers from
the sultan's capital. Ibrahim is then told
by Muhammad Ali to withdraw and
consolidate his position in Syria

Aleppo

rebellions and Anglo-Austrian intervention
force Egypt to withdraw in 1840

OTTOMAN
EMPIRE

1822-27 Egyptian forces operate on
sultan's behalf against insurgents in
Cyprus, Crete and the Morea. Ibrahim is
at the point of supressing Greek
resistance altogether when British,
French and Russians intervene,
destroying the Turko-Egyptian fleet at
Navarino in October 1827. 1828 Egyptian
forces withdraw from the Morea

Rhodes

Crete
1822-23 Egyptian troops crush rebellion

Cyprus
1822-23 Egyptian troops crush rebellion

Homs

Damascus

MEDITERRANEAN SEA

Acre
November 1831 under siege, city falls
May 1832

Jerusalem

Alexandria

El Arish

Cairo

1805 Muhammad Ali, commander of an
Albanian contingent which has served in
the Anglo-Ottoman operations against the
French, establishes his hold over Cairo
and is appointed viceroy by the sultan.
He rules till 1848

1811-15 Egyptian forces under
Muhammad Ali and son, Tusun,
campaign against Saudi-Wahhabi forces
in the Hijaz, which they finally conquer
in 1815 and occupy till 1840

ARABIA

Egypt's Syrian empire 1831-40

June 1821 date of first Egyptian occupation

Egyptian expedition to Arabia

Egyptian expedition to Sudan

Egyptian expedition to Greece

Egyptian expedition to Syria and Turkey

site of important battle

scale 1:14 000 000

El Minya

EGYPT

HIJAZ

NAJD

Dariya

Medina

Yanbu

Aswan

1816 Tusun's expedition against Dariya
fails.
1817-18 a second expedition led by
Ibrahim, Muhammad Ali's eldest son,
leads to its capture after a 6-month siege
and the destruction of Saudi power in
the Najd

RED SEA

Wadi Halfa

Jedda
Mecca

Turabah

Kulakh

SUDAN

Nile

1820-21 Muhammad Ali conquers Nubia,
the Funj Sultanate of Sennar and
Kordofan. Egypt rules the Sudan until
the Mahdist revolt in 1881

NUBIA

Dongola

Suakin
Egyptian 1846-65

Al Qunfidhah

Ed Debba

Korti

Berber

Shendi

Blue Nile

FUNJ

Omdurman

Khartoum

Massawa
Egyptian 1846-65

KORDOFAN

White Nile

Sennar

Bara

El Obeid

Identifying the secular nationalists as their chief enemy, they went so far in their efforts to preserve their independence as to support the crown, which meant implicitly accepting the continued British presence. Religious-minded Egyptians did come forward, however, who were not content with the limp attitude of the *ulama* and the compromises with imperialism they seemed prepared to make. In the 1930s and 1940s a militant political organization grew up, the Muslim Brethren founded by Hassan al-Banna (1906–49), which aimed to impose on Muslims in Egypt and elsewhere, and by violence if necessary, a theocratic Islamic government. On the eve of the Free Officers' revolution in 1952 Egyptian society was still deeply divided. If the balance of power had come to lie with those who looked to a secular future, there was still powerful support in organization and in spirit for an Islamic vision.

Arab aspirations

We now turn to the eastern Arab provinces of the Ottoman empire. Their first attempt to throw off foreign rule failed, blocked by the ambitions of Britain and France. The opportunity came in 1914 after the Ottomans declared war on the Allies. Sharif Husain (died 1931), the hereditary ruler of Mecca and descendant of the Prophet, asked the British to support independence for Arab lands from the Taurus mountains to the Indian Ocean and from the Mediterranean Sea to the Iranian frontier. The British pledged support with the main exceptions of the *vilayats* of Baghdad and Basra, and of areas on the Mediterranean coast north of Palestine. The sharif compromised, which meant shelving some key issues, and raised the standard of Arab revolt on 10 June 1916. His forces advanced into Palestine with the British. They took Damascus on 1 October 1918, where, amid wild rejoicing, one of his sons, Prince Faisal, established an independent Arab

government. Arabs thought their dreams had come true. But the British had made other promises which conflicted with their pledges to Sharif Husain – in May 1916 the Sykes-Picot agreement with the French, and in November 1917 the Balfour Declaration, which supported the establishment of a Jewish national home in Palestine. The Arabs had barely tasted the sweets of freedom before the Allies locked them away again. In 1920 the League of Nations gave the French mandates to rule Lebanon and Syria, and after 21 months of independent government Faisal was chased out of Damascus by the French army. Churchill and other leading British statesmen had the grace to be embarrassed. In the same year the British received mandates for Iraq, for Transjordan and for Palestine, with the obligation to create in the last a Jewish national home.

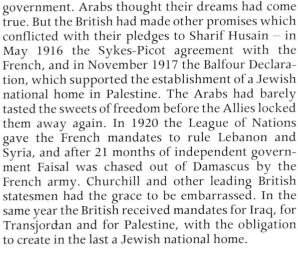

Egyptian society in the 20th century, like that of most Islamic countries, came to comprise two distinct social and cultural layers. There was the Islamic layer, symbolized by the university of al-Azhar, *bottom left*, which still, through the network of schools and teachers attached to it, controlled most Egyptian education, and with whose values most Egyptians identified. There was also the much thinner layer of men and women of European culture and education who participated in the activities of the modern state, leading the nationalist movement and collaborating with the European forces without. *Left* King Faruq of Egypt, in exile, at a nightclub with his close friend, the Italian singer, Irma Minutolo.

Right As soon as the Ottoman empire entered World War I on the German side, Britain and France were left with the problem first of protecting their interests in the region and then of making arrangements which would continue to protect those interests once the war was over.

Top: The Husain-McMahon understanding 1915
The map sets out those areas in which Sharif Husain of Mecca wanted to establish Arab independence after the war, and the more limited area in which the British, represented by Sir Henry McMahon, pledged support for such an ambition.

Center: The Sykes-Picot agreement 1916 and the Balfour Declaration 1917
The agreement between Sir Mark Sykes, representing Britain, and M. Georges-Picot, representing France, May–October 1916, and the promise made by the British Foreign Secretary, Balfour, to the Zionist movement, 2 November 1917, would appear to have conflicted with the spirit of the Husain-McMahon understanding; Arabs at the time, and since, most certainly believed that it did.

Bottom: The new arrangements in the Arab lands 1920–21
The eventual postwar settlement in the Arab lands was reached at the San Remo conference of April 1920 and the Cairo conference of 1921. The outcome, in the form of League of Nations mandates to France and Britain, was essentially the Sykes-Picot agreement revised in favor of French, British and Zionist interests; the Balfour promise for the development of a Jewish national home was written into the Palestine mandate. The Arabs felt cheated. The vision of freedom and democracy, which opened up with the fall of the Ottoman empire, was shattered. Instead they were subject, if only for the mandatory period, to European imperialism, which was pledged to establish an alien people in Palestine. To appease Arab feelings, and to lighten their consciences, the British at the Cairo conference gave two sons of Sharif Husain territories to govern. Faisal, whom the French had expelled from

Damascus, where he had ruled a free Arab state, was made king of Iraq. Abd Allah was made amir of Transjordan. Thus, between 1915 and 1921, in the interaction of British and French imperialism and Jewish and Arab nationalism, the framework for the subsequent political development of the area was laid down.

Husain proposed that Great Britain should recognize the independence of the Arab countries "which are bounded: on the north by the line Mersin-Adana to parallel 37°N and thence along the line Birecik-Urfa-Midiat-Jazirat-Amadia to the Persian frontier; and on the east, by the Persian frontier down to the Persian Gulf; on the south, by the Indian Ocean (with the exclusion of Aden whose status will remain as at present); on the west, by the Red Sea and the Mediterranean Sea back to Mersin."

McMahon agreed to Husain's proposals with the following crucial modifications: "The districts of Mersin and Alexandretta, and portions of Syria lying to the west of the districts of Damascus, Homs, Hama and Aleppo, cannot be said to be purely Arab, and must on that account be excepted from the proposed delimitation." That these modifications were made without prejudice to "our existing treaties with Arab chiefs," i.e. in the Persian Gulf region. That Britain made her pledge in those "regions lying within the proposed frontiers, in which Britain is free to act without detriment to the interests of her ally fronts . . ." That the Arabs recognize ". . . the fact of Great Britain's established position in the two vilayets of Baghdad and Basra."

Husain accepted the modifications regarding Mersin and Alexandretta; he agreed to a short British occupation of Baghdad and Basra without prejudice to the interests of either party; he did not agree to the modifications regarding Syria west of the line from Damascus to Aleppo, but continued to work with the British.

The 1917 Balfour Declaration supports the establishment of a Jewish national home in Palestine, "it being clearly understood that nothing shall be done which may prejudice the civil and religious rites of existing non-Jewish communities in Palestine . . ."

Syria: 1918 Faisal, son of Sharif Husain, establishes an independent Arab government in Damascus.

Palestine: terms of the Balfour Declaration are written into the mandate.

Transjordan: 1921 separated from Palestine, and Abd Allah, son of Sharif Husain, made amir.

Iraq: 1921 after being forced to flee from Syria for opposing the French mandate, Faisal made king of Iraq. Anglo-French oil agreement providing France with 25 per cent of Iraqi oil; in return Mosul included in British mandate.

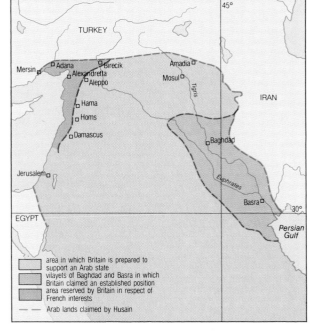

area in which Britain is prepared to support an Arab state
vilayets of Baghdad and Basra in which Britain claimed an established position
area reserved by Britain in respect of French interests
— — — Arab lands claimed by Husain

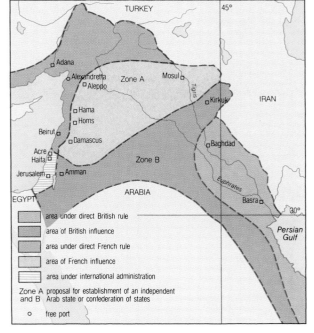

area under direct British rule
area of British influence
area under direct French rule
area of French influence
area under international administration

Zone A and B   proposal for establishment of an independent Arab state or confederation of states
o   free port

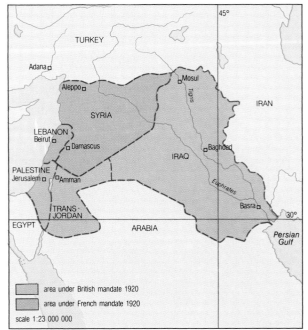

area under British mandate 1920
area under French mandate 1920

scale 1:23 000 000

The dashing of Arab hopes after World War I brought a new militancy to Arab nationalism which was now nourished by a lively resentment both of Anglo-French domination and of Jewish settlement. There was also a growing secularism of thought as those who had had the education of the last Ottoman years and of the mandatory regimes began to make their mark in public life. We can see their impact in the changing relationship between Arab nationalism and Islam. Arabs could not circumvent the problem of Islam in the same way as the Turks. Islam was the great Arab contribution to history, and it had given them unity, law and culture. It was even possible to regard Muhammad as the first Arab nationalist: his message was not easily ignored. There were potential advantages here in that *ulama* could try to reconcile Islam to an Arab national state. Muhammad Abduh (1849–1905), a brilliant rector of al-Azhar, laid the foundation by demonstrating that Islam and modern European thought were reconcilable. His pupil, the Syrian Rashid Rida (1865–1935), went further and asserted at the time of the Arab rising in World War I that the political interests of the Arabs were the same as those of the community as a whole, and that an independent Arab state would put new life into the language and into the *Sharia* which would form its law. But by the 1930s very different views were coming to dominate. Islam was no longer seen as the binding agent of an Arab national state, but just as a strand in a broader Arab culture. Arabic, men argued, was the foundation of national solidarity. This transformation was of major significance. It enabled Christians, who after all had been the earliest promoters of secular nationalism, to appropriate the Arab Muslim heritage. Egyptians and other North Africans could be included in the Arab nation as well and whatever non-Islamic ideas were useful could be exploited. One outcome was the foundation of the socialist Baath, or resurgence party, which came to power in Syria and Iraq in 1963. Arabs could now build a modern state, or states, and treat Islam purely as culture.

Developments in the Arabian peninsula offer a totally different picture. It is, indeed, one unique in the 20th-century history of Islam, the major processes deriving not from the interactions between Islam and the European world but entirely from a rekindling of the spirit of revival which had awoken there in the 18th century. The actors were the same as before, the Saudi family allied to Wahhabi *ulama*. For much of the 19th century their fortunes had fluctuated and the end of the century found the Saudi house in exile in Kuwait. Then the family produced one of the greatest Muslim leaders of the 20th century, Abd al-Aziz Ibn Saud (1880–1953), who from 1902 began to rebuild Saudi-Wahhabi power in the Najd. From 1912 his strength was greatly enhanced as he began to wield a weapon of his own devising, the *Ikhwan* or Brothers. For some time he had been sending Wahhabi *ulama* among the Bedouin to persuade them to forego their un-Islamic practices and shiftless nomadic habits and settle in self-sufficient missionary and military agricultural communities. Here they lived lives of extreme asceticism and literal adherence to the *Sharia*, beating, for instance, women who wore silks or men who were late for prayers. Over 200 such communities were founded, whose members'

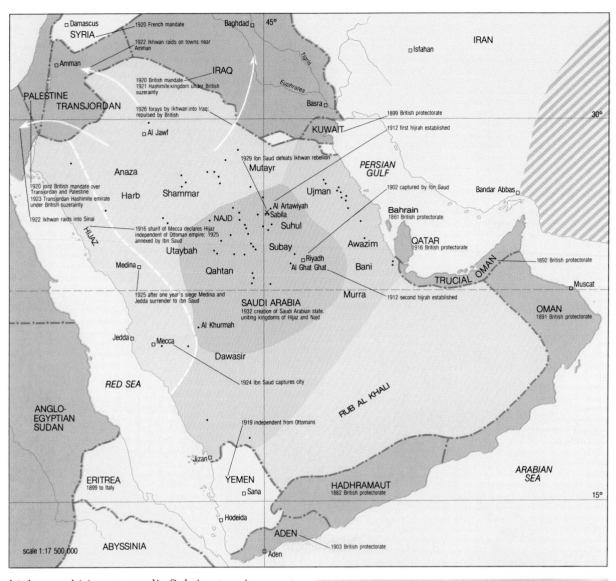

From the beginning of the 20th century the Saudi family, allied with Wahhabi *ulama*, built a state in Arabia as they had done in the 18th century. Aged 21, Abd al-Aziz Ibn Saud began the process in 1902 with a daring night raid when with 40 followers he captured the town of Riyadh, capital of the Najd. He finished the process 23 years later, after conquering the Hijaz from Sharif Husain, which made him master of the land which from 1932 was called the Kingdom of Saudi Arabia. Apart from his remarkable gifts as a leader of men, two facts were central to Ibn Saud's success: no great power wished to intervene in central Arabia; and he created a shock force, committed to die fighting for Islam, in the form of the *Ikhwan*. Over 200 military-cum-missionary agricultural communities, or *hijrah*, committed to Wahhabi religious ideas, were established in the Arabian heartland, as the map reveals. They provided a firm basis for the early Saudi state and led its expansion. Eventually their religious idealism clashed with Abd al-Aziz's desire to create a modern and internationally acceptable state.

extent of Ibn Saud's territory

in 1912

in 1920

in 1925

sharif of Mecca and Medina

. hijrah (a representative distribution, after Habib)

Harb tribal name

area under British mandate or protection

area of British influence

highest ambition was to die fighting to raise men to their own puritan Islamic standard. With the aid of this remarkable force, and unimpeded by the desire of any great power to intervene, Abd al-Aziz gradually spread his rule over Arabia until by 1925 he had emulated the achievement of his ancestors over a century before by conquering the Hijaz and by imposing their fundamentalist views on religious practice in the holy cities of Mecca and Medina.

Once Abd al-Aziz had achieved power and declared himself king, the *Ikhwan* became an embarrassment. They objected to his introduction of motor cars and telephones and they knew no international frontiers in their campaigns against unbelievers, coming to blows with the British in Iraq and Transjordan. He was forced to destroy the demon he had created and most of the *Ikhwan* died at the battle of Sabila in 1929. Nevertheless, the basis of his state, known as Saudi Arabia from 1932, was the *Sharia* which was administered in full through the courts. Modernization took place within the framework of divine law, royal decrees regulating areas where the *Sharia* did not run. In this respect the development of modern Saudi Arabia was quite different from that of any other Muslim state. After oil was discovered in 1938 and power returned to the birthplace of Islam, it was to be a difference of the first significance for Muslims throughout the world.

Left Abd al-Aziz Ibn Saud (seated left), founder of the Saudi Arabian state, with other male members of his family in 1911.

Right: Russian and British imperialism in Iran 1800–1946
From 1800 till after World War II the development of Iran was constantly subject to the commercial ambitions and strategic rivalries of Britain and Russia. The new strength given to Iranian government by the rise of Riza Shah Pahlavi also brought greater independence, although the Russian and British occupation in World War II revealed that Iran's fundamental weakness in relation to the great powers had not changed. An understanding of the way in which outside forces have influenced Iran's destiny during the past two centuries helps to explain the occasionally passionate xenophobia of its politics.

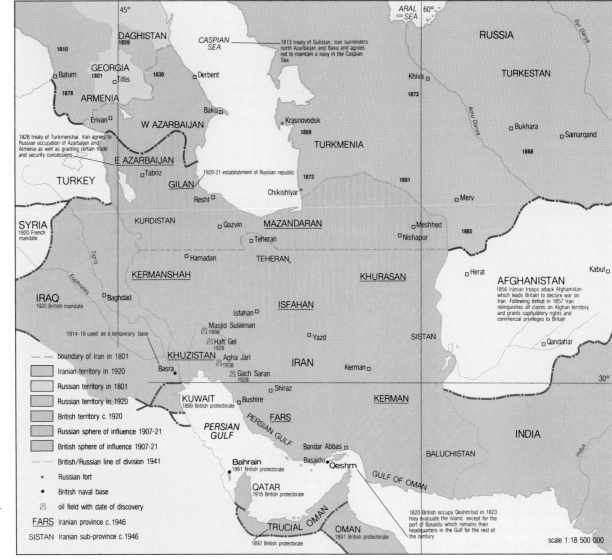

Below Amir Sultan Bin Abd al-Rahman al-Dawish, son of the governor of al-Artawiyah, the first *Ikhwan hijrah*; he fought Abd al-Aziz at the battle of Sabila (1929). He holds part of a bullet-ridden *Ikhwan* war banner on which we can see the words Allah and Muhammad from the full confession of faith which was written all along the banner.

Iran's struggle for independence

The responses of Iran to Europe make interesting comparison with the Ottoman empire and with Egypt. There were similarities, but there were also important differences, notably the later drive for modernization, the weaker power of the state and the greater power of the *ulama*.

Pressure from Britain and Russia was continuous throughout the 19th century and into the 20th century. The Russians aimed to extend their possessions in Iran as far as was feasible and to lay the foundations for the commercial and political domination of the remainder of the country. By 1828 they lived in Iran under their own law, not the *Sharia*. By the 1870s they had made considerable territorial gains on both sides of the Caspian Sea. Between 1907 and 1921 they asserted a sphere of influence in northern Iran and again during World War II. The British were concerned with the defense of India and the development of commerce. They wanted a strong independent Iran able to keep the Russians away from the Persian Gulf and the borders of India. Between 1907 and 1921 they asserted a sphere of influence in southeastern Iran which was extended to the whole of southern Iran in World War II. From the 1870s Anglo-Russian commercial rivalry was also intense. In 1872 Baron de Reuter, a British subject, was granted a countrywide monopoly including railroad construction, mining and banking. Russian counter-demands quickly followed and in 1878 they were granted permission to raise, equip and train an Iranian Cossack regiment. By far the most pervasive and disliked foreign commercial presence was the Anglo-Iranian Oil Company, later British Petroleum, which first struck oil in 1908 and quickly grew to be the country's dominant economic enterprise.

The main reason why Britain and Russia were able to penetrate Iran with such ease was that central government was weak. Iranian society at this time is best seen as a collection of semi-autonomous estates: religious and ethnic minorities (Armenians, Assyrians, Jews, Zoroastrians, amounting to about 10 per cent of the population), tribes (Kurds, Lurs, Bakhtiars etc., amounting to between 25 and 50 per cent of the population), merchants who formed close networks across the land and were the major source of loans to government, and *ulama* whose power, in stark contrast to that of their contemporaries in the Ottoman empire and Egypt, was increasing. We have already seen how under the later Safavids the *ulama* had begun to promote the theory that in the absence of the Twelfth Imam only a *mujtahid*, a scholar deeply learned in the *Sharia* and whose life was without blemish, could rule. The theory was further elaborated in the 18th century so that most *ulama* and most Iranians came to believe that they must seek guidance from a living *mujtahid*. *Ulama* who achieved this status had extraordinary power. It was bolstered, moreover, by the social functions and economic strength of the group as a whole. They had total control over education, the law and the administration of charitable works. They had huge endowments, large landholdings and received annually one-fifth of the disposable income of each devout Shia, half to support the poor and half to support their work. Religious specialists with such powers might well have found popular support hard to win. These *ulama*, however, had a symbiotic relationship with the people; they progressed towards the rank of *mujtahid* not by government appointment, nor by the election of their peers, but through a combination of scholarship and popular standing. They formed a great independent corporation firmly rooted in the people. No ruler could afford to ignore them.

Like the Ottoman sultans and the Egyptian khedives, the Qajar shahs strove to build up the power of central government. The work really began in the reign of Nasir al-Din (1848–96) and as elsewhere attention was paid first to the army. The equivalent of the massacres of the Janissaries and the Mamluks was Nasir al-Din's abolition of the old feudal army and his raising of battalions whose first loyalty was to the state and not to landowners or tribal leaders. A college was established in 1851 to give army officers and bureaucrats Western learning. In the 1860s central government was further strengthened by bureaucratic reforms and the introduction of the telegraph, and in 1873 Nasir al-Din felt secure enough to make the first of his three visits to Europe. Then he tried to hasten the pace of modernization by granting concessions to Europeans: the Reuter concession and the Cossack brigade, as well as rights granted to Christian missionaries to establish schools and hospitals, were part of the process. *Ulama* were bound to oppose

Left Fath Ali Shah Qajar (reigned 1797–1834), the last Iranian monarch truly confident in his world beyond the reach of Europe.

Top Nasir al-Din Shah, who came to the throne 14 years after Fath Ali Shah died, knew that Iran would have to master the secrets of Western power if it was to survive. In his 48-year reign he strove to build up the authority of central government against the *ulama*, the tribes and the merchants, and to introduce all the Western learning and the Western finance he could to help him in the process. He was assassinated in 1896 by a follower of the religious reformer and pan-Islamic thinker, Jamal al-Din al-Afghani.

Above Riza Shah Pahlavi, the next shah markedly to push forward policies of the centralization of power and the adoption of Western learning. Starting life as a boy tending his father's sheep in the pastures of Mazandaran, he grew up to found the Pahlavi dynasty. The Allies forced him to abdicate in 1941 after he brought Iran into World War II on the side of the Axis powers.

Right: The Muslim press in Russia 1917
The map reveals how the community was spread widely from the Baltic coast to Turkestan; Baku and Kazan, the old capital of the Volga Tatars, were the major centers. Turkestan, where most Muslims lived, had relatively the fewest papers, although the number increased greatly between the Revolution of 1917 and 1920.

such developments. The growth of Western education, the presence of missionaries, increasing European influence and the extension of royal power threatened their position. They led a successful protest against the Reuter concession in 1873. They led another successful protest against a British tobacco monopoly in 1891/2, persuading Iranians to forego smoking for several months, and they led the early stages of the constitutional revolution of 1905–11, in which, allied with the merchants of Teheran and a small group of Western-educated radicals, they succeeded in imposing a democratic constitution on the royal regime. At first sight their leadership of the revolution seems paradoxical. It was not. They were concerned to defend the *Sharia* and the Islamic quality of Iranian life against royal government and Western-educated radical alike. They inserted provisions to meet these ends in the constitution which was promulgated in 1906, and when it became clear that their Western-educated allies did not intend to uphold them, they went into opposition.

A dramatic increase in the authority of central government took place after Colonel Riza Khan (1878–1942) of the Cossack brigade seized power in 1921 and used it to make himself shah in 1926. At the heart of this greater government power was a new unified standing army which was both to curb the forces of decentralization and to help modernize society. A secular pattern of development was now imposed. In 1921 a comprehensive and compulsory system of state education with a Westernized curriculum was introduced; in 1935 the university of Teheran was founded; Iranians were sent abroad for further studies. Secular codes of law replaced the *Sharia*, religious courts were stripped of their functions, and only Western-educated men were allowed to sit as judges. Like Ataturk, whom he greatly admired, Riza Shah wanted Iranians to adopt the outward symbols of a secular society. From 1928 men who were not *ulama* had to wear Western dress. From 1935 they had to wear hats with brims.

From 1936 women had to go unveiled, and police were employed to rip the veils from those who dared to ignore the shah's command. Overall, this soldier's achievements were considerable. Iran was freed from much foreign political and economic domination, a modern state of secular style was firmly established in Iranian life and the power of the *ulama* was greatly curtailed. That the *ulama* did not come to suffer the same fate as their Turkish contemporaries was in large part due to World War II, which brought about the shah's abdication and ushered in two decades of relatively weak government. The *ulama* were able to regain some of their losses and to preserve the fabric of an Islamic society within the modernizing Iranian state.

Renaissance and suppression in Russia
For the most part so far we have been studying the responses of Muslims concerned to keep the foreigner out of their lands. Now we turn to the responses of Muslims in a different situation, those already under alien rule in Central, southern and southeast Asia and in Africa. Here responses depended in part on the impact of the colonial power and in part on the position of Islam in society. Two points are clear: because Muslims were being ruled by non-Muslims, whether Christians or atheists, Islam, or at least Islamic culture, usually moved closer to the center of their identity than in Turkey or even Iran; and because colonial regimes often felt weak and had developed a healthy respect for their subjects' religious susceptibilities, they were often cautious in attacking Islamic institutions.

Russian policy in the northern Islamic lands stimulated a revival of Islam in the 19th century. Its roots lay in Catherine the Great's rehabilitation of the Volga Tatars, whose religious and economic freedoms had been much limited since their conquest in the 16th century. Restrictions on their trading activities were lifted which enabled them to monopolize the growing trade between Russia and

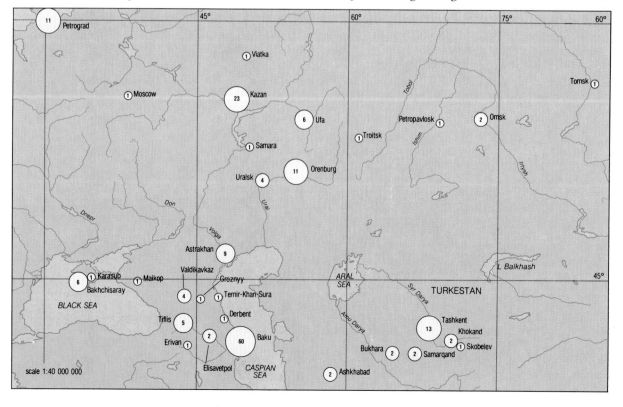

Political Cartoons

Newspapers published by Muslims for Muslims began to be founded from the late 1820s, and the credit for producing the first probably belongs to Muhammad Ali of Egypt. It was not, however, till the late 19th century that a really vigorous press developed and, although censorship both by colonial governments and by Muslim rulers often exercised a severe check on growth, by the end of the first decade of the 20th century there were about 150 newspapers and periodicals in Egypt and 160 in Central Asia, over 370 in Iran and perhaps more in Ottoman Turkey, while even in China at least 100 Muslim papers were founded between 1913 and 1939. Among the outstanding papers should be noted the *Terjuman*, founded in 1883 by the Crimean Tatar reformer, Ismail Bey Gasprinski, the *Aligarh Institute Gazette*, founded in 1866 by the Indian reformer, Saiyid Ahmad Khan, and *al-Jawaib*, the leading Arabic paper of the late 19th century. The cartoons of two leading satirical papers, *Mulla Nasreddin*, published spasmodically from Tiflis in the Caucasus from 1906 to 1917, and *Awadh Punch*, published from Lucknow in north India from 1877 to the 1930s, reveal something of the flavor of this journalism.

Mulla Nasreddin was a vigorously nonconformist weekly, published by a group of progressive writers and poets who attacked all forms of conservatism, especially the religious fanaticism of the Shiite *ulama*, who were denounced in almost every issue for being unable to resist European imperialism effectively, for representing an obstacle to progress and for compromising with the tsarist regime. Landlords and capitalists were attacked, the venality of judges exposed and the stupidity of schoolmasters mocked. On the other hand, the work of the reformer, Ismail Bey Gasprinski, was highly praised. Humorous vignettes, like the ones shown *left* and *opposite far right*, were scattered through the issues of the journal. *Bottom left* Cartoon on the front page of the very first issue establishing its concerns: the Muslims are still asleep; Mulla Nasreddin aims to wake them up. *Bottom right* No caption is needed for this gathering of smugly sleeping *ulama*. It is eloquent with contempt. *Top right* Gasprinski, the educational reformer, is squashed by an unholy alliance of Tatar schoolmaster and Russian school superintendent. In the caption, the schoolmaster declares: "The minds of the young Tatars who go to the new schools are daily corrupted." To which the superintendent replies: "Recently the young Tatars have slipped towards the left. We must strengthen the old schools and forbid the new." *Right* Here again we find Gasprinski in trouble with the *ulama* who are attacking him with accusations that he is an infidel and that his new method of education is against the holy law.

Below In this savage comment on the consolidation of Russian expansion in Central Asia, entitled the "Colonization Problem," a Russian official snaps at some Kirghiz, "Out of here, we need this room for Ukrainians."

Awadh Punch was the literary and humorous magazine of the sophisticated Urdu-speaking landed and service elite of northern India. British rule, Muslim politics, nationalist politics, all were targets for its wit, and like most of the Indo-Muslim press it was especially aware of events in the wider Islamic world.

Above left This distressing scene, published on 12 November 1920, refers to the non-cooperation protest, launched by Muslims to persuade the British to protect the Turkish caliphate, in which a national Muslim university was established and threatened the premier Muslim university at Aligarh. A particularly venomous-looking representative of the *ulama* and Muhammad Ali, founder of the National Muslim University, helped by a Hindu, saw away at a representative of the Aligarh establishment. On the saw is written: "The crescent-shaped saw of the National Free University," while the victim screams "sacrificing old educational centers."

Left Britain, represented by John Bull, negotiates with Egypt astride a donkey, 23 June 1922. Egypt won its much-qualified independence from Britain in February 1922.

her expanding Muslim empire. Tatars spread through the new Russian territories making fortunes where Russian merchants feared to travel. Much of the new wealth was invested in industry around Kazan and the Tatars became the leading entrepreneurs of the Volga region. Religious disabilities were also removed and, subject to a council of *ulama* at Orenburg, the Tatars were free to fashion an Islamic society. Liberty allied to prosperity stimulated progress: literally thousands of Islamic elementary schools were founded, many publishing houses were set up and a distinctive Tatar Islamic culture began to flourish.

At first the Tatars were much influenced by the cultural standards set by the great Uzbeg cities of Bukhara and Samarqand. They copied their dress and customs, they began to veil their women and they attacked those who slipped from a high Sunni orthodoxy. But then, having ridden the wave of Russian expansion, they began to feel Russian competition. In Central Asia Russian administrators began to discriminate in favor of Russian traders, and in the Volga region Russian industrialists were beginning to overtake their less advanced Tatar rivals. The Tatars responded by trying to absorb Russian learning in their Islamic education system. The way was shown by such leading Tatar intellectuals as Shihab al-Din Marjani (1815–89), who, like Muhammad Abduh, declared that modern science was compatible with the Quran, and Abd al-Qaiyum al-Nasiri (1825–1902), who made the Tatar language an effective educational tool. Then a Crimean Tatar, Ismail Bey Gasprinski (1851–1915), pioneered a new phonetic method of learning Arabic and a new curriculum which included secular subjects. This modern method quickly spread and also began to involve instruction in the vernacular. Thus Muslim education came to be divided between the modern style, which was most favored in the lands of the Volga Tatars where one-third of the population was literate, and the traditional style, which still held sway in Central Asia.

The years between the revolutions of 1905 and 1917 presented opportunities, but Muslims could not agree on a common policy. The leading Tatar modernists joined their Christian fellow subjects in demanding political liberalization. They envisaged the creation of an autonomous Muslim regime in which Turkish would be the common language. In 1905 and 1906 three Muslim congresses were held, but only the Tatars and the Azarbaijanis could agree on common political action. Other Muslim delegates thought more in terms of autonomy or even independence for their particular linguistic group. Between the February and October revolutions of 1917 the Tatar modernists made a second attempt to coordinate Muslim Russia, but the congresses which gathered in Moscow and Kazan met the same response; the other Muslim peoples were indifferent to the concept of pan-Turkic unity. For a few months more they played with their dreams of religio-cultural autonomy. Then the Communists took over.

Some men of Muslim culture became Communists, progressing through modernism into a secular view of the world; some, too, had dreams of a "Muslim" future. Mir Sultan Galiev (c. 1900–?), the son of a Tatar schoolteacher, was one. He served on the People's Commissariat for Nationalities under Stalin and founded a Muslim Communist Party. He argued that Muslim society, with the exception of a few big landowners and bourgeois, had been collectively oppressed by tsarist Russians. There was no point in dividing it by creating artificial class struggles; liberation from foreign rule was the key issue. The situation of Muslims in Russia, in fact, was but in miniature that of oppressed colonial peoples throughout the world. Who better than they to bear the torch of revolution into Asia and beyond? Such talk, of course, was heresy, and when Galiev began to organize his fellow Tatars against what he called the "Great Russian Chauvinism," he had to be silenced. He is to be remembered as the first man who dared suggest that Marxism could be nationalized.

For Muslim believers, as opposed to those who were merely Muslim by culture, the development of the revolution was even more of a disaster. The last century of tsarist rule had witnessed a renaissance in their Islamic life. Religious endowments were tolerated; over a hundred thousand hectares of the Crimea, for instance, were devoted to this purpose. The *Sharia* was widely applied, although in most areas restricted to the civil and petty criminal fields. Schools flourished, and if Muslims had come to divide between the traditional and the modernist methods, all learning was contained within an Islamic frame. Fasts were observed; prayers continued in thousands of mosques. Within a decade all had been destroyed: the *Sharia* abolished, religious endowments expropriated, schools closed down. The veil was attacked, the Arabic script no longer used, Qurans were collected and publicly burned. *Ulama* suffered disabilities, defamation and eventually deportation to labor camps. Mosques were shut; of the 24562 mosques in 1914 only 1312, according to official figures, remained in 1942. Muslims were driven to extraordinary ingenuity to perform their rites: in Tashkent they were discovered using the Red Teahouse, the local Communist propaganda center, as a mosque; in Turkestan the shrine of Shaikh Ahmad Yasavi was converted into an "anti-religious" museum, yet prayers continued to be held although now worshipers entered by ticket and masqueraded as "anti-religious" tourists. The resort to such subterfuge tells its own story; Islam had to go underground to survive.

Separatism in south Asia

Under the British in southern Asia Muslims did not suffer wholesale destruction of their institutions. Admittedly, by the end of the 19th century the application of the *Sharia* had been reduced to the domain of family law. On the other hand, the endowments which sustained religious institutions were untouched; the state had merely begun to concern itself with their more efficient administration. The Islamic educational system was also untouched; it was open to Indian Muslims to send as many of their boys to Quran schools and madrasas as they wished. *Ulama* could transmit the core of the Islamic tradition, men could dress as they pleased, women could go veiled. Nevertheless, British rule did seem to bring serious threats to Islam. Muslims saw Christian missionaries setting up schools, preaching on street corners and trying to make converts. In the mid-19th century,

moreover, they knew they were supported by leading British officials, some of whom wrote works deeply unsympathetic to Islam. They saw the steady construction of a secular state system, of schools which taught only European knowledge, of law which owed nothing to the *Sharia*, of government posts for which traditional Muslim education was of no value, and they feared that if they wished to gain access to this new source of power, they would have to desert Islam. They became increasingly aware that they were a minority in India, just over 20 per cent of the population, and were in danger of being overwhelmed by sheer weight of numbers. Such worries became acute as they came to realize the meaning of the growth of electoral government. Devout Hindus, who came to control town councils, could with much popular acclaim make it harder for Muslims to eat beef or celebrate their religious festivals. Hindus, who came to control provincial councils, could destroy the role of the Urdu language and the Perso-Arabic script in public life. Indian Muslims seemed to be faced with a hard struggle to preserve their civilization in a world which was increasingly dominated by European and Hindu ideas and values. They began to despair and their mood was well expressed by the poet, Altaf Husain Hali (1837–1914):

When Autumn has set in over the garden, why
        speak of the springtime of flowers?
When shadows of adversity hang over the present,
        why harp on the pomp and glory of the past?
Yea, these are things to forget; but how can you
with the dawn forget the scene of the night before?
The assembly has just dispersed;
The smoke is still rising from the burnt candle;
The footprints on the sands of India still say:
A graceful caravan has passed this way.

The Muslim response was led by Muslims from northern India, in particular the area known under the British as the United Provinces. Muslims, in fact, were scattered throughout India, the largest concentrations being in the northwest and the northeast, in the Punjab and Bengal, where they formed the majority of the population. But it was in the United Provinces, where Muslim empires had usually been based, that intellectual and cultural traditions remained most vigorous. Here, for instance, were the great families of *ulama* and sufis who had given intellectual and spiritual leadership down the centuries. Many responded to the new order introduced by the British with sullen acquiescence. Those who were more positive made it clear that no concessions were to be made. They were led by men educated in the reformist traditions of Shah Wali Allah and Shah Abd al-Aziz of Delhi. They debated with Christian missionaries, usually had the better of the argument and produced the basis of Muslim apologetic which came to be widely used in India and elsewhere. They declared holy war against the British in the Mutiny uprising of 1857. A decade later they founded a madrasa at Deoband, close to Delhi, which taught a typically reformist Islam, emphasizing the *Hadiths*, the *Sharia* and restrained sufi practice. This school played the central role in sustaining the *ulama* through the coming century, founding many branch institutions and becoming respected for its learning throughout the Islamic world. Other schools of *ulama*, like that of Firangi Mahal in Lucknow, became more active. All were agreed as to how society should be rightly ordered. "The national life," declared one leading scholar in 1894, "is in the *ulama*'s right of ownership ... and they alone have or can have absolute sway over it." They repeated the point to the British when asked how power should be devolved: the only true "Home Rule" for Muslims, declared the leading scholar of Firangi Mahal, was the enforcement of the *Sharia*.

As elsewhere in the Islamic world, there were Muslims who felt that power on this earth could only be satisfactorily answered in its own terms and who were determined that Muslims should have the strength to do so. Their leader was Saiyid Ahmad Khan (1817–98), who came from a service family long associated with the Mughal court in Delhi, but also from a milieu in which the reformist ideas of Shah Wali Allah and Shah Abd al-Aziz were strong. The most remarkable Indian Muslim of the 19th century, indeed a "renaissance man" in the spread of his interests and his achievements, his prime concern was that his coreligionists should continue to wield power in India. "The more worldly progress we make," went his motto, "the more glory Islam gains." He set out to demonstrate that Islam was compatible with modern science, becoming in the process the most radical theologian of his time. In 1877 he founded a college at Aligarh, the Muhammadan Anglo-Oriental College, which offered a Muslim environment in which young Muslims could imbibe Western learning. He discouraged his coreligionists from having anything to do with Indian nationalism, declaring that their interests would be best served through a close relationship with the colonial government. The outcome of his work was to produce men who were Muslim less by faith than by culture, although after being raised in Aligarh's Muslim revivalist air their identification with that culture could be intense. They studied European subjects in English and the ablest went on to Oxford and Cambridge; they also learned how to behave at tea parties and to play cricket rather well. Thus equipped, these men were able to bid for power in the new system created by the British, getting jobs in government service, speaking in council chambers and when need be forming political organizations. A satirist of the time saw what had been taking place:

But most of those who head this modern school
Neither believe in God, nor yet in prayer.
They *say* they do, but it is plain to see
What *they* believe in is the powers that be.

Akbar Allahabadi;
trans. R. Russell and Khurshidul Islam

Men from Aligarh were at the heart of most Muslim political activity down to the partition of India in 1947. Some became Indian nationalists, supporting the Indian National Congress, but most supported separate Muslim political organizations. Opinions vary as to why these Muslims should have been unwilling to throw in their lot with Indian nationalism. Any explanation, however, has to take into account the influence of Muslim revivalism, the policies of the colonial government, the material interests of particular Muslim groups, Muslim fears of the close association between Hindu revivalism and the Indian National Congress, and the powerful sense of community generated by Islam which influenced even those who were Muslim mainly by culture. This said, the growth of separate Muslim political activity was not a steadily rising line on a graph. The All-India Muslim League, the organization of Muslim separatist politics, was founded in 1906. In 1909 it had its first great victory when it succeeded in imposing separate electorates and reserved seats for Muslims on colonial India's growing system of electoral government. But in 1916 it allied itself with the Indian National Congress, in 1919 it was wafted aside by a mass protest over the fate of Turkey, in the 1920s and 1930s it was feeble and in the 1937 general elections it won little more than a fifth of the seats reserved for Muslims. Yet, the result of the next elections in 1946 was a different story: the League won 446 of the 495 seats in the various elected councils. World War II, the failures of the Indian National Congress and the leadership of Muhammad Ali Jinnah (1876–1948) had transformed the political situation. At virtually the last moment before the British left India the League found itself in a position to take separate Muslim political organization to its logical conclusion and to dictate the formation of a Muslim state out of the Muslim majority areas of northeast and northwest India. Thus those Muslims who were trained to seek power in the new state system succeeded in capturing control of a large slice of the subcontinent.

The idea of creating a separate Muslim state on the Indian subcontinent had grown slowly in the two decades before 1947. It was not the ideal solution to Muslim problems as Muhammad Iqbal (1878–1938) emphasized:

Our essence is not bound to any place;
The vigor of our wine is not contained
In any bowl; Chinese and Indian
Alike the shard that constitutes our jar,
Turkish and Syrian alike the clay
Forming our body; neither is our heart
Of India, or Syria, or Rum,
Nor any fatherland do we profess
Except Islam.

Rumuz-i Bekhudi, 1918;
trans. Arberry

Indian Muslims were part of the worldwide Muslim community, which ideally continued to exist as a confessional, social and political unity. But 20th-century reality was very different:

Now brotherhood has been so cut to shreds
That in the stead of community
The country has been given pride of place
In men's allegiance and constructive work;
The country is the darling of their hearts,
And wide humanity is whittled down
Into dismembered tribes ...

Indian Muslims, Iqbal argued, must accept this disappointing reality and create some form of compromise between Islam and the modern national

Muslim separatism in India and the foundation of Pakistan

For many Muslims one of the most heartening events during the retreat of European colonialism was the emergence of the Islamic Republic of Pakistan on the south Asian subcontinent. Although large numbers of the subcontinent's Muslims still lived in Hindu-dominated India, in Pakistan at least Muslims could mold state and society on Islamic lines, if they chose. Ten years before the partition in 1947 few would have thought such an outcome possible. In the general elections of 1937 the All-India Muslim League, the organization of Muslim separatism, won barely more than one-fifth of the seats especially reserved for Muslims. Yet in the next elections of 1945–46 it was able to demonstrate that it had the support of Muslims throughout the land. The drive behind the rise of the League, without which there could have been no Pakistan, came from Muslims of the Muslim-minority provinces, most notably the United Provinces. They had to have the support of Muslims in the Muslim-majority provinces if the League was to be taken seriously, and here it is important to note that it was not long before the partition that the League was able to demonstrate that it had the support of Muslims in Bengal and the Punjab, the two key areas in the new state of Pakistan. Moreover, the actual partition was probably not inevitable till the failure of the Cabinet Mission plan in June 1946; in May 1946 the League had agreed to the Mission's proposals which would have enabled Muslims to create a kind of Pakistan within a federal India. For much of its history the League was led by Muhammad Ali Jinnah, a Bombay barrister. "The impassive face, the slow and measured voice with its exact articulation, the neat Bond Street tailored figure," wrote one contemporary, "formed a mask

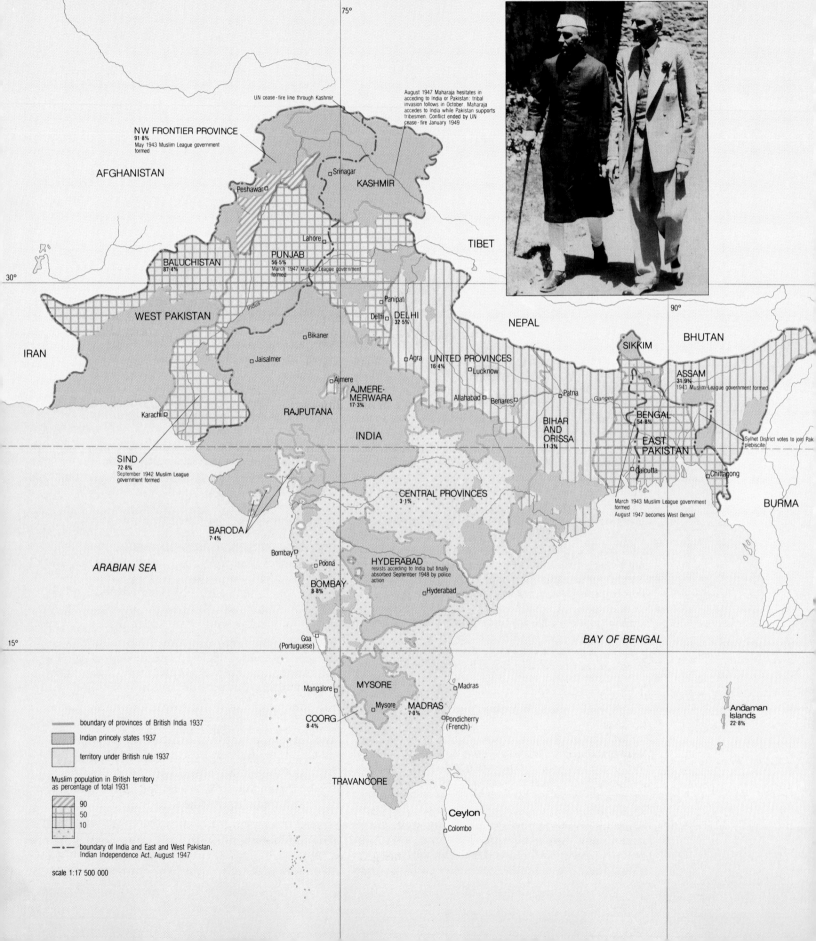

Map legend and labels:

75°
90°

UN cease-fire line through Kashmir

August 1947 Maharaja hesitates in acceding to India or Pakistan: tribal invasion follows in October. Maharaja accedes to India while Pakistan supports tribesmen. Conflict ended by UN cease-fire January 1949

NW FRONTIER PROVINCE
91·8%
May 1943 Muslim League government formed

AFGHANISTAN

Srinagar
Peshawar
KASHMIR
TIBET

BALUCHISTAN
87·4%

PUNJAB
56·5%
March 1947 Muslim League government formed

Lahore

WEST PAKISTAN

30°

Indus

Panipat
Delhi DELHI 32·5%

NEPAL

SIKKIM
BHUTAN

IRAN

Bikaner
Jaisalmer

Agra UNITED PROVINCES
16·4%
Lucknow

ASSAM
31·9%
1943 Muslim League government formed

Ajmere
AJMERE-MERWARA
17·3%

Allahabad Benares
Patna
Ganges

BIHAR AND ORISSA
11·3%

BENGAL
54·8%

Karachi
RAJPUTANA

INDIA

EAST PAKISTAN

Sylhet District votes to join Pak plebiscite

SIND
72·8%
September 1942 Muslim League government formed

Calcutta
Chittagong

BURMA

CENTRAL PROVINCES
3·1%

March 1943 Muslim League government formed
August 1947 becomes West Bengal

BARODA
7·4%

Bombay
Poona

HYDERABAD
resists acceding to India but finally absorbed September 1948 by police action

ARABIAN SEA

BOMBAY
8·8%

Hyderabad

15°

Goa (Portuguese)

BAY OF BENGAL

MYSORE

Mangalore
Madras
Mysore MADRAS
7·0%
COORG
8·4%
Pondicherry (French)

Andaman Islands
22·8%

TRAVANCORE

Ceylon
Colombo

Legend:
— boundary of provinces of British India 1937
Indian princely states 1937
territory under British rule 1937

Muslim population in British territory as percentage of total 1931
90
50
10

–·– boundary of India and East and West Pakistan. Indian Independence Act, August 1947

scale 1:17 500 000

behind which lay an iron will and nerve, a supreme tactical skill, a power to inspire loyalty and impose discipline . . .'' Jinnah's abilities played a remarkable part in the League's success. *Inset* Jinnah (right) walks with Jawaharlal Nehru, leader of the Indian National Congress, during the negotiations over the Cabinet Mission plan at Simla, 1946.

Right During the partition of India, according to one estimate, 12 million were made homeless and half a million people were killed. Here a train, carrying all the Muslims it can, leaves for Pakistan. It was a time of insensate slaughter on all sides. At New Delhi station, as Marshall Hodgson relates, one towering Sikh, raising his sword above an old Muslim woman, was asked, ''Why are you killing her?'' and answered, ''I don't know, but I must,'' as he brought his sword down and cleaved her skull.

state in which the *Sharia* could be enforced. He presented the idea of a separate Muslim state in his presidential speech to the Muslim League in 1930. The state's name, Pakistan, came later from a young Cambridge student: it was a mnemonic from the names of the Muslim-dominated regions of north-west India, *P*unjab, *A*fghania, *K*ashmir, *S*ind and Baluchis*tan*), which also happened to mean ''land of the pure.'' The realization of Pakistan became the central demand of the Muslim League in 1940. The result, however, was distinctly less Islamic than anything Iqbal had in mind. The men who first ruled Pakistan saw it as a modern secular state. Faith, Jinnah told the country's constituent assembly, was to be a personal matter; he had no plans for the enforcement of the *Sharia*. Two further points put their achievement in perspective: many *ulama* refused to support the campaign for Pakistan, denouncing Muslim League leaders as ignorant of Islam and indifferent to the *Sharia*; the problem of the Muslim minority in south Asia remained unsolved as 40 million Muslims were left in India even less well protected than they had been before the partition.

Consolidation in southeast Asia

The experience of Islam under Dutch rule in southeast Asia differed from its experiences either in south Asia or in the northern Islamic lands: there was expansion, reform and considerable institutional development. Far from being thrust to one side by a secularizing colonial state and a competing secular nationalist movement, Islam emerged having carved out a position at the center of modern

Indonesian life. Superficially the story might appear different. In the field of law the Dutch tried to put a fence around Islam and to reduce the territory it held. They introduced their penal and public codes, and tried to extend European law into new areas like inheritance or marriage. They strove to protect the pre-Islamic *adah* or customary law against attempts to replace it with the *Sharia*. In the field of education the Dutch attempted to control the expansion of Muslim schools, and introduced a system of state secular education. Overall, they were raising a new state structure which was infused with a blend of Javanese and Western cultures and which found its expression in the life of the growing cities where many men looked to Karl Marx and the Hindu empire of Majapahit for inspiration. Nevertheless, threatening as these developments may have been, they did not prevent a remarkable advance of Islam in Indonesian society as compared with other Islamic societies of the time.

Much of Indonesia at the end of the 18th century, it will be recalled, was but partially Islamized, while in Java the progress of the faith had been checked. On this island, which dominated the region in population and wealth, Islam was profoundly influenced by Hindu-Javanese culture. The nobility were at best only nominally Muslim, the peasantry subscribed to a highly syncretic folk religion, and it was only in the north and west that Islam had struck deep roots. In the 19th century the interactions between Dutch rule and Javanese society, and between Javanese society and the wider Islamic world, brought a shift in Javanese religious beliefs and practices towards Islam. Dutch rule rested on the nominally Muslim elite and those *ulama* willing to act as officials under them. Many *ulama* stood apart from this system, unwilling to collaborate with a non-Islamic government and determined to keep in their own hands as much of Javanese Muslim life as possible. As the century advanced and colonial rule generated more disturbing change, the Javanese turned to Islam as a protest against the burdens they had to bear. Muslim schools spread throughout the island; they spread elsewhere in the archipelago. The activities of the independent *ulama* were further assisted by the growth of small-scale trade, by the growing presence and austere example of Arab traders and scholars from the ports of southern Arabia, but most of all by a tremendous increase in pilgrimage to Mecca. The numbers rose from 2000 a year in the middle of the century to over 10 000 at the end when Indonesians amounted to 20 per cent of all pilgrims. Those who made the pilgrimage, lived for a moment in a wholly Muslim environment, mingled with people of all races and stations in life and came to appreciate the univers-ality of Islam. They also came to learn of how the faithful were almost everywhere ruled by infidels. They picked up the ideas of revived Islam at the feet of Indonesian *ulama* established in Mecca and joined reformist sufi orders like the Naqshbandiya. They returned full of zeal for reform of religious practices in the villages and inspired by a new hostility to colonial rule.

In the 20th century the hold of Islam over its followers strengthened and gained institutional form. Great stimulus continued to come from abroad. The numbers of Indonesian pilgrims rose to a record 52000 in 1926/7 which amounted to 40 per cent of all Muslims performing pilgrimage. Even more important was the spread of Muslim modernist ideas generated by Shaikh Muhammad Abduh and his circle in Cairo. They taught many Indonesians at al-Azhar, their books came in increasing quantities to southeast Asia and their ideas were broadcast by a rapidly expanding Muslim press. Nor was the process hindered by colonial policy which under the influence of the gifted scholar-administrator, Snouck Hurgronje, tolerated Islam and continued to allow its vigorous institutional development until well into the present century. The Indonesian modernists, like those elsewhere, wished to reform Islamic belief and practice and to adjust it to the requirements of the modern world. It should be noted, however, that this modernist stream re-mained firmly within the channels of Islamic revelation. It was more akin to that of the Tatars than that of the often deracinated products of Saiyid Ahmad Khan's Aligarh College.

In 1912 the modernist drive acquired in-stitutional form with the foundation of the Muham-madiya. By 1938, through intensive missionary work, the Muhammadiya had a quarter of a million members, over 800 mosques and 1700 schools and colleges throughout the archipelago. Their firm line prompted the development of similar organization and similar missionary activity by *ulama* of a more syncretic outlook who founded the Nahdatul Ulama in 1926, although it was never to be as successful as its modernist counterpart. Both organizations avoided overt politics. In fact, Muslims steadily retreated from the vanguard of active resistance to colonial rule. In 1912 they had founded the first

large-scale modern political organization, the *Sarekat Islam* (Islamic League), which in the space of a decade spread through island Indonesia and developed into a radical mass movement, becoming all the while less of an Islamic affair and more of a broad front of protest against economic upheaval, administrative change and colonial rule. In the mid-1920s the movement declined. There was no further significant Muslim political organization till 1938 when the *Partai Islam Indonesia* was formed, by which time it was clear that there was a considerable gulf between those whose vision of the future was fashioned purely in Islamic terms and the growing numbers, concentrated in Java, who saw it in terms of a secular national state. The latter were the Western-educated intelligentsia who drew on a mixture of Western ideologies and Javanese symbols and dominated both the representative institutions created by the Dutch and the Indone-sian nationalist movement. Indeed, it seemed at the end of the 1930s that, if the Dutch were to leave, these men would have exclusive control of the machinery of the state and the marked advances made by Islam over the previous hundred years would be in danger.

This prospect was transformed by the Japanese occupation of 1942–45. The Japanese proscribed political activity and aimed to use Islam to underpin their rule. This enabled Muslims to strengthen their position. After the invasion of March 1942 a department of religious affairs was one of the first

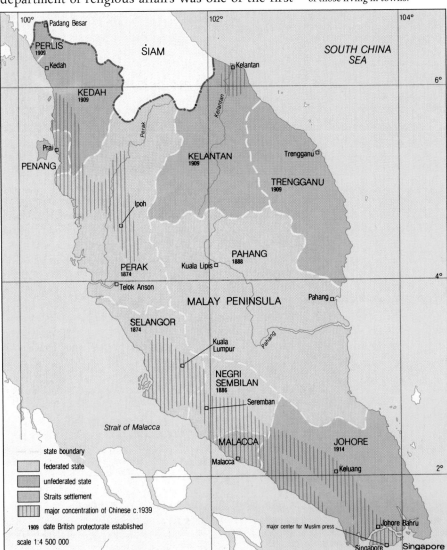

The Malay states in the first half of the 20th century
The British exercised their rule through the sultans of the Malay states who supported established forms of Islam against reformist influences from outside. In consequence, Islamic modernism made little headway here as compared with Indonesia. One important development to note is the migration of largely non-Muslim Chinese into Malaya: up to 1929 there was unrestricted immigration open to all races. In 1947 38 per cent of the population were Chinese, and they amounted to 62·4 per cent of those living in towns.

100°   Padang Besar   102°   104°
PERLIS   SIAM   SOUTH CHINA
1909   SEA
   Kedah   Kelantan
KEDAH   6°
1909
                                    Perak
Prai
                                              KELANTAN   Trengganu
PENANG   1909
                                                          TRENGGANU
                        Ipoh   1909

                                                PAHANG
PERAK   Kuala Lipis   1888
1874
  Telok Anson   MALAY PENINSULA   Pahang   4°

SELANGOR
1874   Kuala
                            Lumpur
                                        NEGRI
                                        SEMBILAN
                                        1886
                                              Seremban
Strait of Malacca   JOHORE
                                    MALACCA   1914
state boundary   Malacca
federated state   Keluang   2°
unfederated state
Straits settlement
major concentration of Chinese c.1939   major center for Muslim press
1909 date British protectorate established   Johore Bahru
scale 1:4 500 000   Singapore   Singapore

Over much of the Islamic world the influences of Islamic reformism, and sometimes of colonial rule, have combined to make architectural styles resemble the buildings of Middle Eastern Islam at the expense of indigenous styles. Consider, for instance, this mosque built over the last 100 years at Tasikmalaya, Java. Above all things, the dome, the common symbol of the religious building in the central Islamic lands, marks it out from earlier southeast Asian mosques with their layered roofs.

offices to be opened. In 1943 the department created the *Masjumi* (Consultative Council of Indonesian Muslims) from the Muhammadiya and the Nahdatul Ulama, and *Masjumi* came to take over the department's functions. By 1944 an official administrative structure had been created for the first time in Java's history in which devout Muslims supervised Muslim life. Similar advances were made in Sumatra. When in late 1944 the secular nationalists were again permitted to play a part in public life, they found the Muslims firmly entrenched and able, after the proclamation of Indonesian independence in 1945, to make further advances. Thus, somewhat curiously, the Japanese helped the Muslims make further progress in Indonesia.

In the Malay states British rule and the Japanese occupation produced a rather different result. Malay society was exposed to many of the same influences as that of Indonesia. There was the growth of pilgrimage, the return of Malays with modernist ideas from Cairo, expansion of a vigorous Muslim press, impressive economic modernization, all taking place within a British policy of non-interference. But the policy which permitted the growth of modernist Islam in Indonesia led to the entrenchment of a traditional, syncretic, heterodox Islam in Malaya. In the last two decades of the 19th century the Malay sultans were able to introduce religio-legal bureaucracies in which secular elites joined hands with "traditionally minded" *ulama* in administering the faith among the Malays. When they were able to gain a foothold, Muslims of a modernist cast of mind found little support. On the one hand, the lives of the Malays had not been as badly disrupted as those of the Javanese because the

impact of economic modernization had fallen on the non-Muslim immigrant groups. On the other hand, the Malay religious authorities were concerned to keep out potentially subversive modernist views. Islamic modernism made little progress. Nor was the situation changed by the Japanese occupation as they preserved the prewar social and political structure and, if anything, deepened the connections between the secular elite and the "traditionally minded" *ulama*.

Expansion in Africa

In Africa south of the Sahara Islam expanded more under colonial rule than anywhere else in recent times. In West Africa the big advances of the 19th century were continued into the 20th. There was steady progress in Guinea, Sierra Leone and the Sudan, and spectacular progress in Senegal, where the Wolof tribe was converted in 50 years, and in Nigeria, where Muslims increased from 50 to 80 per cent in the Hausa lands of the north, from a third to two-thirds among the Nupe of the center and made huge gains among the Yoruba peoples of the southwest. In East Africa Islam spread slowly in Ethiopia and with some speed in Tanganyika, where Muslims grew from a small trading minority at the time of the German conquest to be 40 per cent of the population at independence. Only in the Nilotic Sudan, where in the 19th century the pagan communities of the south had been subjected to ruthless Arab slaving expeditions, was Islam's progress notably checked. The expansion, moreover, has continued to the present, although the pace began to slow with the growth of nationalism in the later days of colonial rule and the growing power of an often secular modern state since independence.

That the government of Christian powers should do so much to further the advance of Islam, especially when Africa was the favored target of Christian missionaries, may seem strange. In fact, some colonial policies directly assisted the expansion of Islam, like the close association which developed between the French administration and the Murid sufi order in Senegal, or the way in which the British confirmed the Muslim rulers of pagan peoples in central Nigeria. The most important aids to the spread of Islam, however, came from the indirect influence of colonial rule: the extension of peace and stable government over large areas enabled peoples to mix as never before and Islam to gain new importance as a set of beliefs and values which might be widely shared. The construction of roads and railroads enabled Muslim traders to penetrate regions hitherto inaccessible: in East Africa they pressed into the hinterland, in West Africa they reached the coast where, for instance, in Lagos and Dakar Muslims grew from being a minute proportion of the population to 50 and 85 per cent respectively. Urban growth itself brought new believers as villagers coming from the pagan countryside to the Muslim-dominated towns adopted Islam in the same way as they began to cover their nakedness in flowing robes. Islam, moreover, had many advantages in the competition with Christianity for pagan souls. Its teachers were African, it seemed to be African in spirit and sensibility, while it offered a much-needed wider understanding of the world without the shame of submitting to the white man's culture. Christianity tended to be the faith of the elite, who received Western education, led nationalist movements and aimed to capture the colonial state.

European rule, whether it acted as a channel for Christian or for purely secular culture, threatened the very existence of Islam. Yet, as we have seen in Indonesia, it could stimulate quite paradoxically a remarkable development of Muslim institutions. Nowhere was this more the case than in sub-Saharan Africa. The tendency derived from the policies of indirect rule which led colonial powers to govern through Muslim institutions and be concerned to preserve them as an insurance against the growth of political opposition. In the French Sudan the government supported Islamic education, and madrasas were established with *ulama* trained in North Africa. In northern Nigeria, where the British, somewhat ironically, exercised their power through the emirates established by the holy wars of Usuman dan Fodio, the *Sharia* was applied more thoroughly than ever before, except that the courts were not allowed to impose those sentences of amputation and stoning which offended British susceptibilities. Even where colonial rule was more direct it could come to rest upon and help to consolidate the authority of sufi orders. In the Nilotic Sudan, where most Muslims were sufis, the British brought forward first the Khatmiya, the order with strong Egyptian connections whose influence had been eclipsed by the rise of the Mahdiya, and then, after Egypt became increasingly nationalistic in the 1920s, the Mahdiya were restored to influence as the order of Sudanese independence against Egypt. Both orders, in

consequence, were able to dig deeper roots in Sudanese society. In Senegal the Muridiya, the extremely heterodox order, which sanctified manual labor and encouraged its devotees to delight in the riches they brought their shaikhs, carved out such a role for its Wolof followers in the colonial economic order that they came to dominate the highly profitable groundnut business. Not every brotherhood was prepared to accommodate itself thus to colonial rule. But most did and thus mitigated the trauma of major transformations, becoming in the process both agents of the colonial government and yet more firmly entrenched in the lives and minds of their followers.

Nevertheless, the protection which the colonial power so often gave to Muslim institutions, although it meant consolidation and advance under colonial rule, threatened a reversal of fortunes once independence was won. What happened varied, among other reasons, according to the proportion of Muslims in the population. In the states where Muslims were a majority (Somalia 100 per cent, Mauritania 90 per cent, Gambia 90 per cent, Niger 85 per cent, Senegal 85 per cent, Guinea 60 per cent, Mali 60 per cent, Sudan 60 per cent, Chad 50 per cent) they could be found, though not invariably, in nationalist politics. Indeed, the extent to which the organizations of Sudanese nationalist politics came to be molded around the Khatmiya and Mahdiya sufi orders was unusual. In those states where Muslims were a minority (Nigeria 47 per cent, Portuguese Guinea 36 per cent, Sierra Leone 30 per cent, Liberia 10 per cent, Upper Volta 22 per cent, Ivory Coast 20 per cent, Ghana 5 per cent, Togo 2·3 per cent, Uganda 5·5 per cent, Kenya 4 per cent, Tanzania 40 per cent) nationalist politics tended to be in the hands of Christians or pagans. There were, of course, some Muslims who had come under modernist influences in North Africa, or who had encountered Wahhabi influences as pilgrims, who supported nationalist movements because they saw them as the way to end not only alien European

We may say the same for this modern mosque in Kano (Nigeria) as for that of Tasikmalaya on the previous page. Its style reveals the influence of the central Islamic lands and compares strikingly with the Sudanic mosques of earlier centuries, pp. 108–09.

influence but also the continued existence of sufi orders, often allied to the colonial power, which they regarded as corrupt. Most Muslims, however, stayed well clear of the politics of secular nationalism and must have witnessed the passing of colonial order with mixed feelings. They may have shared in the joyous celebrations of freedom all about them, but they also knew that their protectors had gone. Outside Mauritania, the Sudan and Somalia, they found themselves in secular modern states ruled by African infidels who were concerned to change their lives more completely than the colonial powers had ever done. Indeed, the Muslims who had long represented advanced civilization to the peoples of sub-Saharan Africa found that they were now the backward peoples as compared with the pagans and the pagans turned Christians, who had acquired the skills of Europe and taken command of the machinery of the state.

In North Africa there was a different situation. The European powers ruled this society in which Islam was deeply rooted in various ways. The French planned the assimilation of Algeria; it was to become another department of France. The Italians had something similar in mind for Libya. The French, on the other hand, merely asserted a protectorate over Tunisia and Morocco, as did the Spanish over the Rif mountains of the north. All the main areas suffered from a tremendous influx of

European colonists. By the 1930s there were 100 000 Italians in Libya, more than 200 000 Frenchmen in Morocco and Tunisia apiece, and 1 000 000 Frenchmen in Algeria. The European settlers occupied the best land and held the highest-paid jobs. In Algeria political rights were open only to those educated Muslims willing to forsake the *Sharia* for French law. Understandably this kind of European impact served to sharpen Muslim self-awareness. Unlike West Africa, traditional Muslim resistance movements continued right up until the 1930s. In Spanish Morocco a former Muslim judge, Abd al-Karim, proclaimed a republic of Rif and from 1921 to 1926 held the might of Spain and France at bay with much military skill. In Libya, the Sanusi sufi order fought the Italian occupation from 1912 to 1918 and again from 1922 to 1931, and did so with such bravery and determination that an Italian army of 20 000 was kept continually occupied, and Mussolini's regime was forced to resort to aerial bombardment and concentration camps before it could prevail. Nevertheless, the influence of the Sanusi order was not destroyed, and it was Saiyid Idris, the temporal head of the order, who was declared king of independent Libya in 1951 after Italian rule had been brought to an end in World War II. Thus Libya, the most backward of the four main states, gained independence first and came to be ruled by a representative of the traditional

The advance of Islam in Africa south of the Sahara since 1800 European colonial rule stimulated the conversion of pagan Africans both to Christianity and to Islam. The latter, because its teachers were Africans and because it offered a much-needed understanding of the world without the shame of submitting to the white man's culture, seems to have fared particularly well in the competition for African souls.

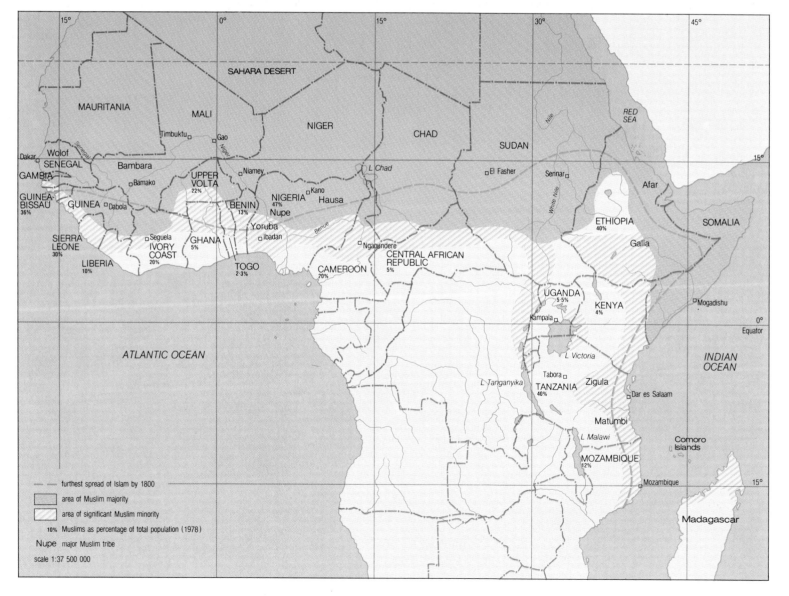

furthest spread of Islam by 1800
area of Muslim majority
area of significant Muslim minority
10% Muslims as percentage of total population (1978)
Nupe major Muslim tribe
scale 1:37 500 000

Islamic order. In the Maghrib, on the other hand, vigorous nationalist movements developed, and independence was only won through struggle with the colonial power. In Tunisia the movement was led by the *Neo-Destour* (New Constitution) Party founded in 1934. A secular nationalist party which embraced a Muslim cultural identity, it won independence in March 1956. In Morocco the movement was organized by the *Istiqlal* (Independence) Party founded in 1943 and led by Sultan Muhammad V, who became the symbol of the freedom movement and thus succeeded in channeling the new political forces within the framework of the maraboutic state. Independence was also won in March 1956. The growth of Algerian nationalism was retarded by the success of French assimilationist policies. In the 1930s observers could see no sign of a sense of Algerian nationality. Only in 1954 was the *Front de Libération Nationale* founded, which won independence eight years later after the most bitter fighting.

The leaders of the freedom movements never doubted that they were Muslims; the presence of large numbers of European settlers made them acutely aware of this as did the racially arrogant style of French rule. Nevertheless, generally they were Muslims by culture rather than by faith, men educated in French or Franco-Arab schools. The influence of Islamic institutions in their societies varied according to French policy and their intrinsic strength. In many places sufi orders were compromised, as in West Africa, by alliances made with the colonial government. Initially Islamic schools fared badly in Algeria where their economic basis was undercut but understandably did better under the protectorate regimes in Tunisia and Morocco. Islamic education throughout the area, however, received a considerable fillip from modernist influences emanating from Muhammad Abduh and his followers in Cairo. In Algeria they inspired an Islamic revival and the establishment of many new schools. In Morocco they had a similar effect and stimulated great scholarly ferment in Fez, intellectual center of the Islamic Maghrib. French law was imposed for all but personal matters in Algeria from 1850, whereas in Morocco and Tunisia

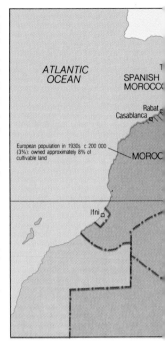

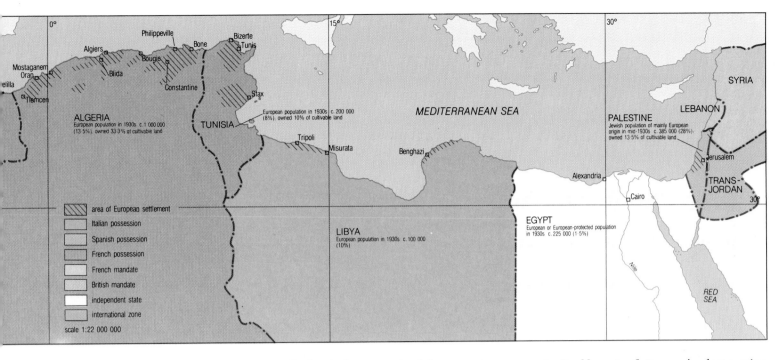

ALGERIA
European population in 1930s c.1 000 000
(13·5%), owned 33·3% of cultivable land

TUNISIA
European population in 1930s c. 200 000
(8%), owned 10% of cultivable land

LIBYA
European population in 1930s c.100 000
(10%)

MEDITERRANEAN SEA

SYRIA

LEBANON

PALESTINE
Jewish population of mainly European
origin in mid-1930s c. 385 000 (28%):
owned 13·5% of cultivable land

TRANS-
JORDAN

EGYPT
European or European-protected population
in 1930s c. 225 000 (1·5%)

RED
SEA

area of European settlement
Italian possession
Spanish possession
French possession
French mandate
British mandate
independent state
international zone
scale 1:22 000 000

Mostaganem / Oran / elilla / Tlemcen / Algiers / Blida / Philippeville / Bougie / Bone / Constantine / Bizerte / Tunis / Sfax / Tripoli / Misurata / Benghazi / Alexandria / Cairo / Nile / Jerusalem

Above: European settlement on the southern and eastern shores of the Mediterranean in the 19th and 20th centuries Only in Russian Central Asia did Muslims have to endure the settlement of Europeans in their lands as they did in this region. Understandably, the settlers came to symbolize the political and economic, and the cultural and psychological, domination of the foreign power, so when independence was won the vast majority had to leave. In Algeria, which the French had regarded as part of France and in which many French families had lived for three or four generations, the process brought terrible bloodshed in a war lasting from 1954 to 1962.

Left This picture speaks eloquently of the Algerian war: a Muslim woman, with her worldly possessions (or is it a baby?) on her lap, begs as a French soldier and French settler pass by.

traditional systems of Islamic law remained intact until the 1950s. In much of North Africa Islamic institutions seem to have suffered no worse than anywhere else.

Nationalism and the decline of Islam

We have witnessed Muslim responses to the rise of Europe primarily at the level of the colonial or "nation" state. There was also a pan-Islamic response, which is significant for what it reveals of the enduring sense of Islamic community in spite of that community's division for hundreds of years into separate empires and sultanates. Its first proponent was Jamal al-Din al-Afghani (1839–97) who hoped, by reforming Muslim religious practice and by uniting all beneath the Ottoman caliphate, to check, if not to sweep back, the rising tide of European power. He influenced Muslim thought in Central Asia, Turkey and India, and had a direct impact on the 1881 revolt in Egypt and on the Iranian constitutional revolution. Afghani's ideas were developed at a purely religious level by his most influential pupil, Muhammad Abduh; we have seen above how the Muslim modernism of this distinguished rector of al-Azhar, his demonstration that modern scientific thought and Islam were reconcilable, was enthusiastically received from Morocco to Indonesia. Afghani's political ideas found increasing support from the beginning of the 20th century. As Ottoman Turkey came under growing pressure from Europe, Muslims protested. When, after World War I, Mustafa Kemal was seen to be fighting for the very existence of Turkey, and therefore the caliphate, major political agitations sprang up, those in India and Indonesia being the greatest mass movements their societies had seen. Understandably Mustafa Kemal's abolition of the caliphate in 1924 was received with incomprehension. For a further 10 years Arab and Indian Muslims held congresses and strove to reestablish the office, but their ambitions were wrecked by the rivalry of potential caliphs and the growing power of nationalism.

That the Muslim response to Europe should have been overwhelmingly within the frame of nation-states was in itself part of Europe's destructive impact on the world of Islam. But within these nation-states the damage wrought by the new European power was much greater. Systems of government had been raised up which did not recognize the *Sharia*, systems of education which did not teach Islamic knowledge. Men who subscribed to no Islamic vision came to control the vastly powerful machinery of the modern state. They aimed to fashion a society secular in outlook and often Western in taste. Those who had guarded and transmitted the molding forces of Islamic society down the centuries were increasingly thrust to one side, and scorned by modern men as incongruous figures in turbans and cloaks, fit only for museums, like their learning and their attitudes. *Ulama* found their knowledge less and less valued by the state, while prospective pupils knew that it was unlikely to get them a living. Sufis were even more severely troubled. They were attacked for their sometimes lax religious practices by *ulama* anxious to present the rational face of Islam to the modern world. Growing state power cut into their social functions as mediators between groups of men or individuals and the state. The cold breath of materialism withered support for their spiritual vision in the hearts of men.

In the middle of the 20th century the fate of the transmitters varied from state to state. *Ulama* had been all but wiped out in Turkey, but in Indonesia had actually strengthened their position. The decline of the sufi orders had been general, but they had nevertheless discovered important political roles in Africa and survived as the main sustainers of Islam in Soviet Central Asia. Some new states declared themselves Islamic republics, like Pakistan, but only one, Saudi Arabia, was concerned to hold the sources of Western strength within an Islamic frame. In general the Islamic vision of progress had been replaced by a secular one. Those who ruled did so because they had mastered the secrets of European power. The consequence was usually that they had been shaped in the secular image of Europe, and it was in this likeness that they now hoped to mold the Muslim masses.

THE REASSERTION OF ISLAM IN THE LATER 20th CENTURY

Against Europe I protest,
And the attraction of the West:
Woe for Europe and her charm,
Swift to capture and disarm!
Europe's hordes with flame and fire
Desolate the world entire;
Architect of Sanctuaries,
Earth awaits rebuilding; rise!
    Out of leaden sleep,
    Out of slumber deep
        Arise!
    Out of slumber deep
        Arise!

Muhammad Iqbal, *Zabur-i Ajam*,
1927; trans. Arberry

The advance of secular culture

From the mid-20th century the fortunes of the Muslims changed for the better. There had been signs of improvement from the 1920s, when the Turks and Iranians began to master their affairs. Now most Muslims won freedom from the formal political control of the Europeans, who had been much weakened by World War II. Syria and Jordan, which were the remaining Arab states under League of Nations mandates, became free in 1945 and 1946. Pakistan achieved independence in 1947 and Indonesia in 1949, forming at the time the two largest Muslim states with a combined population well over 200 million. Then in the decade after 1955 came the turn of the African Muslims, so that by the mid-1960s the Muslims of the Soviet Union remained the only sizeable group still under

The achievement of independence in the Muslim world
Most Muslim peoples won independence from colonial rule between World War II and the late 1960s. Two points should be noted: first that at least one quarter of the Muslims of the world still remained under the rule of unbelievers, most notably in India, China and the Soviet Union; and secondly that independence was often highly qualified. Egypt gained its independence in 1922 but had to endure British forces on its territory until 1954. Iraq gained its independence in 1932 but remained under considerable British influence till the revolution of 1958. For devout Muslims independence could mean very little: they merely exchanged European rule for that of a European-educated elite of distinctly secular outlook.

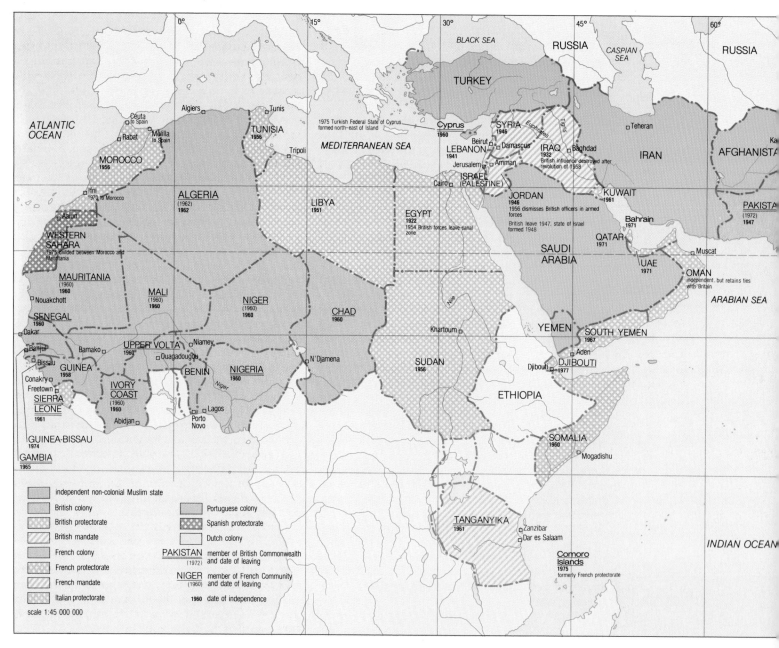

independent non-colonial Muslim state
British colony
British protectorate
British mandate
French colony
French protectorate
French mandate
Italian protectorate
Portuguese colony
Spanish protectorate
Dutch colony
PAKISTAN (1972) member of British Commonwealth and date of leaving
NIGER (1960) member of French Community and date of leaving
1960 date of independence

scale 1:45 000 000

Most prominent of the leaders of the newly independent Muslim peoples was President Nasser of Egypt, who asserted Egypt's interests against those of Britain and France by asking the British to withdraw their forces from the Suez Canal zone in 1954 and then by nationalizing the canal in 1956. Here, Nasser is carried in triumph on 19 June 1954 as he comes to raise the Egyptian flag on the former British headquarters in Port Said after they had evacuated the canal zone.

colonial rule. Independence brought a surge of confidence to Muslim societies and new strength to their governments, as they were now relieved of the weakness of the declining years of alien rule. Muslims could now decide for themselves whether they really wanted to travel the road of Western culture and secular values along which the Europeans had directed them.

On the morrow of independence the first thing the leaders of the new states discovered was that they had not got rid of the West. Their freedom remained hedged about by the power of Europe, and soon that of the USA too. Western military bases were scattered through their lands and Western businesses often had firm grip on the most recently developed and most profitable sectors of their economies. Indeed, decolonization had sometimes brought about an ideal situation for the old colonial powers of continuing to be able to pursue their economic and strategic interests without being burdened by the costs of administration. Among the first Muslim leaders to strive for a more genuine independence was Dr Musaddeq, prime minister of Iran under the young Shah Riza Pahlavi (reigned 1941–79). He refused oil concessions to the Soviet Union, and nationalized the Anglo-Iranian Oil Company which controlled the rich fields of Khuzestan and the world's largest refinery at Abadan. From 1951 to 1953, supported by many *ulama*, left-wingers and the Iranian people, he resisted Western pressure to back down. Eventually a coup was engineered, in which with British and American help the army deposed Musaddeq and pushed the shah to a stronger position in the state. Musaddeq's policies of independence were reversed: other companies joined the Anglo-Iranian Oil Company, now renamed British Petroleum, in exploiting Iran's riches, and treaties were made with Iraq, Turkey, Pakistan and Britain for common defense against the Soviet Union. Iran was aligned to the West even more firmly than before.

The Arabs, on the other hand, had greater success. Colonel Nasser, who had come to power in Egypt after the Free Officers' revolution in 1952, was determined that independence should be real. In 1954 he persuaded the British to withdraw their forces from the Suez Canal zone. In 1955 he turned to the Communist bloc after the USA refused to sell him arms. In 1956 he nationalized the Suez Canal, vital artery of international trade and rich source of tolls. He survived Israeli, British and French invasions to assert triumphantly, as no Muslim leader had done for years, the right of his country to command its own destiny. Moved by his example, Arabs elsewhere, though not with the same enthusiasm, tossed aside their leading strings: in 1956 King Husain of Jordan dismissed his army's British commanding officer; in 1958 units of the Iraqi army destroyed their Hashemite rulers and revoked the British alliance. Nasser had shown how Muslim states might stand more freely in the world.

Nasser's achievement, however, did not make all Muslims more free, not even all Arabs. Some states had gained greater leverage in international affairs, yet they along with most other developing countries still felt their freedom cramped by outside forces. Although leaders like Nasser might be able to shake off the military and economic grip of the old colonial powers, the more subtle influences of colonialism

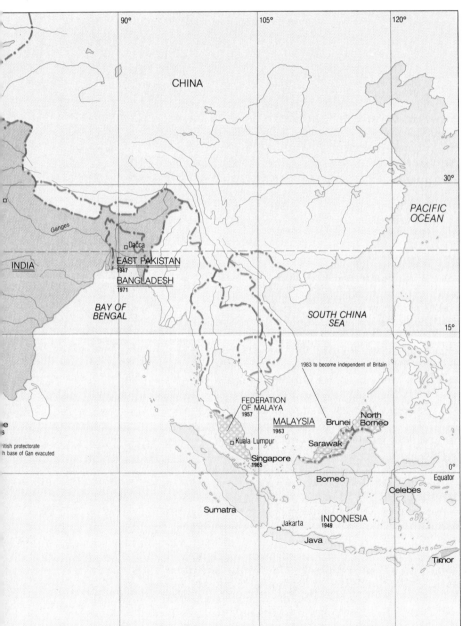

Left Arafat (center) makes a point to Ayatullah Khomeini while Khomeini's son, Ahmad, listens, on 17 February 1979, less than a week after Teheran fell to the revolutionary forces. The open affection which these three men are showing is typical among Muslims who regard each other warmly. Khomeini's feelings for the Palestinian cause were no doubt all the stronger for the fact that Israel had been an important ally of the Pahlavi regime.

still persisted – those of language and of culture, of association and of life experience which continued to draw elites to the former imperial center. In addition the newly free Muslim states suffered from all the problems of the smaller and less advanced countries dealing with those which were larger and more advanced. To survive and to grow they needed to trade, yet in doing so they seemed to run the risk of continuing to foster a position of inferiority in which they supplied raw materials and received finished goods. To overcome their weakness they accepted aid. However, this also limited their freedom: their people had to go to the advanced societies to learn how to operate the latest machines; they depended for years on these societies for spare parts for their modern equipment; their creditors strove to influence their internal policies, and their suppliers of arms their foreign policies; military advisers tried to suborn their armies, and civilian advisers their people. Aid, they often discovered, was just a new form of imperialism. To solve their problems Muslim states learned how to play off one advanced country against another, Western against Communist power. They joined the groupings of non-aligned countries which came together after the Bandung conference of 1955; they experimented with federations of states like the United Arab Republic which bound Syria to Egypt from 1958 to 1961; they came together in an economic cartel, the Organization of Petroleum Exporting Countries (OPEC) in 1960. Nevertheless, throughout the early years of independence the leaders of the new Muslim states must have felt that it was a distinctly phony freedom that they had won.

Nothing brought home the continuing inferiority of the Muslim position more acutely than the existence of the state of Israel in the Arab land of Palestine. It was a feeling exacerbated by the constant flow of immigrants, by the declared expansionist aims of some Israelis and by the humiliation of Arab arms in the wars of 1948, 1956 and 1967, in the last of which much new territory was occupied – the Golan Heights, the Sinai Desert, the West Bank of the Jordan and east Jerusalem. Westerners often make the mistake of considering these developments as problems which engage the Arabs alone. Nothing could be further from the truth. Witness the newspaper coverage in Indonesia or even the southern Philippines whenever Arab and Israeli go to war. Listen to the views of Muslims in India, or recall how Muslim politicians in search of popular support have courted the company of Palestinian leaders. Palestine was the one subject on which all Muslims could unite. Muslims by culture felt the humiliation of their weakness; for those who still believed, there was the added shame of holy places under infidel rule. They saw the Zionist as just another European colonist who should be sent back to Europe as the French had been sent back from Algeria after a hundred years of settlement. These colonists, moreover, were supported in their existence and their expansionist endeavors by Western capital, Western arms and by Western foreign policy, in particular those of the USA. Israel thus reminded Muslims in potent and wounding ways of how they were still weak and subject to the West.

For Muslim believers independence did not bring even this circumscribed freedom, but only a seemingly more hopeless imprisonment and a continuing decline of the faith. More often than not it was the secular elite, educated in Britain, France, the USA, or in the modern universities of the Muslim world like Cairo, Istanbul or Aligarh, who came to untrammeled power. They continued, often with greater confidence and zest than the old colonial rulers, to reduce the role played by Islam in their societies. In Algeria President Ben Bella constructed a socialist society, paying no more than

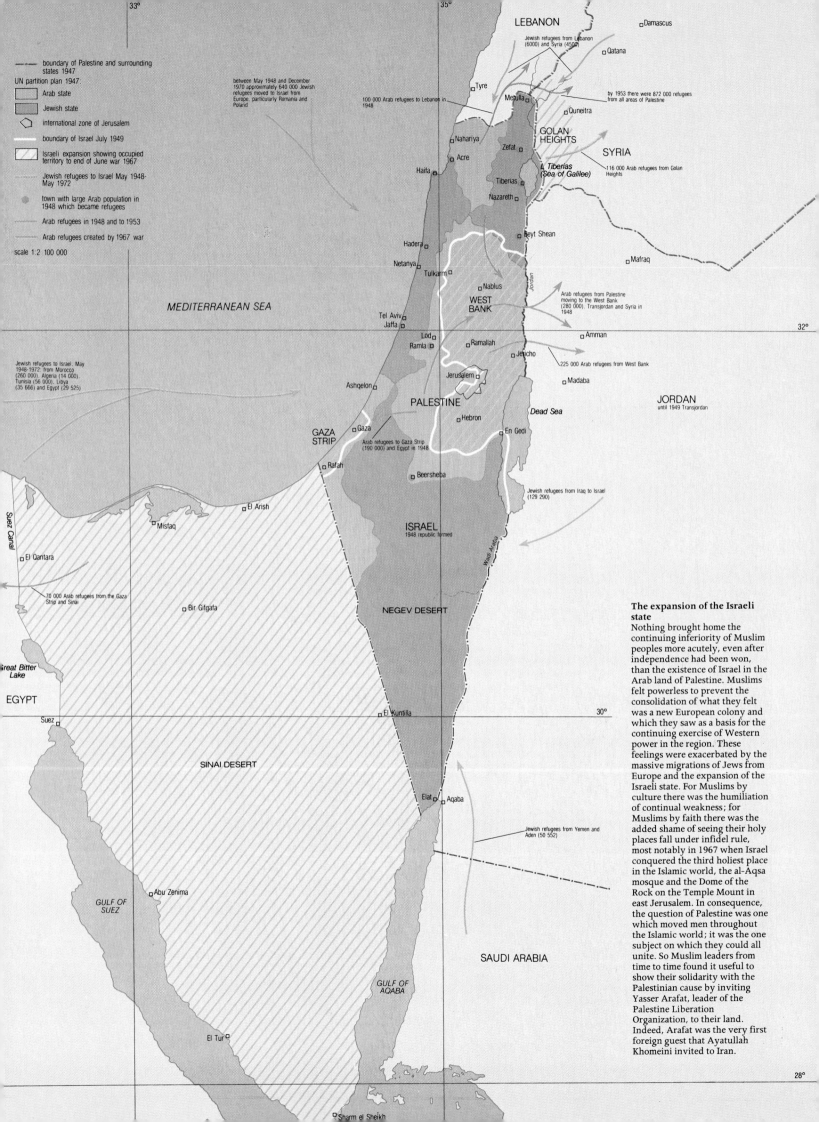

33° 35°

LEBANON □Damascus

Jewish refugees from Lebanon
(6000) and Syria (4500)

□Qatana

□Tyre

Metulla□ by 1953 there were 872 000 refugees
from all areas of Palestine

100 000 Arab refugees to Lebanon in
1948

□Quneitra

□Nahariya GOLAN
HEIGHTS

Zefat□ SYRIA

□Acre

Haifa□ L. Tiberias
(Sea of Galilee)

Tiberias□ 116 000 Arab refugees from Golan
Heights

Nazareth□

Beyt Shean□

Hadera□

MEDITERRANEAN SEA

Netanya□ Mafraq□

Tulkarm□

□Nablus

WEST
BANK

Tel Aviv□ Jordan

Jaffa□ Arab refugees from Palestine
moving to the West Bank
(280 000). Transjordan and Syria in
1948

Lod□ □Amman

Ramla□ □Ramallah

Jericho□ 225 000 Arab refugees from West Bank

Jerusalem□ □Madaba

PALESTINE JORDAN
until 1949 Transjordan

Ashqelon□ Dead Sea

□Hebron

GAZA
STRIP □Gaza En Gedi□

Arab refugees to Gaza Strip
(190 000) and Egypt in 1948

Rafah□

Beersheba□ Jewish refugees from Iraq to Israel
(129 290)

El Arish□

Misfaq□ ISRAEL
1948 republic formed

Wadi Araba

Suez
Canal

El Qantara□

70 000 Arab refugees from the Gaza
Strip and Sinai

Bir Gifgafa□ NEGEV DESERT

Great Bitter
Lake

EGYPT El Kuntilla□ 30°

SINAI DESERT

Suez□

Elat□ □Aqaba

Jewish refugees from Yemen and
Aden (50 552)

GULF OF
SUEZ

Abu Zenima□ SAUDI ARABIA

GULF OF
AQABA

El Tur□

28°

□Sharm el Sheikh

boundary of Palestine and surrounding
states 1947

UN partition plan 1947:

Arab state

Jewish state

international zone of Jerusalem

boundary of Israel July 1949

Israeli expansion showing occupied
territory to end of June war 1967

Jewish refugees to Israel May 1948–
May 1972

town with large Arab population in
1948 which became refugees

Arab refugees in 1948 and to 1953

Arab refugees created by 1967 war

scale 1:2 100 000

between May 1948 and December
1970 approximately 640 000 Jewish
refugees moved to Israel from
Europe, particularly Romania and
Poland

Jewish refugees to Israel. May
1948–1972: from Morocco
(260 000). Algeria (14 000).
Tunisia (56 000). Libya
(35 666) and Egypt (29 525)

**The expansion of the Israeli
state**
Nothing brought home the
continuing inferiority of Muslim
peoples more acutely, even after
independence had been won,
than the existence of Israel in the
Arab land of Palestine. Muslims
felt powerless to prevent the
consolidation of what they felt
was a new European colony and
which they saw as a basis for the
continuing exercise of Western
power in the region. These
feelings were exacerbated by the
massive migrations of Jews from
Europe and the expansion of the
Israeli state. For Muslims by
culture there was the humiliation
of continual weakness; for
Muslims by faith there was the
added shame of seeing their holy
places fall under infidel rule,
most notably in 1967 when Israel
conquered the third holiest place
in the Islamic world, the al-Aqsa
mosque and the Dome of the
Rock on the Temple Mount in
east Jerusalem. In consequence,
the question of Palestine was one
which moved men throughout
the Islamic world; it was the one
subject on which they could all
unite. So Muslim leaders from
time to time found it useful to
show their solidarity with the
Palestinian cause by inviting
Yasser Arafat, leader of the
Palestine Liberation
Organization, to their land.
Indeed, Arafat was the very first
foreign guest that Ayatullah
Khomeini invited to Iran.

Modern Arab Art

Right A detail of the *Monument of Revolution* in Baghdad's Liberation square. The monument, a 50 by 8 meter frieze, was sculpted by Jawad Salim, doyen of the modern art movement in Iraq.

The minds of the Muslim elite, which led the newly independent states of the Muslim world, were profoundly influenced by Europe: this emerges from their art. We have the delicious paradox of the most spectacular work of modern Arab art, the *Monument of Revolution*, which celebrates Iraq's revolution of 1958, when European colonial influence was finally cast off, in sculpture powerfully reminiscent of European models. Today European influence remains strong. Nevertheless, quality which begin to distinguish Arab art, from Morocco to Iraq, are emerging in a preference for abstraction, an aversion to representation, and a fascination for calligraphic forms.

Kamal Amin Awad, Egypt.

Jawad Salim, Iraq.

M. Qadir al-Triqi, Tunisia.

Dia al-Azzawi, Iraq.

lip-service to Islam. In Tunisia President Bourguiba maintained the highly secular pattern of development presaged by the nationalist movement; *Sharia* courts were abolished, *ulama* disappeared from the scene and all traces of Islam were removed from the administration. In Syria the Baathists first smashed the religious opposition to their regime between 1966 and 1970 and then in 1973 tried to force through a new socialist constitution which did not allow Islam a nominal position as the religion of the state. Even when Islam was the very basis of the state, as in Pakistan, the secular elite struggled fiercely to restrict those areas where it had influence; indeed, the very role of Islam as the source of the state's legitimacy seemed to be reduced when the title "Islamic Republic of Pakistan" enshrined in the constitution of 1956 changed to plain "Republic of Pakistan" in that of 1962.

Turning to states where the institutional framework of Islam was especially strong we find the same basic tendency. In Egypt, for instance, Nasser abolished the *Sharia* courts and then in 1961 reorganized al-Azhar as a modern state university under the president's direct control. There was certainly to be a role for the *ulama*, and for sufis too, but only in the service of the Egyptian state. In Iran, from 1959, Muhammad Riza Pahlavi moved forcefully to curb the resurgent power of the *ulama*. Policies they abhorred, like the enfranchisement of women and friendship with Israel, were adopted; their incomes were slashed by land reform, their endowments illegally appropriated and their protests met with arrests and exile. In 1959/60 there were 252 madrasas with 14419 students; eight years later there were 138 madrasas with 7482 students. Even in Iran, where the *ulama* had resisted the attacks of the modern secular state for so long, they could look to the future with little confidence.

Muslim peoples began to see, as the frontiers of the state were pushed deep into the lives of ordinary men and women, how they were beginning to be cast in a different mold, and that mold owed nothing to Islam. Government now reached out into the villages with new purpose. It insisted that children should attend school to receive the rudiments of Western learning; girls were not excused. It redistributed village lands, sometimes with benefit to the poorer peasant, but sometimes too destroying the endowments which supported local holy places. It penetrated the women's world, insisting on vaccinations, urging family planning and interfering with the tried lore of the past. Sons, and sometimes daughters, were carried off for national service and thus indoctrinated in the new national culture which made it hard for them, once released, to slip back into their old village ways. Simultaneously, countryfolk were drawn into the activities of a developing industrial society, constructing roads, building pipelines, working in factories. They began to make their way to the towns and cities, Teheran or Karachi for instance, whose populations grew from a few hundred thousand in the 1940s to over five million in the 1970s. Often squatting in insanitary townships on the outskirts, they gazed upon a world which contrasted sharply with their vision, indifferent though it sometimes was, of the the rightly guided Muslim life: there were cinema hoardings which promised debauch-

ery within, bars where men might lose their minds to wine, women unaccompanied, with their hair flying free and immodestly clothed, much conspicuous wealth, and many foreigners – Americans with their loud voices, British with their lobster complexions, Russians sallow and silent.

A glance at the elite culture of this world reveals how far Muslim minds had been seduced by Europe. Sadiq Hidayat, who is widely regarded as the greatest figure in 20th-century Iranian literature, was powerfully influenced by Sartre with whom he studied in Paris. Modern Egyptian writers sought inspiration from British and Russian work as well as French. The Indian Progressive Writers Association, which was founded in 1936 and came to dominate Urdu literature, reveals the European socialist stimulus in its manifesto: the association aimed "to rescue literature and other arts from the priestly, academic and decadent classes in whose hands they had degenerated for so long"; progressive writing had to "deal with the basic problems of our existence today – the problems of hunger and poverty, social backwardness and political subjugation." Progressive writers drenched themselves in European literature from Tolstoy to Kafka, they warmed to English Romantics like Byron and Shelley, they devoured the works of English socialists of the 1930s, Spender, Auden, Day Lewis and so on, whom they often knew. From Delhi to Cairo and from Teheran to Istanbul, writers experimented with new forms – the short story, the novel, blank verse, free verse – using European models to help them break out of the stifling influence of traditional literary conventions in the way that they wanted their own thoughts set free from the patterns of the past. They talked of politics and poverty, asserted women's rights, discussed female sexuality and mocked piety.

The same influences and the same rejection of Islamic values can be seen in modern Arab painting, which owed more to European fashions than to the great traditions of Arab art and also flouted religious preferences, including most confidently, for example, the female nude within its repertoire. The Islamic prohibition on the making of images, however, seems to have been rather more effective, because only in Egypt and Iraq did strong schools of sculpture come to flourish. Presiding genius of the art was Jawad Salim (1920–61) who studied in Rome, Paris and at London's Slade School of Art. His masterwork, *Monument of Revolution*, which stretches across Baghdad's Liberation Square and celebrates the revolution of 1958, expresses that movement's alien source of inspiration and profoundly secular cast of mind. In its echoes of Picasso's *Guernica* and the sculpture of Jacob Epstein we find the influence of Europe, while the whole is conceived to glorify man, not God. Leaders of modern Muslim states seeking for equality and self-respect in their relations with the West seem nevertheless to have become the vigorous and effective agents of Western civilization in their societies. We can sympathize with the agonized cry of Muhammad Iqbal:

> Turk, Persian, Arab
> intoxicated with Europe,
> And in the throat of each
> the fish-hook of Europe.

The reassertion of the Islamic vision

In recent years Muslims have begun to respond to this transmutation of their civilization under the influence of the West and have reasserted Islamic values and the Islamic vision of progress. They came to sense with growing certainty that the aims of Islam and those of the West were totally opposed. Muhammad Iqbal, although he wrote almost half a century earlier, speaks their mind:

The Westerners have lost the vision of heaven,
they go hunting for the pure spirit in the belly.
The pure soul takes not colour and scent from the
                                        body,
and Communism has nothing to do save with the
                                        body,
The religion of that prophet [Marx] who knew not
                                        truth
is founded upon equality of the belly;
the abode of fraternity being in the heart,
its roots are in the heart, not in water and clay.

Capitalism too is a fattening of the body,
its unenlightened bosom houses no heart;
like the bee which pastures upon the flower
it overpasses the petal, and carries off the honey,
yet stalk and leaf, colour and scent all make up the
                                        rose
For whose selfsame beauty the nightingale laments.
Surpass the talisman, the scent and colour,
bid farewell to the form, gaze only upon the
                                        meaning.
Though it is difficult to descry the inward deaths
call not that a rose which in truth is clay.

The soul of both is impatient and intolerant,
both of them know not God, and deceive mankind.
One lives by production, the other by taxation
and man is a glass caught between these two
                                        stones.
The one puts to rout science, religion, art,
the other robs body and soul, the hand of bread.
I have perceived both drowned in water and clay,
both bodily burnished, but utterly dark of heart.

Muhammad Iqbal, *Javidnama*,
1932; trans. Arberry

Muslims such as these feel that there is another way forward, the Islamic way, and they want to invest it once more with power. It was no longer enough that the European ruler had been expelled; now those aspects of his civilization which had taken firm root in Muslim soil – Western laws, godless learning, decadent culture – must also be grubbed up. Precisely who came forward to urge the Islamic way, or at least an Islamic way, depended on the particular historical development of the state concerned. In a few the transmitters were still strong and free enough to fight for the *Sharia*; in others it was organizations of Western-educated men who took up the cause. The intellectual and spiritual lineage of some went back to the 18th- and 19th-century movements of revival and reform; others found their origin and their impetus, as have many down the ages, in the glaring contrast between the ideal life set out by the Prophet and the grim state of human life around them. Invariably the movement was entangled with the needs of

165

those who sought to gain, or maintain themselves in, power.

In Turkey, where Ataturk had decreed there should be no *ulama*, the sufi orders came forward for Islam. The Naqshbandiya worked secretly in eastern Anatolia where 17 of their leaders were arrested in 1954. The Tijaniya, who came from North Africa in 1949, adopted direct methods, destroying statues of Ataturk for example, because they transgressed the words of the Quran. The Nurcular, a completely new order which found support in university circles, was extremely active, broadcasting its fundamentalist views that all truth lies in the Quran, that secularism is contrary to Islam and that the *Sharia* should be restored. From 1970 such views, despite the constitutional provisions against the association of religion with politics, began to find a foothold in the political system through the efforts of Necmettin Erbakan, a professor of engineering at Istanbul Technical University. In the general elections of 1973 his National Salvation Party won 11·9 per cent of the votes cast. He used the fact that his party held the balance of power in the National Assembly to win concessions for Islam; he used his position as vice-premier to make defiant points, choosing for its symbolism the old sultan's palace of Topkapi Sarai as the site for his address on the 53rd anniversary of the republic.

There is little doubt that the activities of the sufi orders and the National Salvation Party were encouraged by the general rehabilitation of Islam in the fabric of Turkish life which had taken place since the death of Ataturk. Indeed, the great man's body was barely cold before the process began, his sister insisting that the burial prayer be recited for him! Within a few years the National Assembly was debating the question of religious education and in 1949 it was restored to the school curriculum as an optional subject. There followed a decade of Democrat Party government from 1950 which presided over a state-controlled restoration of Islam which no one would have believed possible 20 years before. Arabic replaced Turkish as the language in which men were called to prayer; the state radio began to broadcast on religious subjects; 15000 mosques were built; all Muslim children were required to have religious instruction; schools were established to teach *ulama* and were widely patronized. Turks expressed their faith again openly and with vigor: thousands attended the celebrations of the anniversary of Jalal al-Din Rumi's death which were permitted once more; hundreds of thousands followed government-sponsored Quran courses; the numbers performing the pilgrimage to Mecca, which was allowed again after 1947, rose from over 10000 in 1954 to over 106000 in 1974. There was, moreover, a flood of Islamic literature, much of it the usual aids to devotion, but much too which advanced the Islamic point of view, asserting the superiority of its vision over Western materialism. Friction grew between secularists and Muslims eager to make further gains for Islam; the army, chief guardian of Ataturk's revolution, objected. There was a coup in 1960, after which Prime Minister Menderes, whom some had come to call the "Friend of God," was hanged, and a new constitution promulgated in which the secular ideals of the state were trenchantly reaffirmed. The

right to religious expression was acknowledged providing it was "not in opposition to public order, or morals, or the laws enacted to uphold them . . ." A balance had been struck, legally at least, between secularism and the burgeoning forces of religion. Nevertheless, it has not prevented persistent attempts to reassert Islamic values and to inject them into the political system.

In Egypt Islam returned to the forefront of affairs in a similar fashion and many of its leaders and supporters came from among the Western educated. The process began when Nasser's position weakened after Egypt was badly defeated in the war of 1967 with Israel. Islamic groups were quick to argue that the Egyptians had lost because they were no longer good Muslims. They had been seduced by imported Western ideologies: socialism, nationalism and secularism. The defeat revealed their inadequacy; the solution was to return to Islam. After Nasser died in 1970, popular support for Islam became more evident, as for instance, large numbers of young middle-class Egyptian women began to dress according to Islamic law. Support for Islamic associations grew rapidly: they emerged as the most cohesive and organized force in Egyptian universities, controlling most student unions; the Muslim Brotherhood, banned since they had tried to assassinate Nasser in 1954, began to refound their countrywide organization; several militant and clandestine organizations sprang up on the fringes of the Brotherhood, the *Takfir wal Hijra* (Repentance and Flight from Sin) being the best known, and they demonstrated their willingness to kill to seek their ends.

If one cause of this new Islamic fervor was

In the 1960s and 1970s many governments of Muslim states had increasingly to take into account the Islamic values and preferences of their peoples. It was not an easy policy to adopt, as the ends of the Islamic groups which they came to tolerate could sometimes be fundamentally opposed to theirs. President Anwar Sadat of Egypt tried to use a new respect for Islam and Islamic organizations as one of the pillars of his rule. Here in December 1977 he attends Friday prayers in the mosque of the new city of Serabim near Ismailia on the Suez Canal.

growing disaffection with the leadership of Egypt's secular elite, another, as in Turkey, was government policy. Nasser, himself, turned to Islam in the last years of his rule to distract attention from the disaster of 1967. His successor, Anwar Sadat, considerably developed the policy. He exploited Islamic symbols in order to reach into those layers of Egyptian society as yet barely touched by Western influences and to build up support against Communism and Nasser's followers. His speeches were larded with Islamic imagery and he was careful to ensure that the public saw him regularly on his knees at Friday congregational prayer. He strove to manipulate Islamic organizations. Al-Azhar received unusually large shares of government funds and its rector was promoted in terms of protocol and salary to the rank of prime minister. In return the leaders of Egypt's *ulama* offered strong support both for his domestic policy and for his attempts to make peace with Israel. The Muslim Brotherhood was also drawn into the net. In exchange for being allowed to reestablish their organization, they defended him against attacks from the left. But there was danger in trying to ride the Islamic tiger. Big concessions had to be made to fundamentalism; the works of the sufi master, Ibn al-Arabi, had to be banned for instance, and a constitutional amendment came to be passed making the principles of the *Sharia* the main source of legislation. There was, moreover, no guarantee that the tiger would not devour its rider. In 1979 the Brotherhood opposed the peace negotiations with Israel; in 1981 the *Takfir wal Hijra* assassinated President Sadat.

In Libya the shift towards a form of fundamentalist Islam came not as a result of political responses to growing Islamic feeling among the people but as a result of an army coup in 1969. The 27-year-old Captain Muammar Qaddafi, who led the new government, was, although of Bedouin extraction, set in the mold of a modern technocrat like Erbakan in Turkey or the leaders of the Muslim Brotherhood in Egypt. His belief combined Islamic fundamentalism with the Arab socialism of his hero, Nasser. The early actions of his regime are as clear a statement of Muslim feelings regarding Western influences upon their lives as the world had witnessed up to the time. The Revolutionary Command Council, advised by *ulama* from all over the world, declared that the *Sharia* had ruled Islamic countries for nearly 14 centuries, that when the colonialists took over they had replaced it under the pretext of "civilization" with secular laws and fascist practices, and that the time had now come to redress the wrongs of colonialism by making the *Sharia* "the supreme and principal source of all legislation and practices in this Republic." In similar spirit all signs of Western culture were obliterated: British Petroleum was nationalized, alcohol was forbidden, school textbooks were censored, all street signs had to be in Arabic, even the passports of visitors had to be in Arabic as well as in English and French. As the new regime consolidated its position, greatly helped by its abundant oil wealth, it became evident that Qaddafi's "Third Way" of Islamic socialism, as an alternative to capitalism or Communism, was also a highly individual way, and in Islamic terms revolutionary. He insisted on going further than any reformer before him and in looking to the Quran alone as a source of legitimacy, denying the

authority even of the *Hadiths*. In consequence a theological commission in Saudi Arabia found him guilty of apostasy.

In Pakistan there was a similar sharp assertion of Islam against the legacies of Western colonialism. From the beginning there had been parties determined to make Pakistan into an Islamic state in fact no less than in name; indeed their activities were one reason why the first constitution was not adopted until 1956, nine years after independence. There were parties representing schools of *ulama*, but more notably there was the *Jamaat-i-Islami* which was highly disciplined and like the Muslim Brotherhood attracted much support from the Western-educated middle class. It was founded in 1941 by Mawlana Mawdudi (1903–79), whose writings were admired in much of the Islamic world including Libya where he was one of the chief advisers to Qaddafi's Revolutionary Command Council. Among the ideas he advocated were that the *Sharia*, of course, should be the law of the land; the state should be ruled by one man who should hold power so long as he followed state ideology; this ruler was to be helped by men qualified to interpret the *Sharia*; there should be no political parties and no legitimate opposition; only Muslims could play a part in government, while non-Muslims must vote in separate electorates. For years the *Jamaat-i-Islami* advocated this program, and for years it had little success. The secular elites were in control and the rise to power of Zulfiqar Ali Bhutto's Pakistan Peoples' Party in the early 1970s, with its socialist manifesto, its harping on economic issues and its populist style, seemed finally to confirm their victory. Nevertheless, at the same time the Islamic parties were beginning to gather greater support. The shattering loss of East Pakistan in 1971 brought many to Islam as the ground on which the state could be rebuilt; growing disillusionment with both the capitalist road to development of the 1950s and 1960s and the socialist road of the 1970s led to a willingness to try an Islamic way forward. After the Islamic parties, which formed part of a national alliance of nine parties, failed to win the general elections of March 1977, there was prolonged mass protest. The army stepped in, accepted accusations of ballot-rigging leveled against Bhutto's Peoples' Party and ruled with the support of the national alliance.

The chief martial law administrator, General Zia ul-Haq, instituted a cultural revolution no less dramatic than that of Qaddafi in Libya. There was to be an Islamic system along the lines laid down by Mawlana Mawdudi. The *Sharia* was declared supreme over the law of the land, which was of British origin. Islamic punishments like flogging, amputation and hanging were introduced for "major" crimes ranging from the drinking of alcohol to adultery. Bank interest was abolished; *Sharia* taxes were introduced. Non-Muslims were excluded from playing a part in the state and Western-style democracy was declared un-Islamic — sovereignty belonged to God alone. Remnants of Western influence were attacked: schools teaching in English were told to use Urdu; textbooks were revised; towns, streets and public places were renamed. The people were directed to follow the patterns of an Islamic life; government offices now set aside time for prayers, and fasting in Ramadan was strictly enforced. Thus General Zia ul-Haq strove to break the Western and secular mold and to create a religious one which would make Pakistan more like the Islamic state and society it proclaimed itself to be.

The revolution in Iran of 1978–79 represents the most sudden and successful attempt to break this Western and secular mold. "What has already occurred in Iran," declared a Muslim in 1980, who is also a leading historian of the land, "is at the same time the most unexpected and most joyful triumph of the Islamic *Ummah* in the 20th century." The leaders were *ulama* who from the 17th century had opposed the shahs whenever they threatened Islam or seemed in other ways unworthy to rule. They were in the forefront of protest from that against the Reuter concession in 1873 to that in favor of Musaddeq in the early 1950s. The movement which finally brought them to power began in reply to Muhammad Riza Shah's assault on Islamic institutions and values from 1959 which seemed to promise the ultimate secularization of Iranian society. One scholar, Ayatullah Khomeini (1902–) emerged as the strongest critic of the regime, although neither the most senior nor the most learned of the top-ranking *ulama*. A leading teacher at the Faiziya madrasa in Qum, which was the intellectual heart of Iranian Islam, he had won considerable moral authority as a man who embodied Islam in his simple, devout life and in his active guardianship of the faith. He rejected the quietist stance of many of his fellow *ulama* and spoke out against the Pahlavi regime which he knew to be fundamentally hostile to Islam. "All the idiotic words that have proceeded from the brain of that illiterate soldier," he wrote of Riza Shah, "are rotten and it is only the law of God that will remain and resist the ravages of time." In 1963 he began openly to attack the soldier's son: Muhammad Riza Shah had violated his oath on coming to the throne to protect Islam; he had subordinated Iran to foreign powers, in particular the USA and Israel; he had granted American advisers and their dependants total exemption from Iranian law so that, as Khomeini put it, if an American soldier's dog bit the shah he could gain no redress. He called upon the Iranian army to rise up and overthrow the tyranny which was "working towards the total enslavement of Iran." On 5 June 1963 Iranians rose throughout the land. The army replied with bullets and at least 15 000 died. Khomeini was sent into exile where from Najaf, one of the Shia holy cities of Iraq, he continued his assault.

Around the same time a thinker emerged within Iran, Dr Ali Shariati (1933–77), whose understanding of Islamic and Western learning was so outstanding that he was able to demonstrate in a way which many found intellectually satisfying how the great subjects of Western scholarship might be contained within an Islamic frame. He published much and lectured in colleges and universities throughout the country; the young devoured his thoughts. He was tortured, exiled and died mysteriously in Britain. He had, nevertheless, shown young Iranians how they might reconcile their secular education with Islam. When in 1978 discontent swelled against the Pahlavi regime, many were prepared both to seek an Islamic solution and to look for leadership to the learned man who for

years had spoken out against it unequivocally. Such was Khomeini's authority that by the simple means of tape-recorded messages, transmitted by telephone and through the contacts of the *ulama*, he was able to guide the rising tide of protest which flooded onto the streets and braved the army's guns. In December over five million people, according to several estimates, converged on the vast square in Teheran, where the shah had raised the Shayyad monument celebrating 2500 years of Iranian monarchy, to demand the abolition of that monarchy and the establishment of an Islamic republic. It was a display of popular will without parallel in recent history. The shah was forced to flee. Khomeini returned. To the amazement of Westerners and secular Iranians alike he seemed able to guide the development of the revolution from within no less effectively than he had conducted the mounting protest from without.

Not since the late 17th century, when Muhammad Baqir Majlisi had virtually taken over the government from Shah Sultan Husain, had one of the *ulama* come to exercise such power. While acknowledging that this was the most striking manifestation of the general movement of Islamic reassertion in the 1960s and 1970s, we should also identify those features which were peculiar to Iran. There was the particular theory of Twelver Shiism that in the absence of the Twelfth Imam only a *mujtahid*, deeply learned in the *Sharia* and of spotless life, could rule. Many saw Khomeini as such a *mujtahid* and some wondered if he might not be the Twelfth Imam himself to the extent that the Ayatullah's chief rival was driven to remark, somewhat acidly, that the Twelfth Imam was not expected to return by jumbo jet! There was the martyrdom of Husain (see above, p. 47), the remembrance of which lay at the heart of Shia religious practice and which operated as a metaphor to describe the oppression of the righteous. The shah became Yazid whose forces had slaughtered Husain and his tiny band at Karbala; the young Iranians shot in the street were martyrs. The religious cycle which focused on martyrdom and periods of mourning became a political cycle too; 10 Muharram, when Shias mourn the martyrdom of Husain, was the day when over five million progressed through the streets of Teheran to demand the foundation of an Islamic republic. Then, there was the unusually strong position of the *ulama*, many of whom stood apart from the state, retained popular support and formed a network throughout Iran beyond government control. Such a compound of belief and organization was intrinsically revolutionary. The shah's dash to make Iran the world's fifth strongest industrial power by the 1990s added combustible materials. Bazar traders, the hub of traditional commercial enterprise, felt threatened by the rapid growth of the modern capitalist system. Iranians in general felt affronted as nearly 150 000 foreigners flocked in to run the new high-technology industries and to live a gilded life in secluded colonies. Teheran grew by 200 per cent in 20 years, and so did the other major cities, as countrydwellers came to man the new industries: no single development strengthened the hands of the *ulama* more effectively than this mushrooming of the cities. A revolutionary situation formed as the economy careered out of control. Agriculture broke

Left Women played an important part in the Iranian revolution and many, who had previously been unveiled, adopted the *chador* less for religious reasons than as the symbol of their protest against the shah's regime. This somewhat daunting group of "Guardians of the Revolution" is celebrating Iranian Women's Day, 18 May 1979.

Below The Iranian revolution produced some striking posters. Here Ayatullah Khomeini, as Moses, is victorious over the shah, as Pharaoh, who clings on to the coattails of American imperialism allied to the Israeli state.

down as farmers left the countryside; urban services broke down as the cities became congested. Then the 50 per cent growth in GNP of the years 1973–76 was replaced by rampant inflation, recession and unemployment.

In making the revolution the *ulama* allied with the secular opposition, as they had done in the constitutional revolution of 1905–11 and in the other movements against the crown. Yet, whereas it was the secular leaders who eventually put their stamp on the legislation of the constitutional revolution, this time it was the *ulama* who gained complete control. They proceeded to impose an Islamic impress on the Iranian state and public life which was more complete than anything achieved in Libya or Pakistan. Foreign influences were attacked: pornography and much music were banned, the Anglican Christian community was persecuted and American diplomatic staff were held hostage. Respect for Islamic values was insisted upon: women had to come to government offices with their hair covered, while the contents of the royal wine cellars were publicly smashed as Muhammad Baqir Majlisi had smashed those of Sultan Husain nearly 300 years before. All life was now to be subject to Islamic ends. The *Sharia* became the law of the land and a new constitution was drawn up which embodied Ayatullah

The Iranian revolution of 1978–79 was one of history's great crowd revolutions. It saw unprecedented demonstrations of popular will on the streets of Teheran. The revolution also benefited from the glorification of the martyrs of oppression and the cycle of mourning, which is a prominent feature of Shia Islam. The dead are mourned for 40 days, of which the third, seventh and fortieth days after death are high points. As the revolution claimed more martyrs, the cycle of mourning offered more and more opportunities to express opposition to the regime. The height of passion was reached when the mourning for those mown down by the bullets of the army merged into the month of Muharram when Shias mourn their martyred imams. The tenth day of this month, when they mourn the martyrdom of Husain, is the most highly charged day of the Shia year; and it was on this day in December 1978 that over five million people processed through Teheran and assembled around the Shayyad monument, *left*, the symbol of the Pahlavi dynasty, to demand the "end of the present tyranny" and the foundation of an Islamic republic.

Khomeini's concept of Islamic government. "Islamic government," he wrote,

> is a government of divine law. The difference between Islamic government and constitutional government – whether monarchical or republican – lies in the fact that, in the latter system, it is the representatives of the people or those of the king who legislate and make laws. Whereas the actual authority belongs exclusively to God. No others, no matter who they may be, have the right to legislate, nor has any person the right to govern on any basis other than the authority that has been conferred by God . . . It is the religious expert and no one else who should occupy himself with the affairs of government.

The events we have examined above are just the most striking examples of Islamic reassertion in recent times. There are signs of similar movements elsewhere, though not sustained so long nor yet so vigorous. In Syria, for instance, the Muslim Brotherhood has become increasingly active against a secular Shia-dominated government; in Iraq Shias, moved by Khomeini's achievement in Iran, have agitated against the Baathist socialist regime. In North Africa the attempts of governments to use Islam to bolster their authority at home and their influence abroad have tended, as in Egypt, to strengthen the role of religion in society and politics. The fate of women's emancipation is a measure of the change; in Tunisia, long among the most forward of Muslim states, support for it has declined, while in Algeria the women of the cities are taking once more to the veil. Thousands of miles to the east, Malaysia offers a similar story of men as well as women adopting distinctly Islamic dress, of the rapid growth of private and government missionary movements and of shifts of government policy in an Islamic direction. Still further east, in those states where Muslims form small minorities, the process of reassertion has been revealed less as a movement for Islamic culture and institutions than as one of political separatism. Thus in Thailand's Pattani province Muslims have demanded greater autonomy within the Buddhist state, while in the Philippines the Moros of the south have fought a most bitter and persistent battle for autonomy within, if not separation from, this Christian polity.

Evidence of reassertion, however, is not to be found everywhere. In the Soviet Union, where Muslims have endured for over half a century the most thorough and brutal attempt on the part of the last great colonial power to destroy the religious roots of the community, the situation must be viewed more in terms of survival. Officially, fewer than 300 mosques, 1000 *ulama*, two madrasas and one quarterly journal exist to serve nearly 50 million Muslims, and they are only permitted to continue as levers of social control at home and sources of propaganda abroad. Yet, according to Soviet research, there has been a remarkable persistence of covert Islamic organizations. In Azarbaijan, for example, there are more than a thousand clandestine mosques and 300 shrines to which pilgrimages are made, as well as underground madrasas. Sufi orders remain vigorous, especially in the Caucasus, and are expanding in Central Asia. Soviet sociologists tell us, moreover, how Muslims have resisted assimilation by Russians, generally avoiding intermarriage at all levels of society, and possess a birthrate which means that one in three Soviet citizens will be Muslim by the year 2000. By going underground Islam has survived, and may even rise again as it did after the Mongol conquests.

In Indonesia Islam seems to have retreated in a period when men of secular outlook, and often of Hindu-Javanese background, have dominated the country. During World War II, it will be recalled, Islam made important advances; an Islamic bureaucracy had come to be established in the state and Muslim political parties were vigorous and well placed. Independence brought the first setback when Muslims were unable to make the new country an Islamic state; indeed they were not even able to realize the principle propounded in the Jakarta Charter of 1945, that Muslims should be obliged to observe the *Sharia*. Some rebelled. Under the leadership of S. M. Kartosuwirjo (1905–62) the rebels claimed that there could be no true freedom in a secular state; this could only be found when orthodox Muslims governed, acting in the name of God and in accordance with the *Sharia*. The Dar al-Islam rebellion, as it was known, lasted from 1948 to 1962, ravaging large areas of western Java as well as the historically active Muslim regions of Aceh and south Sulawesi. Most Muslims, however, pursued their aims in peace, although they were no more successful than those who went to war. Muslim political parties failed to capture power in the first general elections of 1955, gaining only 44 per cent of the vote; in the second elections of 1971 their share was reduced to 23·7 per cent. They were denied a voice in government and even lost control of the Islamic bureaucracy. They were clearly losing ground among Indonesians: Western culture attracted the young, Christians were winning converts, support for Javanese mystical sects was growing. Bitter communal riots in 1968 and 1969 expressed Muslim frustrations. Matters improved slightly in the 1970s. In the 1977 elections Muslim political parties increased their share of the vote to 29·3 per cent and Muslim intellectuals began to respond to the new confidence spreading through the Islamic world. There was joy at Egypt's success in the war of October 1973 and pride at an event as distant as the London Festival of Islam in 1976. A new self-assurance began to develop, for instance, in relations with Indonesian Christians. Nevertheless, Islam did not seem to be regaining the ground it had lost in state and society: the numbers of pilgrims to Mecca in the 1970s were below the high figures of the early 20th century, and as a proportion of the Muslim population were much lower.

The growth of pan-Islamic organizations

The reassertion of Islam has not just taken place within the nation-states which emerged as the Western tide receded. There has also been a rekindling of the pan-Islamic spirit, which had languished since the caliphate was abolished and the broad vision of the community was overwhelmed by secular nationalism. Indeed, the new confidence in Islam which we have witnessed in many societies has found its complement in the growth of international organizations to draw

Below: The reassertion of Islam in the 1960s and 1970s The map indicates which states belong to the Islamic Conference, the pan-Islamic political organization established by King Faisal of Saudi Arabia, and where the Islamic summits and the annual meetings of foreign ministers of Muslim states have taken place.

Bottom: The Muslim world and oil In 1978 the Islamic world produced over 45 per cent of the world's oil and controlled over 65 per cent of known reserves. The wealth and power brought by the possession of such a considerable proportion of this key resource have played a major part in the reassertion of Islam. On the one hand they have enabled Saudi Arabia to found pan-Islamic organizations like the Islamic Conference and the World Muslim League; on the other they have enabled Muslim countries to put pressure on the West to respect their views, as they did with the oil embargo and with the sharp increase in oil prices which accompanied the Arab-Israeli war of October 1973.

Right Some of the chief participants in the second Islamic summit at Lahore, February 1974, at prayer. Their varying degrees of reverence hint at the stresses the organization faces with the difference in outlook between those whose vision is Islamic and those whose vision is purely secular. From the left,

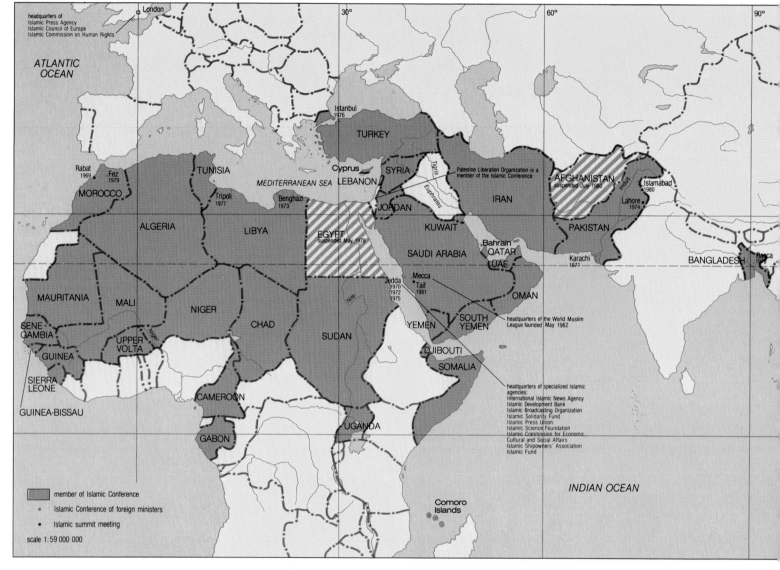

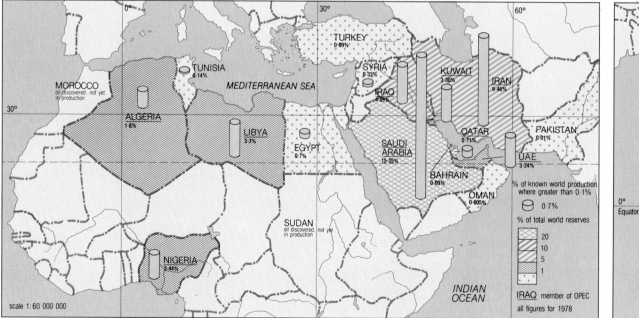

Saddam Husain of Iraq, Zulfiqar Ali Bhutto of Pakistan, Muammar Qaddafi of Libya, King Faisal of Saudi Arabia and the shaikh of Kuwait.

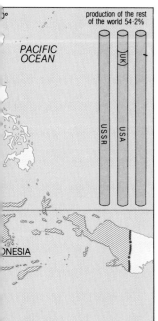

Muslim states together and to concert their actions so that Muslim voices are heard more clearly and their interests are treated more respectfully by the peoples of the world.

Two great pan-Islamic organizations have been established. There is the World Muslim League (*Rabetat al-alam al-Islami*) set up in May 1962 which, as a purely religious organization with bodies affiliated throughout the world, exists to oppose all ideologies inconsistent with Islam and to propagate the faith. It adjudicates on Islamic matters and offers support to Islamic causes. The headquarters is in Mecca and the leading members meet there each year during the pilgrimage. The second great organization is the Islamic Conference, which derived from the impetus of the first Islamic summit conference which met at Rabat in 1969. There followed the first Islamic conference of foreign ministers which decided to establish a permanent Islamic political organization with its secretariat at Jedda. By 1975 there were 43 member states; the first secretary-general was from Malaysia, the second from Senegal; it was a truly pan-Islamic organization. From 1970 the conference of foreign ministers met annually; there were further Islamic summits. Among the issues taken up were the Arab cause against Israel, the Muslim freedom movement in the southern Philippines and the coordination of a common Muslim front in the United Nations. At the same time the conference pressed ahead with the creation of the framework of pan-Islamic institutions: funds were set up to finance cultural centers, liberation movements and major projects; a news agency, development bank and broadcasting organization were established, all with their headquarters in Jedda.

This pan-Islamic enterprise, in which the World Muslim League and the Islamic Conference perform complementary roles, is an important new force in international affairs. It rests on the twin pillars of Muslim belief, transmuted on occasion into secular values, and temporal power. Belief in the importance of the Muslim community is one pillar. God told Muslims that they were the best community, which could not agree upon error. They believe that it is through belonging to this community that their lives become significant: the Islamic era dates not from the birth of Muhammad, nor from the beginning of revelation, but from the flight from Mecca to found the community. The sense of community is fostered by all the key rituals of the faith; the annual pilgrimage to Mecca is its ultimate celebration. If for Muslim believers the community is a living fact, for those who are Muslims only by culture the sense of shared history and the feeling of brotherhood still linger. Thus, if the growth of the World Muslim League around the pilgrimage is yet one more example of how this rite continues to bind the community down the generations, the speed with which Muslim states came to join the Islamic Conference, wise diplomacy apart, illustrates the enduring appeal of Muslim brotherhood – no Muslim leader, however secular, however radical, could find it easy to explain to his people why they should not join the international forces of Islam. Oil is the second pillar. Of the 13 members of OPEC in the mid-1970s, 11 were Islamic countries: Algeria, Gabon, Libya, Indonesia, Iran, Iraq, Kuwait, Nigeria, Qatar, Saudi Arabi and the United Arab Emirates, the two others being Venezuela and Ecuador. The wealth oil brought was used to finance the structure of pan-Islamic organization and its various funds. The international leverage it offered was used both to draw recalcitrant Muslim states into line and to put pressure on the West, as was achieved most dramatically in the oil embargo and the sharp increase in oil prices which followed the Arab-Israeli war of October 1973. Islam and power were united once more.

The hand behind this pan-Islamic enterprise was that of King Faisal of Saudi Arabia (reigned 1964–75), who combined learning and piety with statesmanship of real vision. Influential over his country's policies long before he came to the throne, he was moved to assert Islam internationally for reasons similar to those which spurred devout Muslims in the various states: opposition to Muslim leaders with secular ideologies, and opposition to alien influences over the Muslim world, in particular the state of Israel. The World Muslim League was established to counteract at a religious level the radicalism and revolutionary socialism of Nasser and his followers in the Arab world. The Islamic Conference was the culmination of attempts throughout the 1960s to draw Muslim states together at the political level to struggle against not just revolutionary socialism but the state of Israel. Faisal's plans for Islamic unity were boosted by the 1967 Arab war with Israel in which two revolutionary states, Egypt and Syria, were badly beaten and looked to Saudi Arabia for aid. Moreover, now that east Jerusalem, site of the al-Aqsa mosque, the place towards which the Muslims had first prayed and the third holiest place in the Islamic world, was in Israeli hands, he was able increasingly to present Israel not just as an Arab problem but as an Islamic one. The burning of al-Aqsa in August 1969 brought a rapid consolidation of the Islamic front. Within a month the first Islamic summit met at Rabat. Within a year the first Islamic conference of foreign ministers had also met and made one of its first actions to declare 21 August, the anniversary of the burning of al-Aqsa, an annual day of solidarity with the Palestinian people. Thus Faisal drew the radical Arab states into a wider front by means of which the balance of power between not just the Arabs but the whole Muslim community and the Western and Communist countries could begin to be redressed. In the process, although national rivalries continued to be disruptive, he gave the Muslims of the world the basis of more political unity than they had had since the Umaiyad caliphate.

On 21 November 1979, when Muslims celebrated the beginning of their community's 15th century, they looked about them with greater confidence than they had done for nearly 200 years. The message of the Quran had been transmitted to the modern age. It was vigorously alive, in places still passed on by *ulama* and sufis alone, in others with the full support of the powerful machinery of the modern state, which also administered the *Sharia*. Muslims had succeeded not just in winning their political freedom from the West but were now reasserting their culture and philosophy of life. They were achieving this in their various states; they were beginning to achieve this in the affairs of mankind as a whole. Admittedly, other civilizations of the developing world were doing the same, but none so dramatically or so effectively. Much of the secret lay in power. As this filtered back into Muslim hands, they felt new confidence in the vision of life's purpose built around the Quran. As they began to command their destiny, history once more seemed to be on their side. That clarion call issued by Iqbal over 50 years before seemed to have been answered. They had endured "Europe's hordes with flame and fire," they had resisted "the attraction of the West," and now they were rising "out of slumber deep" to rebuild the earth. But as to the truth of the matter, as the Muslim historians always used to say, "God alone knows."

Muslim population of the world by country
Figures for the numbers of Muslims in the world vary, those from Islamic sources being rather more optimistic than those from elsewhere. The map is based on Western sources (*The World in Figures*, 1980; *CBS News Almanac*, 1978; J. S. Nielsen,

Muslims in Europe, 1981); most figures are for 1976, and most are to some extent estimates. The number of Muslims in China is a matter for considerable speculation, estimates varying from 20 million to 80 million.

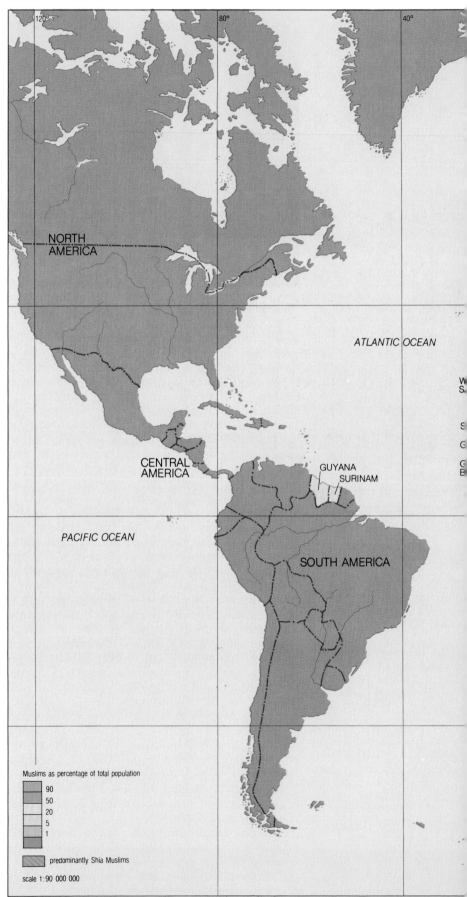

NORTH AMERICA

ATLANTIC OCEAN

CENTRAL AMERICA

GUYANA
SURINAM

PACIFIC OCEAN

SOUTH AMERICA

Muslims as percentage of total population

90
50
20
5
1

predominantly Shia Muslims

scale 1:90 000 000

Islam in the West

Since World War II Westerners have come face to face with Muslims at home. New Muslim communities have grown in their midst; new Muslim confidence has been flaunted beneath their startled gaze. American Blacks converted to Islam as they drew on aspects of African culture to assert their identity. There was new Muslim wealth, notably after the rise in oil prices of 1973. Finally, and in the long run probably most important, there was the establishment of significant Muslim communities by immigration to Britain, France and West Germany.

Right Two signs of the new Muslim confidence in Britain during the mid-1970s were the World of Islam Festival and the opening of this large new mosque in Regent's Park, London.

Far right Motorists in the West became aware of the sudden new Arab Muslim purchasing power in the mid-1970s as this humorous observation of its impact on oil prices reveals.

Above Malcolm X, the American Black Muslim leader, whose pilgrimage to Mecca helped to wean him away from using Islam as a vehicle for Black racialism. "I remember one night at Muzdalifah," he wrote in his autobiography, " . . . I lay awake amid sleeping Muslim brothers and I learned that pilgrims from every land – every color and class and rank, high officials and beggars alike – all snored in the same language."

Right The map illustrates, as far as can be accurately ascertained, the Muslim populations of European societies and the main places from which they came. The Muslims of the Balkans are long established. The new Muslims of western Europe have come largely to do the less well-paid jobs in their host societies.

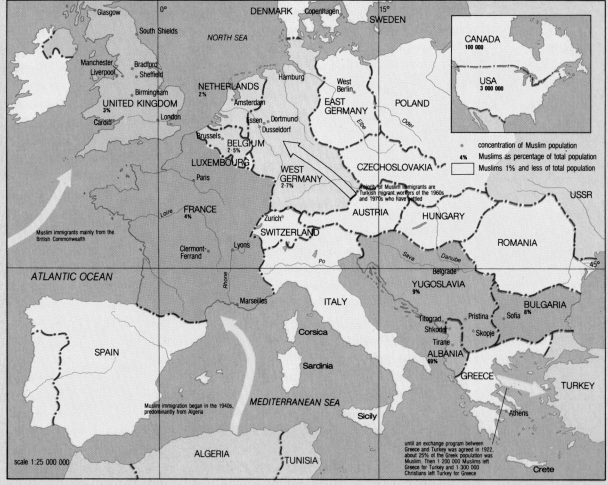

PART TWO

TO BE A
MUSLIM

RELIGIOUS LIFE

*"Glory be to my God,
the Almighty."*

The Quran

The circumstances of the revelation of the Quran and its nature as a book have been described in the first chapter. Here we are concerned with how Muslims regard the book and what part it plays in their daily lives.

Muslims believe that the Quran is the word of God, the direct expression of divine will. Its revelation was a miracle, attested by Muhammad's illiteracy and his ignorance of many of the matters with which it deals, no less than by its literary form which has no like in poetry, in prose or in the recorded versions of the Prophet's normal speech. When God spoke through Muhammad, he intervened in human history for the last time; the revelation is his last word before the day of judgment. The Quran is thus the supreme authority for all mankind, the only road to salvation. It is the measure of truth and the best model for conduct. It is always right and is the purest and most beautiful form of speech. "There was never music in the world before like that," declared one Indian Muslim to a Christian missionary friend. Non-Muslims must read the Quran to begin to have an inkling of its power and of the enormous religious charge it transmits to believers. Even in translation it is possible to sense the superhuman quality, the transcendent power which penetrates the believer's soul:

> O you who believe, hold God in awe. Let a soul look to what he has forwarded for a morrow. Hold God in awe. God is cognisant of all you do. Do not be like those who forgot God and God caused them to forget themselves. These are the wanton with life. The denizens of the fire are not as the denizens of the garden. The denizens of the garden theirs is the triumph.
>
> Had We caused this Quran to come down upon a mountain you would have seen it disintegrating in humility and awe before God. Those similitudes We employ for the sake of men: it may be they will ponder them.
>
> He is God: there is none but him: he knows what is hidden and what is evident. He is the merciful lord of mercy. He is God: there is no god but him. He is the king, the holy, the peace, the faithkeeper, the preserver, the strong, the all-disposing, whose greatness is ever self-affirming. Praise be to God above all that idolaters conceive. He is God, the Creator, the Maker, the Fashioner; his are the beautiful names. All that is in the heavens and in the earth magnifies him. He is ever mighty and wise (59: 18–24).

The Quran accompanies the believer through his life. As a child he will begin to learn it as he begins to talk. He will hear it recited during daily prayers, at his marriage and at the death of loved ones. He will turn to it when in trouble or in need of consolation.

He will perhaps know the whole text by heart and recite it from day to day, seeking spiritual refreshment from the divine presence in the text. One of his greatest pleasures will be to hear a well-voiced *Qari* chanting the holy word in slow melodic phrases, revealing new beauty and uncovering new layers of meaning.

The Quran is as important to Muslims as Jesus to Christians. It is witness of God's care for humankind. The words are to be remembered with the utmost precision; they are to be copied in the fairest of hands. The book is to be made beautiful, its pages, covers and binding an opportunity for craftsmen to praise God through art. The book is cherished, wrapped in a fine cloth and always given a place of honor. It "holds the highest place in Islam," declares a professor of Quran commentary at the 1000-year-old Muslim university of al-Azhar. "For Muslims, the Quran is not only the text of prayers, the instrument of prophecy, the food for the spirit, the favorite canticle of the soul. It is at the same time the fundamental law, the treasure of the sciences, the mirror of the ages. It is the consolation for the present and the hope for the future."

In the name of God, the merciful Lord of mercy. Praise be to God, the Lord of all being, the merciful Lord of mercy, Master of the day of judgment. You alone we serve and to you alone we come for aid. Guide us in the straight path. The path of those whom you have blessed. Not of those against whom there is displeasure, Nor of those who go astray.

I was in his voice despite the vast legacy of incredulity that I had received from the West. When he reached the end of a verse, he paused, and so it came about – an outburst of fervor. And while he chanted, it was like a man in the wilderness chanting his faith. And the voice rose and swelled, changed in tone, became tragic, soared and then floated down on our heads like a seagull gliding gently and softly, little more than a whisper. And so – never again will I go in search of intellectuals, of written truths, synthetic truths, of collections of hybrid ideas which are nothing but ideas. Never again will I travel the world in search of a shadow of justice, fairness, progress, or schemes calculated to change mankind.

Muslims feel the essence of the Quran lies in the opening chapter, the *Fatiha. Far left* The *Fatiha* in a 13th/14th-century manuscript, and (*left*) its translation. Muslims use the *Fatiha* as Christians use the Lord's prayer.
Above Boys learning the Quran in Oman. Accuracy is essential as the schoolmaster makes clear to his pupil (*right*) in the *Ambiguous Adventure* by Cheikh Hamidou Kane.
Top right The Quran has a powerful impact. We see it in the face of the Javanese peasant, we feel it in the words of Driss Chraïbi's autobiographical novel, *Heirs to the Past*, as the hero after 16 years in Paris hears the Quran at his father's funeral.
Far right Ornamental panel from a Moroccan Quran, 16th century.

"Repeat it! Again! Again!"
    The teacher had shifted the grip of his fingernails, and they were now piercing the cartilage at another place. The child's ear, already white with scarcely healed scars was bleeding anew. Samba Diallo's whole body was trembling, and he was trying his hardest to recite his verse correctly, and to restrain the whimpering that pain was wresting from him.
    "Be accurate in repeating the Word of your Lord. He has done you the gracious favor of bringing his own speech down to you. These words have been veritably pronounced by the Master of the World. And you, miserable lump of earthly mold that you are, when you have the honor of repeating them after him, you go so far as to profane them by your carelessness. You deserve to have your tongue cut a thousand times . . ."
    "Yes, master . . . I ask you pardon . . . I will not make a mistake again. Listen . . ."
    Once more, trembling and gasping, he repeated the flashing sentence. His eyes were imploring, his voice was fading away, his little body was burning with fever, his heart was beating wildly. This sentence – which he did not understand, for which he was suffering martyrdom – he loved for its mystery and its somber beauty. This word was not like other words. It was a word which demanded suffering, it was a word from God, it was a miracle, it was as God himself had uttered it.

At the Mosque

"Prayer is like a stream of sweet water which flows past the door of each one of you," runs one tradition. "A Muslim plunges into it five times a day." At dawn, at midday, in the afternoon, just after sunset and in the evening the muezzin calls Muslims to prayer: "God is most great," he cries four times in Arabic. "I bear witness there is no god but God," twice. "I bear witness that Muhammad is God's messenger," twice. "Come to prayer," twice. "Come to success," twice. "God is most great," twice. "There is no god but God!" On hearing this Muslims should prepare for prayer, either in their homes, where women generally pray, or in the mosque, a term derived from the Arabic *masjid* meaning place of prostration, where it is preferred that men should pray if they possibly can. It is obligatory, however, that Muslims attend the mosque only for midday prayer on Friday when they will also listen to a sermon.

The Muslim should go quietly to the mosque and try to be in good time. On arriving he takes off his

Below An old man makes his way across the courtyard of the Umaiyad mosque in Damascus, the earliest surviving monumental mosque in the Islamic world, to make his ablution before prayer.

Below Evening prayers have already begun at the mosque of Mahabat Khan, Peshawar. The congregation, led by an imam, have reached the prostration in a *rakat* of prayer, while latecomers are still washing. It will be possible for them to complete their prayers after the others have finished. Then they will probably linger and talk for a

while before going to their homes. "Unlike a church," declared Muhammad Ali Rampuri, the Indian Muslim leader, "a mosque is not a silent place with a dim religious light, deserted for the greater part of the week; but . . . a very airy and well-lit place, a . . . busy haunt of men."

Bottom right A man washes before prayer at the fountain of the al-Aqsa mosque in Jerusalem. First he must wash his hands up to the wrists three times, then rinse out mouth and nostrils and wash face and arms up to the elbow, each action being performed three times. Then he draws his hands over his head,

ears and neck, and washes his feet up to the ankle three times.

shoes and either leaves them at the entrance or carries them to be placed, with their soles together, just beyond his head at the point where he prays. Then he washes himself, symbolically expressing his desire for inner cleanliness as he removes the dirt from his body. And then he joins the lines of his fellow Muslims facing Mecca and waits for the imam to give the signal for prayers to begin. As he performs a *rakat* or cycle of prayer, his whole body expresses the words he utters: as he says "Glory be to my Lord, the great," he bows; as he says "Glory be to my God, the Almighty," he prostrates himself, placing forehead and nose on the ground as a mark of his submission to God. His attitude throughout should be one of humility, devotion and concentrated attention. He is talking to God and listening to him; if he is not sincere the prayer will have no value.

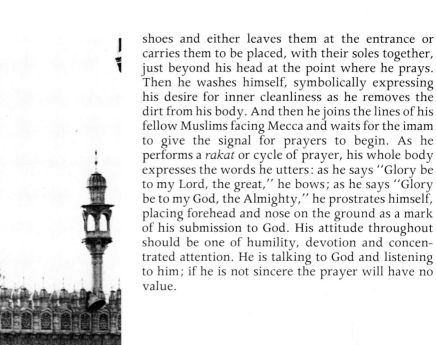

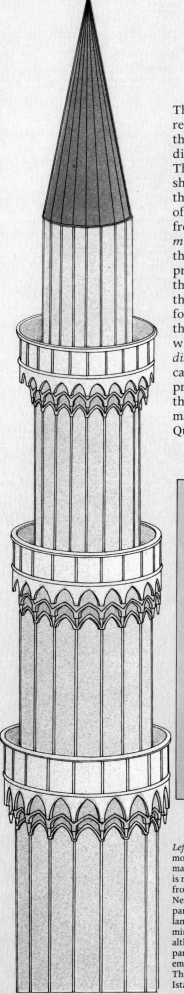

The design of the mosque and its features directly reflect their functions in public worship. Essentially the mosque is a wall so orientated that a line drawn directly from Mecca would strike it at right angles. This ensures that the Muslim knows which way he should face to pray; the niche made in the wall by the *mihrab* emphasizes that direction. The tendency of the building to be square rather than long stems from the desire of worshipers to pray as close to the *mihrab* wall, and therefore to Mecca, as possible: there is no need, as in a church, to accommodate processional worship. The minaret developed to call the people to prayer, and the higher it is, the further the muezzin's voice will carry. Some kind of tank or fountain is essential so that worshipers can perform their ablutions; so also is the *minbar*, or pulpit, from which the imam delivers his Friday sermon. The *dikka*, or platform, is needed so that respondents can transmit the posture of the imam and the appropriate response to a large congregation, although the introduction of the loudspeaker has tended to make it redundant. The *kursi*, or lectern, holds the Quran.

Right The *mihrab*, which indicates the direction of Mecca, is the central feature of any mosque. The niche itself is not sacred, unlike the Christian altar; it is the direction it expresses that is sacred. Indeed, such is the emphasis placed on this that Muslims are careful in aligning privies, graves and even bedrooms to avoid the possibility of inadvertent disrespect. The concave shape is derived from the Christian apse introduced in the early 8th century by Coptic masons. The *mihrab* is usually the most heavily decorated part of the mosque.

Shoes are taken off before entering a mosque so as not to defile it with ritually impure substances. They will either be left in a rack (*below*), or in a trough at the entrance, or the worshiper may carry them with him, as described on the previous page.

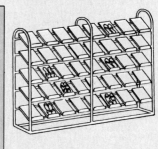

Below A well-designed fountain for washing, which must be done in running water. Normally the partial ablution described on the previous page is sufficient before prayer, but if a man is defiled in a major way, for instance if he has made love to his wife, then he must wash himself completely. The latrines for this purpose are marked on the plan (*left*). Should a Muslim fail to wash correctly, his subsequent prayer is without value.

Left It is not essential that a mosque has a minaret, and in many mosques the call to prayer is made from a roof, a wall, or from the courtyard. Nevertheless, in cities, particularly in the central Islamic lands, mosques usually have minarets. One is the norm, although royal foundations, particularly in the Ottoman empire, tended to have more. The mosque of Sultan Ahmed in Istanbul has six.

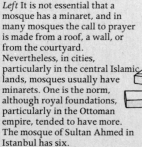

Below The *dikka*, or platform, is usually placed in line with the *mihrab*. Here respondents, usually the muezzins of the mosque, follow the postures of the imam and speak the responses so that the stages of the prayer can be transmitted to a large audience.

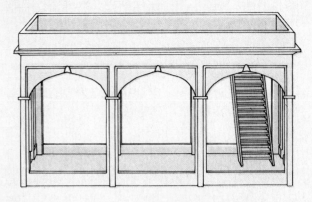

Below The *kursi*, or lectern, holds the Quran, and mosque Qurans are often very large; from there the *Qari*, or cantor, recites. The *kursi* is usually placed next to the *dikka*.

The *minbar*, or pulpit, stands to the right of the *mihrab*. It is essential furniture for a mosque where Muslims propose to gather for midday prayers on Friday. From it the imam, who is leading the prayers, will give his sermon. He will do so from a lower step; only the Prophet preached from the topmost step. The first *minbar* was a simple affair of three steps, and such versions are still preferred in Iran and south Asia. In the Ottoman empire and North Africa, however, a highly decorated *minbar* of monumental scale came to be common.

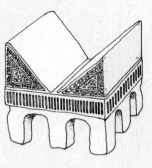

At the Shrine

Muslim piety is manifest as much at the saint's shrine as at the mosque. At the heart of the shrine, in the part usually covered by a dome, lies the tomb of the saint, a holy man, whose example helped many live Muslim lives in the past, and perhaps the founder of a great sufi order. Around him are buried his disciples and followers. It is a place where spiritual blessings are concentrated, where Muslims can come close to those who are close to God, a place where the very dust is precious.

Shrines range from small wayside structures, comprising no more than a tomb and a mosque, to vast complexes containing in addition a ceremonial hall, a madrasa, cells, kitchen, refectory, library and accommodation for guests. Such establishments may have considerable endowments, land and influence in the locality and beyond, which render them, like the shrines of Abd al-Qadir Gilani in Baghdad or Muin al-Din Chishti at Ajmere, the favorite objects for the attentions of the powerful through many centuries. In charge there will probably be the descendants of the saint, actual or spiritual or both. In some places these will be no more than managers, who regard the offerings of the devout, like the lands attached to the shrine, as no more than the rightful perquisites of their custodianship; in others the tradition of spiritual leadership may still run strong, and the living representative of the dead saint may still be actively involved in transmitting his way of knowing God.

While the religious life of the mosque is sober and orthodox, that of the shrine can be warm and ecstatic. Many Muslims attend both, as they find that the two meet complementary religious needs, and most will visit shrines in the locality and in the wider world outside. Behavior at shrines reflects different levels of Islamic understanding. Some might pray to the saint to intercede for them with God, to bring them good fortune or a child. Such prayers, compromising the unity of God, are strongly opposed by the orthodox, who would prefer that Muslims, while in the auspicious presence of a saint, confined their activities to talking directly to God. The high point in the shrine's year is the celebration of the saint's death, the day on which he joined God. There are great festivities, devotees come from afar, spiritual passions are excited, and, depending on the rules of the saint's order, there will be Quran recitations, dancing, or even singing, the program of songs being designed to record how the spiritual tradition descended from the Prophet to the saint.

Shrines have played a central role in conversion to Islam, whether of the shamanistic peoples of the steppes, or pagans in Africa or Hindus in south and southeast Asia. The record is sometimes explicit in the miracles attributed to the saints, while today the shrine may continue to attract new believers. For many the local saint is literally the first rung on the ladder towards submission to the awesome might of God.

Top The representative of a saint, in this case Mawlana Abd al-Ali Bahr al-ulum of Firangi Mahal (died 1810/11), sits in his consulting room where he gives spiritual advice and help. Many come to his daily consultations in Lucknow, India.

Above Pilgrims press to enter the shrine of Saiyid Shah Abd al-Razzaq (died 1723/4) of Bansa, some 50 kilometers from Lucknow, on the day of the new moon, an especially propitious day. Many in this picture are Hindus, as are the majority who seek the benison of this saint: the shrine is famed for relieving women in mental distress.

Right The shrine of Muin al-Din Chishti (died c. 1233) at Ajmere, who established sufism in south Asia. The annual celebration of this saint's death has been the most popular and important sufi celebration in the region for centuries.

several Central Asian, North African and Turkish orders, usually involves a circular anticlockwise rotation.

Below Rumi's tomb, which can be seen from the dance floor, is kept covered by a cloth; beside him rest all his spiritual successors to the present day. "So tangible is the *baraka* [spiritual blessing or power]," declared one scholar after entering the tomb chamber, "that the visitor cannot fail to feel he has entered a powerhouse or accumulator charged with psychic energy."

The Stages of Life

Birth

No sooner has the midwife finished her task than the call to prayer is whispered into the baby's right ear and the commencement of prayer into the left. The full text of the call to prayer, which begins "God is most great," can be found on page 182; the commencement, with which mosque prayers begin, is the same formula with the addition of the words "Lo, the service of worship is ready." Thus the very first word the child hears is God, and he begins his Muslim life with a double exhortation to worship him.

Seven days later the child is named in a ceremony called *aqiqah*. Friends and relatives are invited, the object being to introduce the new Muslim into the immediate world in which he will grow up as well as to give him a name. The head of the baby is shaved completely; a weight in gold, silver or money, equivalent to the weight of the hair, is given to the poor; an animal is sacrificed. The name will generally be chosen from those of the Prophet's family, other prophets mentioned in the Quran, or great Muslims of the past. If the family is especially devoted to a particular saint, the actual choice of name may be left to a representative of the saint's family.

Growing up

Two ceremonies mark childhood, although neither is mentioned in the Quran. The first is the *basmala*. When a child is ready to begin learning, soon after he is four, a family feast is held at which he receives his first lesson. The *basmala* and the first words revealed to the Prophet are recited: "In the name of God, the merciful, the compassionate. Read in the name of the Lord who creates – creates man from a clot. Read and thy Lord is most generous, who taught by the pen, taught man what he knew not" (96: 1–5). The child is then made to recite them, and his education has begun.

The second ceremony is circumcision, which is generally performed on boys between seven and 12, although it is permitted to circumcise a child seven days after birth. In parts of the Islamic world girls also are circumcised, a practice for which religious authority is weak, and some assert does not exist. It is not done much in India, Russia, China, Iran, Afghanistan, Turkey or Arabia, and where it does flourish it would appear to be the persistence of a pre-Islamic custom.

Marriage

"Marriage," declares a prominent Indian guide to correct Muslim behavior, "is God's great blessing for this world and the next. Man is saved from sins, his mind is settled and the heart does not waver." "When the servant of God marries," declared the Prophet, "he perfects half of his religion." Indeed Muhammad laid such emphasis on marriage and so strongly condemned celibacy that even members of ascetic sufi orders tend to be married rather than single.

188

The first call to prayer.

Preparing for circumcision.

Marriage is a contract.

Hurrying to the grave.

Marriage is a contract, not a sacrament. Nevertheless, non-Muslims should not think that it is undertaken lightly. Great emphasis is placed on the importance of mutual love and respect and the care of children; it is preferred that a man cleave to one wife throughout his life. A man is permitted to have up to four wives at once, but only on condition that he treat all of them equally, which means literally giving each the same gifts and passing the night with each in turn. Many feel that such conditions are impossible to meet. The barriers to divorce, for which all a man need say is "I divorce thee" thrice, are also high. The Prophet set his face against divorce. There may be, moreover, a considerable financial penalty. When the marriage contract is made a dowry is agreed, to be paid in two parts, a small sum to be paid before marriage to enable the bride to prepare for the occasion, and a very much larger sum to be paid if the contract is broken.

The marriage ceremony may take place at a mosque, in the home of the bridegroom or that of the bride. Usually the imam of the local mosque is present, but all that is essential is that there are two adult Muslims to witness the exchange of vows between bride and groom, which will be along the following lines:

I, Muhammad, take you, Aisha, daughter, of
Abd Allah, as my lawfully married wife
before God and in front of this company, in
accordance with the teachings of the Quran.
I promise to do everything to make this
marriage an act of obedience to God, to make
it a relationship of love, mercy, peace,
faithfulness and cooperation. Let God be my
witness, because God is the best of all
witnesses. Amen.

Death

When a man is near to death, those at his bedside encourage him to say the confession of faith; just as God was the first word he heard, so it should be the last he utters. After death the body is immediately washed, shrouded and carried to a mosque where the burial service is said. Then the bier will be borne quickly to the grave; the Prophet said that it was good that the righteous should arrive soon at happiness. The body is then buried with the face turned towards Mecca. As it is lowered into the grave those present say: "We commit thee to the earth in the name of God and in the religion of the Prophet." Some Muslims also throw earth into the grave, saying: "From it We created you, and into it We shall return you, and from it raise you a second time" (Quran 20: 55).

Muslims are encouraged not to grieve too much, and among Sunni Muslims mourning continues for no more than seven days. Death is not the end of life; Muslims are only briefly separated from those who die. Through God's grace all who truly submit will enjoy life after death.

The Believer's Year

The Muslim year is based on a lunar cycle, containing 354 days, and so changes annually by 10 or 11 days in relation to the Christian solar calendar. It is divided into 12 lunar months of 29 or 30 days. The months are set out in the calendar (*right*). The year begins with Muharram and, reading from left to right, we move through the year until we reach the last month of Zul-Hijja. The names of the months, some of which refer to the seasons, belong to the pre-Islamic Arab calendar, when a month was added every three years to keep the lunar calendar in harmony with nature. The Prophet is said to have insisted on Muslims adopting a pure lunar year. Each day begins, not at midnight, but immediately after sunset.

Muslims, like believers of other faiths, celebrate festivals to guide them in their devotions. The two main festivals, which Muslims must keep because the Prophet instructed them to do so, are the Id al-Fitr and the Id al-Adha. Fasting in Ramadan is also obligatory. Observance of the other festivals mentioned on these pages is optional. Three further festivals should also be noted: the last Friday in Ramadan, when Muslims make a particular point of attending the mosque to bid farewell to the month of fasting; Shab i-Barat, 15 Shaaban, when God is said to register each year all the actions of mankind, which is celebrated particularly by Indian Muslims; and Ashura, 10 Muharram, when Muslims remember that Noah left the Ark, Moses saved the Israelites from Pharaoh and Husain was martyred at Karbala. It is the most important festival of the Shia year.

MUHARRAM						SAFAR				
Monday		7	14	21	28	Monday		5	12	19
Tuesday	1	8	15	22	29	Tuesday		6	13	20
Wednesday	2	9	16	23	30	Wednesday		7	14	21
Thursday	3	10	17	24		Thursday	1	8	15	22
Friday	4	11	18	25		Friday	2	9	16	23
Saturday	5	12	19	26		Saturday	3	10	17	24
Sunday	6	13	20	27		Sunday	4	11	18	25
JUMADA AL-AWWAL						**JUMADA AL-AKHIR**				
Monday		6	13	20	27	Monday		5	12	19
Tuesday		7	14	21	28	Tuesday		6	13	20
Wednesday	1	8	15	22	29	Wednesday		7	14	21
Thursday	2	9	16	23		Thursday	1	8	15	22
Friday	3	10	17	24		Friday	2	9	16	23
Saturday	4	11	18	25		Saturday	3	10	17	24
Sunday	5	12	19	26		Sunday	4	11	18	25
RAMADAN						**SHAWWAL**				
Monday	1	8	15	22	29	Monday		6	13	20
Tuesday	2	9	16	23	30	Tuesday		7	14	21
Wednesday	3	10	17	24		Wednesday	1	8	15	22
Thursday	4	11	18	25		Thursday	2	9	16	23
Friday	5	12	19	26		Friday	3	10	17	24
Saturday	6	13	20	27		Saturday	4	11	18	25
Sunday	7	14	21	28		Sunday	5	12	19	26

HIJRA, migration, 1 Muharram, the first day of the Muslim year, celebrates the very first day of the Muslim era when in 622 AD Muhammad left Mecca to start a new community in Medina. Hence AH denotes the years of the Muslim era, meaning "After the Hijra," after the migration. The day is usually celebrated by telling the story of how Muhammad and a handful of friends left Mecca for Medina.

RAMADAN, the month of fasting, the ninth month of the Muslim year, when all Muslims who have reached puberty observe their religious obligation to abstain from eating, drinking, smoking and sexual relations during daylight hours. Observation of the rite can be extremely difficult in hot weather. Devout Muslims value the training it offers in spiritual discipline, and in the triumph of mind over matter.

LAILAT AL-QADR, the "Night of Majesty," 27 Ramadan. Ramadan is the month in which the first revelation of the Quran was made to Muhammad. "The Night of Majesty is better than a thousand months. The angels and the Spirit descend in it by the permission of their Lord – for every affair – Peace! it is till the rising of the morning" (Quran 97: 3–5). Muslims spend this night in reading the Quran and in prayer.

...I AL-AWWAL					RABI AL-AKHIR					
...day	3	10	17	24	Monday	1	8	15	22	29
...day	4	11	18	25	Tuesday	2	9	16	23	30
...nesday	5	12	19	26	Wednesday	3	10	17	24	
...sday	6	13	20	27	Thursday	4	11	18	25	
...y	7	14	21	28	Friday	5	12	19	26	
...day	1	8	15	22	29	Saturday	6	13	20	27
...ay	2	9	16	23	30	Sunday	7	14	21	28

...AB					SHAABAN				
...day	3	10	17	24	Monday	2	9	16	23
...day	4	11	18	25	Tuesday	3	10	17	24
...nesday	5	12	19	26	Wednesday	4	11	18	25
...sday	6	13	20	27	Thursday	5	12	19	26
...y	7	14	21	28	Friday	6	13	20	27
...day	1	8	15	22	29	Saturday	7	14	21	28
...ay	2	9	16	23	Sunday	1	8	15	22	29

...QAADA					ZUL-HIJJA				
...day	5	12	19	26	Monday	3	10	17	24
...day	6	13	20	27	Tuesday	4	11	18	25
...nesday	7	14	21	28	Wednesday	5	12	19	26
...sday	1	8	15	22	29	Thursday	6	13	20	27
...y	2	9	16	23	30	Friday	7	14	21	28
...day	3	10	17	24	Saturday	1	8	15	22	29
...ay	4	11	18	25	Sunday	2	9	16	23

MAWLID AL-NABI, the birthday of the Prophet, 12 Rabi al-Awwal. It began to be celebrated from the 10th century and seems to have gained in importance as Muslims have encountered Christianity with its especial emphasis on the birthday of Jesus. Muslims celebrate the day with gatherings to listen to eulogies of the Prophet and descriptions of his life. For sufis, with their especial regard for Muhammad as the "perfect man," the day is particularly important and its observance may sometimes be the culmination of celebrations which begin on 1 Rabi al-Awwal. The Mawlid is the most striking expression of reverence for Muhammad in Islam.

LAILAT AL-MIRAJ, the "Night of the Ascent," 27 Rajab, commemorates the night in the tenth year of Muhammad's prophethood when the Archangel Gabriel conducted him through the Seven Heavens, where he spoke with God, and from which he returned the same night with instructions that included the institution of the five daily prayers. The modern poster (*below*) tells us more of the story. Muhammad is said to have made his journey on Buraq, a winged creature, half-human, half-horse, and his ascent is said to have begun from the al-Aqsa in Jerusalem, which is illustrated in stylized form. Muslims spend the day listening to stories of the Prophet's life.

ID AL-FITR, the "festival of breaking the fast," I Shawwal, used to be the less important of the two Ids; but so great is the joy at the end of the hardship of Ramadan that Muslims have come to celebrate it with much more festivity and rejoicing than the major festival. *Id* itself means "festival" or "time of happiness" in Arabic, and at both festivals Muslims send each other wishes for a blessed and happy occasion with cards like the one shown (*left*).

Id is a time of thanksgiving to God, who has enabled Muslims to overcome the difficulties of Ramadan, and who provides for all man's needs. Muslims begin the day by bathing and changing into new clothes. They then go to the mosque for prayers which are usually so well attended that the crowds of worshipers spill out of the entrance on to the road. (*Far left*, special arrangements seem to have been made to accommodate members of this Id congregation, dressed in their gleaming white new clothes, on a playing field at Balikpapan, Borneo.) After prayers they exchange presents and visit friends and relations. They are also obliged to give to the poor. Throughout the day Muslims try to ponder on the meaning of Islam and to bury their differences with family and friends, so that they can make a new start to life in peace and forgiveness.

ID AL-ADHA, the "festival of sacrifice," 10 Zul-Hijja, is the second obligatory festival; the celebrations may last three or more days. The origins of the festival go back to the Prophet Abraham who demonstrated his willingness to sacrifice all that he loved most dearly for God's sake, which act is commemorated in the last rite of the pilgrimage to Mecca. Muslims throughout the world celebrate this day at the same time as those fortunate enough to be in Mecca. They begin the festival by attending communal prayer, as at Id al-Fitr, and then sacrifice a sheep, a cow or a camel, usually keeping one-third of the meat and giving the rest away to the poor.

Pilgrimage to Mecca

"Labbaika! Labbaika!" the pilgrims cry as they get their first glimpse of the Kaaba, the central sanctuary in the great mosque at Mecca. "Here I am (God), here I am (God), present before you, before you." This is the zenith of a Muslim life, the culmination of years spent striving in the way of the Lord, the moment when yearning can end. "I long for Mecca and its bright heavens," declares the pious Rizwan in Najib Mahfuz's Egyptian novel, *Midaq Alley*. "I long for the whisper of time at every corner and to walk down its streets and lose myself in the holy places ... I can see myself now, my brothers, walking through the lanes of Mecca, reciting verses from the Quran just as they were first revealed, as if I was listening to a lesson given by the Almighty Being. What joy!"

Every Muslim, who is sane, healthy, free from debt and able to pay both his expenses and those of his dependants, while he is away, must perform the pilgrimage at least once in his lifetime. The observances are based on the Quran (2: 196–200; 5: 95–97; 22: 26–33) and the practice of the Prophet Muhammad. They commemorate events in the lives of Abraham, Hagar his wife, and Ishmael his son. The spirit of the rite is one of total self-abnegation. The pilgrim, as he presents himself to God, sacrifices all those things which mark him in the world of men: wealth, family, friends, distinctions of dress, birth and race. He also celebrates the brotherhood of all Muslims. All are equal in dress and in what they must perform, just as they will all stand equal before God on the day of judgment. Nothing, in fact, has done more to foster Muslim solidarity than the coming together of this vast gathering each year through which a fresh charge of spiritual energy is transmitted to the Muslim peoples of the world.

The pilgrimage takes place in Zul-Hijja, the last month of the Muslim year. Before entering the sacred territory around Mecca, the pilgrim takes off his ordinary clothes and puts on the *ihram*, two plain white sheets which symbolize his abandonment of worldly life. He walks seven times around the Kaaba. He runs seven times from Mecca to Marwa and back, recalling Hagar's desperate search for water for Ishmael, and drinks from the Zamzam well where Hagar eventually found water gushing at Ishmael's feet. Soon after sunrise on 9 Zul-Hijja he sets out for the plain of Arafat where from noon until dusk he stands before God and worships him. After sunset he goes to Muzdalifa for the night. Then on 10 Zul-Hijja he moves on to Mina where he stones three pillars in memory of the way Abraham, Hagar and Ishmael rejected Satan's temptings to disobey God's command. He sacrifices an animal in memory of Abraham's willingness to submit to God's will, and then shaves and takes off the *ihram*.

He then makes seven more circuits of the Kaaba and returns to ordinary life. The prayer he offers on his sixth circuit conveys the ardor and joyful submission which mark the performance of the whole rite:

O God, thou hast much against me in respect of my relations with thee and with thy creation. O God, forgive me what is due unto thee and unto thy creation and take it off from me. By thy gracious glory make me well-satisfied without what thou hast disallowed. By obedience unto thee keep me from rebelliousness against thee and by thy goodness keep me from any save thee, O thou who art of wide forgiveness. O God, verily thy house is great and thy countenance is gracious. Thou, O God, art forbearing, gracious, and great. Thou lovest to pardon: therefore, pardon me.

Right The sketch map shows the route taken by pilgrims, on 9 and 10 Zul-Hijja, from Mecca to the plain of Arafat, a distance of about 20 kilometers, and then back via Muzdalifa and Mina.

Pilgrimage to Mecca in 1977
In this year there were 739 319 pilgrims from outside Saudi Arabia, plus 888 270 from within Saudi Arabia of whom a majority were not Saudi Arabian nationals. The number performing pilgrimage from outside Saudi Arabia has increased more than seven times during the past three decades. Of the societies with really large Muslim populations, pilgrims failed to come only from Russia and China, although a few have come in other years. Especially noticeable are the large numbers from the regimes with records of aggressive secularism, for instance Algeria, Iraq and Turkey.

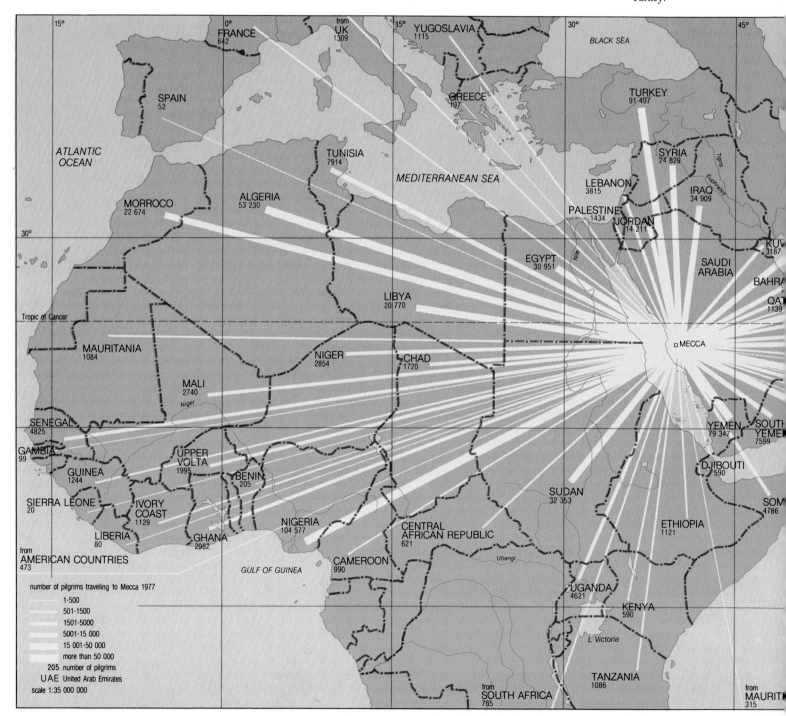

number of pilgrims traveling to Mecca 1977

1-500
501-1500
1501-5000
5001-15 000
15 001-50 000
more than 50 000
205 number of pilgrims
UAE United Arab Emirates
scale 1:35 000 000

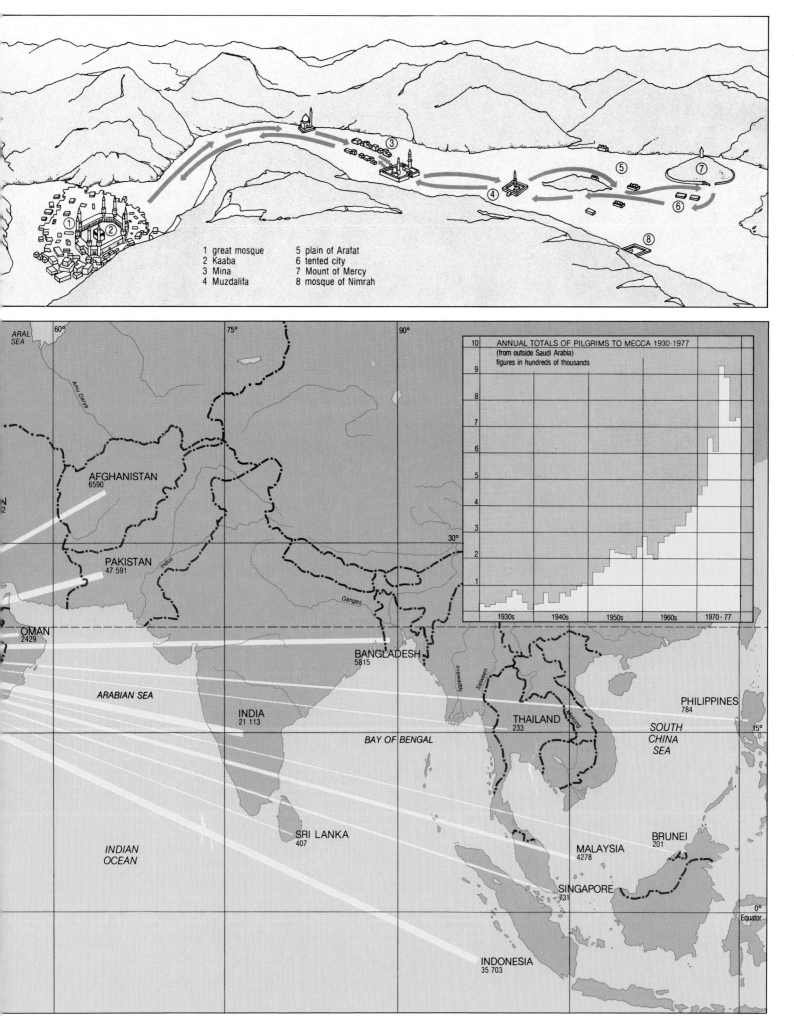

1 great mosque
2 Kaaba
3 Mina
4 Muzdalifa
5 plain of Arafat
6 tented city
7 Mount of Mercy
8 mosque of Nimrah

ARAL SEA

60°

75°

90°

Amu Darya

AFGHANISTAN
6590

PAKISTAN
47 591

Indus

Ganges

30°

OMAN
2429

BANGLADESH
5815

Irrawaddy

Salween

ARABIAN SEA

PHILIPPINES
784

INDIA
21 113

THAILAND
233

SOUTH
CHINA
SEA

15°

Mekong

BAY OF BENGAL

SRI LANKA
407

BRUNEI
201

INDIAN
OCEAN

MALAYSIA
4278

SINGAPORE
731

0°

Equator

INDONESIA
35 703

ANNUAL TOTALS OF PILGRIMS TO MECCA 1930-1977
(from outside Saudi Arabia)
figures in hundreds of thousands

10

9

8

7

6

5

4

3

2

1

1930s   1940s   1950s   1960s   1970-77

Left The vast concourse on the plain of Arafat on 9 Zul-Hijja: the tented city is erected by the Saudi Arabian authorities to protect pilgrims from the sun. We look toward Muzdalifa with the Mount of Mercy, where the Prophet preached his last sermon, in the foreground, and the mosque of Namira in the distance.

Below Pilgrims run seven times from Mecca to Marwa and back, emulating Hagar's desperate search for water.

Bottom Pilgrims make their seven circuits of the Kaaba. The Kaaba, which has been rebuilt several times, is believed to be the first place where the one God was worshiped.

ARTS OF ISLAM

*"And say: Praise be to God! . . .
and proclaim his greatness,
magnifying him."*
Quran 7: 111

Calligraphy

Calligraphy is the highest of the Islamic arts, the most typical expression of the Islamic spirit. ''Thy Lord,'' declares the very first revelation, ''. . . taught by the pen – taught man that which he knew not.'' Moreover, as God spoke in Arabic and his words were first written in the Arabic script, the Arabic language and script were treasured by all Muslims. Only by understanding them could men hope to understand God's meaning. There was no more important task than preserving and transmitting this precious gift; Muslims showed their gratitude by doing so with all the art at their command.

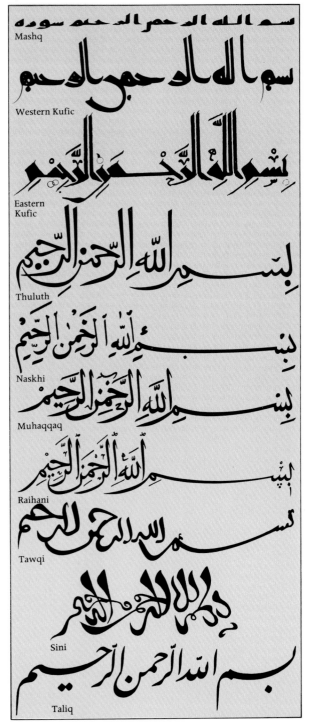

Mashq

Western Kufic

Eastern Kufic

Thuluth

Naskhi

Muhaqqaq

Raihani

Tawqi

Sini

Taliq

Muslims begin all important actions with the phrase Bism Allah al-Rahman al-Rahim. ''In the name of God, the merciful, the compassionate.'' The formula is written (*far left*) in 10 different scripts. The distinctive style of Sini hints at its origin as the script of the Chinese Muslims.

Left The one word, ''Muhammad,'' in Taliq. The enlargement only seems to emphasize the beauty of the form: ''Purity of writing,'' runs a tradition, ''is purity of the soul.''

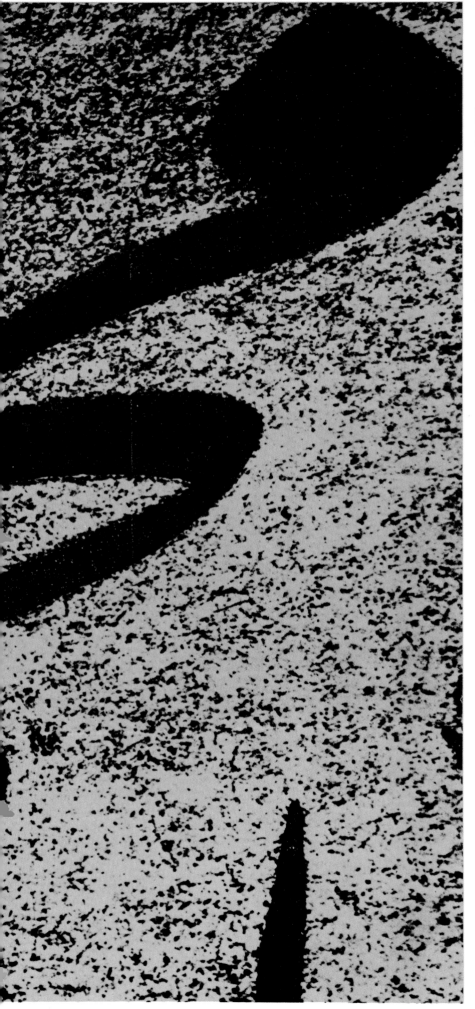

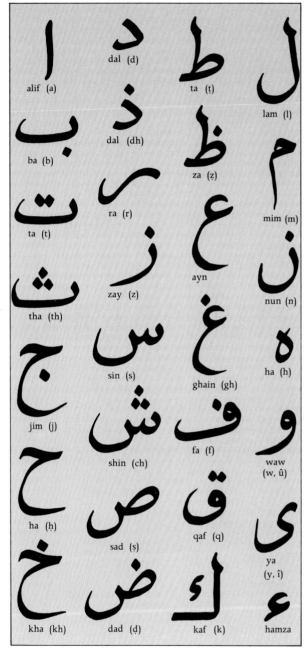

Above The 29 letters of the Arabic alphabet in their unjoined final form. Each letter is accompanied by its Arabic name and its usual transliteration in brackets. Arabic is written from right to left, and most letters change shape, depending on whether their position in the word is at the beginning, in the middle or at the end. All letters, except *alif*, represent consonants. *Wāw* and *yā* are semivowels because, in addition to representing the consonants *w* and *y* respectively, they also represent the long vowels *u* and *i* and the diphthongs *aw* and *ay* (in this book *ai*). The short vowels are represented by orthographical signs placed above or below the letters, for instance بَ (*ba*), بُ (*bu*), بِ (*bi*). Other signs are: *shaddah* ّ , which is placed above a letter to double its consonantal value; *maddah* آ , which means *hamza* plus *alif*; *sukun* ْ , which is placed above a letter to indicate that the consonant is vowelless; and ء *hamza*, a glottal stop. After Y. H. Safadi, *Islamic Calligraphy*, p. 142.

"Good writing," declares a tradition of the Prophet, "makes the truth stand out."

The Arabic script, it is widely agreed, relates directly to the Nabataean script which was itself derived from the Aramaic script. In the 650s the first full versions of the Quran were written down in a form called Jazm which reveals Nabataean influence. This in turn influenced the development of Kufic, a powerful, angular script, which became for centuries the most popular medium for recording the Quran. At the same time cursive scripts developed for bureaucratic and private purposes, and by the mid-10th century the six classical scripts of Islamic calligraphy had been established: Thuluth, Naskhi, Muhaqqaq, Raihani, Tawqi and Riqa. Soon these too were used for Quranic writing, bringing many new possibilities for decorative effect. There were four other important scripts: Tumar, Ghubar, which was often used for miniature Qurans, Taliq, which was greatly encouraged by the Safavids, and Nastaliq, which, although it has not been popular among Arabs, has for nearly four centuries been the favorite script of Iranian, Turkish and Indian Muslims.

Examples of calligraphy have been, and are, highly prized. Tamerlane and his descendants were notable patrons of the art; so too were the Safavids, Mughals and Ottomans. As decoration it is found everywhere: on tombstones and textiles, on pots, weapons and tiles, fashioned into strange shapes and adorning buildings. The words of the Quran are as important a means of beautifying mosques as the figures of Christ in churches: both are gifts of God to man.

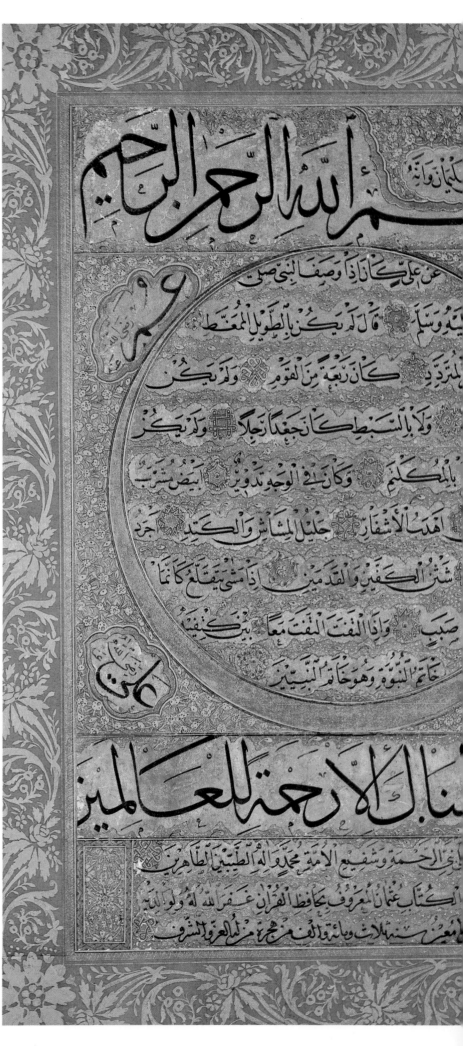

Calligraphers were highly esteemed by the most powerful of Muslim rulers. The Ottoman Sultan, Bayazid II, valued the work of Hamd Allah al-Amasi so highly that he would hold the inkpot as Hamd Allah wrote. *Far left* The calligrapher sits on the ground as he works, with one knee drawn up on which to rest his paper. The tools of his art are set out before him: scissors, a knife for cutting pens, brush and reed pens, and inkpot. The ink was usually made from lamp black mixed with vinegar. From a 16th-century Turkish manuscript of al-Qazwini's, *The Wonders of Creation*.

Great attention was paid to the layout and decoration of the page. *Center* A page of *Hilya-i Nabi* (*Description of the Prophet*) by Uthman Ibn Ali (1642–98). The *basmala* on the top line is in Thuluth; the description in the center and below is in Naskh; around, in Thuluth, are the names of the four caliphs and, below, Quran 21:107.

No less attention was paid to adorning places of prayer, and in particular the *mihrab*, with the words of God. *Left*. The *mihrab* of the Maidan mosque, Kashan. decorated with calligraphy and arabesques.

All kinds of shapes have grown out of the calligrapher's imagination. The boat (*top*) should be called the "galley of faith." The hull represents the seven articles of faith, reading from right to left, "I believe in," then the stern reads "God," the oars "and," and the oarsmen in between, from right to left, "in his angel," "his books," "his prophets," "the last day," "predestination," "good and evil," and "resurrection after death." The sail represents the declaration of faith, "There is no god but God and Muhammad is his messenger."

Above A particularly ingenious representation of the declaration of faith.

Ceramics

Muslims have used color in architecture as no other people, clothing buildings both inside and out with brilliant hues and rich patterns. Glazed tiles are the common medium. The art reached its height under Tamerlaine and his descendants in the cities of Central Asia and Afghanistan. Then there was a late but very fine flowering in the Safavid and Ottoman empires. In North Africa another tradition, no less fine, was maintained. There are four main styles of tile decoration: calligraphic, geometric, floral and arabesque. There are two main ways of using tiles: in mosaics, where pieces of different tiles are cut to fit a pattern, and as whole tiles, colored and patterned to form part of a larger design.

Below A classic arabesque of stylized plant stems, twining upon each other to form a beautiful fretted mosaic, in the drum of the dome of the Lutf Allah mosque in Isfahan.
Right This rich floral panel composed of complete tiles is representative of the best of the Iznik potters' work. It decorates the "Golden Way" traveled by visitors after they had passed through the Harem gate in Topkapi Sarai, Istanbul.
Far right A tiled mosaic dado in the Saadian tombs at Marrakesh, Morocco. Geometric patterns of this kind are typical of the Maghrib.

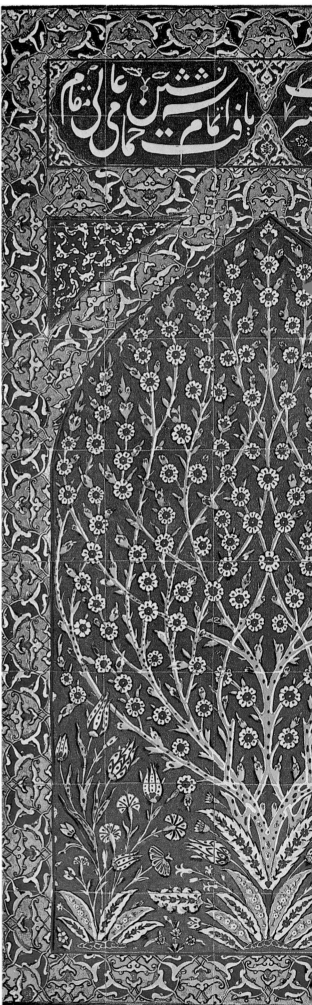

Carpets

The knotting and weaving of carpets and rugs is the classic art of nomads, which found favor among Muslims at large as well as in the non-Muslim world beyond. No product stems more directly from the possibilities and the needs of nomadic life. Women spin into yarn and weave into carpets the wool and hair from the herds managed by their menfolk; they find natural dyes in the plants and insects around them. The products of their looms are the superbly functional furnishings of those who live their lives in tents and on the ground.

Among settled communities carpets served new purposes, covering the sacred areas of shrines and mosques, demonstrating the wealth and connoisseurship of merchants and princes, and producing the stuff of lucrative exports to Europe. Patterns created in both tent and town remained extraordinarily rich and varied, from stylized shapes and geometrical designs, to prayer rugs reproducing the *mihrab* niche, to realistic compositions of men and animals and flowers.

There are five major carpet-producing areas in the Islamic world: Iran, south Asia, Turkey, the Caucasus and Central Asia. Iran has both sustained a rich tradition in the work of its nomadic tribes, for instance the Qashqai, the Lur and the Bakhtiari, and revealed the highest achievement in the hunting, vase and garden carpets of the early Safavid period, when leading painters from the royal studios played

a key role in design. The climate of south Asia is much less hospitable to carpet manufacture than the dry highlands of Iran and Central Asia, and the Mughals found no strong manufacturing tradition after they invaded. Akbar, determined that Mughal glory should not suffer by comparison with the Safavids, introduced 200 Iranian artisans and started the industry in Lahore. Like the painters, who came from Iran to the studios at Fatehpur Sikri, they quickly absorbed indigenous artistic preferences. Turkish carpets reflected the austere religious ideals of the crusading Ottoman state. The typical form was the prayer rug depicting the *mihrab* niche, although in the 18th century patterns of stylized flowers, particularly tulips, began to proliferate, in part as a result of European influence. Most notable are the carpets of Ushak and those of Ghiordes, supreme examples of the prayer rug whose sevenfold borders represent the seven gardens of paradise. Caucasian carpets are unlike those of any other area, being almost entirely geometric in design. They are the especial product of this relatively little-known land of high mountains and deep valleys which harbor many different peoples, languages and traditions from the past. Central Asia from the Caspian's eastern shore to Kashgar in the Tarim Basin is the final area. Its designs were often influenced by China; Bukhara and Samarqand are the best-known types.

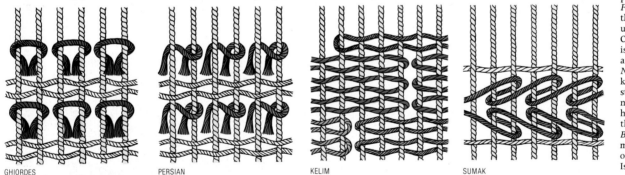

GHIORDES   PERSIAN   KELIM   SUMAK

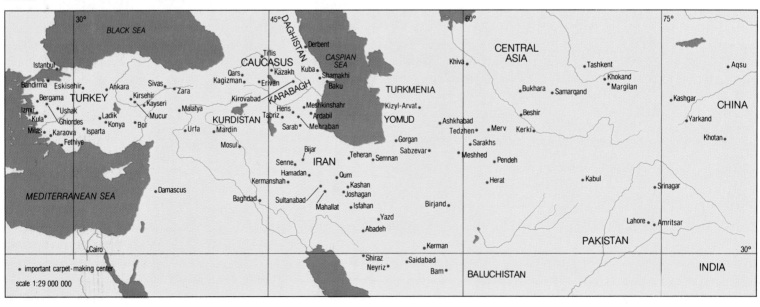

Top left Children are often employed to make carpets as their small fingers can tie finer knots; girls are usually preferred to boys, being the more conscientious workers. Here Turkish girls from the neighborhood of Sivas are weaving a rug on a simple loom of two vertical sidepieces and two crosspieces to which the warp threads are tied. Colored thread is knotted to the warp threads, and, when each row of knots is finished, two woof threads are woven and beaten down tightly by means of a steel comb, which can be seen in the bottom right-hand corner. Rugs woven by nomads are often taken out of the loom, rolled up for days, and then remounted, which can lead to the work being pulled out of shape.
Far left A 19th-century Ghiordes silk prayer rug from Turkey, 165 by 118 cm. It is a good example of this classic style, featuring a *mihrab* niche with columns topped by lotuses on either side and a lamp or ewer suspended in the niche.

Center left Two Caucasian rugs, on the left a 19th-century Kazak rug, 204 by 116 cm, and on the right a 19th-century Bidzhov rug, 204 by 125 cm. Both illustrate the geometric designs typical of the region.
Left A 19th-century rug from Yarkand or Khotan in the Tarim Basin, Chinese Turkestan, 234 by 120 cm. Its design of branches and pomegranates is arresting. Note too the border of swastika rosettes. The swastika, which has been used by civilizations throughout Asia from the Aegean to China for 5000 years, is one of the most common symbols to be found on Islamic rugs. The name is derived from the Sanskrit for well-being and the symbol is usually held to imply good fortune.
Above center A Sumak saddlebag from the Caucasus. The azure, warm red and cream colors are typical of this region.
Above A Turkmen guruband, which is worn by the leading camel of a herd to ward off evil spirits.

SOCIETY AND THE MODERN WORLD

*"The religious ideal of Islam . . .
is organically related to the
social order which it has created.
The rejection of one will
inevitably involve the rejection
of the other."*

Muhammad Iqbal,
Presidential Address to the All-India
Muslim League, Allahabad, 1930

Nomadic Life

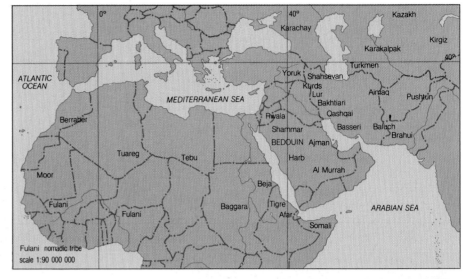

There are two main types of nomads, those who move in search of water and pasture through the year in roughly similar ecological regions, like the camel-herding Bedouin of the Arabian peninsula, and those who move seasonally between complementary ecological zones, from say lowland plains in winter to upland pasture in summer, like the Qashqai or Bakhtiari of Iran. All depend on settled communities: the vision of the Bedouin ranging free across the desert, answerable only to God and nature, is a figment of Western romanticism. The pastoral, agricultural and trading worlds form part of a single economic system, in which nomads supply milk, meat and beasts of burden in exchange for grain, dates, coffee, salt, guns and ammunition.

Nomads have made enormous contributions to Islam. Bedouin armies carried Muhammad's message out of Arabia in the 7th century to much of the civilized world; later Turk and Mongol injected new vitality into the fortunes of the faith. Yet much of Islam was intrinsically hostile to the nomadic way of life: one God replaced many tribal gods, one community replaced many tribal communities. We should not be surprised that many anthropologists stress how little nomads know and care about the Islam to which they all formally adhere. Nevertheless, when nomadic energies have been yoked to reformist organizations, like those of the Sanusi in Libya or the *Ikhwan* in Arabia, they have generated zeal enough to help found a modern state.

The modern state, however, is profoundly opposed to nomads: they do not respect state boundaries, they flout state laws, they contribute to the commonweal only on their terms. They have to be taken in hand and transformed into taxable farmers or laborers. For the first time the state has the power to get its way; there is little the nomad can do against the armored car, the radio, the machine gun or the aeroplane.

Above The map shows the major communities of nomads, herders of sheep, goats and camels, who live in a great swathe of territory through the center of the Islamic world from Turkestan and Pakistan in the east to Mali and Morocco in the west.

Right Although many nomads have been forced to become farmers, some have succeeded in finding an outlet for their nomadic instincts in modern transport like this Afghan lorry driver on the Solang pass. Most taxis and small trucks in Saudi Arabia are owned and operated by recently settled Bedouin.

Below Moroccan nomads survey their flock from inside their tent as day breaks. The tent is divided into a men's section and a women's section, the latter area usually being very much larger than the former. Male visitors may only approach the men's section, which, as in the Muslim house, is the scene of all male social activities.

Above Nomads in Afghanistan say their prayers in a simple mosque, which nevertheless still marks the *mihrab* niche. In the desert it is enough just to scratch the outline of a mosque in the sand.

Left The Qashqai of the Shiraz region in southwest Iran move from winter to summer pasture. Descendants of Turkish nomads who settled in Iran in the 15th century, they number over 400 000. During the 20th century they have been in dire conflict with the central government. In the 1930s they were subjected to brutal attempts at control by Reza Shah; in 1962 Reza Shah's son assumed direct control of tribal movements and land utilization.

Left center Nomads camped in the Unai pass in Afghanistan. Note the typical black desert tent, made of camel and goat hair, which is found throughout the Middle East.

The Village

Right The village of Aqra clings to the mountainside in Iraqi Kurdistan. In their struggle for autonomy Kurdish villagers have fought particularly hard to keep out the agencies of the modern state.
Below Women do much village labor, like these women threshing in southeastern Anatolia. They remain unveiled as are many village women throughout the Islamic world.
Bottom Pilgrimage to Mecca is one of the most important ways in which Islamic consciousness has been raised in the countryside. The wall of this house in Upper Egypt tells the story of the owner's pilgrimage to Mecca and Medina.

Most Muslims have been neither nomads nor townsmen, but villagers. About them we know least of all, in part because they leave few records and few notable buildings, and in part because they have had to keep out of events to survive. Good qualities in a villager were to support established customs, to show that tradition worked. To make innovations, to display initiative, to be fascinated by the new-fangled, was not desirable: such attitudes would surely bring trouble. Village Islam was similarly adapted to local needs. By and large it was an Islam of sufis and saints' shrines. It had grown together with the village community over hundreds of years, and might incorporate aspects of pre-Islamic practice just as the saint's tomb itself might surmount an earlier sacred site.

The 20th century brought increasing challenges to village ways. Improved communications and integration into the national or international economy brought contact with the more self-conscious Islam of the city. Villagers found their tried religious practices condemned, and new ways of being Muslim outlined. Simultaneously, they had to face growing attention from the agents of the modern state, keen both to tax them more heavily and to control them more carefully, and to fashion them after a pattern which owed little to Islam. Alongside the old loyalty to saints, there grew up a new reformist Islam and a new secularism.

The Town

Twin focuses of the Muslim town were traditionally the great mosque, where on Fridays men came together for midday prayer, and the adjacent bazar, whose shops tended to observe a distinct hierarchy in relationship to the mosque: sellers of books and paper were nearby, sellers of textiles further away, till the town limits were reached where the most mundane items were sold. Associated with the bazar were the khans, or urban caravanserais, where travelers would stay, and hammams, or baths, to be recognized by their smoking chimneys and low glass-studded domes, where Muslims could meet the faith's demands for ritual purity and actual cleanliness. This was the man's world, open, accessible, a place of cafés and of easy social intercourse.

Off the bazar branch the major streets of the various quarters. Off these run smaller streets which eventually dissipate in blind alleys. As the stranger leaves the hubbub of the bazar, he becomes aware of an enfolding quietude, broken perhaps by women's voices behind high blank walls, of faces staring, of the sense that this is private space which he is violating. Nor would such reactions be odd as quarters are often inhabited by homogeneous communities, bound by common religious, ethnic or occupational ties. Indeed such quarters were typical and distinctive enough to be regarded as units of administration. The entrance "had a great big gate which was closed at night," writes one 20th-century Cairene. "In the middle of the gate was a small door, behind which was a doorkeeper. This gate was a vestige of the past when it protected the neighborhood from thieves, rebellious mobs, and furious soldiers."

Over the past hundred years the old pattern has been challenged, and in a way which seems to symbolize the challenge of Western civilization to Muslim society itself. New towns have grown up beside the old, often founded by the colonial powers, sometimes by Muslim leaders eager to build for their people the strength of the West. They are rarely planned around a Friday mosque, but around the administrative and symbolic center of the modern state and the banks and offices of international economic enterprise, usually not in Muslim hands – a New Delhi as compared with Shahjahanabad, a North Teheran as compared with South Teheran. They are places of broad boulevards, of cinemas and high-rise apartment blocks, where a Western unsociability may begin to replace the warm companionship of the quarter.

Right The bazar reaches to the entrance of the mosque in Qum, Iran, illustrating the close association of these twin focuses of Muslim urban life.

Left Part of a quarter in the old town of Algiers. Of life in such a quarter AhmadAmin, the noted Egyptian scholar, wrote: "there had not prevailed among us the European tendency which did not value the neighbor whereby a man might live next to another for years without knowing who he was ... All the people of our quarter were neighbors who knew one another's affairs, names, and jobs. They visited each other in sickness, condoled each other in funerals, participated with each other in festivities, and loaned money to each other in cases of need. They used to exchange visits in reception rooms ..."

Right The old city of Sana in the Yemen, which is notable for its tower houses, and (*center*) the new town of Madinat Isa on Bahrain island.

Far right This plan, showing the juxtaposition of old Tunis and the new French colonial town, demonstrates the relationship between the old Muslim urban world and the new one which has grown up beside it. The street plan of the new city, some Tunisians say, takes the form of a cross being driven into the heart of the old city.

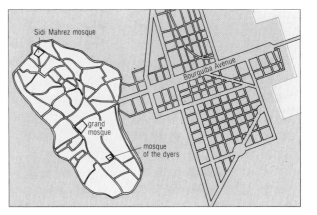

Sidi Mahrez mosque

Bourguiba Avenue

grand mosque

mosque of the dyers

The House

Below left Muslim houses do not seem inviting to the outside world. The high and bare wall and the imposing portal of this house in Fez, Morocco, speak eloquently of the privacy its family seeks within.

Below This pleasant and verdant courtyard of a Cairene house of the Mamluk period suggests what might lie behind the grim and forbidding exterior. Such courtyards, which might also boast a pool or fountain, are typical of the large town houses of the great commercial centers of the Middle East.

Muslim houses vary throughout the Islamic world according to the influence of pre-Islamic types, regional economies, differing climates, building materials and techniques; yet Islamic provisions about the seclusion of women and the central importance of the family have fashioned a common approach to the function of the building. It is first and foremost a private space within which the family can work and relax. It reveals its character to those within, and little is to be guessed about it from outside, where an austere and forbidding face is presented to the world. There will be, perhaps, a completely blank wall. If it is pierced by windows at ground level, they will be small, grilled and high enough to prevent passersby from peeping in. If there are windows higher up, they will be larger, screened and often projecting into the street. All will have been designed so that no one can spy on the doings of the household, and equally so that the inmates cannot intrude on the privacy of others.

The entrance is large, sometimes monumental, sometimes decorated in auspicious colors and symbols, all of which signify the importance of the passage from public to private space. Once inside,

Above Wooden, screened
verandas, supported by stone
corbels, in Jedda old town, Saudi
Arabia. Structures of this kind
are common additions to the
upper rooms of town houses in
the Middle East.

the male visitor is quickly ushered to the men's
reception room, which is usually placed close to the
entrance to reduce the danger of his meeting the
women of the household. It is an important room in
which the economic standing of the family will be
asserted in the profusion and quality of its
decoration and in the prized possessions displayed.
Here men of the neighborhood will gather to relax,
to share in the general Muslim delight in poetry, or
to discuss their faith about which they never seem
to tire of talking.

The greater part of the house, like that of the
nomad's tent which we discussed on p. 212, is the
women's domain. Known in Arabic as the *harim*, a
word related to *haram* meaning "sacred area," it is
forbidden to all men except husbands and those for
whom consanguinity makes marriage impossible.
Often it is designed around a courtyard in which
much of the women's lives will take place. In recent
times the firm division between the public and
private areas of the house has often broken down,
and members of both sexes from within and without
the family mix on social occasions, though not
necessarily with ease. Modern buildings, moreover,
have often matched this changing pattern, making
no architectural allowance for the preferences of
Islam.

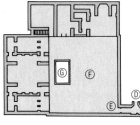

This plan of a house in Isfahan
indicates the care which might be
taken to distance inmates of the
household from outsiders.
"Coming from the public square
(A), the visitor finds himself first
in a small entrance hall (B) but
then has to traverse a long
corridor, passing two other doors
to the outer world (C, D), before
arriving at the entrance (E) to the

main courtyard the house (F),
with its pool (G)" (after Michel).
Once permitted to enter, the male
visitor would be conducted to
the men's reception room.

Below Yemenis enjoy chewing
qat, a leaf with stimulating
properties, in the *mafraj*, or
reception room, of a house in
Sana.

The Position
of Women

Few subjects engage observers of Muslim society more strongly than the position of women. Equally, few subjects arouse so much passion among Muslims themselves. Positions are deeply entrenched. When voices speak, they tend to be those of partisans, of conservatives, of reformers, of male chauvinists, of ardent feminists, of *ulama* for whom the position of women has become the very touchstone of their capacity to defend Islam, of secular leaders for whom the position of women symbolizes the shameful backwardness of their people in the face of the West. Everyone has a position: objectivity is scarce.

It is undeniable that the holy law of Islam seems openly to assert the superiority of man over woman. A man may marry up to four wives at one time, but if a woman takes more than one husband at a time she commits adultery and is subject to the severest penalties in this world and the next. A man may marry a non-Muslim without demanding her conversion, but a woman may only marry a Muslim. A man may seek a divorce unilaterally, but a woman may do so only for limited reasons, before courts, and with difficulty, while custody of the children remains with the father. Furthermore, the man's share of inheritance is twice that of a woman and his witness in court has twice the value of hers. In addition to these juridical marks of inferiority, there are those not specifically mentioned in the Quran but which stem from its general injunctions. Nowhere, for instance, does the Quran state that all women should be secluded in the harem or that they should veil themselves from head to foot when they move outside it. General support for the former practice, however, is found in the following verses: "O wives of the Prophet, you are not like any other women . . . stay in your houses and display not your beauty like the displaying of the ignorance of yore . . ." (33: 32–33). General support for the latter is found in the injunctions to all believers to guard their private parts and the specific injunction: "O Prophet, tell thy wives and thy daughters and the women of believers to let down upon them their overgarments. This is more proper, so that they may be known, and not given trouble" (33: 59). In consequence harem and veil, and the subordination they suggest, have come to be the distinctive badge of Muslim women among most, though not all, of the Muslim peoples of the world.

To these assertions an apologist might reply, first by making a passing reference to the role of Islam in greatly improving the position of women in 7th-century Arabia, and then by stating trenchantly that the spiritual equality of women is stressed throughout the Quran:

> Surely the men who submit and the women
> who submit, and the believing men and the
> believing women, and the obeying men and
> the obeying women, and the truthful men
> and the truthful women, and the patient men

221

and the patient women, and the humble men and the humble women, and the charitable men and the charitable women, and the fasting men and the fasting women, and the men who guard their chastity and the women who guard, and the men who remember God much and the women who remember – God has prepared for them forgiveness and a mighty reward (33: 35).

The husband, moreover, is charged before God with the proper care of his wife. "Be sure to treat your wives well," the Prophet exhorted the faithful in his farewell sermon. "In truth they are yours by trust from God and it is by word of God that you are permitted to consort with them." As to the inferiority imposed upon women by custom and by law, the apologist would deny that there was any actual inferiority, merely a recognition of the different roles which men and women have to play. If women are secluded, it is because they need protection in their functions as wives and mothers. If they inherit only half as much as their brothers, it should be recalled that their husbands are charged with the complete care of the family and that women may use their own resources for what they will. With regard to polygamy, the God-fearing Muslim should be checked by the impossibility of meeting God's command to treat each wife equally; with regard to divorce, by the knowledge that he will have to pay his wife the greater part of her dowry.

Islamic law and Muslim preferences have kept Muslim women out of history. Of course they have exercised influence from the harem, like Roxelana, wife of Sulaiman the Magnificent, or Nur Jahan, wife of Jahangir; but very few have actually sat on the throne – the achievement of Shajar al-Durr, who ruled Mamluk Egypt in 1249–50, was rare. Opportunities for women, however, were transformed by the great process of modernization which began under Western influence. Indeed Western example encouraged a freer role for women outside the home, economic progress made it possible, and modern Muslim governments demanded it, as they sought to exploit the brains and the energy their female populations offered. As a result, women have succeeded in playing an increasingly prominent part in the workings of their societies.

The growing influence of women in general and of highly educated women in particular, however, does not necessarily lead to a total rejection of Islamic values. Recent years have seen an increasing use of the veil throughout the Islamic world, in part by newcomers to the towns aping the culture of the economic groups above them, but in part too by the educated protesting at the non-Islamic route their society may be following. The tremendous fact is that, whether Islamically inspired or not, women now play a substantial part in public affairs, which is the greatest contemporary challenge to the pattern of Muslim life established over 1400 years.

Previous page "Paradise," declared the Prophet, "lies at your mother's feet."

Right Afghan women in the all-enveloping *burqa*. "It's just terrible," complains one Indian girl. "It would be bad enough going out in that heat without a *burqa*, with the sun beating down all day. But just imagine what it's like for us having to cope with an extra layer of clothes! I always arrive drenched to the skin with sweat." Another girl from the same area finds some advantages: "You can pass men in the street without being recognized. Sometimes I want to go to the cinema with my friend so I just tell my husband that we're going to the *bazar* (which he does not question) and off we go. Sometimes we pass him on the way back home, but he's none the wiser."

Below Women wait at the back of Delhi's Juma Masjid while their menfolk pray. They are not specifically forbidden to attend mosque prayers, but it is preferred that they pray at home.

Right center An alternative life-style beckons a veiled woman in Qum, Iran.

Right bottom That women should rule is rare; that a dynasty should rule, as the Begums of India's Bhopal state did from 1844 to 1926, is even rarer. Here Begum Sultan Jahan (reigned 1901–26) leaves to visit the India Office in London, October 1925.

Bottom center Nurses at the Qandahar hospital, Afghanistan, illustrate the new roles which Muslim women are finding outside the home.

Left Women often played stirring roles in the national awakening of their peoples. When the Greeks invaded Turkey in May 1919, Halide Edib, her face unveiled, delivered a passionate speech to a crowd of 50 000 outside the Sultan Ahmed mosque in Istanbul.

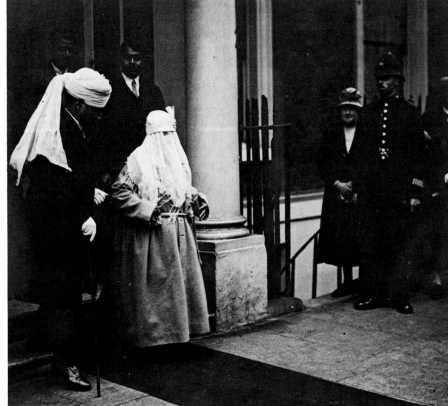

GLOSSARY

alim (plural *ulama*) A learned man, in particular one learned in Islamic legal and religious studies.

amir Military commander, provincial governor.

ayatullah Literally "sign of God." A title conferred by his followers upon a distinguished **mujtahid** among the Shias.

barakat Holiness, divine favòr, often attributed to sufi saints.

basmala Formula with which Muslims begin all important acts: "In the name of God, the merciful, the compassionate."

bida Innovation on a point of law, which is as close as Islam goes to the Christian concept of heresy.

caliph (Arabic *khalifa*, "vicar," "successor") Successor of Muhammad as head of the Muslim community. The title implies continuous religious and political suzerainty over all Muslim peoples but not direct divine revelation.

chador "Tent," the veil for women worn in Iran.

dar el-harb "The land of war," i.e. all territory outside **dar al-Islam** ("the land of Islam"). All territories which did not recognize Islam were under threat of **jihad**.

dar al-Islam "The land of Islam," i.e. all territory which recognizes the law of Islam.

devshirme System of recruitment and training of slaves (especially Christians) for government service in the Ottoman empire. About 10 per cent were sent to the palace school to train for the highest positions in the sultan's service. The rest were set to work on the land and hardened for military service.

dhikr "Recollection" of God, a spiritual exercise to render God's presence throughout one's being.

dhimmi A protected religious minority, tolerated by the Ottomans until the 17th century. Comprising the Jews and Coptic, Greek, Armenian and Syrian Christians, they were allowed to organize themselves as separate communities, or **millets**.

dikka Platform from which men, usually the **muezzins** of the mosque, repeat and amplify the words and actions of the **imam** for the benefit of the congregation.

Fatiha Opening **sura** of the Quran, which Muslims use as Christians would the Lord's Prayer.

fatwa Decision or opinion on a point of Islamic law issued by a **mufti**.

Fulani The largest nomadic society in the world and generators of religious reform in West Africa. In 1680 they began a series of holy wars that led to the establishment of the Islamic states of Futa Jallon, Futa Toro, Khasso, Kaarta, Masina and Sokoto.

ghazi Holy warrior; later a title of honor.

Ghulam Member of an exclusive force of military or palace slaves in the Safavid empire.

Hadith Report of a saying or action of the Prophet, or such reports collectively. The body of *Hadiths* is one of the principal sources of the **Sharia**.

Hajj Pilgrimage to Mecca which every adult Muslim of sound mind and body must perform once in his lifetime.

Hanafi One of the four **Sunni** schools of law, founded by Abu Hanifa (died 767). It was the dominant legal system in the Ottoman empire, Central Asia and India.

Hanbali One of the four **Sunni** schools of law, founded by Ahmad Ibn Hanbal (died 855) and known for its opposition to the speculative and rationalist approaches of the other three schools.

Hijaz Northwest part of the Arabian peninsula, bordering on the Red Sea, which includes the holy cities of Mecca and Medina.

Hijra Flight of the Prophet and his followers from Mecca to Medina in 622 AD from which point the Muslim calendar begins.

Idrisiya Sufi order founded by the Moroccan, Ahmad Ibn Idris, whose influence spread through Africa in the 19th century.

ijaza License or diploma, granting a pupil permission to teach a skill, knowledge of a book perhaps, or a particular sufi way. The certificate records how knowledge has been transmitted from the original fount to the present.

ijma Consensus of the scholarly community on a point of law.

ijtihad Exercise of human reason to ascertain a rule of **Sharia** law. In the 10th century Sunnis considered *ijtihad* permissible only on points not already decided by recognized authorities. The Shias, on the other hand, usually permit full *ijtihad* to their leading scholars.

ikhwan Shock force of "brothers," created by Abd al-Aziz Ibn Saud and committed to die fighting for Islam. Established in over 200 missionary and military communities, or *hijrah*, they enabled him to spread his rule over Saudi Arabia from 1912 to 1929.

imam Leader of mosque prayers, or the leader of the Muslim community. Among Sunnis any great **alim** might be called imam. Among Shias one of the 12 successors of the Prophet, descended from Ali, the legitimate leaders of the Muslim community.

iwan Vaulted hall, an important element of pre-Islamic Central Asian architecture which was adopted for use in mosques and madrasas of the region.

Iznik pottery The chief glory of Ottoman ceramics. It developed in three phases: 1490–1525 blue and white only; 1525–50 Damascus and Golden Horn ware introduced more blues and a sage green; 1550–1700 Rhodian ware employed a full range of design and seven colors.

Janissary Ottoman infantryman, a member of an elite corps of highly trained men, raised initially through the **devshirma** but later hereditary.

jihad "Striving in the way of God," hence holy or "just" war. This may be waged against unbelievers; it may also be waged by an individual against his baser instincts. War on Muslims, or on protected minorities (**dhimmis**), is forbidden.

jizya Tax levied by holy law on unbelievers in Muslim territory, abolished by Akbar.

Kaaba Cube-shaped building in the center of the sanctuary of the great mosque at Mecca where Muslims believe that Abraham built the first house for the worship of the one God; the focus of Islam to which all Muslims turn when praying, circumambulation of which is the climax of the **Hajj**.

Khalwatiya Sufi order based in Cairo whose influence spread through Africa in the 19th century. *Khalwat* means "retreat into prayer."

khan Turkish title, originally the ruler of a state; also a hostel for traveling merchants.

khoja Title given to sufi leaders in Central Asia who were descended from the Prophet and achieved political power from the 16th century. It is also the name given to the followers of the Agha Khan.

Kufic Script used for many early Qurans and monumental inscriptions. Named for the early center of learning at Kufa, Iraq, it is distinguished by the static form of its letters, which are often highly decorated.

kursi Lectern holding the Quran in a mosque.

madrasa School for the teaching of theology and law, Arabic grammar and literature, the *Hadiths* and Quran commentary. Establishment for the training of *ulama* in the Islamic sciences.

Maghrib Literally "the west," the term was applied generally to the area of modern Libya, Tunisia, Algeria and Morocco.

Mahdi Title ("the guided one") assumed by Muhammad Ahmad in 1881 who captured Khartoum in 1885 and established a Mahdist state in the Sudan.

maidan Open space or square in a town.

Maliki One of the four **Sunni** schools of law, founded by Malik Ibn Anas (died 796). Influential throughout Muslim Africa, it usually looked to Cairo.

Mamluk Technically a slave (literally "owned"), later a member of an elite cavalry corps which controlled Egypt from 1260 to 1517.

mansabdar Holder of a civil and/or military appointment, graded according to a decimal ranking system, within the Mughal imperial service.

marabout Term commonly given to sufis in Morocco; it is a French corruption of Arabic and means a man "tied" to God.

Maratha In the general sense, an inhabitant of Maharashtra in western India. From the mid-17th century Maratha Hindu warriors continually raided the Mughal empire.

masjid Place of prostration, mosque.

mawlid Ceremony to celebrate the Prophet's birthday, 12 Rabi al-Awwal.

mihrab Niche in a place of prayer indicating the direction of Mecca. The niche itself (unlike the direction it expresses) is not sacred, but it is the central feature of any mosque.

millet Separate community in which religious minorities, or **dhimmis**, were allowed by the Ottomans to live under their own laws.

minbar Pulpit from which the **imam** delivers his Friday sermon. He does so from one of the lower steps: only the Prophet preached from the top.

muezzin Official at a mosque charged with giving the call to prayer five times a day.

mufti Learned exponent of the **Sharia** who issues **fatwas** when consulted.

mujtahid One who exercises **ijtihad** to inquire into and clarify the intent of the law.

mullah Religious leader, member of the *ulama*, especially in Shia Iran.

Muslim Brotherhood Militant movement for the reassertion of Islamic values which was founded in Egypt and has spread elsewhere in the Arab world. Its attempted assassination of Nasser in 1954 failed; a similar attempt on Sadat by an associated organization in 1981 succeeded.

Naqshbandiya Sufi order which played the major role in the 18th- and 19th-century movement for reform and revival in Asia.

Padri movement Movement for reform in early 19th-century Sumatra.

pishtaq Monumental gateway, usually decorated with colored tiles, a feature of Central Asian madrasas.

qadi Judge appointed to interpret the **Sharia**.

Qari Cantor who recites the Quran.

qiyas Argument by analogy, used to supplement the **Sharia**.

rakat Sequence of movements or "bowings" prescribed for prayer.

Shafii One of the four **Sunni** schools of law, founded by Imam al-Shafii (died 820). Preeminent in southeast Asia, Egypt, Syria and the Hijaz.

shahada Basic statement of Muslim belief: "There is no god but God and Muhammad is the Prophet of God."

shaikh Literally "old man"; the chief of a tribe; any religious leader; in particular an independent sufi "master" in a position to guide disciples in his sufi way.

Shaikh al-Islam The **mufti** of Istanbul and supreme religious authority in the Ottoman state.

Sharia The law of Islam. Based on the Quran and the **Hadiths**, it covers every aspect of Muslim life.

sharif Title (meaning "highborn" or "noble") which came to be applied to descendants of the Prophet.

Shia Group (or "party") of Muslims who, against the orthodox (**Sunni**) view, insist on the recognition of Ali as the legitimate successor (or **caliph**) to Muhammad.

Initially most powerful in Iraq, their particular association with Iran was sealed by the triumph of the Safavids in the 16th century.

silsila Chain of spiritual descent, a sufi lineage.

sipahi Ottoman cavalryman, usually holding a **timar**.

sufism Islamic mysticism. A distinct strand of Muslim devotion, which cultivates the inner attitude with which the believer performs his outward obligations, sufism was an important vehicle for the dissemination of the faith.

sultan The reigning source of authority which came to be the normal Muslim term for sovereign.

Sunni "Orthodox" Islam, basing its teachings on the Quran, the *Hadiths*, and the four schools of law – the **Hanafi, Hanbali, Maliki** and **Shafii**.

sura Chapter of the Quran.

tariqat A sufi's "way" of approaching God.

timar Grant of land in exchange for government service in the Ottoman empire.

Turkoman People who had ruled much of Anatolia after the decline of the Seljuqs. They continue to live in Iraq, Syria and in the lands east of the Caspian.

ulama See **alim**.

Ummah The Islamic community as a whole.

vilayat Administrative unit of land.

vizier Anglicized form of *wazir*, an officer to whom a ruler delegated the administration of his realm; head of the imperial administrative council in the Ottoman empire.

Wahhabi Follower of Muhammad Abd al-Wahhab, who in the mid-18th century led a campaign for spiritual renewal in Arabia. The Wahhabis retained power in the Najd for much of the 19th century and played an important part in founding the Saudi Arabian state.

wayang Javanese shadow theater, based on traditional Hindu cycles of plays, but including one cycle (*wayang golek*) about the Prophet's uncle, Amir Hamza.

zakat Giving of alms.

zawiya Sufi lodge; also *ribat* in Arabic, *khanqah* in Persian, and *tekke* in Turkish.

LIST OF ILLUSTRATIONS

Abbreviations: t = top, b = bottom, l = left, r = right, c = center, tl = top left, etc.

Endpapers: *Asia* by J. Hondius, Amsterdam, 1632: British Library, London.

page
2–5. The *rakat* of prayer: drawings by Lynda Gray. London.
8–9. Drawings by John Fuller, Cambridge.
17. Napoleon commanding his army at the battle of the Pyramids: Mary Evans Picture Library, London.
18. *Summary Execution under the Moorish Kings of Granada*, by Henri Regnault: Musée du Louvre, Paris (photo: Giraudon).
19t. *Odalisque*, by Auguste Renoir: The National Gallery of Art, Washington, D.C. (Chester Dale Collection 1962).
19b. *Dhikr* in Cairo: Mary Evans Picture Library, London.
21. The Kaaba as the center of the inhabited world: from a 16th-century map in the Istanbul University Library, adapted by Andrew Walker, Oxford.
22l. The Angel Gabriel delivering God's message to the Prophet: Edinburgh University Library, Ms. Arabic 20, fol. 47b.
23. 10th-century pen drawing of an Arab horseman: Österreichische Nationalbibliothek, Vienna.
26t. Drawing of the 14th-century tomb tower of Halim Hatun in Gevas, Lake Van, Turkey: John Fuller, Cambridge.
26b. Drawing of a Mongol soldier: John Brennan, Oxford.
27. Page from a Quran written in the eastern Kufic style: Middle East Photographic Archive, London.
28. 16th-century Ottoman tile depicting the praying stations of the four main schools of Islamic law around the Kaaba: Mansell Collection, London.
31. Portrait of a Sufi mendicant or Qalandar, Timurid, late 15th century: Metropolitan Museum of Art, New York (The Cora Timken Burnett Collection, 57.51.30).
33. Incident in the life of Jalal al-Din Rumi: Bodleian Library, Oxford, Ms. OA 24, fol. 78v.
34. Learned man teaching, Mughal, early 16th century: British Museum, London, 1920. 9-17.033.
35. Allegory of drunkenness, by Sultan-Muhammad, Safavid, 16th century: Courtesy Fogg Art Museum, Harvard University, Cambridge, Mass., from the collected works of Hafiz, fol. 135r.
37b. Holy man with disciples and pupils, Safavid, mid-17th century: Keir Collection, Richmond, England (photo: A. C. Cooper).
38. *Another Inadequate Gift*, by Subhat al-Abrar, mid-16th century: Courtesy Freer Gallery of Art, Smithsonian Institution, Washington, D.C., 46.12.15v.
39. Convent of the Mawlawiya order at Konya: Sonia Halliday Photographs, Weston Turville, England.
40tr. Muslim prayer beads or *tasbih*: Roger Gorringe, Crowborough, England.
40cl. The creed, which demands belief in God, his angels, his books, his prophet and the day of judgment.
40br. Recording angels, from *The Wonders of Creation and Their Singularities*, by al-Qazwini, Iraq, 1280: Bayerische Staatsbibliothek, Munich, Cod. Arab. 464, fol. 36I.
41. Moses and the Israelites watching Pharaoh and his host drown in the Red Sea, from the *History* of Hafiz-i Abru, Herat, c. 1425: Keir Collection, Richmond, England (photo: A. C. Cooper).
42. The Archangel Asrafil blowing the last trump, Iraq (Baghdad?), 1370–80: Courtesy Freer Gallery of Art, Smithsonian Institution, Washington, D.C. 54.51v.
43t. Amusements of the *houris* in Paradise, from the *Miraj Namah*, Herat, 15th century: Bibliothèque Nationale, Paris, Ms. Suppl. Turc. 910, fol. 49.
43cl. The punishment of adulterous women, from the *Miraj Namah*, Herat, 15th century: Bibliothèque Nationale, Paris, Ms. Suppl. Turc. 910, fol. 59v.
43cr. Pilgrim caravan, from the *Maqamat* of al-Hariri, Baghdad, 1237: Bibliothèque Nationale, Paris, Ms. Arab. 5847, fol. 94v.
44. Sulaiman's generals at the battle of Szigetvar, from Book Two of the *Huner Namah*, by Nakkas Osman: Topkapi Sarai Museum, Istanbul, 996/1588.H.1524, fol. 277v. (photo: Sonia Halliday).
46t. Shah Ismail in battle against the Turks at Chaldiran,

mural in Chihil Sutun, Isfahan: Alex Starkey, London.
46br. Shah Abbas I, by Bishn Das, Mughal, 15th century: British Museum, London, 1920.9.17.013(2).
47. The shrine of Fatima at Qum: Roger Wood, London.
48. The shrine of Imam Riza at Meshhed: Roger Wood, London.
50tl. Youth drinking wine, designed by Riza Abbasi, silk: Werner Forman Archive, London.
50tr. Muhammad Ali, the gilder, by Riza Abbasi, 17th century: Keir Collection, Richmond, England (photo: A. C. Cooper).
50b. Two lovers embracing, by Afzal al-Husaini, 1646: Victoria and Albert Museum, London, Large Clive Album.
51. The *Court of Gayumarth*, by Sultan-Muhammad(?), from the *Shahnama* of Firdawsi: Arthur A. Houghton Jr. Collection, fol. 20v. (photo: Metropolitan Museum of Art).
52. View of Isfahan: Roger Wood, London.
53. The royal mosque at Isfahan: Erwin Böhm, Mainz.
54. Aerial view of Isfahan, showing the bazar: John Donat, London.
56l. Woven polychrome velvet, early 17th century: Royal Ontario Museum, Toronto, 962.60.1.
56tr. The helmet of Shah Abbas I, 1625–26: British Museum, London, 78.12–30.772.
56br. Hookah base: Bridgeman Art Library, London.
57tr. Textile printing in Isfahan bazar: John Donat, London.
57bl. Painting pots and tiles in Isfahan bazar: John Donat, London.
57br. Interior of Isfahan bazar: John Donat, London.
58t. The Mughal Emperor Babur: British Museum, London, 1921.10–11.03.
58br. Drawing of the Koh-i-Nur diamond: John Fuller, Cambridge.
60t. The Rajput fort of Chitor at Mewar: Robert Harding Associates, London.
60br. The shrine of Shaikh Salim Chishti at Fatehpur Sikri: Douglas Dickins, London.
61. Akbar presiding at a debate in his "House of Worship" at Fatehpur Sikri, from the Chester Beattie *Akbarnama*: Chester Beattie Library and Gallery of Oriental Art, Dublin, Ms. 3, fol. 263v. (photo: Pieterse-Davison International Ltd).
62. Dara Shikoh conversing with holy men, by Govardhan, 17th century: Courtesy Fogg Art Museum, Cambridge, Mass., T1 21 065.3.
63. Awrangzeb at prayer, 17th century: Bibliothèque Nationale, Paris,Oo.51R08.
64l. Inayat Khan dying, attrib. Bishn Das, early 17th century: Boston Museum of Fine Art, 14.679.
64r. Allegorical portrayal of Shah Abbas and Jahangir, by Abul Hassan, early 17th century: Courtesy Freer Gallery of Art, Smithsonian Institution, Washington, D.C., 45.9.
65l. Shah Jahan receiving his sons, by Bichitr, mid-17th century: Royal Library, Windsor.
65tr. Noblewoman of mature age, mid-17th century: India Office Library, London (photo: A. C. Cooper).
65br. Young girl combing her hair: India Office Library, London, Johnson Album.
66t. Himalayan wild goat, by Inayat: Victoria and Albert Museum, London (photo: Mark Fiennes).
66b. Himalayan cheer pheasant, by Mansur; Victoria and Albert Museum, London (photo: Mark Fiennes).
66–67. Zebra, by Mansur: Victoria and Albert Museum, London (photo: Mark Fiennes).
67tr. Indian black buck, by Manohar: Victoria and Albert Museum, London (photo: Mark Fiennes).
67cr. Poppies, from the Large Clive Album: Victoria and Albert Museum, London (photo: Mark Fiennes).
67br. Turkey cock, by Mansur: Victoria and Albert Museum, London (photo: Mark Fiennes).
68l. The Panch Mahal at Fatehpur Sikri: Douglas Dickins, London.
68tr. Agra fort: Josephine Powell, Rome.
68–69. The Juma Masjid in Delhi: Josephine Powell, Rome.
69tl. *Pietra dura* work in the Red Fort, Delhi: Erwin Böhm, Mainz.
69tr. The Rang Mahal in the Red Fort, Delhi: A. F. Kersting, London.
69br. The Red Fort, Delhi: Robert Harding Associates, London.

70tr. The tomb of Sher Shah Suri: Erwin Böhm, Mainz.
70cr. The tomb of Humayun: Josephine Powell, Rome.
70b. The tomb of Akbar: Erwin Böhm, Mainz.
71l. The Taj Mahal: Jane Taylor, Sonia Halliday Photographs, Weston Turville, England.
71tr. One of the four minarets of the tomb of Jahangir: Robert Harding Associates, London.
71br. One of the four minarets of the tomb of Itimad-ud-daulah: Erwin Böhm, Mainz.
74tl. Sulaiman the Magnificent in old age, by Nigari: Topkapi Sarai Museum, Istanbul (photo: Sonia Halliday).
74cl. Sulaiman's seal: Topkapi Sarai Museum, Istanbul (photo: Sonia Halliday).
74bl. Khairuddin, or Barbarossa, by Nigari: Topkapi Sarai Museum, Istanbul (photo: Sonia Halliday).
74br. The Ottoman fleet, 16th century: Topkapi Sarai Museum, Istanbul, Ms. Revan 1272 fol. 23r. (photo: Sonia Halliday).
75. Selim II, by Nigari: Topkapi Sarai Museum, Istanbul (photo: Sonia Halliday).
78. The Sulaimaniye mosque in Istanbul: John Donat, London.
80–81. 16th-century map of Nice: Topkapi Sarai Museum, Istanbul (photo: Sonia Halliday).
80bl. Ottoman cavalry at the battle of Mohacs: Topkapi Sarai Museum, Istanbul (photo: Sonia Halliday).
81tr. Members of the Ottoman Janissary corps: Topkapi Sarai Museum, Istanbul (photo: Sonia Halliday).
81br. The army of Sulaiman the Magnificent at Vienna: Topkapi Sarai Museum, Istanbul (photo: Sonia Halliday).
81bl. Sulaiman the Magnificent at the siege of Rhodes: Topkapi Sarai Museum, Istanbul (photo: Sonia Halliday).
82t. The bedroom of Murad III in Topkapi Sarai: Sonia Halliday Photographs, Weston Turville, England.
82bl. Chinese-influenced blue-and-white ware, 1490–1525: Victoria and Albert Museum, London (photo: Bridgeman Art Library).
82bc. Damascus ware, 1525–50: Victoria and Albert Museum, London (photo: Bridgeman Art Library).
82br. Rhodian ware, 1550–1700: Hanley Museum and Art Gallery, Staffordshire (photo: Bridgeman Art Library).
83t. Topkapi Sarai roofscape: Robert Harding Associates, London.
83bl. 16th-century Turkish fabric: Victoria and Albert Museum, London (photo: Bridgeman Art Library).
83br. The Baghdad kiosk: Erwin Böhm, Mainz.
84tl. Drawing of a statue of Sinan: John Fuller, Cambridge.
84tr. The Shehzade mosque complex in Istanbul: Josephine Powell, Rome.
84bl. The cathedral church of St Sophia: British Library, London, reproduced from G. Fossati, *Agia Sofia*, London, 1852.
85t. The Sulaimaniye mosque complex in Istanbul: Erwin Böhm, Mainz.
85b. The Selimiye mosque complex at Edirne: Roland and Sabrina Michaud, John Hillelson Agency, London.
86l. Plans and sections illustrating the development of Sinan's architectural style: John Brennan, Oxford.
86–87t. Interior of the Sulaimaniye mosque: Henri Stierlin, Geneva.
86–87c. Interior of St Sophia: British Library, London, reproduced from G. Fossati, *Agia Sofia*, London, 1852.
86–87b. Interior of Selimiye mosque: Henri Stierlin, Geneva.
87t. Interior of Mihrimah mosque: Henri Stierlin, Geneva.
87b. Interior of Sokullu mosque: Henri Stierlin, Geneva.
90l. The minaret of Kudus in Java: Vautier Photothèque, Paris.
90r. The tomb of Hasan al-Din at Gowa: John Fuller, Cambridge.
92cl. *Hockerstellung* type of Majapahit kris handle: Rijksmuseum voor Volkenkunde, Leiden, 1018–77.
92bl. Balinese kris handle, 18th or 19th century: Rijksmuseum voor Volkenkunde, Leiden, 3155–140.
92c. Classical central Javanese kris handle, 18th or 19th century: Rijksmuseum voor Volkenkunde, Leiden, 300–1436.
92tl. Female dancer from the 10th-century Shiva temple of Prambanan: Alan Hutchison Library, London.
92bc. Court dancer from Mangkunagaran, Surakarta: Mangkunagara VII of Surakarta.

92tr. A typical *wayang kulit*: Vautier Photothèque, Paris.
92–93c. A traditional central Javanese batik with the *garuda* motif, flowers and birds: Victoria and Albert Museum, London (photo: Mark Fiennes).
92br. Drawing of detail of above: John Brennan, Oxford.
93tl. *Wayang golek* puppet of Umar Maya: Rijksmuseum voor Volkenkunde, Leiden, 300–140.
93br. Silk batik from the north Javanese coast (detail), late 19th century, 315 × 52 cm: Los Angeles County Museum of Art, Costume Council Fund, M.74.18.5.
93tr. Drawing of detail of above: John Brennan, Oxford.
96. The castle of Gondar: Roger Wood, London.
98. The Sankore mosque in Timbuktu: Hoa Qui, Paris.
99. Wayside shrine at Melilla, Morocco: Alan Hutchison Library, London.
100. The *mihrab* of a small mosque outside the mausoleum of Mawlay Ismail in Meknes: Per Hellsten, Uppsala.
102. Abd Allah Khan eating a melon, Bukhara, late 16th century: British Museum, 1948.12–10.010.
105. A group of Chinese Muslims in Turfan: Caroline Blunden, London.
106cl. The courtyard of the Shir Dar madrasa in Samarqand: A. F. Kersting, London.
106bl. The south *iwan* of the Mir-i Arab madrasa in Bukhara: Werner Forman Archive, London.
106–07. The *pishtaq* of the Shir Dar madrasa: A. F. Kersting, London.
107tr. Plan of Registan square: John Brennan, Oxford.
107cr. General view of Registan square: C. M. Dixon, Dover.
107br. The Tila Kara madrasa: Edgar Knobloch, London.
108tl. The Friday mosque in Kano, northern Nigeria: Mansell Collection, London.
108tl. A Chinese mosque in Tao-chou, Kansu: Arnold Arboretum, Harvard University, Cambridge, Mass.
108bl. The Shah Hamadan mosque in Srinagar: Michael Ridley, Bournemouth.
108tr. Dyula-style mosque in Timbuktu: Robert Harding Associates, London.
108cr. Friday mosque in Namou, Guinea: Musée de l'Homme, Paris.
108br. Mosque in the Lake Simkarrak area of Minangkabau, Sumatra: Vautier Photothèque, Paris.
109. The central mosque in Lagos: Alan Hutchison Library, London.
111. Mural of a youth drinking wine, in Chihil Sutun, Isfahan, 17th century: William MacQuitty, London.
115tl. Shivaji the Maratha, Mughal, 17th century: Bibliothèque Nationale, Paris, Od.45 Res.
115cl. Shivaji's claw: Robert Harding Associates, London.
116. Europeanized gentleman, by Levni, Ottoman, 18th century: British Museum, London.
117. Equestrian portrait of Selim III, by Hippolyte Berteaux, Ottoman, 19th century(?): Topkapi Sarai Museum, Istanbul (photo: Sonia Halliday).
120. Abd Allah Ibn Saud, the defeated Wahhabi chief: Equinox archive, Oxford.
121. Lithograph of Medina, from R. F. Burton, *Personal Narrative of a Pilgrimage to al-Medinah and Mecca*, London, 1855.
123. Dipanegara in exile: Universitets Bibliothek, Leiden, Codex Orientalis 7398 (Snouck Hurgronje Collection).
124. Portrait of Imam Shamil, by Thomas Horscheldt: from L. Blanch, *The Sabres of Paradise*, London, 1960.
125t. Landscape at Tali: Roy Lancaster, Winchester.
125b. The seal of Tu Wen-hsiu: from E. Rocher, *La Province chinoise du Yunnan*, Paris, 1880 (photo: Bibliothèque Nationale).
127. The tomb of the Mahdi, Muhammad Ahmad, at Khartoum: Alan Hutchison Library, London.
129l. A North African *zawiya*: Equinox archive, Oxford.
129r. Fulani warriors in a cavalry charge: Equinox archive, Oxford.
133. *The Palmer Family*, by Francesco Renaldi, 1786: India Office Library, London.
135l. Jannissary officer in 1825: Sonia Halliday Photographs, Weston Turville, England.
135r. Ottoman soldiers of the Crimean War: BBC Hulton Picture Library, London.
136. Opening the Hijaz railroad: BBC Hulton Picture Library, London.
137. Poster depicting the new Republic of Turkey as an unveiled woman.
138tl. Ataturk dancing with his daughter: BBC Hulton Picture Library, London.
138br. Muhammad Ali, and the massacre of the Mamluks: Mary Evans Picture Library, London.
139. Muhammad Ali on horseback: BBC Hulton Picture Library, London.
140c. King Faruq of Egypt with Irma Minutolo: Keystone Press Agency, London.
140b. Al-Azhar University, Cairo: Henri Stierlin, Geneva.
142. Abd al-Aziz Ibn Saud with his family: Royal

Geographical Society, London.
143. Amir Sultan Bin Abd al-Rahman al-Dawish holding a bullet-ridden *Ikhwan* war banner: from J. S. Habib, *Ibn Saud's Warriors of Islam*, Leiden, 1978.
144. Fath Ali Shah Qajar: William MacQuitty, London.
145t. Nasir al-Din Shah: Mary Evans Picture Library, London.
145b. Riza Shah Pahlavi: Popperfoto, London.
146cl. Vignette from *Mulla Nasreddin*, No. 2, 1907.
146bl. The awakening of Islam: cartoon from the first issue of *Mulla Nasreddin*, 1906.
146tr. Gasprinski squashed by an unholy alliance of Tatar schoolmaster and Russian school superintendent: cartoon from *Mulla Nasreddin*, No. 17, 1908.
146cr. Gasprinski attacked by *ulama*: cartoon from *Mulla Nasreddin*, No. 42, 1908.
146br. Gathering of sleeping *ulama*: cartoon from *Mulla Nasreddin*, No. 5, 1906.
147tr. The Russian expansion in Central Asia: cartoon from *Mulla Nasreddin*, No. 8, 1909.
147cl. The founder of the National Muslim University and his companions sawing away at a representative of the Aligarh university: cartoon from *Awadh Punch*, 12 November 1920.
147bl. Britain, represented by John Bull, negotiating with Egypt: cartoon from *Awadh Punch*, 23 June 1922.
147r. Vignettes from *Mulla Nasreddin*.
150. Muhammad Ali Jinnah with Jawaharlal Nehru: BBC Hulton Picture Library, London.
151. A train carrying Muslims to Pakistan during the partition of India: Associated Press, London.
153. Tasikmalaya mosque, Java: Vautier Photothèque, Paris.
154. Kano mosque, Nigeria: Peter Fraenkel, London.
156. Street scene during the Algerian war: Popperfoto, London.
159. Nasser in triumph on 19 June 1954: Popperfoto, London.
160. Yasser Arafat with Ayatullah Khomeini and Khomeini's son, Ahmad: Popperfoto, London.
162t. Painting by Kamal Amin Awad: Pamegap, London.
162b. Painting by M. Qadir al-Triqi: Iraqi Cultural Centre, London.
163t. *The Monument of Revolution* in Baghdad's Liberation Square, by Jawad Salim: Pamegap, London (photo: W. Faris).
163b. Painting by Dia al-Azzawi: Pamegap, London.
164. A scene of revolutionary fervor in Iran: Frank Spooner/Gamma, London.
166. President Anwar Sadat at prayer: John Hillelson Agency, London.
169l. "Guardians of the Revolution" celebrating Iranian Women's Day: John Hillelson Agency, London.
169r. Poster from the Iranian Revolution: The Observer Magazine, London.
170. Crowds assembled around the Shayyad monument in Teheran: Frank Spooner/Gamma, London.
173. Muslim leaders at prayer during the second Islamic summit in Lahore: Frank Spooner/Gamma, London.
176tl. Regent's Park mosque, London: Angelo Hornak, London.
176tr. Cartoon by Trog, reproduced by permission of *Punch*.
176bl. Malcolm X: Popperfoto, London.
177. A *mihrab*: John Brennan, Oxford.
178–79. Muslim at prayer: Roland Michaud, John Hillelson Agency, London.
180. The *Fatiha* in a 13th/14th-century manuscript: British Library, London, Ms. Add. 4810 fol. 1b.
181l. Quran school in Oman: Roger Wood, London.
181tr. Javanese peasant reading the Quran: UNESCO, London (photo: World Health Organization).
181br. Ornamental panel from a Moroccan Quran, 16th century: British Library, 1405. fol. 400a.
182l. An old man making his way across the courtyard of the Umaiyad mosque in Damascus: Alan Hutchison Library, London.
182r. Man washing before prayer at the fountain of the al-Aqsa mosque in Jerusalem: Jane Taylor, Sonia Halliday Photographs, Weston Turville, England.
183. Evening prayers at the mosque of Mahabat Khan, Peshawar: Douglas Dickins, London.
184–85. Parts of the mosque: Dick Barnard, Milverton, England.
186tl. The representative of a saint in his consulting room: Francis Robinson, Windsor.
186c. Pilgrims at the shrine of Saiyid Shah Abd al-Razzaq of Bansa: Francis Robinson, Windsor.
186b. The shrine of Muin al-Din Chishti at Ajmere: Robert Harding Associates, London.
186tr. The dance of the Mawlawiya: Sonia Halliday Photographs, Weston Turville, England.
187. The tomb of Mawlana Jalal al-Din Rumi at Konya: Sonia Halliday Photographs, Weston Turville, England.
188t. A newborn baby's first call to prayer: Andrew

Lawson, Oxford.
188b. A boy prepared for circumcision, Turkey: Colorific! London.
189t. A marriage ceremony, England: Courtesy D. Mower, Oxford (photo: B. J. Harris).
189b. A funeral, Karachi: Robert Harding Associates, London.
190l. Prayers at the end of Ramadan, at Balikpapan, Borneo: Vautier Photothèque, Paris.
190–91. The Muslim calendar: John Brennan, Oxford.
190r. An *id* card, exchanged by Muslims at the time of Id al-Fitr and Id al-Adha.
191. Modern poster of the night journey of the Prophet: Equinox archive, Oxford.
192. Pilgrims wearing their *ihram* before arriving at Jedda: Mohamed Amin of Camerapix, Nairobi.
193. The great mosque at Mecca: Mohamed Amin of Camerapix, Nairobi.
195. Location map of Mecca: Dick Barnard, Milverton, England.
196. The plain of Arafat: Mohamed Amin of Camerapix, Nairobi.
197t. Pilgrims running from Mecca to Marwa: Mohamed Amin of Camerapix, Nairobi.
197b. Pilgrims circuiting the Kaaba: Mohamed Amin of Camerapix, Nairobi.
198–99. Glazed brick on the wall of a tomb in Shah-i Zindeh: C. M. Dixon, Dover.
200l. The *basmala* written in 10 different scripts.
200r. "Muhammad" written in Taliq: from A. Khatibi and M. Sijelmassi, *The Splendour of Islamic Calligraphy*, New York, 1976.
201r. The 29 letters of the Arabic alphabet in their unjoined final form.
202l. The calligrapher at work, from al Qazwini's *The Wonders of Creation*, Turkish, 16th century: British Museum, London.
202r. Hilya-i Nabi (Description of the Prophet), by Uthman b. Ali, Istanbul, 1642–98: Chester Beattie Library and Gallery of Oriental Art, Dublin, Ms. Add. (photo: Pieterse-Davison International Ltd).
203tr. Representation of the declaration of faith written in the form of a boat: after Cragg.
203bl. The *mihrab* of the Maidan mosque in Kashan: Islamisches Museum, East Berlin (photo: Angelo Hornak, London).
204l. Arabesque mosaic in the drum of the dome of the Lutf Allah mosque in Isfahan: Henri Stierlin, Geneva.
204r. Floral tiled panel, Iznik: Topkapi Sarai, Istanbul.
205. Tiled mosaic dado in the Saadian tombs at Marrakesh: Josephine Powell, Rome.
206t. Principal knots used in carpet weaving: John Brennan, Oxford.
207tl and r. Details from the Ardabil carpet: Victoria and Albert Museum, London.
207bl. The Ardabil carpet: Victoria and Albert Museum, London.
208tl. Turkish girls from Sivas weaving a rug: Phaidon archive, Oxford.
208bl. Ghiordes silk prayer rug, Turkish, 19th century: Phaidon archive, Oxford.
208tr. Sumak saddlebag from the Caucasus: Private Collection (photo: Andrew Lawson).
208bc. Kazak rug, 19th century: Phaidon archive, Oxford.
208br. Bidzhov rug, 19th century: Phaidon archive, Oxford.
209t. Turkmen guruband: Christopher Legge Collection, Oxford (photo: Andrew Lawson).
209b. Rug from Yarkand or Khotan in the Tarim Basin, 19th century: Phaidon archive, Oxford.
210–11. Man with camel: Middle East Photographic Archive, London (photo: George Wright).
212c. Afghan truck driver on the Solang pass: Roger Gurney, London.
212bl. Moroccan nomads surveying their flock from inside their tent: Colorific! London.
212br. Nomads camped in the Unai pass in Afghanistan: Robert Harding Associates, London.
213t. Nomads in Afghanistan praying in the desert: Alan Hutchison Library, London.
213b. The Qashqai from southwest Iran moving from winter to summer pasture: Robert Harding Associates, London.
214t. Women threshing grain in southeastern Anatolia: Edith Chabrier, Paris.
214b. Painted house wall in Egypt: Alan Hutchison Library, London.
215. The village of Aqra in Iraqi Kurdistan: David Oates, Cambridge.
216l. A street in the old town of Algiers: Alex Starkey, London.
216r. The old city of Sana in the Yemen: Werner Forman Archive, London.
217t. The approach from the bazar to the mosque in Qum,

Iran: Roger Wood, London.
217bl. The new town of Madinat Isa, Bahrein: M. Rice, London.
217br. Plan of Tunis: John Brennan, Oxford.
218l. House front in Fez, Morocco: Colorific! London.
218r. Courtyard of a house in Cairo: Werner Forman Archive, London.
219t. Wooden, screened verandas in Jedda old town: Middle East Photographic Archive, London (photo:

Anthony Hutt).
219c. Plan of a house in Isfahan: John Brennan, Oxford.
219b. Yemeni men chewing *qat* leaves in a house in Sana: Werner Forman Archive, London.
220–21. Woman and child: John Donat, London.
222–23. Afghan women wearing the *burqa*: Roland and Sabrina Michaud, John Hillelson Agency, London.
222b. Veiled woman looking in a shop window in Qum: Colorific! London.

223t. Halide Edib: from Halide Edib, *The Turkish Ordeal*, London, 1928.
223c. Women waiting at the back of the mosque while their menfolk pray: Popperfoto, London.
223bl. Nurses at the Qandahar hospital, Afghanistan: UNESCO (photo: World Health Organization).
223br. Begum Sultan Jahan of Bhopal visiting India Office in London: BBC Hulton Picture Library, London.

BIBLIOGRAPHY

The following booklists are not intended to be comprehensive; they are merely points of departure for further study. Wherever possible we have directed attention to histories, collections of documents or literature in translation as they so often present the most sympathetic path into another world. Wherever books have also been published in paperback, this has been indicated with an *.

Basic works of reference are *The Encyclopaedia of Islam* 2nd edn (ed. J. H. Kramers *et al.*) (Leiden 1954–), which is now just over halfway through the alphabet, and *The Shorter Encyclopaedia of Islam* (ed. H. A. R. Gibb and J. H. Kramers; Leiden 1953), which brings up to date, especially in bibliography, selected articles from *The Encyclopaedia of Islam* 1st edn (Leiden 1913–38). This last is largely out of date but can still be referred to for areas not yet covered in the second edition. Taken together the editions of the *Encyclopaedia* form the basic work of reference for any subject to do with Islam or Islamic civilization, particularly in premodern times. All entries have substantial bibliographies. Further bibliographical guidance may be gained from J. D. Pearson (ed.), *Index Islamicus 1906–55*, which continues to issue supplements, Jean Sauvaget, *Introduction to the History of the Muslim East* (Berkeley, Calif. 1965), and *P. M. Holt, A. K. S. Lambton and B. Lewis (eds.) *The Cambridge History of Islam* (2 vols.; Cambridge 1970). *Marshall G. S. Hodgson, *The Venture of Islam: Conscience and History in a World Civilization* (3 vols.; Chicago, Ill. 1974), mildly idiosyncratic and weaker on the modern period than the premodern, remains a remarkable achievement and the most satisfying treatment of Islamic history as a whole. Those who wish to acquaint themselves with recent research and opinion at a general level should consult: *The Middle East Journal* (1946–), published by the Middle East Institute, Washington, D.C., and *The Muslim World* (1911–), published by the Hartford Seminary Foundation, Hartford, Conn., primarily designed for Christian missionaries. *The Islamic Quarterly* (1954–), published by the Islamic Cultural Centre, London, is edited by Muslim missionaries. Those interested in the latest work of current scholarship might begin by consulting the reviews and articles in: *Revue des études islamiques* (Paris 1927–), *Bulletin of the School of Oriental and African Studies* (London 1917–), and *Studia Islamica* (Paris 1953–).

Western Attitudes to Islam

Trail-breaking work in this field has been done by Norman Daniel, in *Islam and the West: the Making of an Image* (Edinburgh 1960) and *Islam, Europe and Empire* (Edinburgh 1966). Richard W. Southern's *Western Views of Islam in the Middle Ages* (Cambridge, Mass. 1962) offers a first-class summary of what its title announces. A recent overview is also valuable, Maxime Rodinson, "The Western Image and Western Studies of Islam" in *Joseph Schacht and C. E. Bosworth (eds.), *The Legacy of Islam* (Oxford 1974), pp.9–62. The whole subject, however, has come to be dominated in recent years by a book of pugnacity and passion: *Edward W. Said, *Orientalism* (London 1978), which asserts that, practically to the present day, Western studies of Islam tell us more about the West than they do about Islam. Most scholars, while admitting that Said has a point, find his conclusions immoderate. Another approach to this problem is through art and here Philippe Julian, *The Orientalists* (Oxford 1977), reveals in sumptuous illustration the discovery of the East by 19th-century painters.

Part I: Revelation and Muslim History

The First Nine Centuries from 622 to 1500

There are several brief and excellent treatments of Islam in general: *H. A. R. Gibb, *Islam* (retitled 2nd edn; Oxford 1975); *Fazlur Rahman, *Islam* (2nd edn; Chicago, Ill. 1979); *A. Guillaume, *Islam* (2nd edn; Harmondsworth 1976); *Kenneth Cragg, *The House of Islam* (2nd edn; Encino, Calif. 1975). They are all good, but of these the first and oldest, originally published in 1949, remains the best. However, Kenneth Cragg's *House of Islam* is designed to accompany the first-class *anthology he has compiled with Marston Speight, *Islam from Within* (Wadsworth, Calif. 1980), and taken together these two books convey most to the general reader about the development of Islam and about what devout Muslims believe and feel.

The following offer useful general treatments of part or all of the first nine centuries of Islamic history: Bernard Lewis, *The Arabs in History* (4th edn; London 1966); *F. Gabrieli (trans. V. Luling and R. Linell), *Muhammad and the Conquests of Islam* (London 1968); *John J. Saunders, *A History of Medieval Islam* (London 1965); G. von Grunebaum (trans. K. Watson), *Classical Islam: History 600–1258* (London 1970). But the outstanding coverage by one man remains the first two volumes of *Marshall G. S. Hodgson, *Venture of Islam*. Several recent treatments of the life of Muhammad should be noticed: William M. Watt, *Muhammad at Mecca* (Oxford 1953) and *Muhammad at Medina* (Oxford 1956), which bring out the social and political implications of Muhammad's work, and the treatment by the French Marxist scholar *Maxime Rodinson (trans. A. Carter), *Mohammed* (London 1971). Anthologies and translations of documents and literature abound; of excellent value, covering politics and war and religion and society down to a delightful section on Muslim humor, is *Bernard Lewis (ed. and trans.), *Islam: from the Prophet Muhammad to the Capture of Constantinople* (London and New York 1974). But strongly recommended as well are two of the masterworks of the period: Ibn Battuta's *Travels in Asia and Africa 1325–54* (translated and abridged by H. A. R. Gibb; 3 vols.; Cambridge 1971), the introduction to Ibn Khaldun's world history (trans. Franz Rosenthal), *The Muqaddimah: An Introduction to History* (3 vols.; New York 1958). Two excellent illustrated surveys of this period have recently been published: Michael Rogers, *The Spread of Islam* (Oxford 1976), an illustrated survey of Islamic history to 1500 using architectural and archaeological evidence to illustrate various themes, and Bernard Lewis (ed.), *The World of Islam: Faith, People, Culture* (London and New York 1976), to which a powerful team of scholars contributes.

Molding forces of Islamic civilization: Many feel that the best translation of the Quran for overall effect is *A. J. Arberry, *The Koran Interpreted* (London 1980). Notable for its precision is that of Muhammad Ali of Lahore, *The Holy Quran* (6th edn; Lahore 1973), the version used with one exception throughout this book. Ignaz Goldziher, *Muhammedanische Studien* vol. two (Halle 1890; edited and trans. by C. R. Barber and S. M. Stern as *Muslim Studies* vol. two, Chicago, Ill. 1966, London 1971), is the classic study of the growth of the *Hadith*. A popular anthology of *Hadiths* from the six major compilations has been translated and is readily available: Al-Haj Maulana Fazlul Harim (trans.), *Al-Hadis: an English Translation and Commentary of Mishkat-ul-Masabih* (4 vols.; Lahore 1938). On Islamic law, *Noel J. Coulson, *A History of Islamic Law* (Edinburgh 1964), offers an excellent brief introduction to the *Sharia* and modern developments. The following works should also be noted: Joseph Schacht, *The Origins of Muhammadan Jurisprudence* (Oxford 1950; reprint 1979) and *An Introduction to Islamic Law* (Oxford 1964). On sufism useful brief introductions are: *R. A. Nicholson, *The Mystics of Islam* (London 1914; reprint London 1963), and Arthur J. Arberry, *Sufism, an Account of the Mystics of Islam* (London 1950). However, a more substantial work and the outstanding recent introduction is Annemarie Schimmel, *The Mystical Dimensions of Islam* (Chapel Hill, N.C. 1975). The basic works on the early development of sufism are by Louis F. J. Massignon, *La Passion d'al-Hosayn-ibn-Mansour al-Hallaj, martyr mystique de l'Islam exécuté à Bagdad le 26 Mars 922* (2 vols.; Paris 1922), and *Essai sur les origines du lexique technique de la mystique musulmane* (Paris 1922; 2nd edn, Paris 1954). Fortunately there is a readily accessible biography of al-Ghazzali: *William M. Watt, *Muslim Intellectual: a Study of al-Ghazali* (Edinburgh 1963). The most recent study of Rumi's thought is Annemarie Schimmel, *The Triumphal Sun* (Boulder, Colo. 1978). Rumi's works are easily found in translation: *R. A. Nicholson (ed. and trans.), *The Mathnawi of Jalaluddin Rumi* (London 1926); *R. A. Nicholson (ed. and trans.), *Selected Poems from the Divani Shamsi Tabriz* (Cambridge 1898); while for the newcomer to Islam, in prose and extremely approachable, is *A. J. Arberry (ed. and trans.), *Discourses of Rumi* (London 1961). As for Ibn al-Arabi, A. E. Affifi, *The Mystical Philosophy of Muhyid Din-ibnul Arabi* (Cambridge 1939), offers an attempt to reduce Ibn al-Arabi's writings to an orderly system. There is also Henry Corbin (trans. Ralph Manheim), *Creative Imagination in the Sufism of Ibn Arabi* (Princeton, N.J. 1969; London 1970). Ibn al-Arabi's summary of his life's work has recently been translated: Ibn al-Arabi (ed., trans. and introduction by Ralph W. J. Austin), *The Bezels of Wisdom* (London 1980).

The processes of transmission: Scholarly work in this field is still in its infancy; for example, A. L. Tibawi, *Islamic Education: its Traditions and Modernization into the Arab National Systems* (London 1972). "The Ulama of Medieval Damascus and the International World of Islamic Scholarship" by Joan E. Gilbert (unpublished Ph.D. thesis, University of California, Berkeley 1977) sets out before us the scholarly world of the *ulama* of medieval Damascus. The most trenchant exposition of how teachers should be venerated can be found in a fascinating Arabic document of the 13th century: Burham al-Din, al-Zarnuji (trans. G. E. von Grunebaum), *Ta'lim al-Muta'allim at-ta'allum (Instruction of the Student; Method of Learning)* (New York 1947; Oxford 1948). Further work which illuminates the process of transmission, although based on evidence from a later period, is: Francis Robinson, "The Veneration of Teachers in Islam by the Pupils: its Modern Significance", *History Today* (London; March 1980) and Francis Robinson, "The Ulama of Firangi Mahal and their Adab" in B. Metcalf (ed.), *Moral Conduct and Authority: The Place of Adab in South Asian Islam* (Berkeley, Calif., forthcoming). *J. S. Trimingham, *The Sufi Orders in Islam* (Oxford 1971), is the pioneering work on the development of institutional sufism as a worldwide phenomenon, and further evidence can be gleaned from Annemarie Schimmel's *The Mystical Dimensions of Islam*. For a history of one of the major orders see John K. Birge, *The Bektashi Order of Dervishes* (London 1937). Richard M. Eaton, *Sufis of Bijapur 1300–1700: Social Roles of Sufis in Medieval India* (Princeton, N.J. 1978), is a fascinating and path-breaking study of the functions performed by sufis in one region over 400 years.

The Empires of the Heartlands in the 16th and 17th Centuries

Safavids: Just one book serves most excellently as a starting point for further reading on Safavid Iran, R. M. Savory, *Iran under the Safavids* (Cambridge 1980). It is good on the changing relationship between Shiism and the Safavid state. Several good works exist on aspects of Safavid painting: L. Binyon, J. V. S. Wilkinson and B. Gray, *Persian Miniature Painting* (London 1931); B. Gray, *Persian Painting* (London 1930); S. C. Welch, *A King's Book of Kings* (London and New York 1972) and his *Royal Persian Manuscripts* (London 1976). Arthur Upham Pope (ed.), *A Survey of Persian Art* (6 vols.; Oxford 1938–58), is majestic in its range and places Safavid art in the context of the overall development of Iranian art. Anthony Welch, *Shah Abbas and the Arts of Isfahan* (New York 1973), focuses on the remarkable artistic flowering under that great monarch; Wilfrid Blunt and Wim Swann, *Isfahan: Pearl of Persia* (London 1966), provide a colorful introduction to the city of Isfahan.

Mughals: There is no effective up-to-date general history of the Mughal empire, although this deficiency will be made good by the volumes in Gordon Johnson, Christopher Bayly and John Richards (eds.), *The New Cambridge History of India* (Cambridge, forthcoming). The best point at which to begin is the appropriate chapters in *The Cambridge History of Islam* vol. two. M. Mujeeb, *The Indian Muslims* (London 1967), is also useful, and I. Habib, *The Agrarian System of Mughal India, 1556–1707* (Bombay 1963), is an important revisionist study. There are, fortunately, several superb contemporary works in translation, of which the following should not be missed: Babur (trans. A. S. Beveridge), *The Babur-Namah in English* (2 vols.; London 1922), the vital and highly intelligent autobiography of the founder of the Mughal house; Abul Fazl (trans. H. Beveridge), *The Akbarnama* (3 vols.; Calcutta 1907, 1912, 1939), and the same author's description of state and society (trans. H. Blockmann and H. S. Jarrett) *The Ain-i-Akbari* (2 vols.; Calcutta 1872 and 1874), offer a full description by Akbar's close friend and personal adviser; Jahangir (trans. A. Rogers, ed. H. Beveridge), *Tuzuk-i-Jahangir or Memoirs of Jahangir* (2 vols.; London 1909 and 1914), enables us to witness Mughal life and Indian nature through the eyes of this gifted emperor and art connoisseur. There are also two good and readable illustrated books: Bamber Gascoigne, *The Great Moghuls* (London 1971), and Gavin Hambly,

Cities of Mughal India: Delhi, Agra and Fatehpur Sikri (London 1968).

Ottomans: There are two up-to-date general accounts of Ottoman history: Halil Inalcik, *The Ottoman Empire: The Classical Age 1300–1600* (London 1973), and N. Itzkowitz, *Ottoman Empire and Islamic Tradition* (New York 1972). For Ottoman institutions see H. A. R. Gibb and H. Bowen, *Islamic Society and the West* vol. one, parts one and two (Oxford 1950 and 1957), Bernard Lewis, *Istanbul and the Civilization of the Ottoman Empire* (Norman, Okla. 1963), and for a striking first-hand account of the court of Sulaiman the Magnificent and the empire, see Ogier Ghiselin de Busbecq (trans. E. S. Foster), *Turkish Letters* (Oxford 1967). Elias J. W. Gibb, *A History of Ottoman Poetry* (6 vols.; London 1900–09), offers insight into the whole of Ottoman cultural life. A remarkable novel by *Ivo Andric, winner of the Nobel prize for literature, evokes the nature of Ottoman rule in the Balkans over 400 years, *The Bridge on the Drina* (trans. L. F. Edwards; London 1959). Michael Levey, has most lucidly surveyed Ottoman art in general, *The World of Ottoman Art* (London 1975), a subject O. Aslanapa treats in greater detail, *Turkish Art and Architecture* (London 1971). Geoffrey Goodwin's *A History of Ottoman Architecture* (London 1971) is first class. Arthur Stratton has written a biography of the greatest Ottoman architect and archetypal Ottoman figure, *Sinan* (London 1972). Titus Burckhardt shows off Sinan's achievement to great effect in an inspired section of his *Art of Islam: Language and Meaning* (trans. J. P. Hobson; London 1976).

The Further Islamic Lands from 1500 to the 18th Century

This introduces the problem of Islamization which can be followed up in two trail-blazing books: *C. Geertz, *Islam Observed: Religious Development in Morocco and Indonesia* (New Haven, Conn. 1968), the work of a cultural anthropologist who has been influential in breaking down old academic stereotypes of Islam, and Nehemia Levtzion (ed.), *Conversion to Islam* (London 1979), which brings together studies of Islamization from many areas of the Islamic world and is an important step towards the comparative study of the subject.

Southeast Asia: The best introduction to this period is H. de Graaf, "South-East Asian Islam in the Eighteenth Century" in *The Cambridge History of Islam* vol. two. Unfortunately most other work is locked away in journal articles (see the excellent bibliographies in Nehemia Levtzion's *Conversion to Islam*), of which those by S. M. al-Attas, G. W. J. Drewes and A. H. Johns should be noted in particular. Two important books by S. M. al-Attas deal with aspects of sufism in Aceh, *The Mysticism of Hamza al-Fansuri* (Kuala Lumpur 1970) and *Raniri and the Wujudiyah* (Kuala Lumpur 1966). D. Lombard, *Le Sutanat d'Atjeh au temps d'Iskandar 1607–1636* (Paris 1967), examines the sultanate of Aceh at its height.

Africa: The study of Islam in Africa, particularly West Africa, has seen an explosion of activity over the last 20 years and there is an enormous amount of first-class work, but still only in article or thesis form. The most useful starting points are syntheses of recent scholarship to be found in *The Cambridge History of Islam* vol. two; J. F. A. Ajayi and M. Crowder, *A History of West Africa* vol. one (London 1971); R. Oliver (ed.) *The Cambridge History of Africa* vol. three, c.1050–c.1600 (Cambridge 1977), and R. Gray (ed.), *The Cambridge History of Africa* vol. four, c.1600–c.1870 (Cambridge 1975). E. N. Saad, "Social History of Timbuktu: the Role of Muslim Scholars and Notables" (unpublished Ph.D. thesis, Northwestern University, Ill. 1979), is an important piece of recent research. *Thomas Hodgkin (ed.), *Nigerian Perspectives: an Historical Anthology* (2nd edn; London 1975), offers a lively collection of documents. Islamic art in Africa is so far poorly served. *R. A. Bravmann, *Islam and Tribal Art in West Africa* (London 1974), makes a brave start; for architecture one must turn to the brief survey in George Michell (ed.), *Architecture of the Islamic World: its History and Social Meaning* (London 1978). Turning to Morocco, *Jamil M. Abun-Nasr provides an outstanding introduction in *A History of the Maghreb* (2nd edn; Cambridge 1975). *Anthony Hutt offers a pleasant introduction to Moroccan architecture in the context of that of North Africa generally in *North Africa: Islamic Architecture* (London 1977), which can be followed in greater detail in Derek Hill and L. Golvin, *Islamic Architecture in North Africa* (London 1976).

Central Asia and China: Most work on Islam in Central Asia is in Russian. B. Spuler, "Central Asia from the Sixteenth Century to the Russian Conquests," *The Cambridge History of Islam* vol. one, and G. Hambly (ed.), *Central Asia* (London 1978), present the most accessible introductions. Coverage of Islamic architecture in the region after 1500 can be found in: M. Hrbas and E. Knobloch (trans. R. Finlayson-Samsour), *The Art of Central Asia* (London 1965), K. Gink and K. Gombos, *The Pearls of*

Uzbekistan (Budapest 1976). The Muslims in China are even more poorly served than those in Central Asia, and for this period *R. Israeli, *Muslims in China: a Study of Cultural Confrontation* (London 1980), stands alone.

Decline, Reform and Revival in the 18th and 19th Centuries

The ebbing of Muslim power: This is usually presaged and in part explained in the works which deal with the great empires at their height. To those for Iran should be added two works by Laurence Lockhart, *Nadir Shah* (London 1938) and *The Fall of the Safavi Dynasty and the Afghan Occupation of Persia* (Cambridge 1958); the decline of the Mughal empire still awaits its effective historian, although "Symposium: Decline of the Mughal Empire," *Journal of Asian Studies*, February 1976, is a good starting point; to the works on the Ottoman empire might be added the short essay by Bernard Lewis, "Ottoman Observers of Ottoman Decline," in Bernard Lewis, *Islam in History: Ideas, Men and Events in the Middle East* (London 1973).

Reform and Revival: There is no overall treatment of this process at the moment. *Fazlur Rahman offers a brief introduction in chapter 12 of his *Islam* (London 1966). Suggestive articles are: J. Joll, "Muhammad Hayya al-Sindi and Muhammad Ibn Abd al-Wahhab: an Analysis of an Intellectual Group in Eighteenth-Century Medina," *Bulletin of the School of Oriental and African Studies*, part one, 1975, which examines the major school of *Hadiths* at Medina and those who studied at it; Hamid Algar, "The Naqshbandi Order: a Preliminary Survey of its History and Significance," *Studia Islamica*, vol. 44, and A. Hourani, "Shaikh Khalid and the Naqshbandi Order" in Samuel M. Stern, A. Hourani and V. Brown (eds.), *Islamic Philosophy and the Classical Tradition* (Columbia, S.C. 1973), which both illustrate the international connections of the Naqshbandiya and their significance for the revival; and B. G. Martin, "A Short History of the Khalwati Order of Dervishes" in *N. R. Keddie, *Scholars, Saints and Sufis: Muslim Religious Institutions in the Middle East since 1500* (Los Angeles, Calif. 1972). The story of the rise of the first Saudi-Wahhabi empire is told succinctly by G. Rentz, "Wahhabism and Saudi Arabia" in D. Hopwood (ed.), *The Arabian Peninsula* (London 1972). W. R. Roff, "South-East Asian Islam in the Nineteenth Century," *The Cambridge History of Islam* vol. two, describes the three movements of holy war; Peter Carey, *Babab Dipanagara* (Kuala Lumpur 1981), offers the first detailed treatment in English of any of these movements. For a brief discussion of the revivalist movements in India see Peter Hardy, *The Muslims of British India* (Cambridge 1972); Mohiuddin Ahmad, *Saiyid Ahmad Shahid* (Lucknow 1975), is devoted purely to the leader of the Mujahidin movement. For the movement in the Caucasus see A. Bennigsen, "Un Mouvement populaire au Caucase au XVIIIe siècle" in *Cahiers du monde russe et soviétique*, part two, 1964, and Lesley Blanch's romantic study of Imam Shamil, *The Sabres of Paradise* (London 1960; reissued 1978). For a Russian view see Tolstoy's study of Shamil's deputy "Hadji Murad" in Leo Tolstoy, *The Death of Ivan Ilych and Other Stories* (London 1935). Chantal Quelquejay throws light on Baha al-Din's movement in Kazan in "La Vaisisme à Kazan" in *Die Welt des Islams* (N.S.) parts one and two, 1959. For the movement in China see Israeli, *Muslims in China*, and the following very early studies: Marshall Broomhall, *Islam in China: a Neglected Problem* (London 1910); H. D'Ollone, *Mission d'Ollone: recherches sur les musulmans chinois* (Paris 1911); E. Rocher, *La Province chinoise du Yunnan* (2 vols.; Paris 1879 and 1880). For the movement in Africa, in addition to the chapters in the general histories recommended for "The Further Islamic Lands," there is a valuable series of studies in Bradford G. Martin, *Muslim Brotherhoods in Nineteenth-Century Africa* (Cambridge 1976); Martin is concerned to emphasize the interconnections of the movements. In addition, there are three excellent monographs: P. M. Holt, *The Mahdist State in the Sudan 1881–1898: a Study of its Origins, Development and Overthrow* (2nd edn; Oxford 1970); E. E. Evans-Pritchard, *The Sanusi of Cyrenaica* (Oxford 1949); M. Hiskett, *The Sword of Truth: the Life and Times of the Shehu Usuman dan Fodio* (New York 1973).

The Rise of Europe and the Response of Islam until the mid-20th Century

*M. G. S. Hodgson, "The Islamic Heritage in the Modern World," book six of his *Venture of Islam* vol. three, provides an introduction to the period full of ideas. *Bernard Lewis, *The Emergence of Modern Turkey* (2nd edn; London 1968), remains the best study of the transition from Ottoman empire to modern Turkey. For the Ataturk period it is usefully supplemented by a popupar biography, Lord Kinross, *Ataturk: the Rebirth of a Nation* (London 1964). P. J. Vatikiotis, *The History of Egypt* (2nd edn; London 1980), achieves for Egypt what Lewis has for Turkey. But see also R. P. Mitchell, *The Society of the Muslim Brothers* (London 1969). Two autobiographies

offer fascinating insights into Egyptian society and the stresses of modernization: Ahmad Amin (trans. I. J. Boullata), *My Life* (Leiden 1978), and the three volumes of the autobiography of Taha Hussein, a blind man who became Egypt's minister of education, *An Egyptian Childhood* (trans. E. H. Paxton; London 1981), *The Stream of Days, a Student at the Azhar* (trans. H. Wayment; 2nd edn; London 1948), and *A Passage to France* (trans. K. Cragg; Leiden 1976). *A. H. Hourani, in *Arabic Thought in the Liberal Age 1798–1939* (London 1962), has written the authoritative account of the emergence of Arab nationalist thought, and for the later period *Sylvia G. Haim, *Arab Nationalism; an Anthology* (Berkeley, Calif. 1962), should also be consulted. For the emergence of Saudi Arabia see H. St. J. Philby, *Saudi Arabia* (London 1955); J. S. Habib, *Ibn Saud's Warriors of Islam: the Ikhwan of Najd and their Role in the Creation of the Saudi Kingdom, 1910–1930* (Leiden 1978), is a valuable study of the militant religious organization which helped to bring Abd al-Azis Ibn Saud to power. Robert Lacey, *The Kingdom* (London 1981), is an accessible overview. Iran is now well served with surveys of its recent history. There is A. K. S. Lambton, "Persia: the Breakdown of Society," and R. M. Savory, "Modern Persia," in *The Cambridge History of Islam* vol. two; moreover, N. R. Keddie, the leading scholar of modern Iran, has recently published *Roots of Revolution: an Interpretive History of Modern Iran* (New Haven, Conn. 1981). Nevertheless, the classic work on the first Iranian revolution should not be missed: Edward G. Browne, *The Persian Revolution of 1905–1909* (Cambridge 1910). Scholarship on Islam in modern Central Asia has come to be dominated by outstanding French work: A. Bennigsen and C. L. Quelquejay, *Les Mouvements nationaux chez les Musulmans de Russie I: le sultangalievism au Tatarstan* (Paris 1960), *La Presse et le mouvement national chez les Musulmans de Russie avant 1920* (Paris 1964), (trans. G. E. Wheeler and H. Evans) *Islam in the Soviet Union* (London 1967); and H. Carrère d'Encausse, *Réforme et révolution chez les Musulmans de l'empire Russe, Bukhara, 1867–1924* (Paris 1966). For south Asia, *P. Hardy, *The Muslims of British India* (Cambridge 1972), is the established general history of the 19th and 20th centuries, as is Aziz Ahmad, *Islamic Modernism in India and Pakistan 1857–1964* (London 1967), for the development of Islamic thought. For different aspects of Muslim responses to British rule see: C. W. Troll, *Sayyid Ahmad Khan: a Reinterpretation of Muslim Theology* (New Delhi 1978); D. Lelyveld, *Aligarh's First Generation: Muslim Solidarity in British India* (Princeton, N.J. 1978); F. Robinson, *Separatism Among Indian Muslims: the Politics of the United Provinces' Muslims 1860–1923* (Cambridge 1974). What the experience of modernization meant to a leading Mughal poet and courtier can be glimpsed in R. Russell and Khurshidul Islam (trans. and eds.), *Ghalib: 1797–1869* vol. one, *Life and Letters* (London 1969). The best starting point for Iqbal's thought is Muhammad Iqbal, *The Reconstruction of Religious Thought in Islam* (Oxford 1934; reprint, Lahore 1962). His poetry has been translated by Nicholson and Arberry. As yet there is no authoritative analysis of the rise of the All-India Muslim League; the process of partition is described from the British point of view by H. V. Hodson, *The Great Divide: Britain, India, Pakistan* (London 1969). The best introductions to 19th- and 20th-century Islam in southeast Asia remain: W. R. Roff, "South-East Asian Islam in the Nineteenth Century" and H. J. Benda, "South-East Asian Islam in the Twentieth Century" in *The Cambridge History of Islam* vol. two. D. Noer, *The Modernist Muslim Movement in Indonesia 1900–42* (Singapore 1973), studies the progress of the movement. *M. Ricklefs, *A History of Modern Indonesia* (London 1981), is the most recent overview and by a careful scholar. There is relatively little work on Islam in Africa south of the Sahara in recent times: under colonial rule leadership fell into the hands of Christians and pagans. See J. S. Trimingham, *The Influence of Islam upon Africa* (London 1968); two surveys of specific societies, *P. M. Holt, *A Modern History of the Sudan* (3rd edn; London 1967), and I. M. Lewis, *The Modern History of Somaliland from Nation to State* (London 1965); also Donal Cruise O'Brien's, *The Mourids of Senegal: The Political and Economic Organization of an Islamic Brotherhood* (Oxford 1971), which reveals how a sufi order found a major role to play in economic modernization. For North Africa, see again J. M. Abun-Nasr, *A History of the Maghrib*. Scholars have just begun to study in detail the responses of *ulama* and sufis to the rise of European rule and the modern state. A few works must serve as guides: *N. R. Keddie (ed.), *Scholars, Saints and Sufis*, and *An Islamic Response to Imperialism: Political and Religious Writings of Sayyid Jamal ad-Din "al-Afghani"* (Berkeley, Calif. 1968), *S. Akhavi, *Religion and Politics in Contemporary Iran: Clergy-State Relations in the Pahlavi Period* (Albany, N.Y. 1980), D. Green, *The Tunisian Ulama* (Leiden n.d.). For brief introductions to the position of Islam and the *Sharia* in the modern state see: Erwin I. J. Rosenthal, *Islam in the*

Modern National State (Cambridge 1965), and *N. J. Coulson, *A History of Islamic Law.* H. A. R. Gibb's lectures, *Modern Trends in Islam* (Chicago, Ill. 1947), remain stimulating.

The Reassertion of Islam in the Later 20th Century
In addition to the books mentioned above, W. C. Smith, *Islam in Modern History* (Princeton, N.J. 1957), examines the visions of progress of the essentially secular elites which came to power in Muslim societies when the colonial tide receded. The speeches and writings of major leaders are also valuable: Muhammad Ali Jinnah, *Speeches, 3 June 1947–14 August 1948* (Karachi 1948); Jamal Abd al-Nasir, *The Philosophy of the Revolution* (Cairo 1954); Muhammad Riza Shah Pahlavi, *Mission for my Country* (London 1961). As to the reassertion of Islam as a general phenomenon, Md Ayoob (ed.), *The Politics of Islamic Reassertion* (London 1981), has essays of varying quality devoted to different Muslim states. A. S. Cudsis and A. E. Hillal Dessouki (eds.), *Islam and Power* (London 1981), contains an excellent essay by P. J. Vatikiotis on the general problem. For quick summaries of the recent affairs of Arab states see Peter Mansfield, *The Arabs* (revd edn; Harmondsworth 1978). The reemergence of Islam in modern Turkey is covered in Annemarie Schimmel, "Turkish Islam," in A. J. Arberry (ed.), *Religion in the Middle East* (Cambridge 1969), J. M. Landau, *The National Salvation Party: Radical Politics in Modern Turkey* (Salt Lake City, Utah 1976) and J. M. Landau, *Radical Politics in Modern Turkey* (Leiden 1974). The background to and the process of the revolution in Iran are well covered by Keddie, *Roots of Revolution*, M. J. Fischer, *Iran: from Religious Dispute to Revolution* (Cambridge, Mass. 1980), and Hamid Algar's lectures (ed. K. Siddiqui), *The Islamic Revolution in Iran* (London 1980). Fundamental developments among the Muslims of the Soviet Union are studied in H. Carrère d'Encausse, *L'Empire éclaté: la révolte des nations en U.R.S.S.* (Paris 1978). Information on the development of pan-Islamic organization since 1962 will be found in W. A. Beling (ed.), *King Faisal and the Modernisation of Saudi Arabia* (London 1979).

Part II: To be a Muslim

Religious Life
The best way to understand the Islamic life, the joy it can bring as well as the constant tensions between human desire and right conduct, lies in reading novels and biographies. Cragg and Speight's anthology, *Islam from Within*, is revealing, so is Constance Padwick's remarkable collection of Muslim prayers from throughout the world, *Muslim Devotions: a Study of Prayer-Manuals in Common Use* (London 1961), and so is Martin Lings, *A Sufi Saint of the Twentieth Century* (2nd edn; London 1971). Anthropologists have done much to reveal the activities and functions of sufi orders, for example, Ernest Gellner, *Saints of the Atlas* (Chicago, Ill. and London 1969), and Michael Gilsenan, *Saint and Sufi in Modern Egypt* (Oxford 1973). V. Crapanzano, *The Hamadsha: a Study in Moroccan Ethnopsychiatry* (Berkeley, Calif. 1973), examines the possession cults which are so often associated with sufi shrines. Muslim rites and festivals are explained simply by Riadh el-Droubie and Edward Hulmes, *Islam* (London 1980); G. E. von Grunebaum, *Muhammadan Festivals* (London 1976), studies them in greater detail. The pilgrimage, as befits the highpoint of religious life, has attracted most specific attention. C. Snouck Hurgronje, the Dutch scholar-administrator, who visited Mecca in disguise in the early 1880s, wrote a classic study (trans. J. H. Monahan), *Mekka in the Latter Part of the 19th Century* (Leiden and London 1931). It is not an infrequent practice to keep a journal of one's pilgrimage and these offer valuable insights: H.H. Nawab Sultan Jahan Begum (trans. Mrs Willoughby-Osborne), *The Story of a Pilgrimage to Hijaz* (Calcutta 1909); *H. T. Norris (trans. and ed.), *The Pilgrimage of Ahmad . . . an Account of a 19th-Century Pilgrimage from Mauritania to Mecca* (Warminster 1977). *Malcolm X, with the assistance of Alex Haley, *The Autobiography of Malcolm X* (New York 1965, London 1966), tells how the experience transformed his racial outlook. Modern illustrated books can project moving images of the spectacle of the pilgrimage and the spiritual intensity it generates; see Emel Esin, *Mecca the Blessed, Madinah the Radiant* (London 1963), and *E. Guellouz and A. Frikha, *Mecca: the Muslim Pilgrimage* (London 1977). Serious study of the pilgrimage as the greatest annual international meeting in the world over 14 centuries has also begun; see D. E. Long, *The Hajj Today: a Survey of the Contemporary Makkah Pilgrimage* (Albany, N.Y. 1979), and Umar al-Naqar, *The Pilgrimage Tradition in West Africa* (Khartoum 1972). Finally, there is the auto-biography of a German Jew who, as a newspaper correspondent in Arabia in the 1920s, slowly absorbed the Muslim vision of life; it is the moving self-analysis of a perceptive and intelligent European as he journeys into a Muslim consciousness: Muhammad Asad, *The Road to Mecca* (London 1954).

Arts of Islam
Titus Burckhardt's *Art of Islam* offers a sensitive introduction to the relationship between Islam and Islamic art forms. The most comprehensive introduction to calligraphy is Y. H. Safadi, *Islamic Calligraphy* (London 1978), which can be supplemented by Annemarie Schimmel, *Islamic Calligraphy* (Leiden 1970), which carries this fine scholar's especial sufistic angle of vision. For much Moroccan calligraphy, which is not widely known, and for many very beautiful plates, see A. Khatibi and M. Sijelmassi (trans. J. Hughes), *The Splendour of Islamic Calligraphy* (New York 1977). Few works have been devoted to ceramics alone. David Talbot Rice, *Islamic Art* (London 1965), offers a very simple introduction to the context of Islamic art in general. There is also Arthur Lane, *Later Islamic Pottery* (London 1957). Some of the achievement in Iran can be gleaned from Arthur U. Pope's *Survey of Persian Art*, and some of that in Turkey from O. Aslanapa, *Turkish Art*, and Tahsin Oz, *Turkish Ceramics* (Ankara 1957). Books on carpets and rugs, on the other hand, are legion. K. H. Turkhan offers a brief introduction from his long experience in the trade, *Islamic Rugs* (London 1968). Useful wide-ranging treatments are: Jurt Erdmann (trans. C. G. Ellis), *Oriental Carpets, an Account of their History* (London 1961), and R. de Calatchi (trans. V. Howard), *Oriental Carpets* (2nd edn; Rutland, Vt. 1970). On tribal rugs, Jenny Housego, *Tribal Rugs: an Introduction to the Weaving of the Tribes of Iran* (London 1978), is excellent.

Society and the Modern World
Studies of nomadic tribes are plentiful. Important recent studies include: Fredrik Barth, *Nomads of South Persia: the Basseri Tribe of the Khamseh Confederacy* (Oslo 1961, New York 1965), Daniel G. Bates, *Nomads and Farmers: a Study of the Yoruk of Southeastern Turkey* (Ann Arbor, Mich. 1973), T. Asad, *The Kababish Arabs: Power, Authority and Consent in a Nomadic Tribe* (London 1970), *D. P. Cole, *Nomads of the Nomads: the Al Murrah Bedouin of the Empty Quarter* (Chicago, Ill. 1975), and C. Nelson (ed.), *The Desert and the Sown: Nomads in Wider Society* (Berkeley, Calif. 1973). Isaaq Diqs, *A Bedouin Boyhood* (Oxford 1969), gives a first-hand account of growing up Bedouin in Jordan. John S. Habib, *Ibn Saud's Warriors* (Leiden 1978), and E. E. Evans-Pritchard, *The Sanusi of Cyrenaica* (Oxford 1949), illustrate the role nomads could play in making modern states. M. E. Meeker, *Literature and Violence in North Arabia* (Cambridge 1979), is an important recent book on pastoral nomadism and states. Moving to the village world, Joe E. Pierce, *Life in a Turkish Village* (New York 1964), is a straightforward account of growing up in a village; Hamed M. Ammar, *Growing up in an Egyptian Village:* *Silwa, Province of Aswan* (London 1954), is a classic. Village life can be savored in Z. S. Eglar, *A Punjabi Village in Pakistan* (New York 1960), and *Robert A. Fernea, *Shaykh and Effendi: Changing Patterns of Authority among the El Shabana of Southern Iraq* (Cambridge, Mass. 1970). Literature also provides a way in to village life; see the novels of Yashar Kemal, for instance *Memed my Hawk* (London 1961), and *V. M. Basheer (trans. R. E. Asher and A. C. Chandersekaran), *Me Grandad 'ad an Elephant!* (Edinburgh 1980). Regarding the Muslim town, an influential essay has been G. E. von Grunebaum's "The Structure of the Muslim Town" in his *Islam: Essays in the Nature and Growth of a Cultural Tradition* (Chicago, Ill. and London 1955). Three important collections of essays have appeared in recent years: A. H. Hourani and S. M. Stern (eds.), *The Islamic City* (Oxford 1970), I. M. Lapidus (ed.), *Middle Eastern Studies* (Berkeley, Calif. 1969), and L. Carl Brown (ed.), *From Madina to Metropolis* (Princeton, N.J. 1973). J. L. Abu-Lughud, *Cairo: 1001 Years of the City Victorious* (Princeton, N.J. 1971), and F. I. Khuri, *From Village to Suburb: Order and Change in Greater Beirut* (Chicago, Ill. 1975), are important new studies. Again, novels can tell us much about life itself: Najib Mahfuz (trans. T. Le Gassick), *Midaq Alley* (London 1975), is based in Cairo, and Ahmed Ali, *Twilight in Delhi* (2nd edn; Bombay 1966), takes place in the old Mughal city. A. H. Sharar (trans. E. S. Harcourt and F. Hussain), *Lucknow: the Last Phase of an Oriental Culture* (London 1975), is a marvelous description of the persianate urban culture of· this north Indian city. For houses, Guy T. Petherbridge, "Vernacular Architecture: the House and Society" in George Michell (ed.), *Architecture of the Islamic World: its History and Social Meaning* (London 1978), is a good introduction with a useful bibliography. See also James S. Kirkman (ed.), *City of Sanaa: Exhibition Catalogue* (London 1976). There is an outline of the traditional position of women in Islam in Reuben Levy, *The Social Structure of Islam* (Cambridge 1957). Charis Waddy, *Women in Muslim History* (London 1980), offers a survey of the power and achievement of Muslim women. C. Nelson, "Public and Private Politics: Women in the Middle Eastern World," *American Ethnologist*, August 1974, reviews the handling of women as a subject in ethnographic accounts. E. W. Fernea and B. Q. Bezirgan (eds.), *Middle Eastern Muslim Women Speak* (Austin, Texas 1977), and C. Beck and N. Keddie (eds.) *Women in the Muslim World* (Cambridge, Mass. 1978), are two outstanding recent surveys. The case for the position of women in Islam as traditionally understood is argued in B. Aisha Lemu and Fatima Heeren, *Woman in Islam* (London 1976). The argument that Muslim family mores and assumptions are fundamentally opposed to the equality of women is put forward with great passion by Fatima Mernissi, *Beyond the Veil: Male-Female Dynamics in a Modern Muslim Society* (New York 1975). Two books reveal the horrors Muslim women can suffer: L. P. Sanderson, *Against the Mutilation of Women* (London 1981), which deals with female circumcision, and Ian Young, *The Private Life of Islam* (London 1974), which is set in an Algerian obstetric hospital, and is definitely not reading for the squeamish. It is instructive to read the autobiographical works of women who have "beaten" the system: H.H. Nawab Sultan Jahan Begum, *An Account of my Life* (vol. one trans. C. H. Payne, London 1910; vol. two trans. A. S. Khan, Bombay 1922); Halide Edib, *Memoirs* (London 1926); Begum Ikramullah, *From Purdah to Parliament* (London 1963). Literature is again valuable. Some of the work of Assia Djeber, the prominent Algerian woman novelist, can be found in L. Ortzen (ed. and trans.), *North African Writing* (London 1970). The novel by Attia Hosain, first woman graduate from a north Indian *taluqdari* or landowning family, *Sunlight on a Broken Column* (London 1961), which depicts the stresses of changing values for an educated woman against the background of the Indian independence movement, is excellent.

GAZETTEER

Aaiun (Western Sahara), 27°10′N 13°11′W, 14, 158
Abadeh (Iran), 31°06′N 52°40′E, 206
Abeche (Chad), 13°49′N 20°49′E, 95
Abidjan (Ivory Coast), 5°19′N 4°01′W, 14, 158
Abqaiq (Saudi Arabia), 25°56′N 49°40′E, 121
Abu Hamed (Sudan), 19°32′N 33°20′E, 126
Abu Zenima (Egypt), 29°03′N 33°06′E, 161
Accra (Ghana), 5°33′N 0°15′W, 14
Aceh (Sumatra), (Indonesia), 5°30′N 95°20′E, 115, 134
Acre (Israel), 32°55′N 35°04′E, 139, 141, 161
Adana (Turkey), 37°00′N 35°19′E, 73, 132, 139, 141
Addis Ababa (Ethiopia), 9°03′N 38°42′E, 14, 134
Aden (S Yemen), 12°47′N 45°03′E, 14, 73, 95, 121, 134, 142
Adi Langu (Java), (Indonesia), 6°56′S 110°51′E, 91
Adrianople *see* Edirne
Agades (Niger), 17°00′N 7°56′E, 95
Agadir (Morocco), 30°30′N 9°40′W, 88, 95
Agha Jari (Iran), 30°45′N, 49°47′E, 143
Agra (India), 27°09′N 78°00′E, 59, 113, 150
Ahmadabad (India), 23°03′N 72°40′E, 24, 59
Ahmadnagar (India), 19°08′N 74°48′E, 113
Ain Jalut (Jordan), 32°04′N 35°19′E, 24
Ajmere (India), 26°29′N 74°40′E, 24, 36, 59, 113, 118, 150
Aksaray (Turkey), 38°22′N 34°02′E, 32
Albert, L (Uganda/Zaïre), 14
Aleppo (Syria), 36°14′N 37°10′E, 32, 45, 73, 114, 139, 141
Alexandretta (Turkey), 36°37′N 36°08′E, 141
Alexandria (Egypt), 31°13′N 29°55′E, 32, 73, 88, 114, 132, 139, 157
Algiers (Algeria), 36°50′N 3°00′E, 14, 73, 95, 134, 157, 158
Alkalawa (Nigeria), 13°34′N 6°22′E, 128
Allahabad (India), 25°27′N 81°50′E, 59, 113, 150
Almeria (Spain), 36°50′N 2°26′W, 32
Amadia (Iraq), 37°06′N 43°29′E, 141
Amasya (Turkey), 40°37′N 35°50′E, 45
Ambon (Isl), (Moluccas), (Indonesia), 3°41′S 128°10′E, 89
Amman (Jordan), 31°57′N 35°56′E, 14, 132, 141, 142, 158, 161
Amritsar (India), 31°35′N 74°56′E, 59, 206
Amsterdam (Netherlands), 52°21′N 4°54′E, 14, 176
Amu Darya R (USSR), (Oxus), 14, 24, 36, 45, 73, 101, 103, 112, 118, 130, 143, 145, 194
Amur R (Mongolia/USSR/China), 14
Andaman Islands (Bay of Bengal), 14, 150
Andijan (USSR), 40°50′N 72°23′E, 118
Angara R (USSR), 14
Angkor (Cambodia), 13°26′N 103°50′E, 89
Ankara (Turkey), 39°55′N 32°50′E, 14, 24, 73, 114, 118, 132, 134, 206
Anshun (China), 26°15′N 105°51′E, 124
Antalya (Turkey), 36°53′N 30°42′E, 114, 132
Antioch (Turkey), 36°12′N 36°10′E, 45, 114
Antwerp (Netherlands), 51°13′N 4°25′E, 88
Aqaba (Jordan), 29°32′N 35°00′E, 121, 161
Aqsu (China), 41°08′N 80°13′E, 101, 206
Araks R (USSR/Iran/Turkey), 130
Ararat (Mt), (Turkey), 39°40′N 44°23′E, 14
Ardabil (Iran), 38°15′N 48°18′E, 24, 45, 73, 112, 206
El Arish (Egypt), 31°08′N 33°48′E, 139, 161
Al Artawiyah (Saudi Arabia), 26°31′N 45°21′E, 142
Aru (Isl), (Indonesia), 2°23′N 128°07′E, 115
Ashkhabad (USSR), 37°58′N 58°24′E, 145, 206
Ashqelon (Israel), 31°40′N 34°35′E, 161
Asila (Morocco), 35°32′N 6°04′W, 95
Asirgarh (India), 21°31′N 76°22′E, 59
Assaye (India), 20°15′N 75°59′E, 113
Asterabad *see* Gorgan
Astrakhan (USSR), 46°22′N 48°04′E, 88, 101, 112, 126, 145
Aswan (Egypt), 24°05′N 32°56′E, 139
Asyut (Egypt), 27°14′N 31°07′E, 95
Atbara (Sudan), 17°42′N 34°00′E, 126
Atbara R (Sudan), 126
Athens (Greece), 38°00′N 23°44′E, 14, 24, 73, 114, 132, 139, 176
Aurangabad (India), 19°52′N 75°22′E, 59
Aussa (Ethiopia), 11°30′N 40°36′E, 95
Awjila (Libya), 29°05′N 21°12′E, 95
Ayaina (Saudi Arabia), 25°58′N 46°34′E, 121
Azammur (Morocco), 33°20′N 8°25′W, 95
Azov (USSR), 47°06′N 30°26′E, 73, 88, 101, 114

Badr (Saudi Arabia), 17°52′N 43°43′E, 24
Baghdad (Iraq), 33°20′N 44°26′E, 14, 24, 29, 32, 36, 45, 73, 88, 101, 112, 114, 118, 121, 132, 134, 141, 142, 143, 158, 206
Bahrain (Isl), (Persian Gulf), 26°05′N 50°31′E, 73, 121, 142, 158
Bakhchisaray (USSR), 44°44′N 33°53′E, 145
Baku (USSR), 40°22′N 49°53′E, 45, 73, 97, 112, 130, 134, 143, 145
Balakot (Pakistan), 34°28′N 73°24′E, 118
Bali (Isl), (Indonesia), 89, 91
Balkh (Afghanistan), 36°48′N 66°49′E, 24, 45, 59, 88, 101, 103, 112, 130
Balkhash, L (USSR), 14, 24, 36, 45, 88, 101, 103, 112, 118, 130, 145
Bam (Iran), 29°07′N 58°20′20E, 206
Bamako (Mali), 12°40′N 7°59′W, 14, 134, 155, 158
Bandaneira (Isl), (Moluccas), (Indonesia), 4°31′S 129°50′E, 89
Bandar (India), (Masulipatam), 16°13′N 81°12′E, 59, 113
Bandar Abbas (Iran), 27°12′N 56°15′E, 45, 112, 121, 142, 143
Bandar Seri Begawan (Brunei), 4°56′N 114°58′E, 14
Bandirma (Turkey), 40°21′N 27°58′E, 206
Bangalore (India), 12°58′N 77°35′E, 113
Bangka (Isl), (Indonesia), 1°48′N 125°11′E, 91
Bangkok (Thailand), 13°44′N 100°30′E, 14
Bangui (Central African Republic), 4°23′N 18°37′E, 14
Banjarmasin (Borneo), (Indonesia), 3°22′S 114°33′E, 89, 115
Banjul (Senegambia), 13°28′N 16°39′W, 14, 158
Bantam (Java), (Indonesia), 6°00′S 106°09′E, 89, 91, 115
Bara (Sudan), 13°42′N 30°21′E, 139
Baroda (India), 22°19′N 73°14′E, 113
Baros (Sumatra), (Indonesia), (Fansur), 2°02′N 98°20′E, 89, 91, 115
Barqa (Libya), 32°30′N 20°50′E, 73, 95
Basaidu (Qeshm Isl), (Iran), 26°38′N 55°19′E, 143
Basra (Iraq), 30°30′N 47°50′E, 45, 73, 88, 112, 121, 132, 141, 142
Bassein (India), 19°21′N 72°52′E, 59
Batang (Java), (Indonesia), 6°55′S 109°42′E, 115
Batavia *see* Jakarta
Batum (USSR), 41°37′N 41°36′E, 45, 114, 115, 132, 143
Batutulis (Java), (Indonesia), 6°34′S 106°45′E, 91
Al Bayda (Libya), 32°49′N 21°45′E, 126
Baykal, L (USSR), 14
Beersheba (Israel), 31°15′N 34°47′E, 161
Beirut (Lebanon), 33°52′N 35°30′E, 14, 141, 158
Belgrade (Yugoslavia), 44°50′N 20°30′E, 14, 59, 114, 176
Benares *see* Varanasi
Bender *see* Bendery
Bendery (USSR), (Bender), 46°50′N 29°29′E, 73
Benghazi (Libya), 32°07′N 20°05′E, 73, 114, 132, 134, 157, 172
Benkulen (Sumatra), (Indonesia), 3°46′S 102°16′E, 91, 115
Ben Nevis (Mt), (UK), 56°48′N 5°00′W, 14
Benue R (Cameroon/Nigeria), 14, 95, 118, 128, 155
Berber (Sudan), 18°01′N 34°00′E, 139
Berbera (Somalia), 10°28′N 45°02′E, 95, 134
Bergama (Turkey), 39°08′N 27°10′E, 206
Berlin (Germany), (West and East), 52°32′N 13°25′E, 14, 176
Bern (Switzerland), 46°57′N 7°26′E, 14
Beshir (USSR), 38°15′N 64°45′E, 206
Beyt Shean (Israel), 32°30′N 35°30′E, 161
Bhatkal (India), 13°59′N 74°34′E, 59
Bida (Nigeria), 9°06′N 5°59′E, 128
Bidar (India), 17°56′N 77°35′E, 24
Bidderi (Chad), 11°11′N 15°20′E, 95
Bijapur (India), 16°47′N 75°48′E, 24, 59, 113
Bijar (Iran), 35°52′N 47°39′E, 206
Bikaner (India), 28°01′N 73°22′E, 59, 113, 150
Billiton (Isl), (Indonesia), 91, 115
Bilma (Niger), 18°46′N 13°04′E, 95
Binh Dinh (Vietnam), (Vijaya), 13°53′N 109°07′E, 89
Bintan (Isl), (Indonesia), 91
Bin Yauri (Nigeria), 10°46′N 4°45′E, 128
Birecik (Turkey), 37°03′N 37°59′E, 141
Bir Gifgafa (Egypt), 30°28′N 33°11′E, 161
Birjand (Iran), 32°55′N 59°10′E, 206
Birmingham (UK), 52°30′N 1°50′W, 176
Birnin Gwari (Nigeria), 11°00′N 6°50′E, 128
Birnin Kebbi (Nigeria), 12°30′N 4°11′E, 128
Birnin Konni (Niger), 13°49′N 5°19′E, 128
Biskra (Algeria), 34°50′N 5°41′E, 32
Bissau (Guinea-Bissau), 11°52′N 15°39′W, 14, 158
Bizerte (Tunisia), 37°18′N 9°52′E, 157
Black Volta R (Upper Volta/Ivory Coast/Ghana), 14
Blida (Algeria), 36°30′N 2°50′E, 157
Blitar (Java), (Indonesia), 8°06′S 112°12′E, 91
Blue Nile R (Ethiopia/Sudan), 14, 126, 139
Bombay (India), 18°56′N 72°51′E, 59, 113, 118, 134, 150
Bone (Algeria), 36°55′N 7°47′E, 73, 157
Bonn (W Germany), 50°44′N 7°06′E, 14
Bor (Turkey), 37°53′N 34°35′E, 206
Bougie (Algeria), 36°49′N 5°03′E, 32, 73, 157
Bradford (UK), 53°48′N 1°45′W, 176
Brahmaputra R (Asia), 59, 113, 150
Brantas R (Java), (Indonesia), 91
Brava (Somalia), 1°02′N 44°02′E, 95
Brazzaville (Congo), 4°14′S 15°14′E, 14
Brunei (Brunei), 4°56′N 114°58′E, 89, 134, 158
Brussels (Belgium), 50°50′N 4°21′E, 14, 176
Bu Berih (Morocco), 34°16′N 4°50′W, 128
Bucharest (Romania), 44°25′N 26°07′E, 14, 73, 114, 132
Buda *see* Budapest
Budapest (Hungary), (Buda), (Pest), 47°30′N 19°03′E, 14, 73
Bujumbura (Burundi), 3°22′S 29°19′E, 14
Bukar (India), 25°35′N 84°00′E, 113
Bukhara (USSR), 39°47′N 64°26′E, 24, 29, 36, 45, 88, 101, 103, 112, 118, 130, 134, 143, 145, 206
Burhanpur (India), 21°18′N 76°08′E, 59
Bursa (Turkey), 40°12′N 29°04′E, 24, 73, 206
Buru (Isl), (Moluccas), (Indonesia), 115
Bushire (Iran), 28°59′N, 50°50′E, 143
Bussa (Nigeria), 9°55′N 4°26′E, 128
Butung (Isl), (Indonesia), 115

Cairo (Egypt), 30°03′N 31°15′E, 14, 24, 29, 32, 45, 73, 88, 95, 114, 118, 132, 134, 139 157, 158, 206
Calcutta (India), 22°30′N 88°20′E, 59, 113, 134, 150
Calicut (India), 11°15′N 75°45′E, 24, 88
Cambay (India), 22°19′N 72°39′E, 88
Cameroon (Mt), (Cameroon), 4°13′N 9°10′E, 14
Cannanore (India), 11°53′N 75°23′E, 59
Canton (China), 23°08′N 113°20′E, 88, 89, 124
Cardiff (UK), 51°30′N 3°13′W, 176
Carlowitz (Yugoslavia), 45°12′N 19°24′E, 114
Casablanca (Morocco), 33°39′N 7°35′W, 128, 157
Cattaro *see* Kotor
Ceram (Isl), (Moluccas), (Indonesia), 115
Cetinje (Yugoslavia), 42°25′N 18°56′E, 132
Ceuta (Morocco), (Spanish exclave), 35°53′N 5°19′W, 95, 134
Chad, L (Equatorial Africa), 14, 24, 88, 95, 118, 126, 128, 155
Chaldiran (Turkey), 39°10′N 43°52′E, 45, 73
Chandernagore (India), 22°52′N 88°21′E, 59, 113
Chaotung (China), 27°20′N 103°39′E, 124
Chengchou (China), 34°45′N 113°38′E, 124
Chengtu (China), 30°37′N 104°06′E, 124
Cheribon (Java), (Indonesia), 6°46′S 108°33′E, 89, 91, 115
Chikishlyar (USSR), 37°36′N 53°57′E, 143
Chinan (China), 36°41′N 117°00′E, 124
Chingchiang (China), 28°02′N 115°23′E, 124
Chining (China), 40°58′N 113°01′E, 124
Chios (Isl), (Greece), 38°23′N 26°07′E, 73, 139
Chitor (India), 13°13′N 79°06′E, 59
Chittagong (Bangladesh), 22°20′N 91°48′E, 59, 88, 113, 150
Chu R (USSR), 88
Cinto (Mt), (Corsica), 42°23′N 8°57′E, 14
Clermont-Ferrand (France), 45°47′N 3°05′E, 176
Cochin (India), 9°56′N 76°15′E, 59, 113
Colombo (Sri Lanka), 6°55′N 79°52′E, 14, 59, 150
Comoro Islands (Indian Ocean), 14, 95, 134, 155, 158, 172, 175
Conakry (Guinea), 9°30′N 13°43′W, 14, 158
Congo R (Central Africa), 134
Constantine (Algeria), 36°22′N 6°40′E, 157
Constantinople *see* Istanbul
Copenhagen (Denmark), 55°43′N 12°34′E, 14, 176
Cordoba (Spain), 37°53′N 4°46′W, 24, 32
Cracow (Poland), 50°03′N 19°55′E, 73
Cuttack (India), 20°26′N 85°56′E, 113

Dabola (Guinea), 10°48′N 11°02′W, 155
Dacca (Bangladesh), 23°42′N 90°22′E, 14, 59, 113, 158
Dakar (Senegambia), 14°38′N 17°27′W, 14, 155, 158
Daman (India), 20°26′N 72°58′E, 59
Damascus (Syria), 33°30′N 36°19′E, 14, 24, 29, 32, 45, 73, 88, 101, 114, 118, 121, 132, 134, 139, 141, 142, 158, 161, 206
Damavand (Mt), (Iran), 35°56′N 52°08′E, 14
Damghan (Iran), 36°09′N 54°22′E, 45, 103
Danube R (Central Europe), 14, 24, 29, 36, 73, 114, 132, 176
Dar es Salaam (Tanzania), 6°51′S 39°18′E, 134, 155, 158
Dariya (Saudi Arabia), 24°45′N 46°32′E, 118, 121, 139
Dead Sea (Israel/Jordan), 31°30′N 35°30′E, 161
Delhi (India), 28°40′N 77°14′E, 14, 24, 29, 45, 59, 88, 112, 113, 118, 134, 150, 158
Demak (Java), (Indonesia), 6°53′S 110°40′E, 24, 89, 91, 115
Derbent (USSR), 42°03′N 48°18′E, 112, 130, 143, 145, 206
Diu (India), 20°41′N 71°03′E, 59
Diyarbakir (Turkey), 37°55′N 40°14′E, 45, 73
Djibouti (Djibouti), 11°35′N 43°11′E, 14, 158
Dnepr R (USSR), 14, 24, 29, 36, 73, 101, 114, 145
Dnestr R (USSR), 14
Dodoma (Tanzania), 6°10′S 35°40′E, 14
Don R (USSR), 14, 24, 36, 73, 101, 114, 145
Dongola (Sudan), 19°10′N 30°27′E, 126, 139
Dongting Hu, L (China), 14
Dortmund (W Germany), 51°32′N 7°27′E, 176
Drave R (Yugoslavia), 114
Dublin (Republic of Ireland), 53°20′N 6°15′W, 14
Dubrovnik (Yugoslavia), (Ragusa), 42°40′N 18°07′E, 73, 114
Durazzo (Albania), 41°18′N 19°28′E, 132
Durmitor (Mt), (Yugoslavia), 14
Dusseldorf (W Germany), 51°13′N 6°47′E, 176

Ed Debba (Sudan), 18°02′N 30°56′E, 139
Ed Dueim (Sudan), 14°00′N 32°20′E, 126
Edirne (Turkey), (Adrianople), 41°40′N 26°34′E, 73, 114, 132
Elat (Israel), 29°33′N 34°57′E, 161
Elbe R (Czechoslovakia/E Germany/W Germany), 14, 176
Elbrus (Mt), (USSR), 43°21′N 42°29′E, 14
Elisavetpol (USSR), 41°08′N 46°15′E, 145
En Gedi (Israel), 31°27′N 35°23′E, 161
Erivan (USSR), 40°10′N 44°31′E, 45, 112, 130, 132, 143, 145, 206
Erzerum (Turkey), 39°57′N 41°17′E, 45, 132
Eskisehir (Turkey), 39°46′N 30°30′E, 132, 206
Essen (W Germany), 51°27′N 6°57′E, 176
Etna (Mt), (Sicily), 37°45′N 15°00′E, 14
Euphrates R (Turkey/Syria/Iraq), 14, 24, 29, 32, 36, 45, 73, 88, 101, 112, 114, 118, 121, 132, 134, 139, 141, 142, 143, 158, 172, 194
Everest (Mt), (Nepal), 27°59′N 86°56′E, 14

Fancheng (China), 31°06′N 118°04′E, 124
Fansur *see* Baros
El Fasher (Sudan), 13°37′N 25°22′E, 88, 95, 126, 155
Fashoda (Sudan), 9°50′N 32°00′E, 126
Fatehpur Sikri (India), 27°06′N 77°39′E, 59
Fethiye (Turkey), 36°37′N 29°08′E, 206
Fez (Morocco), 34°05′N 5°00′W, 14, 24, 32, 73, 88, 95, 128, 134, 172
Flores (Isl), (Indonesia), 115, 134
Freetown (Sierra Leone), 8°30′N 13°17′W, 14, 158
Frenda (Algeria), 35°04′N 1°03′E, 32
Fuchou (China), 26°09′N 119°17′E, 88

Gach Saran (Iran), 30°12′N 50°50′E, 143
Galle (Sri Lanka), 6°01′N 80°13′E, 59
Gallipoli (Turkey), 40°25′N 26°41′E, 132
Gambia R (Senegambia), 95
Ganges R (India), 14, 24, 29, 36, 45, 59, 88, 113, 118, 134, 150, 158, 194
Gangtok (India), 27°20′N 88°39′E, 14
Gao (Mali), 16°19′N 0°09′W, 24, 73, 95, 118, 155
Gaur-Tanda (India), 25°10′N 87°47′E, 59
Gawilgarh (India), 21°28′N 77°25′E, 113
Gaza (Gaza Strip) (Egypt), 31°30′N 34°28′E, 161
Genoa (Italy), 44°24′N 8°56′E, 73, 88
Ghadames (Libya), 30°10′N 9°30′E, 95
Ghat (Libya), 24°59′N 10°11′E, 95
Al Ghat Ghat (Saudi Arabia), 24°30′N 46°19′E, 142
Ghazna (Afghanistan), 33°33′N 68°28′E, 24, 45, 112
Ghiordes (Turkey), 38°55′N 28°17′E, 206
Ghujduwan *see* Gizhduvan
Ghumara (Morocco), 35°14′N 3°56′W, 128
Gizhduvan (USSR), (Ghujduwan), 40°07′N 64°15′E, 32
Glasgow (UK), 55°53′N 4°15′W, 176
Goa (India), 15°31′N 73°56′E, 59, 113, 150
Godavari R (India), 59, 113
Golkonda (India), 17°24′S 78°23′E, 24, 59, 113
Gombe (Nigeria), 10°17′N 11°14′E, 128
Gondar (Ethiopia), 12°39′N 37°29′E, 126
Gongola R (Nigeria), 128
Gorgan (Iran), (Jurjan), (Asterabad), 36°50′N 54°29′E, 32, 45, 73, 112, 130, 206
Granada (Spain), 37°10′N 3°35′W, 24, 32
Graz (Austria), 47°05′N 15°22′E, 73
Great Bitter Lake (Egypt), 30°15′N 32°20′E, 161
Gresik (Java), (Indonesia), 7°12′S 112°38′E, 89, 91, 115
Gross Glockner (Mt), (Austria), 47°05′N 12°44′E, 14
Grosswardein (Romania), 47°03′N 21°55′E, 73, 114
Groznyy (USSR), 43°21′N 45°42′E, 145
Guadiana R (Spain/Portugal), 14
Gudu (Nigeria), 13°10′N 4°55′E, 128
Gulnabad (Iran), 32°50′N 59°55′E, 112
Guntur (India), 16°20′N 80°27′E, 113
Gunung Bandahara (Mt), (Sumatra), (Indonesia), 3°46′N 97°47′E, 14
Gwalior (India), 26°12′N 78°09′E, 59, 113
Gwandu (Nigeria), 12°30′N 4°41′E, 128

Hadeira (Israel), 32°26′N 34°55′E, 161
Hadejia R (Nigeria), 128
Haft Gel (Iran), 31°28′N 49°35′E, 143
Haifa (Israel), 32°49′N 34°59′E, 141, 161
Hail (Saudi Arabia), 27°31′N 41°45′E, 132
Haiphong (Vietnam), 20°50′N 106°41′E, 89
Halmahera (Isl), (Moluccas), (Indonesia), 115
Halys R (Turkey), 132
Hama (Syria), 35°09′N 36°44′E, 141
Hamadan (Iran), 34°46′N 48°35′E, 24, 45, 73, 112, 114, 143, 206
Hamburg (W Germany), 53°33′N 10°00′E, 176
Hami (China), 42°37′N 93°32′E, 101, 103
Hangchou (China), 30°18′N 120°07′E, 88, 124
Hanoi (Vietnam), 21°01′N 105°52′E, 14
Harar (Ethiopia), 9°20′N 42°10′E, 29, 36, 95
Hari R (Sumatra), (Indonesia), 91
Hebron (Jordan), 31°32′N 35°06′E, 32, 161
Herat (Afghanistan), 34°20′N 62°10′E, 14, 24, 29, 32, 45, 88, 101, 103, 112, 143, 206
Heris (Iran), 38°15′N 47°08′E, 206
Al Hillah (Iraq), (Kufa), 32°02′N 44°25′E, 24
Hodeida (Yemen), 14°50′N 42°58′E, 95, 121, 142
Homs (Syria), 34°44′N 36°43′E, 139, 141
Hooghly (India), 22°59′N 88°24′E, 59
Hormuz (Iran), 27°31′N 54°56′E, 45, 73, 88
Hsian (China), 34°16′N 108°54′E, 124
Huang Ho R (China), 14, 24, 88, 101, 118, 124
Hue (Vietnam), 16°28′N 107°35′E, 89
Humaithira (Egypt), 23°25′N 34°50′E, 36
Hwaiking-fu (China), 35°15′N 114°17′E, 126
Hyderabad (India), 17°22′N 78°26′E, 113, 134, 150

Ibadan (Nigeria), 7°23′N 3°56′E, 155
Ili R (USSR), 101, 103
Illo (Nigeria), 11°32′N 3°33′E, 128
Ilorin (Nigeria), 8°32′N 4°34′E, 128
Inderagiri (Sumatra), (Indonesia), 0°16′S 103°14′E, 115
Inderagiri R (Sumatra), (Indonesia), 91
Indore (India), 22°42′N 75°54′E, 113
Indrapura (Sumatra), (Indonesia), 2°02′S 100°56′E, 91, 115
Indus R (Pakistan/India), 14, 24, 29, 32, 36, 45, 59, 88, 101, 103, 112, 113, 118, 134, 143, 150, 158, 172, 194
Ioannina (Greece), 39°40′N 20°51′E, 139
Ipoh (Malaysia), 4°36′N 101°02′E, 152
Irrawaddy R (Burma), 14, 24, 89, 134, 194
Irtysh R (China/USSR), 14, 24, 36, 101, 103, 145
Isfahan (Iran), 32°41′N 51°41′E, 24, 29, 45, 73, 88, 101, 112, 121, 134, 142, 143, 206
Ishim R (USSR), 14, 145
Islamabad (Pakistan), 33°44′N 75°11′E, 14, 158, 172
Isparta (Turkey), 37°46′N 30°32′E, 206
Issyk Kul, L (USSR), 103
Istanbul (Turkey), (Constantinople), 41°02′N 28°57′E, 24, 29, 32, 45, 73, 88, 114, 118, 132, 139, 172, 206
Izmir (Turkey), 38°25′N 27°10′E, 24, 73, 114, 132, 206
Iznik (Turkey), 40°27′N 29°43′E, 73

El Jadida (Morocco), (Mazagan), 33°19′N 8°35′W, 95
Jaffa (Israel), 32°04′N 34°46′E, 161

Jaffna (Sri Lanka), $9^\circ 40'$N $80^\circ 01'$E, 59
Jaghbub (Libya), $29^\circ 42'$N $24^\circ 38'$E, 118, 126
Jaipur (India), $26^\circ 53'$N $75^\circ 50'$E, 59, 113
Jaisalmer (India), $26^\circ 52'$N $70^\circ 55'$E, 59, 150
Jakarta (Java), (Indonesia), (Batavia), $6^\circ 08'$S $106^\circ 45'$E, 14, 89, 91, 115, 134, 158
Jambi (Sumatra), (Indonesia), $1^\circ 36'$S $103^\circ 39'$E, 91, 115
Jamuna R (India), 59, 113, 150
Japara (Java), (Indonesia), $6^\circ 32'$S $110^\circ 40'$E, 115
Jaunpur (India), $25^\circ 44'$N $82^\circ 41'$E, 24, 59
Al Jawf (Saudi Arabia), $29^\circ 47'$N $39^\circ 52'$E, 121, 142
Jedda (Saudi Arabia), $21^\circ 30'$N $39^\circ 10'$E, 24, 95, 118, 121, 139, 142, 172
Jehol (China), $40^\circ 59'$N $117^\circ 52'$E, 124
Jenne (Mali), $13^\circ 55'$N $4^\circ 31'$W, 24, 95, 118
Jericho (Jordan), $31^\circ 51'$N $35^\circ 27'$E, 161
Jerusalem (Israel/Jordan), $31^\circ 47'$N $35^\circ 13'$E, 14, 24, 32, 73, 114, 121, 132, 139, 141, 157, 158, 161
Jizan (Saudi Arabia), $16^\circ 56'$N $42^\circ 33'$E, 142
Jodhpur (India), $26^\circ 18'$N $73^\circ 08'$E, 59, 113
Johore Bahru (Malaysia), $1^\circ 29'$N $103^\circ 44'$E, 89, 91, 152
Jordan R (Israel/Jordan), 161
Joshagan (Iran), $33^\circ 34'$N $51^\circ 12'$E, 206
Jurjan *see* Gorgan

K2 (Mt), (Pakistan), (Godwin-Austen), $35^\circ 53'$N $76^\circ 32'$E, 14
Kabul (Afghanistan), $34^\circ 30'$N $69^\circ 10'$E, 14, 24, 45, 59, 88, 101, 103, 112, 113, 134, 143, 158, 206
Kaedi (Mauritania), $16^\circ 12'$N $13^\circ 32'$W, 95
Kagizman (Turkey), $40^\circ 08'$N $43^\circ 07'$E, 206
Kairouan (Tunisia), $35^\circ 42'$N $10^\circ 01'$E, 24
Kalgan (China), $40^\circ 51'$N $114^\circ 59'$E, 124
Kama R (USSR), 14
Kampala (Uganda), $0^\circ 19'$N $32^\circ 35'$E, 14, 155
Kanchou (China), $38^\circ 58'$N $100^\circ 30'$E, 101
Kano (Nigeria), $12^\circ 00'$N $8^\circ 31'$E, 24, 88, 95, 118, 128, 155
Karachi (Pakistan), $24^\circ 51'$N $67^\circ 02'$E, 118, 150, 172
Karaman (Turkey), $37^\circ 11'$N $33^\circ 13'$E, 32
Karaova (Turkey), $37^\circ 07'$N $27^\circ 40'$E, 206
Karasup (USSR), $45^\circ 03'$N $35^\circ 06'$E, 145
Karbala (Iraq), $32^\circ 37'$N $44^\circ 03'$E, 24, 45, 121
Karnal (India), $29^\circ 41'$N $76^\circ 58'$E, 112
Kasai R (Zaïre), 14
Kashan (Iran), $33^\circ 59'$N $51^\circ 35'$E, 36, 59, 206
Kashgar (China), $39^\circ 29'$N $76^\circ 02'$E, 24, 45, 88, 101, 103, 118, 206
Kassala (Sudan), $15^\circ 24'$N $36^\circ 25'$E, 126
Kathmandu (Nepal), $27^\circ 42'$N $85^\circ 19'$E, 14
Katsina (Nigeria), $13^\circ 00'$N $7^\circ 32'$E, 24, 95
Kavalla (Greece), $39^\circ 44'$N $20^\circ 55'$E, 139
Kayseri (Turkey), $38^\circ 42'$N $35^\circ 28'$E, 45, 73, 206
Kazakh (USSR), $41^\circ 05'$N $45^\circ 19'$E, 206
Kazan (USSR), $55^\circ 45'$N $49^\circ 10'$E, 24, 88, 101, 118, 145
al-Kazimain (Iraq), $33^\circ 22'$N $44^\circ 20'$E, 45
Kebbi R (Nigeria), 128
Kedah (Malaysia), $6^\circ 06'$N $100^\circ 23'$E, 89, 91, 115, 152
Keffi (Nigeria), $8^\circ 51'$N $7^\circ 47'$E, 128
Kelantan (Malaysia), $6^\circ 07'$N $102^\circ 15'$E, 89, 91, 152
Kelantan R (Malaysia), 152
Keluang (Malaysia), $2^\circ 01'$N $103^\circ 18'$E, 152
Kenya (Mt), (Kenya), $0^\circ 10'$S $37^\circ 19'$E
Kerki (USSR), $37^\circ 53'$N $65^\circ 10'$E, 206
Kerman (Iran), $30^\circ 18'$N $57^\circ 05'$E, 24, 45, 73, 112, 143, 200
Kermanshah (Iran), $34^\circ 19'$N $47^\circ 04'$E, 112, 206
Khartoum (Sudan), $15^\circ 33'$N $32^\circ 32'$E, 14, 118, 134, 139, 158
Khiva (USSR), $41^\circ 25'$N $60^\circ 49'$E, 32, 36, 45, 101, 103, 112, 130, 143, 206
Khokand (USSR), $40^\circ 33'$N $70^\circ 55'$E, 45, 101, 103, 118, 130, 145, 206
Khotan (China), $37^\circ 07'$N $79^\circ 57'$E, 88, 101, 103, 206
Khotan R (China), 103
Al Khurmah (Saudi Arabia), $21^\circ 55'$N $42^\circ 02'$E, 142
Kiev (USSR), $50^\circ 25'$N $30^\circ 30'$E, 73, 101
Kigali (Rwanda), $1^\circ 56'$S $30^\circ 04'$E, 14
Kilimanjaro (Mt), (Tanzania), 14
Kilwa (Tanzania), $8^\circ 55'$S $39^\circ 31'$E, 24
Kilwa Kisiwani (Tanzania), $9^\circ 00'$S $39^\circ 30'$E, 95
Kinshasa (Zaïre), $4^\circ 18'$S $15^\circ 18'$E, 14
Kirkuk (Iraq), $35^\circ 28'$N $44^\circ 26'$E, 141
Kirovabad (USSR), $40^\circ 39'$N $46^\circ 20'$E, 206
Kirsehir (Turkey), $39^\circ 09'$N $34^\circ 08'$E, 206
Kizyl-Arvat (USSR), $39^\circ 00'$N $50^\circ 23'$E, 206
Konya (Turkey), $37^\circ 51'$N $32^\circ 30'$E, 24, 32, 36, 73, 114, 118, 139, 206
Korbi (Sudan), $18^\circ 06'$N $31^\circ 33'$E, 139
Kotor (Yugoslavia), (Cattaro), $42^\circ 27'$N $18^\circ 46'$E, 73, 114
Krasnovodsk (USSR), $40^\circ 01'$N $53^\circ 00'$E, 143
Krishna R (India), 14, 24, 59, 113, 150
Kuala Lipis (Malaysia), $4^\circ 11'$N $102^\circ 00'$E, 152
Kuala Lumpur (Malaysia), $3^\circ 08'$N $107^\circ 42'$E, 152, 158, 172
Kuba (USSR), $41^\circ 23'$N $48^\circ 33'$E, 206
Kucha (China), $41^\circ 43'$N $82^\circ 58'$E, 88
Kuchuk Kainarji (Bulgaria), $43^\circ 57'$N $27^\circ 50'$E, 114
Kudus (Java), (Indonesia), $6^\circ 46'$S $110^\circ 48'$E, 91
Kueilin (China), $25^\circ 21'$N $110^\circ 11'$E, 124
Kufa *see* Al Hillah
Al Kufra (Libya), $24^\circ 19'$N $23^\circ 17'$E, 95, 126
Kukawa (Nigeria), $12^\circ 55'$N $13^\circ 31'$E, 95
Kula (Turkey), $38^\circ 33'$N $28^\circ 38'$E, 206
Kulakh (Saudi Arabia), $21^\circ 16'$N $40^\circ 55'$E, 139
Kulja (China), $44^\circ 00'$N $81^\circ 32'$E, 101, 103
Kunming (China), (Yunnan-fu), $25^\circ 04'$N $102^\circ 41'$E, 101, 124
El Kuntilla (Egypt), $30^\circ 00'$N $34^\circ 41'$E, 161
Kut (Iraq), $32^\circ 30'$N $45^\circ 51'$E, 132
Kutahya (Turkey), $39^\circ 25'$N $29^\circ 56'$E, 139
Kuwait (Kuwait), $29^\circ 20'$N $48^\circ 00'$E, 14
Kuybyshev (USSR), (Samara), $53^\circ 10'$N $50^\circ 10'$E, 145

Ladik (Turkey), $38^\circ 16'$N $31^\circ 57'$E, 206
Lagos (Nigeria), $6^\circ 27'$N $3^\circ 28'$E, 14, 95, 118, 158
Lahore (Pakistant), $31^\circ 34'$N $74^\circ 22'$E, 24, 59, 88, 112, 113, 134, 150, 172, 206
Lamu (Kenya), $2^\circ 17'$S $40^\circ 54'$E, 95
Lanchou (China), $36^\circ 01'$N $103^\circ 45'$E, 88, 101, 118, 124
Lemberg (USSR), $49^\circ 50'$N $24^\circ 00'$E, 73
Leningrad (USSR), (Petrograd), $59^\circ 55'$N $30^\circ 25'$E, 145
Lenin Peak (Mt), (USSR), $39^\circ 21'$N $73^\circ 01'$E, 14
Lepanto *see* Naupaktos
Libreville (Gabon), $0^\circ 30'$N $9^\circ 25'$E, 14
Lilongwe (Malawi), $13^\circ 58'$S $33^\circ 49'$E, 14
Lisbon (Portugal), $38^\circ 44'$N $9^\circ 08'$W, 14, 24, 88
Liverpool (UK), $53^\circ 25'$N $2^\circ 55'$W, 176
Lod (Israel), $31^\circ 57'$N $34^\circ 54'$E, 161
Loire R (France), 14, 176
Lombok (Isl), (Indonesia), $8^\circ 29'$S $116^\circ 40'$E, 115
Lomé (Togo), $6^\circ 10'$N $1^\circ 21'$E, 14
London (UK), $51^\circ 30'$N $0^\circ 10'$W, 14, 172, 176
Luanda (Angola), $8^\circ 50'$S $13^\circ 15'$E, 14
Lucknow (India), $26^\circ 50'$N $80^\circ 54'$E, 113, 150
Lusaka (Zambia), $15^\circ 26'$S $28^\circ 20'$E, 14
Luxembourg (Luxembourg), $49^\circ 37'$N $6^\circ 08'$E, 14
Lyons (France), $45^\circ 46'$N $4^\circ 50'$E, 176

Macassar (Celebes), (Indonesia), $5^\circ 09'$S $119^\circ 28'$E, 24, 89, 115
Madaba (Jordan), $31^\circ 44'$N $35^\circ 48'$E, 161
Madras (India), $13^\circ 05'$N $80^\circ 18'$E, 59, 113, 150
Madrid (Spain), $40^\circ 25'$N $3^\circ 43'$W, 14, 59
Madura (Isl), (Indonesia), $6^\circ 50'$S $113^\circ 10'$E, 91
Madurai (India), $9^\circ 55'$N $78^\circ 07'$E, 59
Mafraq (Jordan), $32^\circ 20'$N $36^\circ 12'$E, 161
Mahallat (Iran), $33^\circ 54'$N $50^\circ 28'$E, 206
Mahanadi R (India), 59, 113, 150
Maikop (USSR), $44^\circ 37'$N $40^\circ 48'$E, 130, 145
Majapahit (Java), (Indonesia), $7^\circ 34'$S $112^\circ 47'$E, 89, 91
Malabo (Equatorial Guinea), $3^\circ 45'$N $8^\circ 48'$E, 14
Malacca (Malaysia), $2^\circ 14'$N $102^\circ 14'$E, 24, 29, 88, 89, 91, 115, 134, 152
Malatya (Turkey), $38^\circ 22'$N $38^\circ 18'$E, 32, 45, 73, 206
Malawi, L (Malawi/Mozambique/Zambia), 14, 155
Malazgirt (Turkey), (Manzikert), $39^\circ 09'$N $42^\circ 30'$E, 24
Maldive Islands (Indian Ocean), 134, 158
Malindi (Kenya), $3^\circ 14'$S $40^\circ 05'$E, 95
Malta (Isl), (Mediterranean Sea), 73
Manchester (UK), $53^\circ 30'$N $2^\circ 15'$W, 176
Mangalore (India), $12^\circ 54'$N $74^\circ 51'$E, 59, 113, 150
Manzikert *see* Malazgirt
Maradi (Niger), $13^\circ 29'$N $7^\circ 10'$E, 128
Mardin (Turkey), $37^\circ 19'$N $40^\circ 43'$E, 206
Margherita (Mt), (Uganda), $0^\circ 22'$N $29^\circ 51'$E, 14
Margilan (USSR), $40^\circ 29'$N $71^\circ 44'$E, 206
Marrakesh (Morocco), $31^\circ 49'$N $8^\circ 00'$W, 24, 88, 95, 128
Marseilles (France), $43^\circ 18'$N $5^\circ 22'$E, 88, 176
Martapura (Borneo), (Indonesia), $3^\circ 25'$S $114^\circ 47'$E, 89, 115
Mary (Iran), (Merv), $37^\circ 42'$N $61^\circ 54'$E, 24, 45, 88, 101, 103, 112, 118, 130, 143
Masjid Sulaiman (Iran), $31^\circ 59'$N $49^\circ 18'$E, 143
Massawa (Ethiopia), $15^\circ 37'$N $39^\circ 28'$E, 73, 95, 121, 139
Massenia (Chad), $11^\circ 21'$N $16^\circ 09'$E, 95
Masulipatam *see* Bandar
Matankari (Niger), $13^\circ 47'$N $4^\circ 00'$E, 128
Mataram (Java), (Indonesia), $8^\circ 36'$S $116^\circ 07'$E, 91
Mazagan *see* El Jadida
Mecca (Saudi Arabia), $21^\circ 26'$N $39^\circ 49'$E, 24, 29, 32, 73, 88, 95, 118, 121, 126, 134, 139, 142, 172, 194
Medina (Saudi Arabia), $24^\circ 30'$N $39^\circ 35'$E, 24, 29, 73, 95, 118, 121, 139, 142
Megiddo (Israel), $32^\circ 35'$N $35^\circ 11'$E, 132
Mehraban (Iran), $38^\circ 03'$N $47^\circ 09'$E, 206
Meknes (Morocco), $33^\circ 53'$N $5^\circ 37'$W, 95
Mekong R (China), 12, 24, 29, 88, 118, 124, 134, 194
Melekes (USSR), $54^\circ 14'$N $49^\circ 37'$E, 145
Melilla (Morocco), (Spanish exclave), $35^\circ 20'$N $3^\circ 00'$W, 157
Menado (Celebes), (Indonesia), $1^\circ 32'$N $124^\circ 55'$E, 115
Menghua (China), $25^\circ 15'$N $100^\circ 20'$E, 124
Merowe (Sudan), $18^\circ 30'$N $31^\circ 49'$E, 126
Mersin (Turkey), $36^\circ 47'$N $34^\circ 37'$E, 141
Merv *see* Mary
Meshhed (Iran), $36^\circ 16'$N $59^\circ 34'$E, 45, 101, 103, 112, 143, 206
Meshkinshahr (Iran), $38^\circ 24'$N $47^\circ 40'$E, 206
Methoni (Greece), $36^\circ 49'$N $21^\circ 42'$E, 139
Metulla (Israel), $33^\circ 17'$N $35^\circ 34'$E, 161
Milas (Turkey), $37^\circ 19'$N $27^\circ 48'$E, 206
Mindanao (Isl), (Philippines), 115
El Minya (Egypt), $28^\circ 06'$N $30^\circ 45'$E, 139
Misfaq (Egypt), $31^\circ 02'$N $33^\circ 09'$E, 161
Missolonghi (Greece), $38^\circ 21'$N $21^\circ 26'$E, 139
Misurata (Libya), $32^\circ 24'$N $15^\circ 04'$E, 157
Mizdah (Libya), $31^\circ 25'$N $13^\circ 02'$E, 126
Mogadishu (Somalia), $2^\circ 02'$N $45^\circ 21'$E, 14, 24, 88, 95, 118, 134, 155, 158
Mohacs (Hungary), $46^\circ 00'$N $18^\circ 40'$E, 73, 114
Moldoveanu (Mt), (Romania), $45^\circ 37'$N $24^\circ 49'$E, 14
Mombasa (Kenya), $4^\circ 04'$S $39^\circ 40'$E, 95
Monrovia (Liberia), $6^\circ 20'$N $10^\circ 46'$W, 14
Mont Blanc (Mt), (France/Italy), $45^\circ 50'$N $6^\circ 52'$E, 14
Moro (Sudan), $10^\circ 51'$N $30^\circ 06'$E, 95
Moscow (USSR), $55^\circ 45'$N $37^\circ 42'$E, 14, 101, 145
Mostaganem (Algeria), $35^\circ 54'$N $0^\circ 05'$E, 128, 157
Mosul (Iraq), $36^\circ 21'$N $43^\circ 08'$E, 32, 45, 112, 141, 206
Moulouya R (Morocco), 128, 157
Mount Giri (Java), (Indonesia), $7^\circ 25'$S $112^\circ 31'$E, 91
Mozambique (Mozambique), $15^\circ 00'$S $40^\circ 44'$E, 95, 155
Mucur (Turkey), $39^\circ 05'$N $34^\circ 25'$E, 206
Mukalla (S Yemen), $14^\circ 34'$N $49^\circ 07'$E, 121
Mukden (China), $41^\circ 50'$N $123^\circ 26'$E, 124
Mukha (Yemen), $13^\circ 20'$N $43^\circ 16'$E, 121
Muko-muko (Sumatra), (Indonesia), $2^\circ 30'$S $101^\circ 05'$E, 91
Mulhacen (Mt), (Spain), $37^\circ 04'$N $3^\circ 19'$W, 14
Multan (Pakistan), $30^\circ 10'$N $71^\circ 36'$E, 24, 45, 59, 112, 113
Murcia (Spain), $37^\circ 59'$N $1^\circ 08'$W, 32
Murzuq (Libya), $25^\circ 56'$N $13^\circ 57'$E, 95
Muscat (Oman), $23^\circ 37'$N $58^\circ 38'$E, 14, 88, 121, 134, 142, 158
Musi R (Sumatra), 91
Mweru, L (Zaïre/Zambia), $9^\circ 00'$S $28^\circ 40'$E, 14
Mysore (India), $12^\circ 18'$N $76^\circ 37'$E, 59, 113, 150

Nablus (Jordan), $32^\circ 13'$N $35^\circ 16'$E, 161
Nadia (India), $23^\circ 22'$N $88^\circ 32'$E, 24
Nagapattinam (India), (Negapatam), $10^\circ 45'$N $79^\circ 50'$E, 59
Nagpur (India), $21^\circ 10'$N $79^\circ 12'$E, 113
Nahariya (Israel), $33^\circ 01'$N $35^\circ 05'$E, 161
Nahavand (Iran), $34^\circ 13'$N $48^\circ 21'$E, 112, 114
Nairobi (Kenya), $1^\circ 17'$S $36^\circ 50'$E, 14, 134
al-Najaf (Iraq), $31^\circ 59'$N $44^\circ 19'$E, 45
Najran (Saudi Arabia), $17^\circ 31'$N $44^\circ 19'$E, 121
Nancheng (China), $27^\circ 36'$N $116^\circ 35'$E, 124
Nanking (China), $32^\circ 03'$N $118^\circ 47'$E, 124
Naples (Italy), $40^\circ 50'$N $14^\circ 15'$E, 73
Narmada R (India), 59, 113
Nasser, L (Egypt/Sudan), 14
Naupaktos (Greece), (Lepanto), $38^\circ 23'$N $21^\circ 50'$E, 73
Navarino (Greece), $37^\circ 15'$N $21^\circ 40'$E, 139
Naxos (Isl), (Greece), $37^\circ 06'$N $25^\circ 24'$E, 73
Nazareth (Israel), $32^\circ 42'$N $35^\circ 18'$E, 161
N'Djamena (Chad), $12^\circ 10'$N $14^\circ 59'$E, 14, 158
Negapatam *see* Nagapattinam
Negombo (Sri Lanka), $7^\circ 13'$N $79^\circ 51'$E, 59
Nen R (China), 14
Netanya (Israel), $32^\circ 20'$N $34^\circ 51'$E, 161
New Delhi *see* Delhi
Neyriz (Iran) $29^\circ 14'$N $54^\circ 18'$E, 206
Ngaoundere (Cameroon), $7^\circ 20'$N $13^\circ 35'$E, 155
Ngazargamu (Nigeria), $13^\circ 00'$N $12^\circ 32'$E, 95, 128
Nguru (Nigeria), $12^\circ 53'$N $10^\circ 30'$E, 128
Niamey (Niger), $13^\circ 32'$N $2^\circ 05'$E, 14, 155, 158
Nias (Isl), (Indonesia), 91, 115
Niger R (W Africa), 14, 24, 29, 88, 95, 118, 128, 131, 134, 155, 158, 172, 194
Nile R (NE Africa), 14, 24, 29, 32, 36, 73, 88, 95, 101, 114, 118, 126, 131, 134, 139, 155, 157, 158, 172, 194
Nish (Yugoslavia), $43^\circ 20'$N $21^\circ 54'$E, 114, 132
Nishapur (Iran), $36^\circ 13'$N $58^\circ 49'$E, 24, 32, 45, 103, 112, 143
Nouakchott (Mauritania), $18^\circ 09'$N $15^\circ 58'$W, 14, 158

Ob R (USSR), 14, 101, 103
El Obeid (Sudan), $13^\circ 11'$N $30^\circ 10'$E, 126, 139
Oder R (Poland/E Germany), 14, 176
Oka R (USSR), 14
Olympos (Mt), (Greece), $40^\circ 05'$N $22^\circ 21'$E, 14
Omdurman (Sudan), $15^\circ 37'$N $32^\circ 29'$E, 126, 139
Omsk (USSR), $55^\circ 00'$N $73^\circ 22'$E, 103, 145
Oran (Algeria), $35^\circ 45'$N $0^\circ 38'$W, 157
Orenburg (USSR), $51^\circ 50'$N $55^\circ 00'$E, 103, 145
Ouagadougou (Upper Volta), $12^\circ 20'$N $1^\circ 40'$W, 14, 158
Oyo (Nigeria), $7^\circ 50'$N $3^\circ 55'$E, 128

Padang (Sumatra), (Indonesia), $1^\circ 00'$S $100^\circ 21'$E, 91, 115
Padang Besar (Malaysia), $6^\circ 38'$N $100^\circ 14'$E, 152
Pagarruyung (Sumatra), (Indonesia), $0^\circ 45'$S $100^\circ 42'$E, 91
Pahang (Malaysia), $3^\circ 50'$N $103^\circ 19'$E, 89, 91, 152
Pahang R (Malaysia), 152
Painan (Sumatra), (Indonesia), $1^\circ 21'$S $100^\circ 34'$E, 115
Pajang (Java), (Indonesia), $7^\circ 22'$S $100^\circ 50'$E, 89, 91
Palembang (Sumatra), (Indonesia), $2^\circ 59'$S $104^\circ 45'$E, 89, 91, 115
Panarukan (Java), (Indonesia), $7^\circ 40'$S $113^\circ 55'$E, 89, 91
Panipat (India), $29^\circ 24'$N $76^\circ 58'$E, 59, 113, 150
Paoting (China), $38^\circ 24'$N $115^\circ 26'$E, 124
Pariaman (Sumatra), (Indonesia), $0^\circ 36'$S $100^\circ 09'$E, 91, 115
Paris (France), $48^\circ 52'$N $2^\circ 20'$E, 14, 24, 73, 176
Pasai (Sumatra), (Indonesia), $5^\circ 12'$N $96^\circ 40'$E, 24, 29, 88, 89, 91, 118
Passarowitz (Yugoslavia), $44^\circ 37'$N $21^\circ 12'$E, 114
Pate (Isl), (Kenya), $2^\circ 08'$S $41^\circ 02'$E, 95
Patna (India), $25^\circ 37'$N $85^\circ 12'$E, 59, 113, 150
Patras (Greece), $38^\circ 14'$N $21^\circ 44'$E, 139
Pattani (Thailand), $6^\circ 50'$N $101^\circ 20'$E, 89, 91, 115
Pegu (Burma), $17^\circ 18'$N $96^\circ 31'$E, 89
Peking (China), $39^\circ 55'$N $116^\circ 26'$E, 14, 24, 88, 101, 124
Pemba (Isl), (Tanzania), $13^\circ 00'$S $40^\circ 30'$E, 134
Penang (Isl), (Malaysia), $5^\circ 26'$N $100^\circ 16'$E, 15
Pendeh (USSR), $35^\circ 16'$N $62^\circ 37'$E, 206
Perak (Malaysia), $4^\circ 17'$N $100^\circ 36'$E, 115
Perak R (Malaysia), 152
Perlak (Sumatra), (Indonesia), $4^\circ 50'$N $97^\circ 48'$E, 91
Peshawar (Pakistan), $34^\circ 01'$N $71^\circ 40'$E, 59, 112, 150
Pest *see* Budapest
Petrograd *see* Leningrad
Petropavlovsk (USSR), $54^\circ 53'$N $69^\circ 13'$E, 145
Philippeville (Algeria), $36^\circ 53'$N $6^\circ 54'$E, 157
Philippopolis *see* Plovdiv
Phnom Penh (Cambodia), $11^\circ 35'$N $104^\circ 55'$E, 14
Pingliang (China), $35^\circ 27'$N $106^\circ 31'$E, 124
Pipli (India), $20^\circ 13'$N $85^\circ 50'$E, 59
Plassey (India), $23^\circ 41'$N $88^\circ 29'$E, 113
Plovdiv (Bulgaria), (Philippopolis), $42^\circ 08'$N $24^\circ 45'$E, 132
Po R (Italy), 176
Poitiers (France), $46^\circ 35'$N $0^\circ 20'$E, 24
Pondicherry (India), $11^\circ 59'$N $79^\circ 50'$E, 59, 150
Poona (India), $18^\circ 34'$N $73^\circ 58'$E, 59, 150
Porto Novo (Benin), $6^\circ 30'$N $2^\circ 47'$E, 14, 158
Poti (USSR), $42^\circ 11'$N $41^\circ 41'$E, 130
Poyang Hu, L (China), 14
Prague (Czechoslovakia), $50^\circ 06'$N $14^\circ 26'$E, 14
Prai (Malaysia), $5^\circ 22'$N $100^\circ 17'$E, 152
Pristina (Yugoslavia), $42^\circ 39'$N $21^\circ 10'$E, 176
Pulicat (India), $13^\circ 26'$N $80^\circ 20'$E, 59
Puy de Sancy (Mt), (France), $45^\circ 32'$N $2^\circ 48'$E, 14
Pyongyang (North Korea), $39^\circ 00'$N $125^\circ 47'$E, 14

Qadisiya (Iraq), $31^\circ 18'$N $44^\circ 54'$E, 24
Qandahar (Afghanistan), $31^\circ 36'$N $65^\circ 47'$E, 45, 59, 112, 143
El Qantara (Egypt), $30^\circ 52'$N $32^\circ 20'$E, 161
Qars (Turkey), $40^\circ 35'$N $43^\circ 05'$E, 45, 112, 114, 130, 132, 206
al-Qasr al-Kabir (Morocco), $35^\circ 04'$N $5^\circ 56'$W, 95
Qatana (Syria), $33^\circ 27'$N $36^\circ 04'$E, 101
Qatif (Saudi Arabia), $26^\circ 30'$N $50^\circ 00'$E, 121
Qazvin (Iran), $36^\circ 16'$N $50^\circ 00'$E, 45, 73, 112, 143
Qeshm (Isl), (Iran), $26^\circ 58'$N $56^\circ 17'$E, 143
Qiru (Chad), $19^\circ 36'$N $19^\circ 36'$E, 126
Quelimane (Mozambique), $17^\circ 53'$S, $36^\circ 51'$E, 95
Quezon City (Philippines), $14^\circ 39'$N $121^\circ 02'$E, 14
Quilon (India), $8^\circ 53'$N $76^\circ 38'$E, 59
Qum (Iran), $34^\circ 39'$N $50^\circ 57'$E, 24, 45, 206
Quneitra (Syria), $33^\circ 08'$N $35^\circ 49'$E, 161
Al Qunfidhah (Saudi Arabia), $19^\circ 09'$N $41^\circ 07'$E, 139
Qusair (Egypt), $26^\circ 04'$N $34^\circ 15'$E, 95

Raba (Nigeria), $9^\circ 14'$N $4^\circ 59'$E, 128
Rabat (Morocco), $34^\circ 02'$N $6^\circ 51'$W, 14, 128, 157, 158, 172
Rae Bareli (India), $26^\circ 14'$N $81^\circ 14'$E, 118
Rafah (Gaza Strip), (Egypt), $31^\circ 18'$N $34^\circ 15'$E, 161
Ragusa *see* Dubrovnik
Ramallah (Jordan), $31^\circ 55'$N $35^\circ 12'$E, 161
Ramila (Israel), $31^\circ 56'$N $34^\circ 52'$E, 161
Rangoon (Burma), $16^\circ 47'$N $96^\circ 10'$E, 14
Rathambhor (India), $25^\circ 32'$N $76^\circ 02'$E, 59
Rembang (Java), (Indonesia), $6^\circ 45'$S $111^\circ 22'$E, 115
Rengat (Sumatra), (Indonesia), $0^\circ 26'$S $102^\circ 35'$E, 91
Resht (Iran), $37^\circ 18'$N $49^\circ 38'$E, 112, 143
Rhein *see* Rhine
Rhine R (W Europe), (Rhein), 14, 73, 176
Rhodes (Isl), (Greece), 73, 139
Rhône R (France), 176
Riyadh (Saudi Arabia), $24^\circ 39'$N $46^\circ 46'$E, 121, 134, 142
Rome (Italy), $41^\circ 53'$N $12^\circ 30'$E, 14, 73
Rudolf, L (Kenya), 14
Rufiji R (Tanzania), 95

Sabila (Saudi Arabia), $26^\circ 24'$N $45^\circ 08'$E, 142
Sabon Gari (Nigeria), $12^\circ 13'$N $6^\circ 02'$E, 128
Sabzevar (Iran), $36^\circ 13'$N $57^\circ 38'$E, 206
Safi (Morocco), $32^\circ 18'$N $9^\circ 20'$W, 95
Saidabad (Iran), $29^\circ 28'$N $55^\circ 44'$E, 206
Saigon (Vietnam), $10^\circ 46'$N $106^\circ 43'$E, 89
Salween R (China/Burma), 14, 24, 89, 124, 194
Samara *see* Kuybyshev
Samarqand (USSR), $39^\circ 40'$N $66^\circ 57'$E, 24, 29, 32, 45, 59, 88, 101, 103, 112, 118, 130, 134, 145, 206
Samarra (Iraq), $34^\circ 13'$N $43^\circ 52'$E, 24, 45, 112
Sambas (Borneo), (Indonesia), $1^\circ 22'$N $109^\circ 15'$E, 115
Samos (Isl), (Greece), 73
Samsun (Turkey), $41^\circ 17'$N $36^\circ 22'$E, 132
Samudra (Sumatra), (Indonesia), $5^\circ 09'$N $97^\circ 09'$E, 89
Sana (Yemen), $15^\circ 24'$N $44^\circ 14'$E, 14, 73, 121, 142
Sarab (Iran), $37^\circ 56'$N $47^\circ 35'$E, 206
Sarajevo (Yugoslavia), $43^\circ 52'$N $18^\circ 26'$E, 132
Sarakhs (Iran), $36^\circ 32'$N $61^\circ 07'$E, 32, 206
Save R (Yugoslavia), 114, 176
Scutari *see* Shkoder
Sebastapol (USSR), $44^\circ 36'$N $33^\circ 31'$E, 114
Seguela (Ivory Coast), $7^\circ 58'$N $6^\circ 44'$W, 155
Selima (Sudan), $21^\circ 22'$N $29^\circ 19'$E, 95
Semipalatinsk (USSR), $50^\circ 26'$N $80^\circ 16'$E, 103
Semnan (Iran), $35^\circ 30'$N $53^\circ 25'$E, 206
Senegal R (Guinea/Mali/Senegambia), 14, 24, 95, 155
Sennar (Sudan), $13^\circ 31'$N $33^\circ 38'$E, 88, 95, 126, 139, 155
Senne (Iran), $35^\circ 18'$N $47^\circ 01'$E, 206
Senta (Yugoslavia), (Zenta), $45^\circ 55'$N $20^\circ 06'$E, 114
Seoul (South Korea), $37^\circ 30'$N $127^\circ 00'$E, 14
Serampore (India), $22^\circ 44'$N $88^\circ 21'$E, 59
Seremban (Malaysia), $2^\circ 42'$N $101^\circ 54'$E, 152
Seringapatam (India), $12^\circ 25'$N $76^\circ 41'$E, 113
Seville (Spain), $37^\circ 24'$N $5^\circ 59'$W, 24, 32
Sfax (Tunisia), $34^\circ 45'$N $10^\circ 34'$E, 157
Shamakhi (USSR), $40^\circ 38'$N $48^\circ 37'$E, 112, 130, 206
Shanghai (China), $31^\circ 06'$N $121^\circ 22'$E, 124
Sharm el Sheikh (Egypt), $27^\circ 51'$N $34^\circ 16'$E, 161
Shaykan (Sudan), $19^\circ 01'$N $30^\circ 19'$E, 126
Sheffield (UK), $53^\circ 23'$N $1^\circ 30'$W, 176
Shendi (Sudan), $16^\circ 41'$N $33^\circ 22'$E, 139
Shiraz (Iran), $29^\circ 38'$N $52^\circ 34'$E, 24, 29, 32, 45, 73, 88, 112, 143, 206
Shkoder (Albania), (Scutari), $42^\circ 03'$N $19^\circ 01'$E, 132, 176
Shunte-fu (China), $37^\circ 47'$N $114^\circ 30'$E, 124
Siak (Sumatra), (Indonesia), $0^\circ 50'$N $120^\circ 05'$E, 91
Siberut (Isl), (Indonesia), $1^\circ 20'$S $98^\circ 50'$E, 91
Sibir (USSR), $68^\circ 29'$N $158^\circ 30'$E, 101
Silebar (Sumatra), (Indonesia), $4^\circ 07'$S $102^\circ 30'$E, 115
Simeulue (Isl), (Indonesia), $2^\circ 30'$N $96^\circ 00'$E, 91
Simpang-Kiri R (Sumatra), (Indonesia), 91
Singapore (SE Asia), $1^\circ 18'$N $103^\circ 50'$E, 14, 89, 91, 115, 152, 158, 194
Singkel (Sumatra), (Indonesia), $2^\circ 16'$N $97^\circ 47'$E, 89, 91, 118
Sinkat (Sudan), $18^\circ 55'$N $36^\circ 48'$E, 126
Sinop (Turkey), (Sinope), $42^\circ 02'$N $35^\circ 09'$E, 45, 73, 132
Sinope *see* Sinop
Sirhind (India), $30^\circ 39'$N $76^\circ 28'$E, 59
Sivas (Turkey), $39^\circ 44'$N $37^\circ 01'$E, 32, 45, 73, 114, 132, 206
Siwa (Egypt), $29^\circ 11'$N $25^\circ 31'$E, 95
Skobelev (USSR), $40^\circ 23'$N $71^\circ 17'$E, 145
Skopje (Yugoslavia), $42^\circ 00'$N $21^\circ 28'$E, 176
Sofala (Mozambique), $19^\circ 49'$S $34^\circ 52'$E, 88, 95
Sofia (Bulgaria), $42^\circ 40'$N $23^\circ 18'$E, 14, 73, 114, 132, 176
Sokoto (Nigeria), $13^\circ 02'$N $5^\circ 15'$E, 118, 128, 134
Solo R (Java), (Indonesia), 91
South Shields (UK), $55^\circ 00'$N $1^\circ 25'$W, 176
Spalato *see* Split
Split (Yugoslavia), (Spalato), $43^\circ 31'$N $16^\circ 28'$E, 73
Srinagar (India), $34^\circ 08'$N $74^\circ 50'$E, 59, 113, 150, 206
Suakin (Sudan), $19^\circ 08'$N $37^\circ 17'$E, 73, 95, 121, 126, 139
Suchou (China), $39^\circ 47'$N $98^\circ 30'$E, 101
Suez (Egypt), $29^\circ 59'$N $32^\circ 33'$E, 161
Suez Canal (Egypt), 161
Sujilmasa (Morocco), $31^\circ 53'$N $3^\circ 03'$W, 95
Sukadana (Borneo), (Indonesia), $1^\circ 15'$S $109^\circ 57'$E, 115
Sultanabad (Iran), $34^\circ 05'$N $49^\circ 42'$E, 206
Sumbawa (Isl), (Indonesia), $8^\circ 50'$S $118^\circ 00'$E, 89, 115, 134
Sungpan (China), $32^\circ 40'$N $103^\circ 30'$E, 124
Surabaya (Java), (Indonesia), $7^\circ 14'$S $112^\circ 45'$E, 115
Surat (India), $21^\circ 10'$N $72^\circ 54'$E, 113
Sutlej R (India/Pakistan), 14, 24, 45, 59, 112, 113, 150
Syr Darya R (USSR), 14, 24, 36, 45, 101, 103, 112, 118, 130, 143, 145

Szigetvar (Hungary), 46°01′N 17°50′E, 73

Tabora (Tanzania), 5°02′S 32°50′E, 155
Tabriz (Iran), 38°05′N 46°18′E, 24, 45, 73, 88, 101, 112, 114, 118, 130, 143, 206
Tafilalt (Morocco), 31°24′N 4°08′W, 128
Taif (Saudi Arabia), 21°15′N 40°21′E, 172
Tai-pei (Taiwan), 25°05′N 121°32′E, 14
Taju (Iran), 36°34′N 54°46′E, 32
Takedda (Niger), 17°26′N 6°37′E, 95
Talas (USSR), 42°30′N 72°13′E, 24
Tali (China), 25°45′N 100°06′E, 118, 124
Tamanrasset (Algeria), 22°50′N 5°28′E, 95
Tana, L (Ethiopia), 12°00′N 37°20′E, 95, 126
Tanganyika, L (Zaïre/Tanzania/Burundi/ Zambia), 14, 155
Tangier (Morocco), 35°48′N 5°50′W, 24, 88, 95, 128, 157
Tanjungpinang (Bintan Isl), (Indonesia), 0°55′N 104°28′E, 91
Tanjungpura (Borneo), (Indonesia), 0°02′S 113°32′E, 89
Tanta (Egypt), 30°48′N 31°00′E, 36
Taodeni (Mali), 22°38′N 3°58′E, 95
Tapti R (India), 59, 113
Tara (USSR), 56°55′N 74°24′E, 101
Tarim R (China), 24, 88, 101, 103
Tashkent (USSR), 41°16′N 69°13′E, 24, 45, 88, 101, 103, 118, 130, 134, 145, 206
Tatsienlu (China), 30°05′N 102°04′E, 124
Tatung (China), 40°12′N 113°12′E, 124
Tbilisi (USSR), (Tiflis), 41°43′N 44°48′E, 45, 73, 112, 130, 143, 145, 206
Tedzhen (USSR), 37°26′N 60°30′E, 206
Tegal (Java), (Indonesia), 6°52′S 109°07′E, 91, 115
Teheran (Iran), 35°40′N 51°26′E, 14, 45, 73, 112, 134, 143, 158, 206
Tel Aviv (Israel), 32°05′N 34°46′E, 161

Telok Anson (Malaysia), 4°00′N 101°02′E, 152
Temesvar (Romania), 45°45′N 21°15′E, 73, 114
Temir-Khan-Sura (USSR), 43°48′N 47°22′E, 145
Terhazza (Mali), 23°38′N 5°22′W, 95
Ternate (Isl), (Moluccas), (Indonesia), 0°50′N 127°19′E, 89
Tetouan (Morocco), 35°34′N 5°22′W, 128
Thatta (Pakistan), 24°41′N 67°34′E, 59, 113
Thessalonica (Greece), 40°38′N 22°58′E, 132
Thimbu (Bhutan), 27°32′N 89°43′E, 14
Tiberias (Israel), 32°48′N 35°32′E, 161
Tiberias, L (Israel), (Sea of Galilee), 32°45′N 35°38′E, 161
Tidore (Isl), (Moluccas), (Indonesia), 0°40′N 127°25′E, 89
Tiflis see Tbilisi
Tigris R (Turkey/Iraq), 14, 24, 29, 32, 36, 45, 73, 88, 101, 112, 114, 118, 121, 132, 134, 139, 141, 142, 143, 158, 172, 194
Tiku (Sumatra), (Indonesia), 0°18′S 99°57′E, 91, 115
Timbuktu (Mali), 16°49′N 2°59′W, 24, 29, 88, 95, 118, 134, 155
Timor (Isl), (Indonesia), 9°00′S 125°00′E, 115, 134
Tirane (Albania), 41°20′N 19°49′E, 14, 176
Titograd (Yugoslavia), 42°28′N 19°17′E, 176
Tlemcen (Algeria), 34°53′N 1°21′W, 24, 32, 36, 37, 95, 157
Toba, L (Sumatra), (Indonesia), 2°40′N 98°50′E, 91
Tobol R (USSR), 145
Tobolsk (USSR), 58°15′N 68°12′E, 101
Tokar (Sudan), 18°37′N 37°41′E, 126
Toledo (Spain), 39°52′N 4°02′W, 24
Tomsk (USSR), 56°30′N 85°05′E, 145

Tondibi (Mali), 16°57′N 0°18′W, 95
Tranquebar (India), 11°04′N 79°50′E, 59
Trebizond (Turkey), 41°00′N 39°43′E, 45, 73, 88, 114, 132
Trengganu (Malaysia), 5°20′N 103°07′E, 89, 91, 152
Trincomali (Sri Lanka), 8°34′N 81°13′E, 59, 113
Trinkitat (Sudan), 18°39′N 37°49′E, 126
Tripoli (Libya), 32°58′N 13°12′E, 14, 73, 88, 95, 134, 157, 158, 172
Tripolis (Greece), 37°31′N 22°22′E, 139
Troitsk (USSR), 54°08′N 61°33′E, 145
Tsangpo R (China/India/Bangladesh), 14
Tsuntsuwa (Nigeria), 13°40′N 6°11′E, 128
Tuat (Algeria), 27°12′N 2°29′E, 95
Tuban (Java), (Indonesia), 6°55′S 112°01′E, 89, 91
Tulkarm (Jordan), 32°19′N 35°02′E, 161
Tunhuang (China), 40°05′N 94°45′E, 101
Tunis (Tunisia), 36°50′N 10°13′E, 14, 32, 73, 88, 95, 134, 157, 158
El Tur (Egypt), 28°14′N 33°36′E, 161
Turabah (Saudi Arabia), 21°15′N 41°34′E, 139
Turfan (China), 42°55′N 89°06′E, 101, 103
Turkestan see Yasi
Tus (Iran), 36°30′N 59°31′E, 32
Tushki (Sudan), 21°56′N 31°12′E, 126
Tyre (Lebanon), 33°16′N 35°12′E, 161
Tyumen (USSR), 57°11′N 65°29′E, 101

Ubangi R (Congo), 14, 194
Ufa (USSR), 54°45′N 55°58′E, 101, 145
Ulaanbaatar (Mongolia), 47°54′N 106°52′E, 14
Umm Abida (Iraq), 31°38′N 45°11′E, 36
Umm Diwaykarat (Sudan), 12°10′N 32°38′E, 126

Ural R (USSR), 14, 24, 36, 73, 101, 103, 130, 145
Uralsk (USSR), 51°19′N 51°20′E, 145
Urfa (Turkey), 37°08′N 38°45′E, 132, 206
Urgench (USSR), 41°35′N 60°41′E, 101, 103
Urumchi (USSR), 43°43′N 87°38′E, 101, 103
Ushak (Turkey), 38°42′N 29°25′E, 206

Valdikavkaz (USSR), 44°58′N 35°22′E, 145
Varanasi (India), (Benares), 25°20′N 83°00′E, 24, 59, 113, 150
Venice (Italy), 45°26′N 12°20′E, 73, 88
Viatka (USSR), 58°30′N 49°40′E, 145
Victoria (Hongkong), 22°16′N 114°13′E, 14
Victoria, L (Uganda/Kenya/Tanzania), 14, 95, 131, 155, 194
Vienna (Austria), 48°13′N 16°22′E, 14, 73, 114
Vientiane (Laos), 17°59′N 102°38′E, 14
Vijaya see Binh Dinh
Vijayanagar (India), 15°20′N 76°25′E, 24, 59, 113
Vistula R (Poland), 14, 176
Vitim R (USSR), 14
Volga R (USSR), 14, 24, 29, 36, 73, 88, 101, 114, 130, 145
Volta R (Ghana), 95

Wadi Araba R (Egypt), 161
Wadi Halfa (Sudan), 21°46′N 31°17′E, 126, 139
Wad Medani (Sudan), 14°24′N 33°30′E, 126
Walata (Mauritania), 17°15′N 6°55′W, 95
Wargla (Algeria), 32°00′N 5°16′E, 73, 95
Warsaw (Poland), 52°15′N 21°00′E, 14
Waw al Kabir (Libya), 25°21′N 16°41′E, 126
West Berlin see Berlin
Wetar (Isl), (Indonesia), 7°50′S 126°10′E, 115

White Nile R (Uganda/Sudan), 14, 126, 131, 139, 155
Woina Dega (Ethiopia), 11°47′N 37°39′E, 95
Wuhu (China), 31°23′N 118°25′E, 124

Xi Jiang R (China), 14

Yanam (India), (Yanaon), 16°45′N 82°16′E, 113
Yanaon see Yanam
Yanbu (Saudi Arabia), 24°07′N 38°04′E, 121, 139
Yangtze R (China), 14, 24, 29, 88, 101, 118, 124
Yaounde (Cameroon), 3°51′N 11°31′E, 14
Yarkand (China), 38°27′N 77°16′E, 101, 103, 206
Yasi (USSR), (Turkestan), 43°38′N 68°16′E, 36, 101, 103
Yassy (Romania), 47°09′N 27°38′E, 73, 114, 132
Yazd (Iran), 31°55′N 54°22′E, 45, 112, 143, 206
Yenisei R (China), 101
Yola (Nigeria), 9°41′N 12°32′E, 128
Yunnan-fu see Kunming

Zabid (Yemen), 14°10′N 43°18′E, 95
Zaila (Somalia), 11°21′N 43°30′E, 88, 95
Zambezi R (Southern Africa), 14, 95
Zanzibar (Zanzibar Isl), 6°10′S 39°12′E, 24, 88, 95, 134
Zara (Turkey), 39°55′N 37°44′E, 206
Zaria (Nigeria), 11°01′N 7°44′E, 24, 95, 118, 128
Zefat (Israel), 32°57′N 35°27′E, 161
Zenta see Senta
Zinder (Niger), 13°46′N 8°58′E, 95, 128, 134
Zurich (Switzerland), 47°23′N 8°33′E, 176

INDEX

Page references in italics refer to illustrations or their captions. Note that in names with the form "al-," the "al-" has been ignored in alphabetization; thus "al-Afghani" appears before "Afghanistan." Short forms of names with "Ibn" (e.g. Ibn Khaldun) appear under I.

Abadan 159
al-Abbas (Prophet's uncle) 23
Abbas (I) the Great (Safavid shah) 45–46, 46, 47, 49, 52, 56, 56, 64, 74
Abbas II (Safavid shah) 112
Abbasid dynasty 23, 25, 26, 30
Abd al-Ali Bahr al-ulum, Mawlana 186
Abd Allah (Prophet's father) 22
Abd Allah (amir of Transjordan; later king of Jordan) 140, 141
Abd Allah II (khan of Bukhara) 101, 103, 104
Abdallahi (Mahdi's successor) 126
Abd Allah Ibn Saud (Wahhabi leader) 120
Abd al-Aziz Ibn Saud see Ibn Saud
Abd al-Ghani of Nablus (Naqshbandi shaikh) 120
Abd al-Hamid II (Ottoman sultan) 136, 136
Abd al-Haqq, Mawlana 63, 120
Abd al-Karim of Rif) 155
Abd al-Qadir Gilani 37
shrine of 186
Abd al-Qadir (Algerian leader) 129
Abd al-Qaiyum al-Nasiri (Tatar scholar) 147
Abd al-Rauf of Singkel (reformer) 94, 120, 125
Abdus Samad (Safavid, later Mughal, painter) 63
Abraham (prophet) 20, 22, 28, 41, 43, 191, 192, 194
Abu Hanifa (jurist) 29
Abul Fazl (Indian freethinker) 61
Abul Hassan (Mughal painter) 64
Abu Madyan (North African sufi) 39
Abu Taleb Khan (Indian traveler) 18
Aceh 87, 90, 93, 94, 115, 116, 120, 121–22, 130, 171
adah see under law
Adal 96, 98
Adam (patriarch) 41, 43, 46
Adamawa 129
Adi Langu 91–93
al-Afghani, Jamal al-Din 145, 157
Afghanistan 58, 130, 130, 132, 134
Afsharid dynasty 112
Afzal al-Husaini (Safavid painter) 51
Afzal Khan (Bijapur general) 115
Aghlabid dynasty 25
Agra 58, 68, 68
Taj Mahal 63, 69, 70, 71; tomb of Itimad-ud-Daulah 69, 71
Agung, Sultan (of Mataram) 93
Ahmad III 116
Ahmad Abdali (king of Afghanistan) 115, 120
Ahmad Ardabili, Mulla 49
Ahmad Baba (scholar of Timbuktu) 98, 99
Ahmad Gran (East African leader) 96, 96
Ahmad Ibn Hanbal (jurist) 29
Ahmad Ibn Idris (Moroccan sufi) 125, 128
Ahmad al-Mansur (Moroccan sharif) 97, 99
Ahmad Shah Bahadur (Mughal emperor) 115
Ahmad Yasavi (sufi shaikh)
shrine of 104, 148
Ain Jalut, battle of 26
Ajmere
shrine of Muin al-Din Chishti 186, 186
Ajudhia 58
Akbar 47, 58, 60, 61, 62, 62, 68, 68
as patron of arts 63, 64, 206; and Divine Faith 61–62; Akbarnama 61, 63; tomb of 70, 70
Alam II, Shah (Mughal emperor) 113, 115
Alamgir II (Mughal emperor) 115
Alawite dynasty 97, 98, 100

alcohol 111, 112, 169
Algeria 17, 125, 129, 131, 155, 156, 157, 160–63
Algiers 19, 216
Ali (Prophet's cousin and son-in-law) 23, 36, 39, 46, 47, 47
Aligarh
Muhammadan Anglo-Oriental College 147, 149; Aligarh Institute Gazette 146
Ali Riza (Safavid calligrapher) 49
Allah 39, 40
names of 40
Allahabadi, Akbar, quoted 149
All-India Muslim League 149
Almohad dynasty 39
Almoravid dynasty 27, 39
Altaf Husain Hali, quoted 148
Ambon 90
Amin, Ahmad, quoted 216
Amir Hamza (wayang character) 93, 95
And-Agh-Muhammad family (of Timbuktu) 98
Andijan 124
angels 40, 40, 42
Anglo-Iranian Oil Company 144, 159
Ankara 27; statue of Sinan 84
Ansariya (sufi order) 126
Aqit family (of Timbuktu) 98
Aquaviva, Rudolf (Jesuit) 61
Arabi see Ibn al-Arabi
Arabia 22, 23, 25, 26, 120, 121, 130, 132, 142; see also Saudi Arabia
Arabian Nights (Thousand and One Nights) 18, 23
Arabic see under languages
Arabs 22, 23, 24–25, 25–26, 27, 131, 134, 140–42, 140, 159–60; Romantic views of 18; and Israel 160, 160
Arafat, Yasser 160, 161
Arafat, plain of 194, 194, 197
Arakan 90
architecture 26, 49, 94–95, 153, 154
bazars 49, 216, 216; convents 39; fountains 183, 184, 218; garden tombs see mausolea; hammams (baths) 216; houses 218–19, 218, 219; khans (caravanserais) 216; madrasas 104–05, 106, 106–07; mausolea 39, 63, 70, 70, 71, 84, 104; see also tombs and shrines; minarets 90, 95, 184, 184; mosques 23, 49, 52, 52, 63, 84, 84, 85, 95, 98, 100, 105, 108, 108–09, 153, 154, 176, 182, 183, 184, 184, 216, 216; palaces 49, 52, 82, 83; tombs and shrines 26, 36, 39, 47, 90, 186; town planning 49, 52, 68, 107, 216
Chinese influence 105, 108; Hindu influence 68, 68, 108; Western influence 109, 216, 218
Ardabil 45
Ardabil carpet 206
Aristotle 16
arithmetic 33
armies
Arab 22; Egyptian 120, 121; Moroccan 100; Mughal 58–60; Ottoman 46, 76, 80, 81, 135, 135; Safavid 46, 46, 110
see also guns
art
manuscripts 43, 49, 50, 63, 64, 180, 181, 203; murals 46, 111; paintings 26, 34, 39, 41, 42, 49, 50, 50–51, 63, 78–79, 203; portraits 46, 64, 65, 74, 78, 103, 116; sculpture 162, 162, 163
patronage 49, 202, 203
animals in 66, 67; eroticism in 49, 50, 50, 51, 65; realism in 64, 64, 66, 67
Hindu influence 63, 64; Western influence 64, 116, 162, 163
Asiatic Society of Bengal 20
Askia Muhammad (of Songhai) 97
Askia dynasty (of Songhai) 99
al-Asqalani (Hadiths scholar) 32
Asrafil (angel) 42
Assassins 47
Astrakhan 100, 101, 103, 110
astronomy 26, 78
Ataturk (Mustafa Kemal) 132, 136–38, 136, 138, 157, 166

Athens 22
Augustine, St 31
Aussa 98
Averroes 16
Avicenna 16
Awad, Kamal Amin (Egyptian artist) 162
Awadh 113, 115
Awadh Punch 146, 147
Awrangzeb (Mughal emperor) 58, 62, 62, 63, 63, 113, 114–15
Azarbaijan 45, 72, 130, 171
al-Azhar see under Cairo
Azrail (angel) 42
al-Azzawi, Dia (Iraqi artist) 162

Baath party 141, 163
Babur (Mughal emperor) 58, 58
memoirs 64; Baburnama 63
Badakshan 58
Baghdad 22, 23, 24, 26, 29, 34, 83, 132, 140
Nizamiya madrasa 33; shrine of Abd al-Qadir Gilani 186; Monument of Revolution 162, 162, 163
Bagirmi 97
Baha-al-Din Muhammad Amili, Shaikh 52
Baha-al-Din Vaisi (Naqshbandi leader) 124
Bahira (monk) 16
Baizawi, Abd Allah Ibn Umar (Quranic commentator) 34
Bakhtiari 206, 212
Baki, Abdul (Ottoman poet) 77
Balakot, battle of 122
Balfour Declaration 140, 140, 141
Bali 92
Balkans 22, 131
Balkh 101
Baluchis 112
Baluchistan 58
Bambara 116, 125–26, 129
Bandung conference 160
al-Banna, Hassan (Egyptian fundamentalist) 140
Bantam 91
Banza
shrine of Saiyid Shah al-Razzaq 186
Baqi-billah, Khwaja 62
Barbarossa see Khairuddin
Barthold, V. V. 20
Basra 140
batik 92, 93, 94
Bayazid II (Ottoman sultan) 203
Bedouin 141, 212, 213
Bektashis 116
Belgrade 72, 80
Benares 22, 58
Ben Bella, Ahmed 160–63
Bengal 27, 58, 113, 115, 148, 150
Faraizi movement 122
Berar 58
Berbers 26, 30, 97
Berteaux, Hippolyte 116
Bessarabia 116
Bhopal
Begums of 222
Bhutto, Zulfiqar Ali 167, 173
Bible 16, 41
Bibliothèque Orientale (1697) 16
Bichitr (Mughal painter) 64
bida 30
Bihar 58
Bihzad (Safavid artist) 26, 49, 50, 63, 104
Bijapur 58, 115
Bishn Das 46, 64
Bombay Tract and Book Society 17
Bondu 129
Borneo 90, 94
Bosnia 27
Bosphorus 27, 72, 82
Bourguiba, Habib 163
British
attitudes toward Muslims 17, 18, 176, 176
allied with Ottomans 130
and Arab nationalism 140–41, 140
in Egypt 138, 147, 158, 159, 159; in India 68, 115, 122, 130, 133, 147, 148; in Iran 143, 143–45, 159; in Malay States 153; in Sudan 126, 128; in West Africa 131, 154

British East India Company 113, 133
Bucharest, treaty of 132
Budauni, Abd al-Qadir (historian), quoted 61
Buddhism 94
Bukhara 44, 101, 130, 130, 147
as center of learning 104; madrasas 106, 106; school of painting 103, 104
Bukhari see Hadiths, compilations of
Buraq 191
Burhan al-Din, Shaikh (legal writer) 34
Burma 27, 90, 94
Bursa 79, 82
Burton, Sir Richard 120
Buyid dynasty 25, 26
Byron, Robert, quoted 52
Byzantine empire 16, 23, 26

Cairo 22, 23, 26, 132
conference 140
al-Azhar (university) 33, 120, 138, 140, 163, 167; mosque of Ahmad Ibn Tulun 23
calendar 61, 190
Ramadan 190
festivals 190–91
caliphate 23, 24, 25, 26, 27, 136
calligraphy 27, 49, 50, 52, 74, 200, 202, 203
carpets and rugs 46, 49, 56, 79, 104, 206, 206, 209
cartography 81
Catherine (II) the Great 103, 145
Caucasus 23, 26, 124, 206, 209
Celebes 91
Central Asia 100–06, 101, 103, 116, 124, 146, 147
carpets 206, 209
see also individual khanates; nomads, invasions by
ceramics 28, 49, 56, 57, 79, 82, 82–83, 86, 107, 204, 204
porcelain 56
Ceuta 34
Chad 154
Chaghatai 101; see also Mongols
Chaldiran, battle of 45, 46, 47, 72, 80
Chelebi, Euliya (Ottoman traveler) 78
Chelebi, Katib (Ottoman encyclopedist) 78
Chelebi, Khoja (Ottoman jurist) 77
Cheribon 91
China 22, 90, 101
Muslims in 22, 27, 104, 105, 116, 124–25, 124, 130, 146, 174
Chinese see under languages
Chishtiya (sufi order) 37
Chitor 61
Chraibi, Driss, quoted 181
Christianity
and Islam 16, 20, 22, 39, 61, 148, 154, 155; missionary activity of 17, 61, 130, 132, 144, 148, 154, 155; under Muslim rule 26, 72, 77, 116
Christ Jesus 16, 20, 22, 40, 41, 180
Churchill, Winston 140
Circassians 27, 46
coins 104
colonialism 17, 94, 130–31, 131, 132, 133, 134, 145, 155, 157, 159–60; see also individual colonial powers
communications 136, 136, 142, 154
Communism 147–48
Comoros islands 129
Confucianism 88, 104, 124
Constantinople 22, 27, 72, 80; see also Istanbul
Cordoba 25
crafts see under individual commodities
Crete 72
Crimea 22, 100, 101, 103
crusades 16, 24, 26, 110
Ctesiphon 23, 24
Curzon, George Nathaniel, Lord 107
Cyprus 72
Cyrenaica 23, 128

Dafur 96
Dagistan 124
Dakar 154
Damascus 23, 24, 32, 34, 132, 140
Umaiyad mosque 182

dance 92, 94; see also under sufis
Dante 16
Dara Shikoh (Mughal prince) 62, 62
al-Darqawi, Ahmad (sufi) 129, 129
David (king of Israel) 41
Deccan, the 58, 115
Delhi 26, 58, 63, 68, 69, 112, 113, 115, 122
Chandni Chowk 68; Juma Masjid (Friday mosque) 68, 68; Rang Mahal 69; Red Fort 63, 68, 69, 113; tomb of Humayun 70
New Delhi 68, 216; Shahjahanabad 63, 68, 216
Deodand
madrasa 148
Demak 90, 91
devshirme 73–74, 76, 79
dhikrs see under Islam
dhimmis 77
dikkas 184, 185
Dipanegara 121, 123
Diyarbakir 45
dress 147, 148, 153, 171, 191
pilgrims' (ihram) 192, 194; Western 135, 136, 145; women's 138, 145, 147, 166, 169, 171, 192, 221, 222, 222
Dutch 17, 90, 91, 93, 94, 115, 116, 121, 123, 151–52
Dutch East India Company 94, 130
Dyula 109, 116

Edib, Halide 222
Edirne
Selimiye mosque 74, 79, 84, 85, 86
education 18, 140, 146, 147, 147, 148, 151
Muslim 33–34, 77, 99, 104, 148, 154, 166, 181; Westernized 135, 151, 163
madrasas 33–34, 77, 104–05; semaniye madrasas 77, 78, 78
Egypt 23, 25, 26, 27, 34, 72, 77, 147, 158, 159, 159, 163, 166–67, 174
British in 130; French in 17, 17, 130; Westernization of 132, 138–40, 138, 140
press in 146
United Arab Republic 160
Elizabeth I 46, 97
Erbakan, Necmettin 166
Eritrea 126
Ethiopia 96, 96, 126, 153
expansionism 22–23, 24–25, 27
Mughal 58, 58; Ottoman 72, 72–73; Safavid 45, 45
in Africa 95–97; in southeast Asia 89, 90–95

Faisal II (king of Saudi Arabia) 140, 140, 141, 172, 173, 173–74
Faiz Baksh, Begum 133
Faqir Allah
Rag Darpan 63
Faraizi movement 122
Farghana 101, 103
Faruq (king of Egypt) 140
Fatawa-i Alamgiri 63
Fatehpur Sikri 61, 63, 68, 70
"House of Worship" 61; Panch Mahal 68; shrine of Shaikh Salim Chishti 61
Fath Ali Shah (Qajar shah of Iran) 145
Fatimid dynasty 25, 26, 47
Fez 156
Firdawsi 25
Shahnama 25, 49, 51
Flaubert, Gustave 17
Forster, E. M., quoted 70
Free Officers (Egypt) 140
French 16, 23, 140
attitudes towards Muslims 16, 17, 17, 18, 176
privileged under Ottomans 116
and Arab nationalism 140–41, 140, 141
in Algeria 129, 131, 155, 156, 157; in Egypt 17, 17, 130; in Morocco 131, 155; in North Africa 130–31, 155, 157; in Tunisia 131, 155, 156; in West Africa 126, 128, 130–31, 153
French Asiatic Society 20
Front de Libération Nationale (Algeria) 156

Fulani 116, 125, 128–29, *128, 129*
Funj 96, 98
Futa Jallon *128*, 129
Futa Toro *128*, 129
Fuzuli, Sulaiman (Ottoman poet) 77

Gabriel (angel) 22, *22*, 40, *42*, 191
Galiev, Mir Sultan 147–48
Galland, Antoine 18
Gambia 154
Gao 27, 97, 116
garuda 93
Gasprinski, Ismail Bey 146, *146*, 147
Gengis Khan 26, 58, *58*
geography 78
Georgians 46
Germany 130
  and Turkey 135, 140
  Muslim emigration to 176
Gezira, the 96
al-Ghali, Muhammad, Shaikh 125
Ghana 27, 98, 154
ghazis 27
Ghazna 25
al-Ghazzali 33, 94, 129; on Quran 28; role in Islam 31, 39; travels of *32*, 34
Ghulam Allah (Sudanese leader) 98, 99
Gibb, Sir Hamilton Alexander 20
Gibbon, Edward 16
Giri 91
Gladstone, W. E., quoted 18–20
Gobir 97
Goethe, J. W. von 18
Gokalp, Ziya 136
Goldziher, Ignaz 20
Golkonda 58, 115
Gondar *96*
government 44; *see also under* Mughal, Ottoman, Safavid *empires*; *Sharia*
Gowa
  tomb of Hasan al-Din *90*
Granada 22, 26
Great Exhibition (1851) *58*
Guinea 98, 153, 154
Gujarat 27, 58, 115
guns 45, *46*, 58, 80, *81*
  gunpowder 44, *44*, *61*
Gwalior *68*

Habsburgs 72, 76, 80, 116
Hadiths (traditions) 23–24, 27, 30, 31, *32*
  compilations of 29; quoted 29, 39, *40*; in reform movements 119; in *Sharia* 28–29; taught 33, *119*, 120, 129, 148
  see also Sharia
Hafiz (Shams-al-Din Muhammad; Persian poet) 26, 32, *34*, 49
Hafiz-i Abru
  History 41
Hagar (Abraham's wife) 43, 192, 194, *197*
Halim Hatun
  tomb tower of *26*
al-Hallaj (sufi martyr) 31
Hamd Allah al-Amasi (Ottoman calligrapher) *203*
Hamza of Fansur (heterodox scholar) 94
Hamzanama 63
Hanafi (school of law) *28*, 29, *29*, 77
Hanbali (school of law) *28*, 29, *29*, 119, 120
haqiqa 32
Harar *96*, 98
al-Hariri
  Maqamat 43
Harun al-Rashid (caliph at Baghdad) 23
Hasan al-Din (Macassarese leader) 91
  tomb of *90*
Hassan Bey (Mamluk officer) *138*
Hausa *see under* languages
Hausas 97, 129, 153
Heber, Bishop Reginald 17
Hector 16
Henriquez, Francis (Jesuit) *61*
Herat 104
  school of painting 26, *43*, 49, 50
Herzegovina 27
Hidayat, Sadiq 163
hijra 22, 122, 190
hijrah 143
Hikayat Raja Pasai 89
Hinduism 22, 58, 63, 114, 148
  Mughals tolerant of 61, 62, 120
  in Java 88, 91, 92, 94, 95, 151
Hira, Mount 22, *22*
historiography 23, 78
Holland *see* Dutch
holy law *see Sharia*
holy war *see jihad*
Hugo, Victor, quoted 17
Hulagu (Mongol chief) 26
Humayun (Mughal emperor) 58, *58*
  tomb of 70, *70*
Hunernama 79
Hungarians 72
Hurgronje, Snouck 20, 152
Husain (Prophet's grandson) 23, 47, 168, 169, 190
Husain (sharif of Mecca) 140, *142*
  Husain-McMahon understanding (1915) *140, 141*
Husain (king of Jordan) 159
Husain, Saddam *173*
Husain, Sultan *see* Sultan Husain
Hyderabad *113*, 115

Iberian peninsula 22
  see also Granada; Portugal; Spain
Iblis 40
Ibn al-Arabi 62, 89, 94, 120, 167
  heterodoxy of 31–32, 119; travels of *32*, 34
Ibn Battuta (traveler) 27, 30, 34, 78
Ibn Fartuwa (historian) 100
Ibn Khaldun (philosopher) *32*
Ibn Mawlana, Shaikh (of Pasai) 91
Ibn Saud, Abd al-Aziz (king of Saudi Arabia) 141, 142, *142, 143*
Ibn Taimiya (Hanbali scholar) 120
Ibrahim al-Kurani (Medinan scholar) 94, 120
Ibrahim Pasha (Ottoman vizier) 116
Idris Aloma (king of Kanem-Bornu) 97, 100
Idrisid dynasty 25
Idrisiya (sufi order) *118–19*, 128
ihram see under dress
ijma 29
ijtihad 29–30
Ikhwan (Brothers) 141–42, *143*, 212
Ilorin 129
imams 23, *28*, 46, 47, *47*
Inayat (Mughal artist) *66*
Inayat Khan (Mughal noble) 63, *64*
India 17, 18, 22, 26, 58, 112, *113*, 114–15, 143
  Muslim reformers in 122
  partition of *150, 151*
  All-India Muslim League 149, *150*, 151; Mutiny 68, 148; National Congress 149; Progressive Writers' Association 163
  see also Mughal empire
Indonesia 17, 151–53, 158, 171
  see also Java *etc.*
industries *see under individual commodities and empires*
Iqbal, Muhammad 149–51
  quoted 134, 149, 158, 163, 165, 174, 211
Iran 23, 45, 112, 114, 130, *130*, *134*, 159
  Islamic Revolution in 168, 169–71; press in 146; relations with European powers *143*, 143–45, *145*, 159; as Shia state 101, 144; Westernization of 144, 145, 163, 168–69
  carpets 206, *206*
  see also Safavid empire
Iraq 23, 72, 120, *140, 141*, 159, 162
  British mandate over 140
Isfahan 49, 52–53, 54–57, *54–57*, 112
  Ali Qapu palace 49, 52; bazar 56–57, *56–57*; Chahar Bagh 49, 52; Chihil Sutun *46, 111*; Friday mosque *56*; Lutf Allah mosque 49, 52, *52*, *204*; Maidan 49, 52, *52*, 56; royal mosque 49, 52, *52*
  Kuh-i-Sufi 52, *52*
Ishmael (Hagar's son) 43, 192, 194
Iskander Muda (sultan of Aceh) 90, 94
Islam
  beliefs: 40–43, 133; hell 42, *43*; judgment, day of 40, 42, 192; paradise 16, 42, *43*; resurrection 189; *shahada* 40
  and polytheism 94, 99
  religious practices 42–43; ablutions *182, 183, 184*; almsgiving 43, 191; burial 188; circumcision 188; *dhikrs* 19, 34, 37, *40*, *186*; fasting in Ramadan 43, 167, 190, 191; "five pillars" 40; marriage 188; mosques, behavior at 182–85, *182–85*; pilgrimage 43, *43*, 47, 191, 192–97, *192–97*; prayer *34*, 42, *63*, 167, 179, 182, *182*, 183, 184, *184*, 188, 191, 194; pork, prohibition of 91; rosaries *34, 40*
  festivals *see under* calendar
  fundamentalism in 119, 120, *121*, 122–24, 141–42, 166, 167, 169; revival movements in 118–22, *118–19*, *121*, 124–29, 130; sensuality in 16, 17, *19*, 42
  challenged by European values 132–34; reconciled with modern European thought 141, 147, 149, 157, 168; reduced to personal religious preference 136–38, 151; reinstated 165–71, *172*
  pan-Islamism 122, 136, 149–51, 157, 171–74, *172*
  see also jihad; Quran; shrines
Islamic Conference *172*, 173, 174
Ismail I (Safavid shah) 45, *45*, *46*, 47, 49, *51*, 72
Ismailis (Shia sect) 47
Israel 159, 160, *160*, *161*, 163, 166, 167, 168, 174
Istanbul *72*, 76, 132
  Baghdad kiosk *83*; mausolea: of Khairuddin 84; of Roxelana 84; of Sulaiman the Magnificent; mosques: of Princess Mihrimah 84, *86*; of Rustam Pasha 79, 84; Shehzade mosque 79, 84, *85*, *86*; of Sokullu Mehmed Pasha 84, *86*; Sulaimaniye mosque 77, *78*, 79, 84, *85*, *86*; of Sultan Ahmed 79, *184*; St Sophia 79, 84, *84*, *86*; Topkapi Sarai 78, 79, 82, *83*, 84, *204*
  university of 135
  Golden Horn *78*, 82, *83*; Seraglio Point 82
Istiqlal Party (Morocco) 156
Italians 130
  in Libya 128, 131, 155
Ithna Ashari *see under* Shias
Ivan (IV) the Terrible 103
Ivory Coast 98, 154
iwans 105, *106*
Iznik
  ceramics center 79, 82, *204*

Jacob (patriarch) 41
Jaghbub 128
Jahangir (Mughal emperor) *46*, 58, 60, 62–63, 68
  as patron of arts 63, *64*, 66; memoirs 64; tomb of 70, 71
Jahriya *see under* Naqshbandiya
Jains 61
Jalal al-Din Rumi, Mawlana *see* Rumi
Jamaat-i-Islami 167
Jamal al-Din al-Afghani *see* al-Afghani
Jami (Persian poet) 26, 62
  quoted 32; *Haft Awrang 39*, 49
Janid dynasty (of Bukhara) 101
Janissaries 74, 80, *81*, 116, 135, *135*
Japan 90
  occupation of Indonesia by 152–53
Java 22, 27, 44, 88, 89, 90, *90*, 91, 93, 94, 171
  cultural impact of Islam on 92, *92–93*, 94–95, *153*; Dutch in 116, 151–52; Muslim reform in 121, *123*, 152
  see also Mataram
al-Jawaib 146
al-Jazuli
  The Proofs of the Blessings 100
Jedda 173
Jedisan 116
Jenne 27, 116
Jerusalem 34, *161*
  al-Aqsa mosque *161*, 174, *183*, 191
  Dome of the Rock *161*
Jesuits 61
Jesus *see* Christ Jesus
Jews 61, 77, 116, 140, *141*, *161*
Jibril Ibn Umar (of Agades) 129
jihad 16, 17, 103, 118, 119, 124
  "striving in the way of God" 40
  in Africa 96, 125–26, 128, 129, *129*; in India 148; in southeast Asia 91
Jinnah, Muhammad Ali *150–51*, 151
jizya 61, 63
Job (patriarch) 41
Jones, Sir William 20
Joseph (patriarch) 41
Jordan 158
  see also Transjordan
Jumna river 63, 68
Jungaria 101
Jurjan 34
al-Jurjani *32*

Kaaba *see under* Mecca
Kaarta *128*
Kabul 58
Kairouan
  mosque 23
Kane, Cheikh Hamidou, quoted *181*
Kanem-Bornu 97, 99, *129*
Kano 97, 99
  mosques *108*, *154*
Kansu 27, 101, 104, 124, *124*, 125
Kara Mustafa (Ottoman vizier) 76
Karbala, battle of 23, 47, 120, *121*, 168, 190
Karim Khan, Muhammad (Zand chief) 114
Kartosuwirjo, S. M. 171
Kashan
  Maidan mosque *203*
Kashgar *101*, 103
Kashmir 58, 66
Katsina 97
Kazakhs 130
Kazan 22, 100, *101*, 103, 110, 124, 147
Kemal, Mustafa *see* Ataturk
Kenya 154
Khairuddin 72, *74*
  mausoleum of 84
Khalid Baghdadi, Mawlana 122–24
Khaljis 27
Khalwatiya (sufi order) *118–19*, 120, 125–26, 129
  see also Sammaniya; Tijaniya
Khan Alam (Mughal envoy) *46*
Khandesh 58
Khartoum 126, *126*
  tomb of Mahdi *126*
Khasso *128*
Khatmiya (sufi order) 154
Khiva *101*, 103, 130
  madrasas 106
Khokand 103, 124, 130
  madrasas 106
Khomeini, Ahmad *160*
Khomeini, Ayatullah Ruholla *160*, *161*, 168, 169–71, *169*
Khurasan 26, 45, 100, 101
Khuzestan 159
Kilwa 22, 88, 96
Kipchaks 26
Kitchener, General H. H. *126*
Knights of St John 72
Koh-i-Nur *58*
Konya
  shrine of Rumi *39*, *186*
Koprulu, Ahmed 76
Koprulu, Mehmed 76
kris 92, *92*
Kubrawiya (sufi order) 104
Kuchuk Kainarji, treaty of 116
Kudus *90*, 91, 95
Kufa 23, *27*
  Kufic script *see under* scripts
al-Kurdi, Mahmud 125
Kurdistan *214*
kursis 184, *185*

Lagos 154
  mosque *109*
Lahore 68, *71*, 115
Lake, General G. 115
Lanchou 124
Lane, Edward 17
languages
  Arabic 24, 25, 27, 28, 33, 99, 147, 166, 167; Chinese 125; Hausa 99; Malay 94, 125; Persian 25, 63, 101, 125; Tatar 147; Turkish 101, 147, 166; Urdu 63, 125, 148, 167
Lausanne, treaty of *132*
law 23–24, 27–30, 98
  adah (customary law) 30, 44, 151; dynastic law 44; schools of law *28*, 29, *29*; Westernized codes 135, 136, 143, 145, 156–57
  see also Sharia
Lawrence, T. E. 18
League of Nations mandates 140, *140*, 158
Lebanon 140
Lebe Lontang 94
Lepanto, battle of 72, *74*
Levey, Michael *86*
Liberia 154
Libya 128, 131, 155, 155–56, 167, 212
Lisbon 26
literature 23, 26
  Malay 94; Mughal 64; Ottoman 77–78; Persian 25, 26, 32, 49; Sudanese 99–100
  European influence on 163
Liu Chih
  True Annals of the Greatest Saint of Arabia 104
Livingstone, D. 17
London
  Regent's Park mosque *176*
Lucknow 146
  Firangi Mahal 149, *186*
Lur 206
Lutfi Pasha (Ottoman vizier) 74
Luther, M. 16, 31

Macassar 90, 91
Macaulay, T. B., quoted 18
McDonald, D. B. 20
McMahon, Sir Henry *140*
Madagascar 22
Madinat Isa *216*
Madras *113*
madrasas *see under* architecture; education
al-Maghili (of Tlemcen) 99, 129
Maghrib 25, 77, *129*
Mahabharata 63, 64, 95
Mahdism 125, 126, *126*
Mahdiya (sufi order) 126, 128, 154
Mahfuz, Najib, quoted 192
Mahmud II (Ottoman sultan) 135, *135*
Mahmud of Qandahar 112, *112*
Ma Hua-lung 125
Majapahit 90, 91, 151
Makhdum-i-Azam (Naqshbandi shaikh) 103
Malacca 90, *90*
Malay *see under* languages
Malaysia 22, 27, 90, *90*, 130, *152*
Malcolm X 176, *176*
Maldive islands 30
Mali 27, 154
Malik Bin Anas 29
  Muwatta 98
Maliki (school of law) *28*, 29, *29*, 77, 99
Malta 72
Malwa 115
Ma Ming-hsin 124
Mamluks 26, 27, 72, 138, *138*
Manchus 124
Mangit dynasty (of Bukhara) 101
Manohar *67*
mansabdars 58–60, 115
Man Singh (raja) *68*
Mansur, Imam (Caucasian reformer) 124
Mansur (Mughal painter) 63, 66, *66*, *67*
Manucci, Niccolo *69*
Manzikert, battle of 26
Manzur Khan (Chaghatai ruler) 103
Maqsud (of Kashan) 206
marabouts 39, 97, *98*, 100
Maracci, L. 20
Marathas *58*, 113, 115
Marrakesh 97, 99
  madrasa 100; mausolea 100, *204*; el-Badi palace 100
marriage 30, 188
Marwa 43, 194, *197*
Marxism 148, 151
Mary, the Virgin 20, 22, 40
Masina *128*, 129
Masjumi 153
Massignon, Louis 20
Mataram *90*, 93, *115*, 116
Ma Te-hsin 125
mathematics 23, 78
Mathnawi see under Rumi
Mauritania 154
Mawdudi, Mawlana 167
Mawlawiya (sufi order) *33*, 39, *39*, *186*
Mawlay Idris I (Moroccan king) tomb of *98*, 100
Mawlay Ismail (Moroccan sharif) *100*
  palace of 100
mawlid see under Muhammad
Mecca 22, 34, 42, 72, 77, 120, *121*, 173, 190
  Kaaba *28*, 119, 192, 194, *197*; mosque *192*; well of Zamzam *28*, 194
  pilgrimage to 18, 43, 120, 136, 152, 166, 173, 191, 192, *192*, 194, *194*, *197*, *214*
medicine 23, 33, 78
Medina 22, 72, 77, *121*
  Muhammad's tomb 120, *120*
  Muhammad's flight to 22, 122, 190; teaching of *Hadiths* at *119*, 120, 129
Mehmet II (Ottoman sultan) 74, 80
Mehmet (Ottoman artist) 78
Meknes
  mausoleum of Mawlay Ismail 100, *100*; palace of Mawlay Ismail 100
Melilla *98*
Menderes, Adnan 166
Meshhed 112
  shrine of Imam Riza (Eighth Imam) *47*, 206
metalwork 49, 56, *56*
Mewar 58, *61*
Michael (angel) *42*
mihrabs 42, *86*, 184, *184*, *203*
Mina
  pillars at 43, 194
Minangkabau 90, 116, 120
  mosque *108*
minbars 184, *185*
Mindanao 22, 94
Minutolo, Irma *140*
Miraj Namah 43
Mir Saiyid Ali (Mughal painter) 63
Mogadishu 96
Mohacs, battle of 72, *81*
Moluccas 27
Mombasa 96
Mongke, Great Khan 26
Mongols 22, *24–25*, 26, *26*, 30, 44, 45
  Chaghatai 26, 103, 104; Golden Horde 26, 100; Il-Khans 26; Oirots 103–04
Montesquieu, C. L., Baron de 18
Morocco 22, 44, 97, *98*, 100, 125, 131, 155, 156, *212*
Moses (patriarch) 22, 41, *41*, 190
Mosul 34, 76, *141*

Moukhtar Bey (railroad engineer) *136*
Mozart, W. A. 18
muftis 77
Mughal empire 16, 44, *45*, 58–71, *58*
army 58–60; decline *113*, 114–15, *115*; government 58–60; Hindu subjects 58–60, 63, 64
architecture 63, 68, *68–69*, 70, *70–71*; art *34*, 63, 64, *64*, *65*, 66, *66*, 67; carpets 206; literature 64; music 63
Muhammad 16, 22–23, *22*, 39, 46, 190, *197*
biography 22
example followed 119, 124, 125, 141, 191, 192; as Prophet of Islam 40, 41, 180
mawlid 119, 191
Life of 17
quoted 30
Muhammad V (sharif of Morocco) 156
Muhammad Abd Allah Hasan (Somali leader) 128
Muhammad Abduh, Shaikh (rector of al-Azhar) 141, 152, 156, 157
Muhammad Abd al-Wahhab (Arabian reformer) 120
Muhammad Ahmad (the Mahdi) 126
Muhammad Ali Pasha (viceroy of Egypt) *114*, 120, *121*, 135, 138, *138*, *139*, 146
Muhammad Ali (of Shiraz) *51*
Muhammad Ali (founder of National Muslim university) *147*
Muhammad Baqir Majlisi (Shiite fundamentalist) 112, 120, 168, 169
Muhammad Hayya al-Sind (Indian reformer) 120
Muhammad al-Hifnawi (rector of al-Azhar) 120
Muhammad Ibn Salih (sufi leader) 128
Muhammad Ibn Saud (Wahhabi leader) 120
Muhammadiya 152
Muhammad al-Muntazar (Twelfth Imam) 46
Muhammad Riza Shah Pahlavi (shah of Iran) 159, 163, 168, *169*, *213*
Muhammad Rumfa (king of Kano) 97
Muhammad Shaibani Khan (Uzbeg chief) 45
Muhammad Usman Mirghani (Sudanese leader) 128
Muin al-Din Chishti 61
shrine of 186, *186*
Muir, Sir William 17
Mujaddidi (reformist movement) 63
Mujahidin (reformist movement) 122
mujtahids 47, 49, 144, 168
Mulla Nasreddin 146, *146*, *147*
Mumtaz Mahal (wife of Shah Jahan) 63, *71*
Murad III (Ottoman sultan) 79, *82*
Murad IV (Ottoman sultan) *83*
Murad, Hajji *124*
Muridiya (sufi order) 153
Musadeqq, Dr Muhammad 159, 168
Musa al-Kazim (Seventh Imam) 47
Muslim *see Hadiths*, compilations of
Muslim Brethren (*or* Muslim Brotherhood) 140, 166, 167, 171
Mussolini, Benito 155
Mustafa al-Bakri (sufi reformer) 120, 125
Muzdalifa *194*, *197*
Mysore 17
mysticism *see* sufis

Nadir Khan (later Nadir Shah) *58*, 112–14, *112*, 115, 116
Nahdatul Ulama 152
Naima, Mustafa (Ottoman chronicler) 72, 78
Namon
Friday mosque *109*
Napoleon 17, *17*
Naqshbandiya (sufi order) 39, 104, 114, *118–19*, 152, 166
active as reformers 62, 114, 120, 122–25, 129
Jahriya branch 124
Nasir al-Din (Qajar shah of Iran) 144, *145*
Nasser, Gamal Abdul 159, *159*
Nasuh (Ottoman mathematician) 79
Nasir al-Din Tusi 26
nationalism 133–34, 140, 157, *158*
African 154–55, 156; Arab 140–42; Egyptian 138–39, 140; Indian 149, *150*, 151; Indonesian 152–53; Turkish 136
Nehru, Jawaharlal *151*
Neo-Destour Party 156
New Sect (in China) 124–25, *124*
Ngazargamu 97, 98
Nice *81*
Nigari (Ottoman artist) *74*, 78
Niger 154
Niger Basin 44
Nigeria 131, 153, 154
Nishapur 34
Nizam al-Din Awliya (sufi saint), quoted 39
Nizam Shah *58*
Noah (patriarch) 41, 190
nomads 212, *212*, *213*
invasions by 25–26, 44, 96, 101
Normans 26
North Africa 23, 25, 72, 88, *94*, 95–100, *96*
see also Maghrib
Nupe 129, *129*, 153
Nubia 96
Nurcular (sufi order) 166
Nur al-Din al Raniri *see* al-Raniri
Nur Jahan 71, 222

Ockley, Simon 20
oil 20, *141*, 142, 144, 159, 167, *172*, 173, 176
Old Sect (in China) 124
Oman 96, 114, *181*
Organization of Petroleum Exporting Countries (OPEC) 160, 173
Orissa 58
Osman I (founder of Ottoman empire) 72
Ottoman empire 16, 27, 44, 45, *45*, 46, 72–87, *72–73*, 97
army *46*, 74, 76, 80, *81*; decline *114*, 115–16, 131–32, *132*; fleet 72, *74*, 76; government 72, 72–76; relations with European powers 116, *116*, 131–32, 134–36, *140*; relations with Safavids 72, 80, *83*; *Sharia* 77, 135
architecture 79, 82, *82–83*, 84, *84–87*, *116*; art 78–79, *116*; carpets 79, 206; ceramics 79, 82, *82*, 204, *204*; literature 77–78; sciences 78
Oxus river 23

Padri movement 120
Pakistan *150*, 151, 157, 158, 163, 167
Palestine 23, 26, 72, 140, *141*, 160, *160*
Palestine Liberation Organization (PLO) *161*
see also Israel
Palmer, William *133*
Palmyra 18
Panipat, battle of 58
Partai Islam Indonesia 152
Pasai 90
Passarowitz, treaty of 116
Pate 96
Peking 26
Persian *see under* languages
Persians 24, 25, 27, 45
see also Iran; Safavid empire
Peshawar
mosque of Mahabat Khan *182*
Philippines 27, 90, 94
philosophy, Greek 23, 94
Picot, Georges *see* Sykes-Picot agreement
pietra dura 69, *71*
pilgrimage *see under* Islam, religious practices; shrines
piracy 72
pishtaqs 105, *107*
Pococke, Edward 20
Poitiers, battle of 23
polo 52, *52*
Polydore Vergil 16
population, Muslim *174*
in Africa 154; in Europe *176*
porcelain *see under* ceramics
Portugal 25
and Muslim world 44, 72, 90, 96, 97
Portuguese Guinea 154
prophets 41, *41*, 46
the Prophet *see* Muhammad
Pugachev revolt 103
Pyramids, battle of 17

Qaddafi, Muammar 167, *173*
al-Qadi al-Hajj family (of Timbuktu) 98
Qadiriya (sufi order) 37, 39, 62, 104, 128, 129
qadis 30, 77
see also Sharia; *ulama*
Qajar dynasty *112*, 114, 144
Qalandars (sufi order) *31*, 37
Qandahar 58
Qarmatian movement 47
Qashqai 206, 212, *213*
al-Qasr al-Kabir, battle of 97
al-Qazwini *40*
The Wonders of Creation 203
qiyas 29
Qizilbash 45, 46, 47
Qum *216*
Faiziya madrasa 168; shrine of Fatima *47*
Quran 16, 20, 27, 29, 41, 43, 180, *180–81*, 184, *185*, 192
basis of Islamic revival 119, 120, 167, 174; content 27–28, 40, 42, 133, 180; interpretations 46; *Fatiha* 42, 181; quoted 22, 43, 180, *180*, 188, 199, 221, 222; revelation 22, 23, 28, 180, 190; scripts *27*, 202; taught 33, *181*, 188; translated 16, 20, 28, 94, 125
and sufis 30, 31, 119
qutbs 31

Rabia (sufi saint), quoted 30
Rajputs 58, *61*
Ramadan *see under* calendar; Islam, religious practices
Ramayana 63, 64, 95
Rampuri, Muhammad Ali, quoted *183*
Rangoon 68
al-Raniri, Nur al-Din 94
Sirat al-Mustaqim 94
Ranjit Singh *58*, 115
al-Rashid, Ibrahim (sufi leader) 128
Rashid al-Din 26
World History 22
Regnault, Henri *19*
Renaldi, Francesco *133*
Renan, Ernest 20
Renoir, P. A. *19*
Reuter, Baron Paul Julius
Reuter concession 143, 144, 145, 168
Rhodes 72, *81*
Rida, Rashid (Arab nationalist) 141
Rif republic 155
Risalah 17
Riyadh *142*
Riza, Imam (Eighth Imam)
shrine of *47*, *206*
Riza Abbasi (Safavid artist) *50*, *51*
Riza Shah Pahlavi (shah of Iran) *143*, 145, *145*, 168, *213*
Robert of Ketton 16
Roman Catholic Church 16
Romanticism 17–18
Roxelana (wife of Sulaiman the Magnificent) 222
mausoleum of 84
Rumi 31, 32, *33*, 39, 166, *186*
shrine of *39*, *186*
Russia
conquers Muslims 17, 44, 101, *101*, 103, *103*, 116, 124, *124*, 130, *130*, 147; persecutes Muslims 103, 148
Muslims in 145–48, 171; Muslim press in *145*, 146, *146*, *147*, 171
Bolsheviks 130, 147, 148
and Iran *142*, 143–44

Saad al-Din Taftazani *see* al-Taftasani
Saadi (Persian poet) 26, 49
Bustan 56
al-Saadi (historian) 100
Saadian dynasty 97, *98*, 100
Sabila, battle of 142, *143*
Sacy, Silvestre de 20
Sadat, Anwar *166*, 167
Safavid empire 16, 44, 45–57, *45*, *47*
agriculture 44; army 46, *46*, 110; decline 110–13, *112*; government 46–49; and Shiism 46–49, 72; *ulama* 47–49, 112, 120
architecture 49, 52, *52–53*, 54, *54–55*; art 46, 49, 50, *50–51*; carpets 206, *206*
see also Iran
Safaviya (sufi order) 39, 44, 45, 112
Saffarid dynasty 25
Safi I (Safavid shah) 110–12
Safi al-Din (sufi leader) 45
Saghananughu 98
Said Khan (Chaghatai ruler) 103
Saiyid Shah Abd al-Razzaq (saint)
shrine of *186*
Saiyid Ahmad (of Rae Bareli) 122
Saiyid Ahmad Khan (Indian reformer) 146, 149
Saiyid Idris (king of Libya) 155
Saladin 16
Sale, G. 20
Salihiya (sufi order) 128
Salim, Jawad (Iraqi artist) *162*, 163
Salim Chishti, Shaikh (sufi saint) 61, *61*, 63, 68
Samanid dynasty 25
Samarqand 23, 26, *32*, 45, 58, 104, 132, 147
Bibi Khanum mosque *107*; madrasas 105, 106, *106*, *107*; Registan square *107*
Samarra
mosque 23
Samman, Muhammad, Shaikh (sufi leader) 120, 126
Sammaniya 126
Samori Ture (West African leader) 129
Sana *216*
San Remo, treaty of 17, *140*
Sanusi (sufi order) *126*, *128*, 155, 212
al-Sanusi, Muhammad Ali (sufi leader) 128
Sarekat Islam (Islamic League) 152
Sarkin dynasty 99
Sartre, J.-P. 163
Sasaram *70*
Sassanian empire 23, 24
Saudi Arabia 120, 142, *142*, 157, 174, *194*, 212
scholarship
European 20; Muslim 23–24, 26, 31, *32*, 33–34, 94, 98–99
see also education; *ulama*
scripts *27*, *201*, 202, *203*
Arabic 25, 94, 200, *201*, 202; Perseo-Arabic 148; Roman 136
decorative *52*, 202, *203*; Kufic 27, 202
see also calligraphy
Second Vatican Council 20
secularism 133–34, 158–63, 174, *194*
in Egypt 166; in Iran 145, 162; in Turkey 135–36, 166; Western 20, 157
in art 49, 162
Seleucia 23
Selim I (Ottoman sultan) 72
Selimnama 79
Selim II (Ottoman sultan) 72, *74*
Selim III (Ottoman sultan) 116, *116*
Seljuqs 25–26
Senegal 153, 154
Serabim *166*
Serbia 116
Seville 34
Sèvres, treaty of 131–32
Shadhiliya (sufi order) 39, 129
al-Shafii, Muhammad Ibn Idris (jurist) 29
Shafii (school of law) *28*, 29, *29*
Shah Abd al-Aziz (scholar of Delhi) 115, 122, 148, 149
Shah Abd al-Qadir (of Delhi) 125
Shah Jahan (Mughal emperor) 58, 62, 63, *64*, *68*, 68, *71*
tomb of 70
Shahjahanabad *see under* Delhi
Shah Murad (khan of Bukhara) 101, 104
Shah Rukh Beg (khan of Khokand) 103
Shah Wali Allah (Indian scholar) 120, 122, 125, 148, 149
Shaibanid dynasty 101, 103
Shaikh al-Islam 77
Shajar al-Durr (ruler of Egypt) 222
Shamil, Imam (Caucasian reformer) 124, *124*
Shams al-Din (sufi) *33*
Shams al-Din (of Pasai) 94
Sharia 29–30, *29*, 31, 32, 32–33, 89, *89*, 141
and sufism 32, 32–33, 39; superseded 134, 135, 136, 148; transmitted 33, 148
in India 63, 122; in Indonesia 151, 171; in Iran 169–71; in Libya 167; in Ottoman empire 74, 77; in Pakistan 151, 167; in Saudi Arabia 141, 142; in West Africa 97, 154
see also law; *ulama*
Shariat Allah, Hajji (Faraizi leader) 122
Shariati, Dr Ali 168
Sharur 45
Shehu Amadu (Fulani leader) 129
Shensi 101, 125
Sher Khan Sur (later Sher Shah, sultan of Delhi) 58
tomb of *70*
Shias 31, 44, 72, 77, 171
origins 23
and Safavids 39, 44, 45; and Sunnis 47
Twelver Shiism (Ithna Ashari) 45, 46–49, *47*, 112, 168
Ashura (ritualized mourning at) 47, 168, *170*, 190; shrines 47, *47*, 120
Shihab al-Din Marjani (Tatar scholar) 147
Shiraz *32*, 114
Shivaji (Maratha general) 115, *115*
shrines 36, 39, 47, *47*, 104, 186, *186*, 206
marabout ic *98*, 100
see also architecture, mausolea; architecture, tombs and shrines
Sicily 22, 24, 26, 110
Sierra Leone 153, 154
Sikandra
tomb of Akbar 70, *70*
Sikhs 113, *151*
silk *see under* textiles
silsila 36
Sinan Pasha (Ottoman architect) *74*, 79, 84, *84–87*, 108
Sind 23
Sirhindi, Shaikh Ahmad 62–63, 114, 120, 122
slavery 61, 76, 133
"slaves of the royal household" 46, 110
see also devshirme
socialism 161–63, 167, 174
Socrates 16
Sofala 96
Sokoto 129, *129*, 131
Somalis 96, 128, 154
Songhai 27, 97, 99
Soviet Union *see* Russia
Spain 23, 24, 25, 26, 97, 110
and Morocco 131, 155
Srinagar
Shah Hamadan mosque *108*
Stanhope, Lady Hester 18
Sudan 96, 97, 98, 125, 126, 130, 153, 154
Suez Canal 130, 159, *159*
sufis *25*, 27, 30–33, *31*, *33*, *36*, *37*, *39*, 61, 62, 77, 94, *94*, 118, 163, 171, 190
advance and unify Islam 39, 89–90, 91, 96, 97–98, 104; redundant 134, 136, 157; reform and revitalize Islam 118–29, *118–19*, 166; wary of temporal powers 39, *39*, 93, 154
sufism: *khalifas* 36; *khojas* 103–04, 124; *Kiyayi* 93; orders of 36–39, *36*, 104; persecuted 31, 77; *shaikhs* 31, 34–36, 39, 45; transmitted 36, *37*, 93
dancing 33, *33*, *34*, 39, *186*; devotions (*dhikr*) *19*, *33*, 34, *34*, 37; pilgrimage to shrines 33, 36, 39, 104, *182*
Sulaiman (II Qanuni) the Magnificent 72, 74, *74*, 80, *81*
patron of arts 78
Sulaimannama 79
Sulaiman I (Safavid shah) 110–12
sultanate 76, 136
the universal 26
Sultan Bin Abd al-Rahman al-Dawish, Amir *143*
Sultan Husain (Safivid shah) 112, 168, 169
Sultan Jahan, Begum of Bhopal *222*
Sultan-Muhammad (Safavid artist) *34*, *51*
Sultan Sulaiman *see* Tu Wen Hsiu
Sulu islands 90
Sumatra 22, 27, 44, 88, 89, *90*, 91, 92, 95, 153
see also Aceh
Sunan Kali Jaga (sufi leader) 93
Sunnis 104
and Shias 47, 101
Suri dynasty 58, 68
Surnama 79
al-Suyuti, Jalal al-Din 98, 99, 129
Sykes, Sir Mark
Sykes-Picot agreement 140, *140*
Syria 23, 25, 26, 72, 120, *141*, 171, 174
French mandate over 140, 158
United Arab Republic 160
Szigetvar *44*

Tabriz 26, 45, 49, 50, 78
library 49, 50, *51*
al-Taftasani, Saad al-Din 26, *32*, 94
Taghaza 97
Tahirid dynasty 25
Tahmasp (Safavid shah) 45, 46, 49, 50, *51*, 58, *58*
Tajiks 130
Takfir wal Hijra 166, 167
Talas river, battle of 23
Tali *125*
Tamerlaine (Timur Lang) 26, 27, *32*, 44, 50, 58, *58*, 68, 100, 202
mausoleum of 104
Tanzania (Tanganyika) 129, 153, 154
Tao-chou
mosque *108*
Taodeni 97
Tarim Basin 22, 27, 101, 103, *103*, 116
Tariqa Muhammadiya 119, 122, 125
Tashkent 23, 26, 101, 148
Tasikmalaya
mosque *153*
Tatar *see under* languages
Tatars 116, 124, 145, *146*, 147, 148
technology, imported 132, 168
Teheran 18, 114, 168, *170*, 216
Shayyad monument 168, *170*; university 145
Terjuman 146
Ternate 90
textiles 49, *50*, 56, *56*, *57*, 79, *82*, *93*
silk 46
Thousand and One Nights see Arabian Nights
al-Tijani, Ahmad (sufi leader) 125
Tijaniya 125–26, 166
tiles *see* ceramics

timars 73, 76
Timbuktu 27, 97, 98, 116, 126, 128
 as center of learning 98–99
 mosques 98, *109*
Timur Lang *see* Tamerlaine
Timurnama 63
Todar Mal (Indian minister) 58
Togo 154
Tolstoy, L. N. *124*
trade 23, 56, 90–91, 110, 116
 with Europeans 26, 76, 116,
 145–47, 160; with nomads 212
 routes *24–25*, 27, *88*; (Old) Silk
 route 88, *88*, 101, *124*; trans-
 Saharan 97; spice *90*, 91
 as spreader of Islam 27, 88–89, 92,
 94, *94*, 95–96, 97
Transjordan 140, *141*
Transoxania 26, 100, 101, *103*, 112–14
al-Triqi, M. Qadir (Tunisian artist)
 162
*True Nature of Imposture Fully
 Displayed* 16
Tughluqs 27
Tulunid dynasty 25

Tunis 34, 72, *216*
Tunisia 131, 155, 156
Turfan *101*, 103, *105*
Turkestan 103, 124, *136*
Turkey *132*, 136–37, *136*, 146, 157,
 166, *222*
 carpets 206, *209*
Turkish *see under* languages
Turkomans 45, 72–73, 74, 76, 130
Turks 25–26, *26*, 27, *134*
Tus 34
Tu Wen-hsiu (Sultan Sulaiman) 125,
 125
 seal of *125*
Twelvers *see* Shias, Twelver Shiism

Uganda 154
Ukraine 72
ulama 31
 as reformers 118–19, *118–19*, 129;
 and sufis 31, 39; superseded 134,
 135–36, 157; and temporal powers
 39, 44, 99, 106, 112, 116, 167; as
 transmitters of Islam 33–34, *34*, 90,
 94, 96, 97–98, 174; as travelers *32*

in Africa 97–98, *98*, 99, 126, 154; in
 Aceh 93, 94; in Central Asia 104,
 106; in Egypt 138–40, 163; in India
 148, 148–49; in Iran 144, 144–45,
 146, 168, 169; in Java 121, 152; in
 Mughal empire 61, 63; in Ottoman
 empire 74, 76–77, 116, 135, 136; in
 Russia 147, 148, 171; in Safavid
 empire 47–49, 112; in Sumatra 120;
 in Turkey 166
Ulugh Beg 26
Umaiyad dynasty 23, 25
Umar Tall, Hajji (Fulani leader) 125,
 128
United Arab Republic 160
United Provinces (of India) 148, *150*
United States of America 159, 160,
 168, *169*
Upper Volta 98, 154
Urban (Hungarian engineer) 80
Urdu *see under* languages
Usuman dan Fodio 129, *129*, 154
Uthman (third caliph) 23
Uzbegs 44, 45, *45*, 46, 100, 101, *101*,
 103

Van, Lake 26, *26*
Venice 72, 76
Victoria, Queen *58*, *125*
Vienna 72, 76, 80, *81*, 114
Vijayanagar empire 22, 58
Volga river 22
Voltaire 16

Wadai 97, 128
Wafd party 138
Wahhabis 120, *120*, *121*, 125, *138*,
 141, *142*
Walata 98
warfare *see* armies; guns
Wattasid dynasty 97
wayang theater 92, *93*, 95
Wolof 153, 154
women in Islam 20, 163, 166, *169*,
 171, *214*, 221–22, *222*
 circumcision 188; dancing 92, *138*;
 harim 218; marriage 188
 liberation of *138*, 145; oppression
 of 133, *138*; seclusion of 218
World of Islam Festival 171, *176*
World Muslim League *172*, 173, 174

Yakub Beg 124
Yazdigird III 47
Yazid I (caliph) 23, 168
Yemen 72, 132
Yoruba *129*, 153
Young Turks 136
Yuan dynasty 27, 101, 105
Yunnan 27, 101, 104, 125, *125*

Zaghlul, Saad (founder of Wafd) 138
Zahid of Gilan, Shaikh 45
Zaidis (Shia sect) 46–47
Zaila 96
Zands *112*, 114
Zanzibar 130
Zaria 97
zawiya *126*, 128, *128*
Zia ul-Haq 167
Zionism *140*, 160
Zoroastrians 61

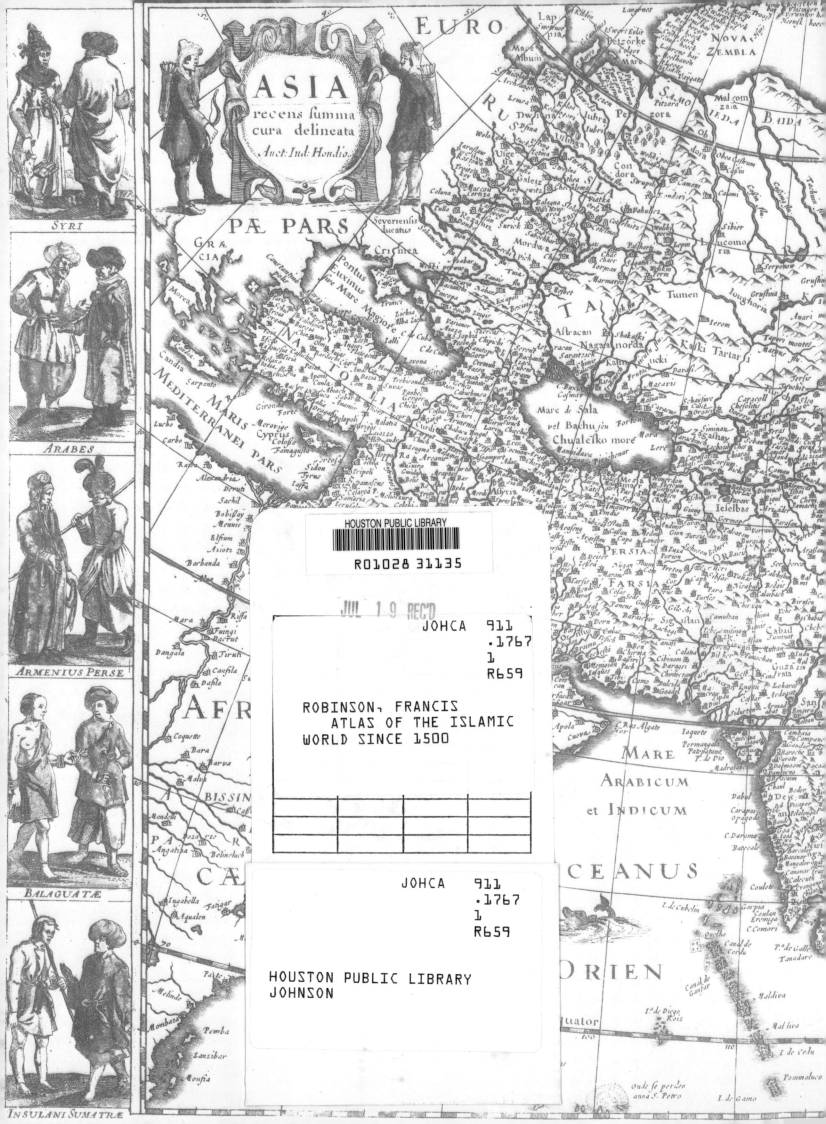